The

GOLDEN AGE OF SHIPPING

The
GOLDEN
AGE OF
SHIPPING

*The Classic Merchant Ship
1900–1960*

Editor: Robert Gardiner

Consultant Editor: Ambrose Greenway

CONWAY
MARITIME PRESS

Series Consultant	DR BASIL GREENHILL CB, CMG, FSA, FRHistS
Series Editor	ROBERT GARDINER
Consultant Editor	AMBROSE GREENWAY
Contributors	JOHN BOWEN DAVID BURRELL DR IAN BUXTON LAWRENCE DUNN ROY FENTON AMBROSE GREENWAY GRAEME MacLENNAN EDWARD PAGET-TOMLINSON IAN STOCKBRIDGE KENNETH D. TROUP PATRICK WATSON RICHARD WOODMAN

Frontispiece: *A characteristic of the ship types built between 1900 and 1960 was a profile that instantly identified its purpose and, furthermore, remained fundamentally unchanged for a half-century. The motor tanker* Seminole, *shown here on trials in May 1921, is a case in point. Although there were some engines-amidships tankers built, the vast majority employed the engines-aft, bridge-amidships layout, demonstrated here, until the all-aft arrangement became popular in the 1960s; combined with the lack of cargo-handling gear, this proclaimed the ship a tanker to all but the most ignorant observer.* Seminole *was built for the Anglo-American Oil Co (later better known as Esso) by Vickers and measured 6923grt.* (CMP)

© Brassey's (UK) Ltd 1994

First published in Great Britain 1994 by
Conway Maritime Press, an imprint of Brassey's (UK) Ltd
33 John Street, London WC1N 2AT

British Library Cataloguing-in-Publication Data
Golden Age of Shipping: Classic Merchant
Ship, 1900–60. – (Conway's History of the Ship Series)
　I. Greenway, Ambrose II. Gardiner, Robert
　III Series
　623.8

ISBN 0 85177 567 5

Designed by Tony Hart
Typeset by Datix International Ltd, Bungay
Printed and bound by The Bath Press, Bath

Contents

Preface

This title is the ninth in an ambitious programme of twelve volumes intended to provide the first detailed and comprehensive account of a technology that has shaped human history. It has been conceived as a basic reference work, the essential first stop for anyone seeking information on any aspect of the subject, so it is more concerned to be complete than to be original. However, the series takes full account of all the latest research and in certain areas will be publishing entirely new material. In the matter of interpretation care has been taken to avoid the old myths and to present only the most widely accepted modern viewpoints.

To tell a coherent story, in a more readable form than is usual with encyclopaedias, each volume takes the form of independent chapters, all by recognised authorities in the field. Most chapters are devoted to the ships themselves, but others deal with topics like 'Shipbuilding' that are more generally applicable, giving added depth to the reader's understanding of developments. Some degree of generalisation is inevitable when tackling a subject of this breadth, but wherever possible the specific details of ships and their characteristics have been included (a table of typical ships for each relevant chapter includes a convenient summary of data from which the reader can chart the evolution of the ship type concerned). With a few historically unavoidable exceptions, the series is confined to seagoing vessels; to have included boats would have increased the scope of an already massive task.

The history of the ship is not a romanticised story of epic battles and heroic voyages but equally it is not simply a matter of technological advances. Ships were built to carry out particular tasks and their design was as much influenced by the experience of that employment – the lessons of war, or the conditions of trade, for example – as purely technical innovation. Throughout this series an attempt has been made to keep this clearly in view, to describe the *what* and *when* of developments without losing sight of the *why*.

The series is aimed at those with some knowledge of, and interest in, ships and the sea. It would have been impossible to make a contribution of any value to the subject if it had been pitched at the level of the complete novice, so while there is an extensive glossary, for example, it assumes an understanding of the most basic nautical terms. Similarly, the bibliography avoids very general works and concentrates on those which will broaden or deepen the reader's understanding beyond the level of the *History of the Ship*. The intention is not to inform genuine experts in their particular area of expertise, but to provide them with the best available single-volume summaries of less familiar fields.

Each volume is chronological in approach, with the periods covered getting shorter as the march of technology quickens, but organised around a dominant theme – represented by the title of the book – that sums up the period in question. In this way each book is fully self-sufficient, although when completed the twelve titles will link up to form a coherent history, chronicling the progress of ship design from its earliest recorded forms to the present day.

This volume deals with the merchant ship in the first part of the twentieth century, a period in which a variety of specialist types developed recognisable characteristics that were not to change radically until the shiphandling innovations of the 1960s – as analysed in *The Shipping Revolution* volume in this series. Although there was steady and significant progress in merchant ship design between 1900 and 1960, it is often presented as a time of relative stasis in comparison with the earlier replacement of sail by steam

and the succeeding introduction of many new ship types. It is also a period which is very familiar to many who grew up with an interest in shipping, so we feel that the much-abused term 'classic' is justified in the context of these vessels.

The firm definition of most ship types before 1960 makes the organisation of this volume easier than most, although there is some necessary overlap in a few areas – tramps sometimes carried bulk cargoes, and some fruit ships carried passengers – so a few types rate a mention in more than one chapter. Chronologically, this volume follows *The Advent of Steam*, which was thematically devoted to the new technology of steam machinery, paddle and screw propulsion, and iron and steel hulls. It did not concern itself in detail with the introduction of particular ship types, like the tanker and the refrigerated ship, so although *The Golden Age of Shipping* nominally covers the period from 1900 to 1960, if necessary the relevant chapters begin their stories in the nineteenth century.

The major problem with all histories of merchant ships is the sheer number of vessels involved. In some cases the most historically significant stand out as the basis for a narrative, but more often the writer can only make a personal selection of typical examples to represent development. In this volume a conscious effort has been made to choose both photographs and entries in the data tables which augment rather than illustrate the text, with a view to including the maximum number of ships. Even so, it is likely that many readers' favourite vessels will not be mentioned, but in the context of the aims of *The History of the Ship* this is perhaps inevitable.

Robert Gardiner
Series Editor

Introduction

By the time the twentieth century dawned, the steamship had truly come of age. During the eighty or so years it had been in operation, it had grown in size from just over 100 to around 20,000 gross tons and the perfection of the triple expansion reciprocating engine in the 1880s had provided it with a form of propelling machinery that for economy and reliability could not be matched by the sailing ship. Steel, a lighter and more flexible material, had replaced iron in its construction and its safety and that of its crew had been greatly increased by the adoption of loading lines, thanks to the efforts of Samuel Plimsoll.

In addition to the reciprocating engine, the final years of the extraordinarily inventive Victorian age had produced two further revolutionary means of propulsion that were to have a marked effect on shipping as the new century progressed – the steam turbine and the internal combustion engine. The former first proved itself in a merchant ship in 1901 but was restricted to high speed ships such as liners and cross-channel steamers until the addition of gearing made it more suitable for general tonnage. Nearly a decade was to pass before the diesel was taken up for deepsea use but it steadily gained ground after the First World War, particularly in Scandinavia. In 1926 Lord Kylsant, one of the great British proponents of the motorship, used the prophetic words 'It is quite possible – and personally I believe it is probable – that many of you will live to see the time when steamers will have become as rare on the high seas as sailing ships are today.' By the end of the sixty-year period under review he was well on the way to

By 1900 steam had replaced sail on most oceanic routes and was threatening to displace sailing craft in the coasting trade. Although wind-power was free, it was unpredictable and in the very light conditions depicted here the steam coaster Dalegarth *would have had a distinct advantage over the schooner* June *(originally built in 1827 but lengthened in 1855 and again in 1869). (Ambrose Greenway collection)*

being proved right, with the use of steam turbines virtually confined to the largest liners and tankers.

As a result of other innovations, ships fitted with refrigerating machinery had been transporting meat and dairy products to the United Kingdom from as far away as Australia and New Zealand for nearly twenty years and specialised tankers for the carriage of oil in bulk had been in operation for only a year or two less.

With all these revolutionary developments in place by 1900, it only remained for them to be applied and refined, affording the merchant ship over fifty years of steady evolutionary development before the next significant changes began to manifest themselves. During these 'Golden Years' ships increased in size and complexity but changes were by and large cosmetic and were not enough to render them unrecognisable to seafarers from the early part of the century. It was an age when the drive for efficiency was by no means at the expense of appearance and the naval architects and shipbuilders of the

period combined to produce some of the finest looking ships ever to grace the oceans.

On the economic front, shipping continued to be affected by the usual fluctations in trade but also had to contend with two destructive World Wars which straddled the most severe and prolonged period of depression yet seen. In terms of ownership, Great Britain's pre-eminent position – it controlled nearly half the world's tonnage before 1914 – was steadily eroded as other nations expanded their own fleets, many doing so to avoid further dependence on British shipping which had been suddenly denied to them during the First World War. In shipbuilding too, Britain's long-held lead was finally relinquished to Japan in the late 1950s.

Passenger ships

To the world at large, the undoubted stars of the shipping scene were the large passenger liners and in particular those operating on the busiest of all ocean passenger routes across the Atlantic Ocean. Great emphasis

In the early part of this century, coaling was an essential aspect of shipping that was both dirty and labour intensive. Although a few coal-burning steamers lasted until the late 1950s, increasingly widespread use of oil to fuel both steamships, many of which were converted to oil-firing, and motorships between the two World Wars led to the gradual disappearance of scenes like this. (Ambrose Greenway collection)

edent, opted for turbo-electric machinery in a number of fine liners built around 1930.

The 1930s marked a return to racing, sparked off by Norddeutscher Lloyd, whose vastly more powerful *Bremen*, aided by a more advanced hull form incorporating a bulbous forefoot, finally broke *Mauretania*'s long-standing record in 1929, despite the latter's grand gesture in reply of her fastest crossing ever. The Atlantic record switched next to Italy's *Rex* and then to France's giant turbo-electric *Normandie* in a race spurred by growing nationalism. The completion of Cunard's reply, *Queen Mary*, was delayed by the Depression but after swapping the record several times with her French rival, she

was placed on speed which gained not only prestige but also custom and this accounted for the adoption of the more efficient turbine from 1905 onwards. Cunard's subsidised 25kt quadruple screw sisters *Lusitania* and *Mauretania* of 1906–7 marked such an advance in speed that nothing to match them was built until 1929, leading rivals like White Star and Hamburg-Amerika to concentrate instead on slower but larger ships, where the emphasis was more on luxury.

The United States began to place restrictions on immigration during the early 1920s and steerage accommodation was gradually replaced by cabin class in a new generation of liners, an increasing number of which were motor-driven following the example set by Swedish America Line's *Gripsholm* in 1925. Diesels were taken up for ships serving the Cape and South America whilst P&O and Furness Withy, following American prec-

Finally opened in August 1914 after a long and arduous construction period but not fully operational until April 1916 due to landslips, the Panama Canal shortened the voyage between the US East and West coasts by some 8000 miles and that between Europe and the US Pacific coast by nearly 6000 miles. In the course of its 51 mile length, ocean ships are raised or lowered 85ft in three separate lock systems with chambers measuring 1000 by 110ft. In this view a heavily laden freighter with a deck cargo of timber is being eased into the Pedro Miguel Locks by shore-based 'tugs' known as electric mules, two of which are visible on either side of her funnel (CMP)

finally took the honours as the war clouds gathered once again over Europe. The same period was to witness a rise in the popularity of cruising whilst internally, a more spacious and practical form of styling was introduced with Orient Line's *Orion* in 1935.

The war put paid to many plans and seven years were to pass before the world's largest liner, *Queen Elizabeth*, was able to join her sister in Cunard's successful weekly express service. No other nation was able to match this but America's outstandingly fast *United States*, designed for the dual role of Atlantic liner and wartime troop transport, created a sizeable impression following her 35kt record debut in 1952.

Many other new liners were built in the 1950s, with the new tourist class occupying correspondingly more space as first class declined, paving the way towards the one-class ship. Passenger comfort was assisted by fin stabilisers, an invention of the 1930s first fitted to a liner in P&O's *Chusan* in 1950. All looked set for a rosy future as passenger figures grew but increasing numbers were turning to air travel. The coming of long-distance jet aircraft, especially the reliable Boeing 707, accelerated the process and the passenger liner was quickly forced to abandon its traditional role and turn instead to cruising in order to survive.

In his survey on passenger liners Laurence Dunn has eschewed the normal well-trodden path in favour of a slightly different tack, drawing on his extensive knowledge and records to take a 'walkabout' look at a series of carefully chosen vessels, representative of the main developments in liner design.

Cargo ships

Although less dramatic than passenger ships in terms of public perception, ordinary dry cargo ships formed the largest and most important group of shipping throughout most of the period under review. Split between cargo liners which offered regular voyages and tramps which sought cargo on a random basis, they were responsible for moving the major portion of manufactured goods, foodstuffs and raw materials around the world.

The cargo liner was initially operated by only a handful of the more developed shipping nations, such as the UK and Germany, but it was not long before companies from other countries in mainland Europe, Scandinavia and Japan entered the business, often switching from existing tramp operations. Cargo liners came in many different guises, many of them being refrigerated, but common to all were tweendecks and extensive cargo gear. Apart from a steady increase in size and the widespread adoption of both diesel and geared turbine propulsion, their basic design remained much the same until the 1950s. Even so, changes made then were quickly overtaken by the onset of containerisation. The same lack of major change applied equally to the refrigerated banana ship which appeared early on in the new century. However, a new type of fast motor fruit ship, developed in Scandinavia, began to be built in increasing numbers after 1930.

Unlike the cargo liner, the tramp steamer had unencumbered holds into which could be loaded any kind of cargo in bulk or bagged form. Tramp shipping entered the

During the period under review, the steam turbine was the most widely used motive power for fast passenger liners, though it was to be increasingly challenged by the diesel for medium speed ships from the mid 1920s onwards. The first oceangoing merchant ships to employ turbines were the 10,700 ton Victorian *and* Virginian *built by Workman Clark at Belfast in 1905 for Allan Line's Canadian service. The latter, depicted here on trials in the Firth of Clyde, became Swedish American Line's* Drottningholm *after the First World War and was re-engined with geared turbines in 1922. Sold to Home Lines in 1948, she was finally broken up in 1955 after fifty years of service. (Ambrose Greenway collection)*

new century with confidence. The South African wars were still continuing, the triple expansion engine provided an economical form of propulsion and coal supplies were cheap and plentiful. Welsh coal out and Black Sea grain home were the staple cargoes of many British tramps, a typical example measuring about 5000grt and burning around 42 tons of coal a day for a speed of 10kts. By 1914 their numbers stood at around 2200 ships and already a few owners were taking the first hesitant steps towards the adoption of diesel propulsion, though it was not until the 1920s that companies such as Andrew Weir's Bank Line and King Line started to take it up seriously.

Following the First World War economic slump and increased foreign competition made the life of UK tramp owners difficult. Many went under and more followed during the Depression, lacking the capital reserves of the liner companies which began to poach tramp cargoes to survive. Despite a trade revival in the late 1930s and a measure of Government subsidy, by the time war came

Heralding the end of a glorious era, a Boeing Stratocruiser airliner overflies the world's largest passenger liner Queen Elizabeth *(83,673grt). Although the number of passengers crossing the North Atlantic was steadily increasing, those going by sea reached a peak of 1,036,000 in 1957, but this figure was bettered by air travellers in 1958 and ten years later the jet airliner had all but cornered the market. The same was soon to apply to other routes and the regular passenger liner was consigned to history.* (CMP)

again in 1939 the UK tramp fleet had shrunk to around 800 ships (*c*3.8m tons). After the Second World War the development of specialised ore carriers made further inroads

into one of the trampship's traditional cargoes, whilst both Greek and flag of convenience fleets grew to the detriment of the UK fleet. From 1960 onwards its eclipse was hastened by the development of the general-purpose motor bulk carrier, which was not only larger but also comparatively cheaper to build and operate.

Bulk carriers

Coal was still very much king when the new century dawned but a liquid alternative in

the form of oil from America and Russia was already a rising star. Easier to extract and transport as well as cleaner and more efficient to use, it would in time topple coal from its long-held position as the world's most widely used fuel.

By 1900 almost fifteen years had passed since *Gluckauf*, the generally accepted precursor of the modern engines-aft oil tanker, left the Swan shipyard on Tyneside and the subsequent surge in tanker construction had seen deadweight tonnage rise to around 8500 tons. Larger sizes became possible after 1908 thanks to the Isherwood system of longitudinal framing, which gave greater hull strength and carrying capacity. Meanwhile American output was soaring following the development of new oilfields in Texas, and other sources in Mexico and the Middle East were

Cross-channel ships, like North Atlantic liners put a premium on speed and so were early beneficiaries of turbine propulsion, and turbines became the norm on Channel routes. However, between the wars Belgian Railways broke with this orthodoxy by building a number of fast diesel-propelled ships. One of these, Prins Albert *(built 1937, 2938grt) is shown here postwar.* (John G Callis)

beginning to be exploited as Russian production declined. By 1914 the world's tanker tonnage was still comparatively small at 1,500,000grt.

To cope with a dramatic rise in oil production after the First World War, many new tankers were built and an increasing number of these were motorships. This was particularly true of new tonnage ordered by Norwegian owners specifically for charter or tramp work. By 1939 the world tanker fleet had risen sharply to nearly 11,500,000grt, more than seven times the 1914 figure and although losses during the ensuing war were heavy, these were partly compensated for by standard type replacements, the most famous and successful being the American T2 design.

Oil demand, already greatly stimulated by the war, continued its rapid upward trend with the Middle East now the major supplier. However, economic and political decisions led to a change in policy which resulted in the oil companies moving the refining process away from the sources of supply to the areas of greatest consumption. To keep the newly built refineries supplied, larger crude carrying oil tankers of around 28,000dwt began to be built from 1950 onwards by companies such as Shell and British Petroleum. Within five years tanker size had all but doubled with vigorous new independent owners such as Ludwig, Niarchos and Onas-

sis – who fully appreciated economies of scale and the use of flags of convenience – leading the way.

The sudden closure of the Suez Canal in 1956 increased at a stroke the voyage between the Arabian Gulf and Europe by some 4500 miles, creating a shortage of tonnage and leading to higher transportation costs. To obviate the problem and maintain prices at a reasonable level, a further substantial jump in size became necessary and the first 100,000dwt tanker, *Universe Apollo*, was delivered in 1959, by which time the world tanker fleet had risen to 39,000,000grt.

The specialised deepsea bulk carrier, which owed its origin to a long line of coastal colliers dating back to the pioneering *John Bowes* of 1852, took much longer to develop than the tanker. Coal and grain were mostly carried in ordinary tramp steamers and the same was largely true of metallic ores. However the great weight of the latter led to the building of specially strengthened ships, which gradually began to follow the practice of Great Lakes ore steamers in having their engines placed aft. With one or two notable exceptions such as the 20,000dwt *Svealand* of 1925, these remained on the small side and it was not until after the Second World War that larger vessels began to be commissioned as depleted local ore supplies were outstripped by industrial demand, leading to the development of new sources much

further away. In a move to combat unprofitable ballast voyages, a new type of combination carrier was developed which could carry either ore or oil. Additionally, a new type of general-purpose dry bulk carrier of around 15,000–20,000dwt with large hatches and both accommodation and engines aft evolved during the late 1950s. This type would proliferate during the 1960s and quickly replace the last of the traditional tramp ships.

Coastal shipping

In the coastal trades Britain again led the way during the early part of the century and its raised quarterdeck coasters were familiar sights in the rivers and creeks of northern Europe, whilst its short sea traders ventured to the Baltic and Mediterranean.

Badly mauled during the First World War, British coastal shipping was then faced with increased competition from the railways, fol-

The versatile and heavily geared cargo liner running to a fixed schedule came to dominate the ocean routes during the first half of the 1900s but the amount of time spent loading and discharging – roughly equal to that spent at sea – led to its replacement by the more efficient containership and roll-on, roll-off ship from the mid 1960s onwards. Amongst the foremost operators of such tonnage was Alfred Holt whose 'Blue Funnel' ships were familiar sights on the Far East run. The 9400dwt Meriones, *built by Scotts of Greenock in 1922, was one of eleven similar ships, turbine driven save for the first two, that were amongst the first to have rounded stems. (CMP)*

lowing the reorganisation in 1923, and a new form of road transport embodied in the motor lorry. On top of this, other countries developed their coastal fleets as part of their industrialisation process and the family run Dutch motor coaster began to proliferate, making considerable inroads into trades formerly dominated by Britain. A number of British owners fought back with their own motorships, notably the large Coast Lines group and F T Everard.

By the 1950s coal shipments were declining, leading to a reduction in colliers which hitherto had formed a large proportion of coastal shipping, whilst road competition became increasingly severe. Experimentation with unit loads, leading to containerisation and the coming of new roll-on, roll-off freight ships marked the beginnings of a period of substantial change.

Fishing

The seas on which ships sailed were also abundant providers of food, the harvesting of which was one of man's oldest professions. In general, though, fishing had been carried out in a rather haphazard way by small sailing craft specially designed to suit local conditions. The coming of steam changed all this and led to the development in the UK of two distinct types, the deep trawler which towed a cone shaped net, the mouth of which

was kept open by 'otterboards', and the drifter, which laid long lines of drifting vertical nets that trapped fish by their gills. To begin with, some of the trawlers were organised into disciplined fleets backed up by support ships and fish carriers, an idea that would be resuscitated in a big way by the Communist Bloc after 1960. Apart from increasing size, made necessary as trawlers were forced to go further afield and the fitting of refrigeration plant to maintain the ice used for packing fish, trawler design remained much the same until the 1950s when the first new refrigerated factory trawlers began to appear. These were much larger and were fitted with stern ramps, similar to those used in whale factories.

The whale had long been hunted as a source of both food and oil, the latter initially used for lighting purposes but later refined to form an important ingredient of margarine, soap and explosives. By 1900 Norway was pre-eminent in commercial whaling,

largely as a result of Svend Foyn's invention of a special harpoon gun firing barbed projectiles with explosive heads. Thus armed, small but sturdy steam whalecatchers were able to extend operations from the Northern Hemisphere down to the Antarctic, where shore bases were established in South Georgia, and the South Shetlands. In time these were supplemented by converted merchant ships fitted with tanks and machinery for extracting whale oil which acted as static factory vessels. Despite these developments the whale industry was still subject to violent fluctuations.

After the First World War licensing systems set up by the British began to restrict the Norwegians in the far south and they looked for a means of moving the hunt for whales into ocean waters. The answer was supplied by an old whaling hand, Carl Larsen, who obtained sufficient finance to buy an old British cargo ship and convert her into a self-contained factory ship capable of operating for long periods at sea. In late 1923 the *Sir James Clark Ross*, accompanied by several catchers, left Norway on the first pelagic whaling expedition to the whale-rich Ross Sea. The potential of this new form of whaling was soon apparent and a number of

other merchant ships were converted in the ensuing years. Stern ramps to enable whale carcasses to be hauled directly on board – another Norwegian invention – were incorporated from 1925 onwards. Most of these conversions took place in British shipyards, which in 1929 delivered the first new stern ramp whale factory ships, some of which were fitted with spotting aircraft. Japan and Germany both took up the concept and the impetus of these new vessels led to the industry reaching an all-time peak in the winter of 1937–38.

The Second World War decimated the factory ship fleet and although these were to some extent replaced by new tonnage, dwindling whale stocks and increasing restrictions occasioned by mounting public concern led to a fairly rapid decline in the industry. Ironically some of the last factory ships to be built, for Holland and Russia, were the largest ever but their day had already passed.

Service ships

Amongst other specialised ships were the so-called service vessels. Best-known of these was the tug – a powerful deep-draughted vessel with high bows, broad beam and a long open after deck. The largest of these carried out long distance ocean towage of unwieldy items such as dredgers and floating docks and were also used to assist ships in distress, later examples being specifically stationed at various maritime locations to await just such eventualities. The Dutch soon made a name for themselves in the latter two fields, in particular the firm of P Smit which went on to develop powerful motor tugs of

4000 horsepower in the 1930s, but this figure had doubled by 1960 to cope with the rapid increase in tanker size.

Smaller tugs were used for shiphandling purposes and these harbour tugs gradually increased in size and power, commensurate with a general increase in vessel size. Diesels were introduced in the 1930s but it was not until the 1950s that the motor tug seriously began to challenge its steam counterpart. By this time, however, the first examples of Voith-Schneider cycloidal propulsion units capable of providing thrust in any direction were being experimented with, paving the way for a new design of 'tractor' tug.

The general expansion of trade demanded improved communications and although wireless began to be used early in the twentieth century, there was still an increasing requirement for cable ships to lay new submarine telegraph links and to repair existing ones. Fitted with special bow and stern sheaves and circular tanks, which in the largest examples could hold over 3000 miles of cable, these ships grew in size and complexity throughout the period.

The desire to share in increased trade also led the northernmost countries such as Russia to develop large icebreakers in order to keep sea lanes open as long as possible during the winter months. The powerful *Yermak*, British built in 1898, spawned a long line of similar icebreakers and, apart from the gradual introduction of diesel-electric machinery, it was not until the 1950s that new designs began to emerge from Finnish shipyards. In 1959 the Russian built *Lenin* ensured a place in maritime history as the world's first nuclear powered merchant ship.

Conclusion

As the 1950s progressed, the traditional passenger liner began to lose its custom to the new and infinitely faster long-distance airliner and the classic type of cross-channel ferry started to succumb to a steady increase in vehicular traffic, which demanded a different type of vessel. At the same time cargo ship operators, already beset by rising crew costs, were forced to seek new ideas to overcome increasing time spent in port as a result of cargo handling practices that were largely unchanged since the beginning of the century and damaging industrial action by dock labourers.

The winds of revolutionary change, still for over sixty years, began to stir once more and in a comparatively short time had produced the container ship, which would quickly displace the traditional cargo liner and Empire Food Ship; the roll-on, roll-off ship – a development of the wartime tank landing craft – that would soon come to dominate the short-sea routes; as well as new types of heavy lift-ship and multi-purpose reefers.

In the bulk trades, large new multi-purpose dry bulkers would replace the last of the old style tramps, whilst crude oil tankers would mushroom in size and smaller ones became increasingly specialised for the transportation of new petroleum, chemical and gas products. In the fishing industry, the traditional side trawler would soon give way to factory stern trawlers capable of filleting and freezing their catch immediately, whilst the whaling fleets would disappear altogether.

Faced with these new developments, shipping's Golden Age passed quietly into history, taking with it many famous house-flags and funnel colours. In the harsher, accountant-led world of the Shipping Revolution, ownership would be disguised rather than flaunted and straight lines would replace the luxuries of rounded sterns and sweeping sheerlines.

Ambrose Greenway

To meet the needs of the rapidly expanding pelagic whaling industry in the 1920s, many merchant ships, including passenger ships and tankers, were converted into whale factory ships. Yngvar Hvistendahl's Skytteren, *seen here being escorted into Cape Town on her way home to Norway at the end of a whaling season by the large harbour/salvage tug* Ludwig Wiener, *was originally the* Suevic, *one of four former White Star liners so converted. (Alex Duncan)*

1

Passenger Vessels

The Passenger Liner - its Development 1900 - 1960

Introduction

It would be fascinating to learn the reactions of bygone ship designers and operators should they be able to see the products of recent decades – the successors of the ships they had known so well. Amazement and incomprehension would surely come first, then a somewhat bewildered admiration as they began to appreciate the degree of comfort and safety which has been achieved, not in one stage, but over many.

The turn of the century was not only of significance calendar-wise but also in terms of propulsion, since the steam reciprocating engine was on the point of losing its monopoly to the infinitely more compact turbine which, by its performance, opened up new vistas in terms of speed. By then electric light and mechanical ventilation had ceased to be novelties but, judged by present standards, navigational aids were woefully primitive.

Since it was on the North Atlantic that the passenger liner was born and developed, it is appropriate to start there and view the position as it appeared in 1900. At long last the giant

Great Eastern of 1858 had been eclipsed, at least in terms of length by *Oceanic,* a one year-old, 17kt ship of 17,274grt. Although no flyer, she was easily the largest afloat, her owners White Star Line having decided to turn from the record breakers for which they had become known, to larger, somewhat slower ships, which by their size and increased steadiness, could offer far more in the way of passenger comfort.

In contrast, Cunard Line, long believers in the prestige value of record-breakers, were in a period of near eclipse, their 22kt *Campania* and *Lucania* (both built 1893, 12,950grt) having been outpaced by more modern German tonnage in the form of the *Kaiser Wilhelm der Grosse, Deutschland* and then *Kronprinz Wilhelm* of 1902. The French Line had greatly improved its image, its fleet now being headed by the new 21kt, 11,000 ton *La Lorraine* and *La Savoie.* The other North Atlantic flyers then in service belonged to an earlier generation. Built in 1890 or just before, and of around 10,000 tons apiece, they were the White Star *Teutonic* and *Majestic* and Inman Line's clipper-stemmed *City of New York* and *City of Paris.*

The last of the North Atlantic flyers to be driven by reciprocating engines was the 23½kt, 19,000 ton *Kronprinzessin Cecilie* of 1906. Regarded as a potential record breaker once

her engines had been run in, she was frustrated in this by Cunard's 31,000-ton turbine-driven *Lusitania* and *Mauretania.* Once more supreme in terms of speed, Cunard retained this position until the advent of *Bremen* in 1929.

The twentieth century was two decades old when the use of oil took over from coal. After this interval of time one is apt to overlook the benefits this brought, especially to long routes. To take merely the passengers' viewpoint, they were rid of the tedium and grime as they stopped at Aden and the like so that depleted bunkers could be replenished by hordes of bent backs carrying countless sacks of coal. Coupled with the introduction of turbines —infinitely more compact than the old machinery— much additional space became available for cargo or accommodation. To appreciate the size of the later quadruple-expansion engines it is worth harking back to *Kaiser Wilhelm II* (built 1903, 19,361grt), a four-funnelled, three-masted liner in which the tops of the engines reached almost to the top of the hull itself. These engines were placed aft, under the second of the three masts, while their boilers and coal bunkers reached forward to the bridgefront. As a further reminder of those now seemingly primitive days, the space between the bridgefront and the stem was filled on two decks by seven vast dormito-

As the world's largest liner the Oceanic *(1899/17,274grt) brought nineteenth century shipbuilding to a spectacular close. She joined White Star service when that company's one-time record-breakers, the* Majestic *and* Teutonic *were nine and ten years old, and so long past their prime. The* Oceanic *represented a complete change in White Star policy, a switch from high speed to large size and maximum comfort. Long in relation to breadth, she measured 704ft × 64ft and her twin screws and triple-expansion machinery gave her a speed of 19kts or more. Of passengers she carried 410 first, 300 second class and some 1000 steerage. With the outbreak of war in 1914 she became an auxiliary cruiser, but within a few weeks stranded in fog near the Shetlands and became a total loss.* (Ambrose Greenway collection)

The Armadale Castle *(1903/11,973grt) was built for the Union-Castle mail service between Southampton and Cape Town. This was an area in which traditional designs persisted, for she was the seventh of a series of ten ships (some two-, and others three-masted) which started with the 7537 ton* Norman *of 1894. Like the much larger* Oceanic *of 1899 they had an open based superstructure which was long and low in relation to hull length. The* Armadale Castle *was unusual in having been built not at Belfast by Harland & Wolff like most Union-Castle ships, but by Fairfield and measured 590ft × 65ft. First listed as carrying 351 first, 200 second and 270 third class, this was later cut to 312 first and 235 tourist class. Twin screws and quadruple expansion machinery gave a legend speed of 17kts, but by 1936 when she was sold for demolition at Blyth, this had dropped to 15½kts. (Ambrose Greenway collection)*

ries which contained berths for 770 of the luckless third class.

She was one of the long slim-hulled generation and so, like most of those reviewed on a later page, had two long fore and aft passages to provide access to her midship cabins. She had some thirty rows of these, each four abreast (two port, two starboard). To appreciate the changes made between then and the 1990s, plans of a current 55,000-ton cruise ship show two similar but dead straight passages, each of them serving some seventy rows of cabins, one on each outboard side and two amidships. This was only slightly different from all but the very largest ships built during the intervening years – except that the older ones normally had cabins on the outboard side only with all toilets, bathrooms, etc grouped on the other (midship) side of all the alleyways. Some may query why the layout of none of the giant ships is summarised below. The answer is

simple – sheer complexity. Over the years ships had not only become larger in terms of gross tonnage, but also more tubby in terms of length/breadth. The *Europa* of 1930 provides a good example, since on her second class D deck – this amidships – she needed four (not two) fore and aft passages – plus cross ones – to serve the cabins which were ten abreast.

One of the major problems which arose in planning the accommodation layout was that the rooms – be they large or small – had to be built around certain fixed features, such as the engine room uptakes and the trunked hatches which linked the cargo holds with the open deck high up. The placing of the several dining rooms could be particularly difficult, since their respective galleys had to be very close at hand. Sometimes one galley could be placed between two dining rooms and so serve both, and with the aid of an escalator, a third. In a few giant ships the engine room uptakes were divided, only joining at the base of the funnels.

This made possible a magnificent sequence of public rooms but, in turn, created other problems.

During the period under review, the first class cabins/staterooms and their social rooms

The Mooltan *(1905/9621grt) was the fifth of the P & O Line's well known 'M' class ships of which ten were built between 1903 and 1911, most of them on the Clyde. The 9500 ton* Moldavia *headed the series which ended with 12,350 ton* Medina. *The first five and the last pair were designed for the important Bombay service and had speeds of 16½–17kts, but the* Mooltan *was one of the slightly faster ones which could continue on to Australia. She measured 520ft × 58ft; fitted with twin screws and quadruple expansion engines, she had a listed speed of 18kts. She carried two classes only, 348 first and 166 second. The Indian passenger list, in particular, was more formal than was usual, passengers being largely made up of senior army officers and high ranking officials – or Indian dignitaries. To minimise cargo handling noise all the 'M' ships relied on hydraulic cranes, not derricks. Of the ten ships in this series five were sunk during the 1914–18 war, the* Mooltan *being lost while in the Mediterranean. (CMP)*

The Adriatic (1907/24,541grt) was the last and largest of the White Star 'big four' which were built after the Oceanic had justified herself, likewise the company's switch to size rather than speed. The Cedric of 1901, Celtic and Baltic all had the same two-funnelled, four-masted profile, one which for the larger ships remained one of the international favourites from 1900 to 1909. Of the fourteen or so built then the Adriatic remained the largest. A twin-screw ship with quadruple expansion engines, she had a speed of 17–18kts and measured 726ft × 75ft. Used on the New York run, her UK terminal varied between Liverpool and Southampton. Besides her very large cargo capacity she was designed to carry 400 first, 465 second and over 1300 steerage class passengers. Later, however, her accommodation was down-graded to cabin, tourist and third classes. After briefly outliving the Cunard–White Star merger of 1934, she was scrapped in Japan. (Ambrose Greenway collection)

were grouped amidships, the exception being the dining room, which was normally placed lower and rather further forward. Those for the second class were generally one or two decks lower and extended from just aft of amidships to just beyond the mainmast. As for the third class – often very numerous – they were placed yet lower down and nearer the stern and also, quite often, right forward near the bows.

Publicity illustrations of first class cabins naturally stressed the better grades or de luxe suites and these generally left nothing to be desired, but for the ordinary first class cabins the picture was rather different. Fitted with essentials such as a wardrobe and drawers for clothes, beds or berths, a dressing table, mirror and washbasin, it was for many decades, merely a place of retreat, where one could rest, sleep and dress. For other needs one was expected to cross the passage and queue for either toilet or bath. But that really belongs to the past – except for some still surviving elderly and low grade ships.

One of the most successful liners of her period, the Cunard Line's Aquitania *(1914/45,467grt) was built by John Brown & Co, at Clydebank. The last North Atlantic liner to be given four funnels, she had a remarkably pleasing sheer line – one to which the height of her funnels conformed, and in contrast to those of the* Olympic. *Used during the war as an armed merchant cruiser, hospital ship and troopship, she later operated from both Liverpool and Southampton. Conversion from coal to oil in 1920 reduced her stokers from 300 to 50. She measured 901ft × 97ft and her four screws and geared turbines gave a speed of 22–24kts. As built she carried some 600 first, 600 second class and 2000 in the steerage, but later these figures were several times reduced. Twenty years' service on the New York run was followed by nine years of wartime trooping and a final two years on an austerity service to Halifax, after which – in 1950 – she was scrapped on the Clyde. (Ambrose Greenway collection)*

The side promenade decks were, for many years, open to the winds and the gradual introduction of glass side-screens added greatly to their popularity – especially if the windows could be readily adjusted. On most liners the first class rooms were good enough to more than satisfy the average passenger, but in the more prestigeous ships the trend in decor was more extreme – with period style furnishings, evocative of stately home grandeur, but which owed more to fantasy than fact.

The break came with the completion of Orient Line's *Orion* in 1935, the product of something rare – good teamwork between enlightened and art-conscious owners and an interior designer of like calibre who was responsible not just for one or two rooms, but for all. *Orion's* layout and decor offered nothing dramatic but, instead, settings which made for comfort and relaxation, even on her long voyages (to and from Australia) and this in both hot and cold weather. It was because of these and other features that she was something more than just *the* passenger ship of the year.

For decades undue exposure to direct sunlight was regarded as harmful to delicate skins, so, when out East, passenger ships carried a vast amount of protective canvas awnings. In the early part of this century an interior swimming pool was definitely seen as a prestige symbol, but never did it achieve the relaxed atmosphere of its open air counterpart on deck, one which had evolved from a mere temporary canvas erection. After a dip one wanted to dry off in the sun – and so old style awnings became just a memory. But not however in local service ships stationed in the East, where the aim is to escape from the glaring sunlight.

Two developments which added enormously to voyage enjoyment were the introduction of stabilisers and air-conditioning. The great Italian liner *Conte di Savoia* of 1932 was fitted with three Sperry gyro-stabilisers and was advertised as 'the ship which cannot roll', but of the several alternative systems which followed it was the Denny-Brown, with its extendable fins which became the most popular. Given them during a 1959 refit, P&O's *Chusan* was claimed to be the world's first large liner to be fully stabilised.

The Vaterland *(1914/54,282grt) was the largest liner so far built and although impressive, certainly had no claim to outward elegance – while an excess of topweight demanded the removal of certain fittings. The second of an intended trio for the Hamburg America Line, she gave her owners only minimal service. Interned at New York and first used as the American troopship* Leviathan, *she was later operated by the United States Lines for whom, without a suitable running mate, she proved herself a prestigious loss-maker. Withdrawn in 1934, she was sold in 1938 for demolition at Rosyth. A quadruple screw turbine driven ship with a speed of 23½kts or over, she was originally fitted to carry some 2100 passengers in three classes as well as over 1700 steerage. (CMP)*

As for air-conditioning, this in its earliest form, was applied only to dining rooms and special suites, but during the 1950s there was a steady stream of passenger liners going to shipyards to be made fully air-conditioned.

THE SHIPS REVIEWED AND THEIR TRADES

Alsatian	North Atlantic
Amazon	South Atlantic
Baloeran	Europe – Far East
Calypso	North Sea
Duchess of Bedford	North Atlantic
Kenya Castle	UK – East Africa
Lady Nelson	Eastern Canada – Caribbean
Leicestershire	UK – Burma
Manunda	Australian Interstate
Ophir	In Far East
President Cleveland	Trans-Pacific
Santa Maria	USA – West coast of South America
Southern Cross	Round the world
Suecia	North Sea

Calypso, 1898

The *Calypso*, 3820grt, spent sixteen years with Ellerman's Wilson Line, Hull – better known as the Wilson Line. One of their older units, her popularity on the company's UK–Scandinavia services was remarkable, since in her early years she had traded to an area known for warmth rather than cold.

As *Bruxellesville* she had been built by Sir Raylton Dixon & Co, Middlesbrough for Compagnie Belge Maritime du Congo, of Antwerp and measured 365ft (111.2m) length overall and 44.2ft (13.5m) breadth, her load draught being just under 23ft (7m). Steam triple-expansion machinery of 2400ihp gave a speed of 12kts. Service to West Africa underwent no great change after her 1901

transfer to the associated Woermann Line and as *Alexandra Woermann*, she continued on her old run until the advent of the First World War. Subsequently surrendered and put under White Star management, this ended in 1920 when she became *Calypso*. When she entered Ellerman's Wilson service, *Calypso* was used mainly on the run between Hull and Oslo, but if operational requirements demanded occasionally ran from Hull to Gothenburg, Copenhagen, Danzig and other Scandinavian and Baltic ports. She was used in 1933 to initiate a series of Northern cruises, her passenger capacity being given as sixty first, twenty second and sixty third class. On these she sailed fortnightly, the fares charged ranging between £10 and £18, with £20 for private occupancy.

Calypso – advertised as being of 7500 tons displacement – had a well deck forward, and then a combined bridge deck and poop which reached to the stern – the promenade deck, as it was named. If one boarded via the well deck and took the stairway to the promenade deck, the first door gave access to the entrance hall and, by it, the main staircase. Forward of this hall was the dining room, which measured a mere 15ft × 22ft. Either side of its long centreline table – which seated fourteen – there were five small tables, each set in an alcove, surrounded on three sides by padded seating. Food was brought in from a galley situated the other side of the hall. At the after end of the superstructure there was one two-berth cabin and, near the stern, a tiny card room. Ascend to the sun deck and there were two rooms to choose from, the lounge and, just aft of it, the smoke room, both small enough to be termed 'snug'.

Take the stairway down to the main deck

hall and there, reaching forward, was a centreline passage which, after taking a 'T' formation, served some thirty cabins, mostly two- or three-berth. Return to the hall and the familiar two passages reached aft to serve another thirty similar rooms. Close to the stern there was one final public room, a full-width lounge and cocktail bar, its capacity being about thirty.

Alsatian, 1913

When completed late in 1913 the 18,481grt *Alsatian*, attracted much attention as the largest liner yet designed for the UK – Canada trade and also the first transatlantic liner to have a cruiser stern. Built on the Clyde for Allan Line Steamship Co Ltd, she was a product of the Wm Beardmore shipyard in Glasgow while her sister, *Calgarian*, was delivered a few weeks later by Fairfield. Originally coal-fired, but later converted to burn oil, she had four screws and a waterline length of 600ft (182.9m). Her breadth was 70.2ft (21.4m) and when loaded to her marks, at 28.5ft (8.7m), she had a displacement tonnage of 28,500. Steam turbines of 21,400shp gave her a service speed of 18kts. A ship with a considerable amount of cargo space – much of it insulated – she had five holds, three of them being forward. She catered for three classes of passengers, 263 first, 506 second and 956 third class. For these she carried twenty-two conventional lifeboats, supplemented by twenty-eight of the collapsible Englehardt type.

For her first class passengers the two most important decks were B, which contained public rooms, and C on which their top-grade cabins were situated. It should be noted that C deck was the ship's top continuous deck but, from a point near the mainmast, was open underneath to provide the third class after promenade. To complete the first class world, the dining saloon was on D

The Windsor Castle *(1922/18,967grt) and the* Arundel Castle *of 1921 were the first Union-Castle liners to be built under the Kylsant regime and were their owners' first to have four funnels, turbine drive and a cruiser stern. A Clyde-built ship, the* Windsor Castle *measured 662ft × 72.5ft, carried three classes of passengers (235/360/275) and had a speed of 17kts. To achieve the 20kts required by a new mail contract both ships were re-engined in 1937, when they were also lengthened forward and given a much more handsome two-funnelled profile. Her end came in 1943 when, as a troopship, she was sunk off North Africa. (Ambrose Greenway collection)*

deck, just forward of amidships. Near it were a few more first class cabins, singles, which were arranged three deep from the ship's sides.

Second class passengers boarded her at C deck level at a point near the mainmast and by their entrance hall. There they found the bureau and main staircase, which went up two decks and down two, and immediately aft was the main lounge and, in the same position – but one deck higher – was the smoking room. To reach the second class dining saloon they would go down to D deck, its entrance being at the foot of the stairway. A full-width room, it could seat 290 persons at long tables taking up to 12 a side. As for the cabins, these were on E deck, where they occupied one third the length of the ship. Hardly luxurious, they were for two or four persons and arranged three deep in from the ship's sides. A few others however were sited near the centreline.

The third class accommodation (some 956 in all) was divided, most of it forward, the rest aft. To take the former first, the boarding point was under the foremast at D deck level, while the dining room was nearer amidships on F deck and could seat 340 persons at long tables, some taking 11 a side. The open promenade was between the foremast and the bridge front and the two small public rooms were beneath on E deck. Alternatively they had bare but enclosed 'tween deck space on D deck. Those who were berthed aft boarded the ship on E deck (near the mainmast). The two public rooms and promenade were above on D deck, but the dining room – for 176 – was fractionally forward on F deck. So too were the cabins, but right aft near the stern.

Having dealt with the general layout as it affected each class, a final look at the first class seems called for. Their main entrance hall on C deck was at the head of two long passages which extended the length of the superstructure. The cabins, mainly for one or two persons, were two deep, some lacking a porthole. Of special interest were several intercommunicating cabins which could be used as two-or three-room suites. These naturally had their own bathrooms, obviating the need to cross the passage. Above, on B deck, the sequence of social rooms commenced (from forward) with the library and writing room, lounge, card room, second entrance hall and smoking room. Outside was open promenade space, the forward part of which was protected by a glazed screen – North Atlantic weather was not always that attractive!

Duchess of Bedford, 1928

The *Duchess of Bedford* (20,123grt) was the first of four sisterships built in 1928–29 for Canadian Pacific Steamships, expressly designed for service between Liverpool and ports in eastern Canada. She was one of three built by John Brown & Co, Clydebank, the others being *Duchess of Richmond* and *Duchess of York*. It had been intended that *Duchess of Atholl*, built by Wm Beardmore & Co, Dalmuir, should be the first, but a broken sling caused a large piece of machinery to be dropped and smashed when it was being lowered into position. It had long been customary for elderly liners to be down-graded from first to cabin class, but for Canadian Pacific the 'Duchess' ships represented the third generation to be specially designed as such. In service they proved to be extremely successful and popular.

The Almeda *(1926/12,838grt) was one of five new ships with which the Blue Star Line started their London–River Plate passenger and refrigerated cargo service. In doing so they took on the Royal Mail group which already had three services running there, these with their 'A', 'D' and earlier 'Highland' class ships. Like her sisters* Andalucia, Arandora, Avelona *and* Avila, *the* Almeda *soon had* Star *added to her name, this to avoid confusion with their larger rivals. As built the Blue Star ships measured 535ft × 68ft; turbine-driven with a speed of 17kts (faster than most of the opposition), they carried some 160 first class passengers. Trade depression subsequently caused one vessel to shed her passenger accommodation and another to become a famous cruise ship. The remaining three had their performance improved by being lengthened forward and given Maier bows. Tragically, all were sunk during the Second World War. (Laurence Dunn collection)*

To take *Duchess of Bedford* as typical of the four, when built she had a passenger capacity of 578 cabin, 480 tourist and 518 third class passengers, the last named being mainly settlers and students. For cargo she had seven holds – four of them forward, her deadweight tonnage being 9500. Her overall length was 601ft (183m) and breadth 75ft (23m), while her load draught was 27ft (8.2m). Her twin screws were driven by Parsons single-reduction geared turbines of very advance design. These developed 20,000shp and took steam from three main boilers and gave a service speed of 17½kts, although she could quite easily average 18kts, and at times proved capable of 20kts.

A two funnelled ship with two masts and a cruiser stern, *Duchess of Bedford* had a well balanced profile. Studied in detail, her fore deck (A) ran right to the stern, although its after portion was 'open' beneath to provide crew working space. Above this was a 520ft (159m) long stretch of white painted side plating, this being the base of the promenade deck. Beneath A deck were B, C and D decks, all of which were mainly given over to cabins, as indeed was the forward part of E deck. For imaginary exploration the best point of entry was at A deck, through side doors just aft of the forward funnel. Inside was the entrance hall and main staircase. The latter took one down two decks (to C) and the cabin class dining saloon. Domed, spacious and full-width, it could seat 244 persons. Immediately aft was the very large galley area, so placed that it could also serve the tourist class dining saloon. Similar in size to the other one, it too, had to offer two sittings for meals. Down on D deck, the third class dining saloon was immediately under that for the cabin class. Also on this deck

were cabins for over 500 passengers, those for the third class being forward and the cabin class aft.

To return to the starting point, the entrance hall on A deck, it was on this level that the majority of the cabin class were accommodated. Their cabins, generally for two or three persons, were arranged in groups of four, two inner and two outer, reached by a series of short thwartships passages branching off the main fore and aft passages. Toilets and baths were mostly grouped inboard, near the centreline. Aft, and beyond the cabin area, was a spacious lounge which was flanked by glass protected promenades.

On the 'Duchess' ships the main sequence of social rooms was on the promenade deck above. Flanked by open decks, these included the forward observation/drawing room, side gallery and writing room, then, further aft, two much larger ones, the main lounge and smoking room. On the topmost level – the boat deck – there were fourteen two-cot cabins which, when required, could be turned into suites. Other features on this deck were the playroom and deck for children and the gymnasium.

Lady Nelson, 1928

The *Lady Nelson*, 7970grt, was the first of five twin screw passenger and refrigerated cargo steamers built for Canadian National Steamships, Montreal to further trade between eastern Canada and the many West Indies islands. Outwards they were intended to carry manufactured goods and return with island products, such as bananas, oranges and the like. She was one of three ships designed to operate on what was known as the longer

The Vulcania *(1928/23,970grt) and her sister* Saturnia, *the world's most powerful motorship when built a year earlier, belonged to Cosulich Line which was absorbed into the Italia fleet in 1937. With their massive appearance, thick-set funnel and closely placed masts, they introduced a new style to the Atlantic. They measured 632ft × 80ft and carried approximately 1800 passengers in four classes. They were essentially prestige ships but opulence in first class was offset by gems of Italian artistry. Re-engined in 1935–36, raising their speed from 19kts to 21kts, they were taken over by the United States in 1943 and used as troopships. Released in 1946, they resumed commercial service with modified accommodation, running from Genoa and later Trieste to New York. Withdrawn in the mid-1960s,* Saturnia *was scrapped but* Vulcania *was sold to SIOSA, operating as* Caribia *in the West Indies emigrant trade and later cruising in the Mediterranean before finally being broken up in Taiwan in 1974. (CMP)*

route. After an initial call at Bermuda, they visited nearly a dozen other island ports as far south as Demerara before returning by the same route. Two other ships were used on the shorter and inner route to Bermuda, Nassau and Jamaica and these differed slightly in detail to meet local requirements.

A product of the Cammell Laird shipyard at Birkenhead, *Lady Nelson* had a deadweight tonnage of 6370 and an overall length of 438ft (133.5m), her breadth and draught being 59ft (18m) and 24ft (7.3m) respectively. Two sets of Parsons single-reduction geared turbines of 5700shp and four oil-fired boilers gave a service speed of 14–15kts. She was of three-island type and between her four holds she had a bridge deck 225ft (68.6m) long. It was on and under this that she had her passenger accommodation – for 107 first and 32 second class. In addition she could carry 100 deck class passengers on short inter-island runs.

Her principal decks were known as the upper, bridge, promenade and boat decks.

The Rangitiki *(1929/16,755grt) was the first of three motor liners built on the Clyde for the New Zealand Shipping Co. Designed to operate via the Panama Canal, they measured 553ft × 70ft and carried some 100 first, 85 second and 410 third class passengers. She, like the* Rangitane *and* Rangitoto, *were large cargo carriers – their deadweight tonnage was almost 13,200 – yet despite this they had a remarkably elegant and well balanced profile. Very early in her career the* Rangitiki *had her funnels shortened and some kingposts removed, this to reduce topweight. With the war over, she and the surviving* Rangitata *were given new Doxford diesels which raised their speed to 15½kts. The* Rangitiki *made her final passage to Spanish breakers in 1962. (CMP)*

One boarded the ship at bridge deck level and on opening the door found the entrance hall, purser's office, main stairway and, nearby, two very luxurious de luxe suites. Going aft two long passages gave access to three de luxe cabins (one single and two doubles), then a sequence of cabins able to take from one to three persons. On the centreline was a block of toilets, the barber's shop and medical area. Beyond this enclosed area and extending to the mainmast, was the second class open promenade deck. The ship's main social rooms were on the promenade deck above. Approached by the main stairway was the first class lounge – which faced forward – and the equally large smoking room. Aft of the funnel casing was the similar sized garden lounge. Here there was a generous amount of covered deck space and more, which was open, on the deck above.

Returning to the main staircase and descending to the upper deck, one entered the first class dining saloon, a domed and full-width room with small tables for two, four or six persons. The galley area which was just aft, also served the second class dining saloon, which was on the starboard side and had its seats arranged at three long tables. The traditional two fore and aft passages stretched aft towards the stern and these served the remaining cabins. Nearly twenty in all, these had three and four berths. Just beyond, and approximately under the mainmast, were two small cabin class rooms, the lounge and smoke room.

Ophir, 1928

The Netherlands passenger and cargo ship *Ophir*, 4115grt, was typical of many small and medium sized vessels built in Holland for service in the Dutch East Indies (now Indonesia) but which never returned to Europe. *Ophir* was built at Amsterdam by Netherlands Shipbuilding Co for that one-time giant, Koninklijke Paketvaart Maatschappij (KPM) which, although controlled from Amsterdam, had its eastern base at Batavia (now Jakarta).

Her length overall was 386ft (117.7m) and breadth 52ft (15.8m), while on a load draught of just under 19ft (5.8m), she had a deadweight tonnage of 2620. Twin screws and a pair of Werkspoor diesels of 5000bhp gave a speed of 15kts. She had four cargo holds, two forward and two aft and these were served by a mix of derricks and electric cranes. The hull had two continuous decks, the lower one being topped by three islands, a 154ft (47m) long bridge deck, also a forecastle and poop, both some 50ft (15.2m) in length. The space between them was bridged over to provide large deck spaces which were covered, but open at the sides. These provided the temporary quarters of the customary scores of deck passengers who, with their bedding and personal belongings, just camped on deck. As distinct from these, *Ophir* provided cabin accommodation for some 110 passengers.

The best means of entry was by the gangway which led to the main deck and so to the entrance hall. There, in addition to the usual bureau, was the main staircase which led to two other decks, one up and one down. The main deck was almost entirely filled with cabins, two long rows of them, with twenty each side. These, mostly two- or three-berth, extended as far as the mainmast. Go down to the main deck and here and there were a few more cabins, but the major feature was the first class dining saloon which faced forward and had small tables for four or six persons. Amidships and on the port side was the hospital, mail room and a dormitory – presumably for those who preferred something better than a bare deck to sleep on.

A couple of levels up, the upper deck had two major rooms. These were the first class saloon – which seated some forty persons and, located aft, the second class dining saloon which could seat some sixty persons. Stretching aft, beyond the last two hatches, was the second class promenade space.

Above, on the promenade deck, there were two blocks of cabins, but these were for the deck and engineer officers. On this level *Ophir* carried two lifeboats each side, while near the stern she had another four stowed abreast.

Santa Maria, 1928

The United States passenger and cargo liner *Santa Maria*, 8060grt, was the first of a pair ordered by Grace Line for their old-established service between New York, the Panama Canal and ports along the west coast of South America. Delivered by the Furness Shipbuilding Co in the spring of 1928, she was joined a few months later by her sistership *Santa Barbara* which came from the same yard. The largest in the Grace Line fleet, they had an overall length of 486ft (148.1m), their breadth being 84ft (25.6m). Of 7500dwt, they had a load draught of just over 25ft (7.6m). Twin screws and two eight-cylinder Sulzer diesels of 8000bhp gave a loaded speed of 16½kts.

A handsome ship, *Santa Maria* had two funnels although the forward one was a dummy. Of her five cargo holds the three largest were forward, two having hatches trunked through the accommodation. On the shelter deck, the upper of her two continuous decks there was a short raised forecastle and a bridge deck which was 250ft (76m) in length. This in turn carried a superstructure two decks high and some 160ft (49m) long. It was in and under this central mass that the passengers, some 150 of them, all first class, were accommodated.

The easiest means of access was by gangway to the bridge deck, where double doors led one to the main hall and stairway. On the forward side was the purser's office and behind it, two passages which led to a pair of cabins and two large two-room de luxe suites which looked out forward. Running aft from the hall were the usual twin passages – port and starboard – which gave access to the best first class cabins, these mostly two berth and complete with bathroom. Beyond these was a smaller staircase and the barber's shop.

It was the deck above, the promenade, on which the social rooms were grouped, these in two blocks. At its top the main staircase ended in the leading block in which were the social hall and dance room. Separated from these by some open deck was the second block which contained the smoking room and veranda cafe. On the topmost deck (one up) there were a number of penthouse-like cabins and a sports area, but the forward part was the domain of the captain and officers.

Take the same main staircase down to its foot on the upper deck and there, just forward was the lofty and full-width dining saloon which could seat all at small tables. Otherwise the rest of this deck, and also the forward part of the one below, was occupied by passenger cabins.

Manunda, 1929

The Australian interstate liner *Manunda*, 9115grt, was built on the Clyde by Wm Beardmore & Co for Adelaide Steamship Co. A twin screw motorship which measured 447ft (136.2m) in length and 60ft (18.3m) breadth, she had two Harland & Wolff-B&W type diesels of 10,000bhp which gave a service speed of 15½–16kts. She was built before the days of stabilisers and air-conditioning and when private cabin facilities were luxuries reserved only for special suites and the like. Her designed route stretched along the whole of Australia's southern and eastern coasts, from Fremantle in the southwest, then via intermediate ports, to Cairns in the northeast. That *Manunda* carried a considerable amount of cargo largely contributed to her reputation for steadiness.

She was of shelter-deck design and this deck was topped by a long raised forecastle, the foremast being at its after end. Separating this from the bridge front was the second of her four hatches. Those for the midship and after holds were trunked upwards to passenger decks above. For her passengers, 176 first and 130 second class, she offered the use of four decks, the lowest, inside the hull, being the upper deck. Those above were named the shelter, promenade and boat decks.

It was best to board the ship by the midship gangway and then go forward along the shelter deck until one came to the entrance hall. There, opposite the main staircase, was the purser's office which was flanked by two short passages leading forward to some fourteen cabins, mainly two-berth. From the other side of the entrance hall two long passages stretched towards the stern. Along these were grouped the great majority of the passenger cabins. Mostly two-berth, they were laid out in 'Bibby' style, each having its own porthole. Many of those aft were interchangeable, first or second.

The two restaurants, first and second class, were just beneath, on the upper deck. The one forward, full width and square in shape, was situated immediately under the bridge. The galley area, just aft, also served the second class restaurant. About half the size of the other, it could nevertheless seat about ninety persons. From its after side stretched two long passages and around these were grouped the balance of the second class cabins. If one took the main staircase up to the front of the promenade deck, one entered the big and domed music room. Almost adjacent were the remaining cabins, about ten, and all of them two-berth.

The Empress of Japan *(1930/26,032grt) was designed for the Canadian Pacific Line's trans-Pacific service between Vancouver and Yokohama. The fastest on that run, she initially operated with three others, notably the* Empresses *of* Asia *and* Russia *– earlier products of the Fairfield yard and which had the same well balanced profile and easy sheerline. A turbine-driven ship with a speed of 21–23kts, she measured 666ft × 84ft. Of passengers she carried 400 first, 164 second and 100 third class, also over 500 steerage. Renamed* Empress of Scotland *in 1942, she spent the next few years on the Liverpool–St Lawrence run. In 1958 she was sold to the Hamburg-Atlantic Line and reconstructed to emerge as the two-funnelled* Hanseatic. *A fire at New York in 1966 caused much damage and soon after she was scrapped at Hamburg. (Ambrose Greenway collection)*

The Jean Laborde *(1931/11,414grt) was built for the Messageries Maritimes, of Marseilles for use as required on the Company's Indian Ocean service or that to French Indo-China. Shown as built with black hull and funnels, she measured 491ft × 62ft and had accommodation for some 140 first, 90 second, and 75 third class passengers, also almost 600 steerage. Her speed in early days was 15–16kts, but in 1936 she was lengthened forward, given a raked stem and more powerful diesels, which raised her speed to about 18–19kts. At the same time she was given an all-white livery, one which vastly improved her appearance. Laid up at Marseilles in 1940, she was later scuttled there by the retreating Germans. Raised, she was found fit only for scrap. She was one of six MM ships built 1929–33 each with two square, cowl-topped funnels. Much criticised at the time – public opinion was then far more conservative – they did bring their owners useful publicity in stressing MM ownership.* (Ambrose Greenway collection)

Continuing aft the engine casing divided the wide deck space into two and these areas were popular for deck chair addicts and for evening cinema shows. Beyond this area lay the final first class venue, the smoking room.

A short distance beyond was the mainmast and at its base was the deckhouse which contained the second class smoking room and music room. Very close to the stern was a final deckhouse and there one found the hospital. As for the ship's topmost deck – the boat deck – this had a row of officers' cabins, the lifeboats – and plenty of open deck.

Suecia and Britannia, 1929

The Swedish North Sea passenger ships *Suecia* and *Britannia* had long and very successful careers on the London–Gothenburg route. Both were built on the Tyne by Swan, Hunter & Wigham Richardson, the first on the berth at Wallsend from which the first *Mauretania* was launched. Structurally alike, they differed only in the style of decor chosen for their public rooms, one in Scandinavian style and the other English. Owned by Rederi-AB Svenska Lloyd, Gothenberg, when new they were the largest and fastest to operate between the two countries and had a gross tonnage of 4216, the figure for deadweight being 2420. Their overall length was 370ft (112.8m), breadth 50ft (15.2m) and load draught just over 20ft (6.1m). Originally coal-burners, but later converted to oil, each had a single screw, three Parsons type geared turbines of 5700shp and a service speed of 17kts. Their passenger capacity was 218 first and 44 third class.

The ships had two continuous decks – main and shelter. The latter was topped by a long raised forecastle which was separated (originally) from the bridge front by a break – and No 2 hatch. There were five holds and hatches, the third one – trunked to boat deck level – being served by a single kingpost stepped just forward of the funnel. The boat

deck, which had four boats aside, ended midway between the funnel and mainmast, but the one below continued to that mast. Right aft there was another deckhouse which contained the third class saloon and pantry.

To return to the bridge deck and its several public rooms, the forward lounge was set inside a long glass screen, the space between serving as a pleasant and sheltered veranda. Aft of this lounge and at the head of the main staircase was the first class smoke-room and, beyond it, the aft-facing veranda cafe. Below, at the forward end of the superstructure, was the nearly full-width dining saloon while, on the other side of the foyer, there was a small private dining room. The rest of this deck was devoted to two-berth cabins, these opening off the traditional pair of fore and aft passages.

The main deck below had two similar passages, these serving the great majority of the passenger cabins, nearly all of which were two-berth. These extended from mast to mast, while right aft, was a separate deckhouse which contained twelve third class cabins, most of them four-berth. One unusual feature of the main deck was the placing of the galley amidships, where it reached from the centreline to the port side, while on the opposite side were arranged all the heads.

Baloeran, 1930

The 16,981grt *Baloeran* was built in 1930 for the Rotterdam Lloyd mail, passenger and cargo service between the Netherlands and the Dutch East Indies – now Indonesia. She was built at the Fijenoord shipyard at Rotterdam and was later joined by her sister *Dempo* which came from Flushing. *Baloeran* had a length overall of 574ft (175m) and a breadth of 70ft (21.3m), while on a draught of just over 28ft (8.5m) she had a deadweight tonnage of 8736. Twin screws and two Sulzer diesels of 14,000bhp gave a service speed of

18kts. Her passenger capacity was 234/252 first, 280/253 second, 70 third and 48 fourth class. There were also an extra forty-two berths for children.

The round voyage took just over two months, much of it near the tropics. For this reason the base of her superstructure was set in by 4ft, the overhang of the full-width promenade deck being enough to give some shade to the upper row of the cabins. With a profile then unique, she had her masts set unusually close to the funnel, made possible by the use of electric cranes – not derricks – for the working of her four holds. Not visible from the waterline was another unusual feature, the placing of her swimming pool on the forecastle.

If boarding *Baloeran* via the forward gangway, this took one to the upper deck and the entrance to the first class vestibule. In this were the main staircase and lifts. Down on the next (second) deck you faced the entrance to the first class dining saloon, a full width room which could seat 234 passengers. Something unlikely ever to be seen again, it was three decks high with the lower of the two galleries specially enlarged to take the orchestra. Beyond the adjacent pantry area was the engine room casing. Then the pattern was reversed with another pantry close to the second class dining saloon. Less impressive, this had only one gallery, and opening out of this room was the main second class staircase, a feature which marked the vertical division between the first and second classes.

Aft of this, and on three decks (second, upper and bridge), were grouped the second class cabins. Long and narrow, but each with its own porthole, these were fitted out for two, three and sometimes four persons. Take this staircase up to the promenade deck and there were the second class public rooms – the smoking rooms and social room, while just astern of these were the children's nursery and playdeck. Yet higher was their veranda cafe and open deck, which extended to the stern.

The seventy third class passengers were accommodated in two to four berth cabins situated near the stern on the third deck. Above, two decks higher, was their dining room (long tables), but it was to the next deck up (bridge deck) that they had to go for their smoking room and open promenade space. As for the fourth class, their cabins, mainly four to six berth, were located near the bows on the second deck – nearly under their social room in the forecastle.

To return to the forward first class staircase, this served two decks of first class cabins, those on the upper and bridge decks. Each with its own porthole, they were for one, two or three persons. One unusual feature was the frequent provision of one bathroom for two cabins; otherwise one still had to cross the passage. Above, on the promenade deck, the two main public rooms were the circular shaped social hall and the adjacent smoking room. Slightly aft and flanking the engine casing was a compact group of fourteen cabins, mostly single berth, with adjacent bathrooms. The only other feature of note here was the nursery area.

Taking the same main staircase – or lift – to the top boat deck level one found one of the ship's most attractive open-air features, a spacious area, ideal for deck chairs. Covered, but open sided and with adjustable glazed screens, it was the ideal place from which to view the world. This was not quite all, for on the deck above and just forward of the funnel, was a well laid out sports deck.

President Cleveland, 1947

The *President Cleveland*, 15,456grt, was the first of a pair built 1947–48 for American President Lines (APL). The first US postwar passenger ship, she and *President Wilson* were the largest liners built on the Pacific coast and together cost $46 million to build. They brought new standards of luxury to the Pacific and for many years formed the backbone of the company's fleet. Based on San Francisco, the main ports served were Honolulu, Yokohama, Manila, Hong Kong and Kobe. Originally laid down as the last two of a series of type P2 naval transports, they were bought by APL when they were at a very early stage of construction at Bethlehem Alameda Shipyard. As completed they had air-conditioning (except in some passenger areas and crews quarters), flume stabilisers and seven cargo holds.

Their main dimensions were length overall 610ft (185.9m), breadth 76ft (23.2m) and load draught 30ft (9.1m). Twin screws and GEC turbo-electric machinery of 20,000shp gave a service speed of 19kts. Over the years their accommodation was subject to some change, but they are described here when they carried 304 first, and 380 tourist/economy class passengers.

Of the seven decks the promenade was the most important. Right forward it was an open deck, but amidships it became the base of the superstructure where, inside the hull plating, it contained the main first class social rooms.

To get an idea of her internal layout it is best to work downwards from the top. Here, on the sun deck, the main feature was the games area laid out between the funnels. Below, on the boat deck, there was more open deck space but also, at its after end, the

children's play deck and room. Returning to the promenade deck, there the sequence of social rooms was divided into three by the main foyer and one forward, each with its own staircase and lift. Facing forward was the main lounge and, after the first foyer, two small rooms which flanked the engine casing – the library and writing room. Pass one of these and one entered the smoking room, beyond which was the main foyer and its shopping centre. Yet further aft was the cocktail bar and the even larger veranda with its dance floor. Outside was the first class swimming pool and lido area.

The upper deck, from mast to mast, was devoted to first class cabins, which were reached by the usual port and starboard passages. These cabins were for one, two or three persons. Most of them had their own facilities and often a bath. Here too, on each side, were a number of de luxe suites while, adjacent to them and, at the after end of the superstructure, was the small and select Marco Polo lounge.

Beyond this lay the domain of the tourist class. Here, besides the swimming pool and lido area was the main lounge flanked by

The Queen Mary *(1936/80,774grt) – then known as '534' – was laid down at Clydebank at the very end of 1930 with the announcement that she and a proposed consort would be fast enough to take the place of the three then employed on the Southampton–New York run. Financial difficulties coupled with the deep depression caused a long cessation of work and it was May 1936 before she finally entered service. An early record crossing was soon bettered by the* Normandie, *but the* Mary *finally won with a speed of 31.69kts. After proving invaluable as a wartime troopship she returned to commercial service in 1947. Her propensity for rolling was countered in 1958 when she was fitted with two sets of stabilisers. Withdrawn in 1967, she sailed via Cape Horn for Long Beach, California, where she still lies as a museum/hotel complex.* (CMP)

enclosed promenades. On A deck, the next down, the main feature other than tourist class cabins, was the big lounge, beyond which was a playdeck for children. Going down to the next level, the two major features of B deck were the first class dining saloon and, just aft, that for the tourist class, whose cabins – apart from the hospital area – filled the after part of the ship, also the corresponding part of C deck below.

Leicestershire, 1949

The passenger and cargo liner *Leicestershire*, 8908grt, was built for the Bibby Line's long-established service between Liverpool, Colombo and Rangoon. Like her near sister, *Warwickshire* of 1948, she was built on the Clyde by the Fairfield Shipbuilding & Engineering Co. The trade for which they had been designed had started in 1889 and it was hoped that, after the Second World War had ended, some semblance of normality would return. That however, was not to be and so in 1965 both ships were sold, *Leicestershire* to become the Typaldos-owned *Heraklion*. Converted into a passenger/car ferry with side doors, she foundered in 1968 during a particularly violent Mediterranean storm. Seen historically, *Leicestershire* acquires a special interest in representing the very last of a long proven type.

A single-screw ship of 9614dwt, her length was 498ft (151.8m) overall, breadth 70ft

(21.3m) and load draught 27.5ft (8.4m). Geared turbines of 7000shp and two water-tube boilers gave her a service speed of 15½kts. Given one wide funnel, she had no mainmast, its place being taken by two pairs of kingposts and eight derricks. She had five holds, the hatch for the third being trunked to boat deck level at a point between the bridge and funnel. To serve this hatch were two pairs of kingposts, each of which carried two derricks. *Leicestershire* had accommodation for seventy-six passengers, all first class, nearly all of whom had their cabins on the 195ft long bridge deck. The rest, twelve in number, had their cabins below, near the purser's office. Boarding via the forward end of the bridge deck and entering the foyer, this had three cabins each side, while the familiar pair of fore and aft passages provided access to another nineteen cabins which stretched away aft. These were for two or three persons who, for their ablutions, had just to cross the passage. However right forward and beyond the foyer, there were two special staterooms, each with its own bathroom.

The promenade deck – which was one up – had much of its length protected by a glazed screen and inside this were most of the social rooms. Of these the lounge faced forward, while aft of the funnel casing was the smoking room and veranda cafe. Nearer the stern was a special play area and room for children. The aftermost feature of this deck was a generous size swimming pool.

Above there was the boat deck, but that was the domain of the officers. The most important room was the full width, forward facing dining saloon which seated eighty-four persons and was situated at the base of the superstructure on the boat deck. Close by was a group of four three-berth cabins, the hairdresser, shop and the always important purser's office.

Kenya Castle, 1951

The *Kenya Castle*, 17,042grt, was one of three medium sized passenger and cargo steamships built by Harland & Wolff, for Union-Castle Line. Originally designed for use on the company's round Africa service, they were given a major refit in the early 1960s and put on another route, via Suez and East African ports to Durban.

She and her sisters *Braemar Castle* and *Rhodesia Castle* measured 576ft (175.6m.) length overall and 74ft (22.5m) breadth and, with twin screws and geared turbines of 14,400shp had a service speed of 17½kts. She carried 526 cabin class passengers and had a considerable amount of space for cargo. Her superstructure had its base on A deck which, in open form, extended to the stem and also continued aft to the stern although, from the mainmast aft, it was open sided. The upper part of the eye-catching white hull plating contained the higher grade cabins, while the promenade deck above had the main public rooms.

Down on D deck (within the hull) there was an even longer array of cabins of somewhat lower grade, more of these being grouped at the after part of C deck. However the most important feature of C deck was the dining saloon, a full width room with small tables for some 260 persons (*ie* two

The Willem Ruys *(1947/23,114grt) marked the end of long rivalry between the ship's owners, the Royal Rotterdam Lloyd and the Amsterdam-based Nederland Line. When, in the late 1930s, reason dictated that each firm should build and operate only one more passenger ship, the Nederland Line responded with the very different looking Oranje. Laid down rather later, the* Willem Ruys *spent the war years looming over the shipyard at Flushing. Finally launched in July 1946, she commenced her maiden voyage in December 1947. Eleven years later her trade to the Dutch East Indies (now Indonesia) died. Used briefly on the North Atlantic, the* Willem Ruys *was then remodelled for a round-the-world service. In 1964 she was sold to the Flotta Lauro and as the* Achille Lauro *started a new cruise ship career. (CMP)*

sittings). Opposite the entrance to the dining saloon were the lifts and staircase which served all four decks.

To start at the top – promenade – deck, the major rooms were the forward facing lounge and, at the opposite end, the smoking room. Between them, and flanking the engine room casing, were the long narrow gallery/library and cocktail bar. Beyond the smoking room there was just open deck space. Take the lift or stairs to the A deck foyer, and from there stretched two long passages which served some fifty cabins. Designed to take from one to three persons, these had either a shower or bath. Only six were inside rooms. At the after end of these passages were the club room (port side) and the nursery play deck area. Beyond was the full width and roofed-in dance area. Go through its swing doors and one was by the swimming pool.

Retrace one's steps to the forward lift and descend to B deck and one was in the main entrance foyer – the focal point of the ship and which contained the bureau, shop, hairdressers and the purser's office.

The foyer was also at the head of the traditional pair of long fore and aft passages. It started with a few single-berth cabins,

each with its own bathroom, but the rest were for two, three or four persons – whose facilities lay just across the passage. Some of those aft were inside rooms, but most were arranged in Bibby Line fashion, each having its own porthole. Another fifty-six cabins were on C deck and stretched from amidships aft. Mainly for one to three persons, only half were outside rooms. Indicative of the period in which she was built, *Kenya Castle* had only limited air-conditioning, the areas so blessed being the dining and social rooms, the top (A deck) cabins and a few other places such as the hospital. Otherwise mechanical ventilation and punkah louvres were the rule.

Southern Cross, 1955

Among passenger ships, when built *Southern Cross* was unique, since never before had a liner of her size had her engines placed aft. Nor had one been built which carried passengers only – and no cargo whatsoever. The separation of these two elements was of particular importance since it cut out the risk of unexpected port delays and the disruption of a prearranged schedule.

Southern Cross, of 20,214grt, was built and engined by Harland & Wolff, of Belfast for the Shaw, Savill & Albion Co and designed to make four round-the-world voyages per year. When sailing eastabout she did so via South Africa and returned via Panama, the reverse applying when she sailed westabout. Her length overall was 604ft (184.1m), breadth 76.8ft (23.4m) and when down to her marks – at a little short of 26ft (8m) – she had a displacement of 20,420 tons. Twin screws, double-reduction geared turbines and three Foster-White boilers together gave her a speed of 20kts. Of passengers she carried 1160 – all tourist class.

The placing of her engines right aft gave her designers hitherto undreamed of scope in the arrangement of her passenger accommodation. Her profile had a flush deck line and a long superstructure which was topped by a massive bridge structure and tall, tapered mast and a smallish, streamline funnel placed right aft. It was the promenade deck, stretching from the stem almost to the stern which served as the base for the superstructure, the decks below being known as the main, saloon, A, B and lower decks. In

The Gripsholm *(1957/23,190grt) was built in Italy for Swedish America Line's transatlantic service. Nicknamed 'The Golden Yacht', she was the largest Scandinavian passenger ship to date and much use was made of light alloy in the construction of her superstructure. Fully air-conditioned, she carried 150 first and 612 tourist class passengers with an additional 80 interchangeable berths, nearly all cabins having their own bathrooms. In 1968 she switched to cruising with just the odd Atlantic positioning voyage but high labour costs forced her sale in 1974 to Greek shipowner Karageorgis, for whom she continued to cruise as* Navarino. *Her further sale to Sally Line late in 1981 was thwarted when a drydock in which she was being refitted capsized, almost causing her to be totally lost. Eventually repaired and sold to Regency Cruises, she is still operating in American waters as* Regent Sea. *(Ambrose Greenway collection)*

turn, the promenade deck was topped – in order of ascent – by the lounge, sun and upper bridge decks. Starting again at promenade level, this had a rather narrow walkway all round, while the space inside was almost completely filled with cabins. These had from one to six berths and were mostly arranged six abreast, a layout made possible by the use of an extra (third) fore and aft passage. More cabins grouped in similar fashion filled varying sized areas of the decks below. However, the saloon deck had two major features, the large and full-width restaurants which were placed one forward and one aft of the midship galley area. Situated three decks down and at the base of the lift and main staircase, was the larger of two swimming pools, the other being high up at the forward end of the sun deck.

The focal point of *Southern Cross* was the lounge deck which took its name from a magnificent forward facing room – alongside which were the smaller writing room and library. Aft of the main stairway were several other large rooms – the smoking room, the lofty and galleried cinema/lounge and the full-width taverna with its dance floor and bar. Here folding doors led out on to the open deck beyond. The sun deck (above) had as its key features the swimming pool and lido area, both of which were well sheltered by screens. Yet higher, on the lower bridge deck, was the really notable feature of the ship, one only made possible by placing her funnel and machinery aft. This was the sports deck which was over 100ft (30m) long and well protected by screens.

To round off, *Southern Cross* had two features then relatively new – the fitting of Denny-Brown stabilisers and a major air-conditioning plant. The latter was made necessary by the high proportion of inside cabins and by the climatic variations through which she passed and was capable of supplying 9 million BTU (British Thermal Units) per hour.

Amazon, 1959

The *Amazon* (20,368grt) was the first of a trio for Royal Mail Lines, London, and started her maiden voyage from London in January 1960, her sisters *Aragon* and *Arlanza* following a few months later. A Belfast-built ship, *Amazon* had an overall length of 585ft (178m) and a breadth of 78ft (24m). Twin screws and Harland & Wolff/B&W diesels of 20,000bhp gave a service speed of 17½kts. Her passenger capacity was 107 first, 82

second (some interchangeable) and 275 third class, many of the last named being seasonal workers who embarked at Vigo for South America. After Vigo, the ship called at Lisbon before making for Salvador, Rio de Janeiro, Santos, Montevideo and Buenos Aires.

The first British passenger liner to rely solely on alternating current, she was fully air-conditioned and fitted with stabilisers. Below decks she had five holds with 435,000cu ft of insulated space and another 45,000cu ft for general cargo. To handle this she had 20 derricks and electric winches. Her profile was tall in relation to length, an unusual feature being the separation of the bridgehouse from the main part of the superstructure and its passengers. A traditional Royal Mail feature this, it sprang from the belief that officers were more efficient if the two were kept well apart. As a result passengers had no access to the forward part of the ship, while the massive size of the bridge certainly restricted their view ahead.

The promenade (B) deck was the ship's uppermost continuous deck and it was on this that the bridge and superstructure were built. Above it was the upper promenade (A) deck and lido deck. The next one up, the boat deck, had little of interest to passengers, but the uppermost, the observation deck, had two tennis courts for first class. The promenade and upper promenade decks were devoted to first class cabins, but some on the lower level were interchangeable. These cabins were a mix of singles and doubles; some were inside, but most had their own facilities – as did a forward facing pair of de luxe rooms. There were also another sixteen first class cabins situated on C deck, close to the entrance hall.

The first class social rooms extended the length of the lido deck. These comprised a forward facing lounge with side verandas, a children's playroom, a side gallery for reading and writing, and a smoking room. Aft of this was the lido cafe and swimming pool area. As for their restaurant, this was on C deck, its location being under the bridge.

Most of the cabin class passengers were berthed just aft of amidships on C and D decks. These cabins had from one to four berths apiece; many were inside rooms. For relaxation those in the cabin class had two open promenade decks, one forward and the other aft of the superstructure. The latter which included the swimming pool and lido were overlooked by their main social room – the lounge – which was flanked by a cocktail bar and library.

Although the 275 third class passengers

The P & O Line's Canberra *(1961/45,733grt) entered service a year after her counterpart, the Orient liner* Oriana. *With a common service speed of 27kts the two were designed to replace three 22kt ships on the UK–Australia run, these being the 28,000 ton* Orcades, Oronsay *and* Orsova. *Slightly the larger of the two, the* Canberra *measured 818ft × 102ft. While her original passenger capacity was 596 first and 1616 tourist class she now – as a cruise ship –carries 1737 open class. Seldom have two passenger liners built for the same route differed so much. While the Vickers-Armstrongs built* Oriana *was given geared turbines placed amidships, the* Canberra, *which came from Belfast, had turbo-electric machinery of 88,000shp. Her engines-aft layout made possible a very fine lido area amidships, but reputedly created problems of trim. Apart from her high reputation as a cruise ship, she will be remembered historically for her valuable contribution to the Falklands conflict, when she was affectionately nicknamed 'The Great White Whale'.* (Ambrose Greenway collection)

had their cabins (two to four berth) on D and E decks, their relaxation areas were several decks up. Their swimming pool was on the after deckhouse, just by the docking bridge, while on C deck they had a large covered promenade area. Doors from this led forward to their smoke room and lounge, both of which were on the port side very close to their restaurant.

Laurence Dunn

Cross-channel steamers

As a distinctive type of ship the cross-channel steamer is an interesting one. Often referred to as 'a miniature liner', it was peculiarly British in origin and its design presented naval architects with the challenge of combining both large passenger capacity and space for mail with high speed and great manoeuvrability into a small hull, often with very shallow draught, moreover one capable of withstanding the worst kind of weather that might be encountered in the open waters it was required to traverse all the year round.

The cross-channel steamer can be divided into two different categories. The fast day steamer carried over 1000 passengers on the shortest routes (20–30 miles) such as those crossing the Dover Strait and the St George's Channel as well as on longer ones (around 60 miles) such as Dover–Ostend, Newhaven–Dieppe and Holyhead–Dun Laoghaire (formerly Kingstown). The other type was the slower overnight steamer which operated on routes of 100 miles or more, such as those linking Liverpool and Glasgow with Belfast and Dublin. Services running out of Southampton to Le Havre, the Channel Islands and St Malo also came into this category, as did those crossing the southern part of the North Sea from Harwich to the Hook of Holland and Antwerp.

Cross-channel steamer services began in 1819 when the small paddle steamer *Rob Roy* started running between Glasgow and Belfast and it was not long before a variety of different services sprang up, run by a number of private operators. From the outset all were served by paddle steamers, a type particularly well suited to the shallow tidal harbours of the eastern English Channel, an area where they continued to hold sway until the beginning of the twentieth century. However the arrival of the more efficient screw form of propulsion, coupled with the development of the triple expansion engine, led to them being quickly adopted for ships

operating on the deepwater routes out of Southampton and across the Irish Sea.

As most of the ports being used had a railway connection, it was inevitable that the railway companies became more involved and they gradually took over the running of the majority of the services, having first obtained the necessary parliamentary powers to run steamships. The exceptions were services to Ireland from the Clyde, Liverpool and Holyhead, the mail contract in the latter case being held by the City of Dublin Steam Packet Co. This concern, formed in 1824, ran some of the finest channel steamers to be built before the turn of the century, namely the *Ulster* quartet built by Laird Bros in 1896–97. At 2633grt they measured 360ft in length and were fitted with sleeping berths for 238 first class and 124 second class passengers. Two reciprocating engines fed by coal-fired boilers provided 9000ihp for a service speed of 23kts. Previously it had been the practice for male and female passengers to be segregated in separate sleeping saloons but this began to change following the delivery in 1894 of London & South Western Railway Co's new Le Havre overnight steamers *Alma* and *Columbia*, which were amongst the first to be fitted with individual cabins.

Although many British shipbuilders were involved in the construction of channel steamers, one particular shipyard, William Denny & Bros of Dumbarton on the River Clyde, was to have a greater influence on their design and development than any other, greatly assisted by the fact that it had its own ship testing tank. By the turn of the century it had already been responsible for nine cross-channel paddle steamers and a similar number of screw driven vessels. Fol-

lowing the invention of the steam turbine by Charles Parsons, Denny's worked with him to produce the world's first commercial turbine steamer, *King Edward*, in 1901. A slightly larger ship, *Queen Alexandra*, followed a year later and their combined success and smooth running led the shipyard to approach two railway companies, the South Eastern & Chatham and the London, Brighton & South Coast, with the idea of adopting this novel form of propulsion for their next steamers. Both were persuaded and the SECR ship, *The Queen*, was the first to enter service in June 1903, after attaining 21¾kts on trials from triple screws directly connected to three Parsons turbines. An elegant two-funnelled ship with a low flush hull and a gross tonnage of 1676, she set a pattern that was to last for a good number of years.

The new ship created widespread interest when she commenced running between Dover and Calais, being the first to make the crossing in under one hour. Her success and that of the LBSCR ship *Brighton*, delivered two months later, which demonstrated its superiority when tried against its near identical but reciprocating-engined sister *Arundel* – another Denny product dating from 1900 – confirmed the suitability of the turbine for cross-channel application. One drawback, however, lay in reduced stern power (some 60 per cent of ahead power), which resulted in slightly less manoeuvrability.

It was not long before there were many imitators both in the UK – Denny built two turbine steamers for the Irish Sea in 1904 – and around the world. Japan, which needed ships for a railway connection across the Tsugaru Strait separating the two main islands of Honshu and Hokkaido, also went to

Although no new paddle steamers were built for UK cross-channel routes after 1900, several of the largest and fastest examples remained in service until the 1920s. Marie Henriette built by John Cockerill in 1893 for the Belgian Marine Administration's Ostend–Dover service was amongst the most powerful with 9100ihp compound diagonal engines producing a trial speed of over 22kts. She was lost through stranding on the Cherbourg Peninsula in October 1914 when transporting wounded troops. (Ambrose Greenway collection)

Riviera and her sister Engadine, *both Denny products of 1911, were slightly faster developments of the original turbine cross-channel steamer* The Queen. *They were amongst the first to provide space for the carriage of motor cars, though these had to be crane loaded into the hatches placed forward and aft of the superstructure. Both ships were converted to carry seaplanes during the First World War, canvas shelters fore and aft being replaced in 1915 with large rectangular hangars abaft the second funnel. In 1933* Riviera *started a second career with Burns & Laird Lines, running between Ardrossan and Belfast as* Lairds Isle *until 1957. (CMP)*

Denny for its first two turbine ships in 1907. Speeds increased rapidly as higher powers were installed. The Belgian Marine Administration's *Princesse Elisabeth*, the first of several cruiser-stern turbine vessels built by John Cockerill, Hoboken, attained over 24kts on trials in 1905, making her the fastest merchant vessel of the day until the advent of *Lusitania*, though this was bettered by Isle of Man Steam Packet Co's *Ben-my-Chree* of 1908, which made 25¼kts.

The overnight services to Ireland did not require high speed in order to avoid arriving too early in the morning, 16–17kts being regarded as sufficient; for this reason turbines were not adopted. Typical of the prewar Irish Sea ships was *Patriotic* built by Harland & Wolff for Belfast Steamship Co's Belfast–

Liverpool service in 1912, a ship of 2254grt with a single funnel and a much larger accommodation block than found in the fast day ships.

All the early turbine steamers employed direct drive but by 1910 Charles Parsons had perfected a gearing system which reduced propeller speed, leading to greater efficiency and smoother operation. This was first tried in London & South Western Railway's *Norman-nia* and *Hantonia* built for the Southampton–Le Havre overnight service by Fairfield Shipbuilding & Engineering Co Ltd in 1911. Fitted with four single reduction turbines geared to twin screws, they proved highly successful in service – confounding their many initial critics – and the new arrangement quickly became standard for most ships of this type, including fast day ships such as the 25kt *Paris* built by Denny on torpedo boat lines for the Newhaven–Dieppe joint service in 1913.

The first World War saw many channel steamers taken up for government service, being employed on tasks as varied as armed boarding steamers, troop transports, ambulance ships and even seaplane carriers.

By the early 1920s the refinement of a raised forecastle appeared in the newer Harwich continental ships, a feature that was to be progressively extended further aft in later

ships such as the 4200grt *Vienna* of 1929, reaching almost to the stern in the even larger post Second World War *Amsterdam* and *Arnhem*. The many British railway companies were reorganised into four new companies from January 1923. One of these was the Southern Railway, which soon co-operated with Denny in the design of a new type of fast day steamer with a single funnel, enclosed promenade decks and much improved accommodation, the first being *Isle of Thanet* and *Maid of Kent* in 1927, with the smaller and faster *Worthing* following a year later. One of the best known of this type, *Canterbury*, was specially built in 1929 to be the link in the luxury 'Golden Arrow' train service between London and Paris which had been inaugurated in 1927. Of 2912grt, she initially carried only 300 first class passengers but was soon altered to carry second class passengers as well.

Meanwhile a competitor to the steam turbine – the internal combustion engine invented by Dr Rudolf Diesel at about the same time as Parsons' original breakthrough – had been steadily gaining ground after rather a slow start. First applied to a short sea passenger ship in the Det Forenede D/S (United Steamship Co) North Sea packet *Parkeston* in 1925, it attracted the attention of

The elegant and popular Lady of Mann *(3104grt/23kts) was built at Barrow by Vickers-Armstrongs in 1930 to celebrate the centenary of the Isle of Man Steam Packet Co, which linked that island to Liverpool, Fleetwood, Ardrossan and Dublin. Built at Barrow by Vickers-Armstrongs, her design marked a peak in the evolution of the steamships built for the company up to that time, all of which were different. The same shipyard was also responsible for building its first sisterships* Fenella *and* Tynwald *in 1937. Although both were lost during the Second World War, they introduced a lower and leaner profile that was continued in a series of six well-known ships built between 1947 and 1955, all of them turbine driven. (Ambrose Greenway collection)*

Belfast Steamship Co (part of Coast Lines Group since 1919) which ordered three new motor vessels from Harland & Wolff for its Liverpool night service. The first of these and the world's first cross-channel motor ship, *Ulster Monarch*, appeared in 1929, introducing a three-island type hull topped by a solid superstructure and two squat motor ship type funnels. The design proved so successful that, apart from her two sisters, a further ten similar vessels were built for Coast Lines up to 1957.

Although more costly to install than turbines, diesels were far more economical to run and could be shut down in port. At the same time equal power was available for going astern, an important consideration with channel ferries which either had to manoeuvre through locks or turn off a harbour entrance and reverse some considerable way into their berth.

The next step in the development of the diesel-engined cross-channel ship occurred in the early 1930s when the Belgian Marine Administration was persuaded to alter its plans for a new turbine steamer, in favour of a radical new motor ship designed by its technical adviser, Monsieur Grimard. Built by Cockerill, the 3050grt *Prince Baudouin* astounded the maritime world in August

1934 when she achieved a maximum speed of 25¼kts – the fastest yet attained by a motor vessel – during deepwater trials off the Scheldt, proving the efficiency of diesel propulsion for fast ships with lightly built hulls. Her looks were also entirely new, with a low squat funnel, short vertical masts and many large windows in her superstructure. A sister, *Prins Albert*, proved marginally faster on trial in 1937 but their basic design, with the same installed power and speed, set the pattern for all subsequent traditional Belgian mail ships.

For a long time the motion of fast channel ferries had been a source of great discomfort to many travellers. Many means were tried to alleviate this, including an early stabilising system built into *The Queen* consisting of a travelling weight on rails which unfortunately had the opposite effect and was quickly dispensed with. It was not until 1934 that Denny–Brown perfected the retractable gyro-controlled fin stabiliser, which was first

successfully demonstrated in Southern Railway's Channel Islands steamer *Isle of Sark*. The latter incidentally was the only British channel steamer to adopt a Maierform bow.

The Zeeland Steamship Co of the Netherlands, which had retained reciprocating machinery for two fast ships built as late as the early 1920s, switched directly to diesel propulsion for a notable pair of 4135grt sisters built at Flushing by De Schelde just before the Second World War. *Koningen Emma* and *Prinses Beatrix* were 23kt ships with a long forecastle merging into the superstructure and a novel arrangement of lifeboats, six of which were positioned much lower than usual at weather deck level. They and many others of their type again proved invaluable in many different ways during the war years and they were especially useful during the evacuation of France and the later invasions of southern Europe and Normandy. Many did not return to their normal routes when peace was declared and others were not

The Newhaven–Dieppe route was unique in being jointly owned by both British and French railway companies, their respective one-third and two-thirds shares relating to the rail distances between both capital cities and the English Channel. With a crossing of 64 nautical miles, it required faster than average ships to maintain it, as did the similar length Dover–Ostend and Holyhead–Dun Laoghaire routes. Southern Railway Co's shallow draught Brighton, *seen crossing the Newhaven bar on a blustery day, was built by Denny in 1933 and was capable of 25kts. Her enclosed promenade deck provided much greater protection from the spray generated by high speed than the tarpaulins which had to be almost permanently rigged in the older open decked steamers. (Newhaven Historical Society)*

Following on from the pioneering Ulster Monarch *trio, Harland & Wolff's Belfast shipyard built several improved Irish Sea motor vessels in the 1930s, the largest of which were British & Irish Steam Packet Co's 4303grt* Leinster *and* Munster *of 1937–38, which provided comfortable accommodation amidships in single and double cabins for over 400 saloon passengers with a further 100 berthed aft in steerage. The cattle doors in the well decks were particular features of ships in the Irish trade, but the prominent belting around the hull was common to all channel steamers to avoid damage during constant docking and undocking manoeuvres.* (B Fielden)

released from government service until a year or two later.

Among postwar replacements, the 24kt *Brighton* built for the Newhaven service in 1950 introduced light tripod masts which became a feature of other Denny-built ships during the decade and were also adopted by the Belgians. It is significant that both British and French railways remained faithful to the steam turbine for almost all their cross-channel passenger ships, except the 5000grt *Hibernia* and *Cambria* built by Harland & Wolff in 1949 for the Holyhead–Dun Laoghaire service.

By the end of the decade increasing numbers of car ferries meant that the writing was on the wall for the predominantly passenger carrying channel ferry. In 1960 Zeeland Steamship Co adopted an unusual stream-lined design for its last ship of this type, the 6228grt motor vessel *Koningen Wilhelmina*, which had her machinery placed well aft, exhausting through a long, low funnel. Three years later British Rail's Eastern Region re-

ceived the 6584grt *Avalon*, last and largest of all the British conventional turbine ferries, destined to be converted into a car ferry in 1975.

The very last of this long line of channel passenger ferries was the Belgian *Prinses Paola* of 1966, a ship of 4356grt with air-conditioned accommodation for 1700 passengers arranged over six decks.

Train ferries

With the spread of railway systems in the nineteenth century, it soon became necessary to find ways of crossing natural barriers such as rivers that were too wide to be bridged in the ordinary way. At first this had to be achieved by the tedious and time consuming process of unloading passengers and freight from a train, loading them on to a steamer and then reversing the process on the opposite side. The alternative was the dedicated train ferry, a type which first made its appearance in 1849 in the shape of the pontoon-like paddle steamer *Leviathan* built by Robert Napier & Co of Greenock for the North British Railway Co for carrying wagons across the River Tay. Similar ships were later built for the Forth and Tay crossings but these were rendered redundant by the completion of bridges.

The United States adopted similar types of paddle train ferry, one of the largest being

The Belgian Marine Administration's Roi Leopold III *typified the fast diesel-propelled English Channel packet of the 1950s. The first of three ships built by Cockerills during 1956–1958 in anticipation of extra traffic generated by the Brussels World Expo of the latter year, she was a direct development of the pace-setting* Prince Baudouin *of 1934, employing identical 12-cylinder Sulzer engines. Up to 1700 passengers (in two classes) could be accommodated on her five passenger decks in addition to around 30 cars in two holds, the after one of which was trunked through the promenade deck. Note also the light tripod masts.* (FotoFlite)

The 2795grt icebreaking train ferry Prince Edward Island *was built for the Canadian Government's Department of Transport by Armstrong Whitworth in 1915 to transport wagons across the strait separating Cape Tormentine, New Brunswick and Boden, Prince Edward Island. Following icebreaker practice, she had three propellers (one forward, two aft) and her unusual layout of twin paired funnels was later taken up by Japanese National Railways for a series of train ferries built in 1948 for the Tsugaru Strait crossing between Honshu and the northern island of Hokkaido.* (CMP)

the Southern Pacific Railway's 3549grt *Solano*, built in 1879 for crossing the Strait of Carquinez in California, which could accommodate a whole train including the locomotive. Even she was outdone by the 5375 ton *Contra Costa* built for the same route in 1914. The service was terminated in the 1930s when a bridge was built. On the Great Lakes, however, a new type of train ferry was introduced in 1896 with *Pere Marquette* which operated across Lake Michigan for the Chesapeake & Ohio Railway. A twin screw steamship of 2443grt, she could be described as the first truly modern train ferry with a low train deck almost totally enclosed in a normal ship's hull on which was placed the accommodation block, navigating bridge and two normally positioned funnels. Rail access was over the stern and she could carry up to thirty large freight wagons. Her design set the pattern for over twenty similar ships built for several Great Lakes routes up to 1930.

Meanwhile train ferry development was also taking place in Denmark, a country split into three by stretches of water known as the Great Belt and Little Belt. The latter was the first to be crossed by a train ferry, a simple double-ended paddle steamer containing a single section of track, but a larger type capable of carrying eight wagons on two tracks evolved for the longer (11 miles) Great Belt crossing between Korsør and Nyborg. By the turn of the century these train ferries had gained a rudimentary bridge-type super-

structure over the train deck amidships and their success led to the opening of international train ferry routes linking Copenhagen with Malmö in 1900, Gedser with Warnemünde in 1903 and Trelleborg with Sassnitz in 1909. The latter was the longest at 57 miles and necessitated the construction of four ice-strengthened ships with normal built-up bows to cope with open sea conditions. *Deutschland* and *Preussen* were built for German State Railways by Stettiner Maschinenbau in 1908, whilst Swedish State Railways received *Drottning Victoria* from Swan Hunter in 1909 and *Konung Gustav V* from

Lindholmen, Gothenburg in 1910. About 372ft in length with gross tonnages of around 3000, they were propelled by two triple-expansion engines driving twin screws for a speed of about 16kts. Their twin track train decks could carry eight passenger carriages or alternatively eighteen freight wagons. Coincidental with the start up of this service, Italian State Railways commissioned a train ferry linking Reggio di Calabria with the Sicilian port of Messina across the strait of that name. Common to all these routes was an almost complete lack of tide, greatly facilitating loading and discharge.

The 3133grt train ferry Schwerin *was built for German State Railways by F Schichau in 1926 to augment the link between Gedser and Warnemünde run jointly with its Danish counterpart and to match the latter's* Danmark *(2915grt) which had entered service in 1922. Capable of both bow and stern loading, these two ships were amongst the first to adopt lifting bow visors, a feature that was to become increasingly widely used in roll-on, roll-off, car ferries after 1960. Schwerin could carry 7 large or 20 small carriages on two tracks and was propelled at 15.5kts by two triple-expansion engines.* (Ambrose Greenway collection)

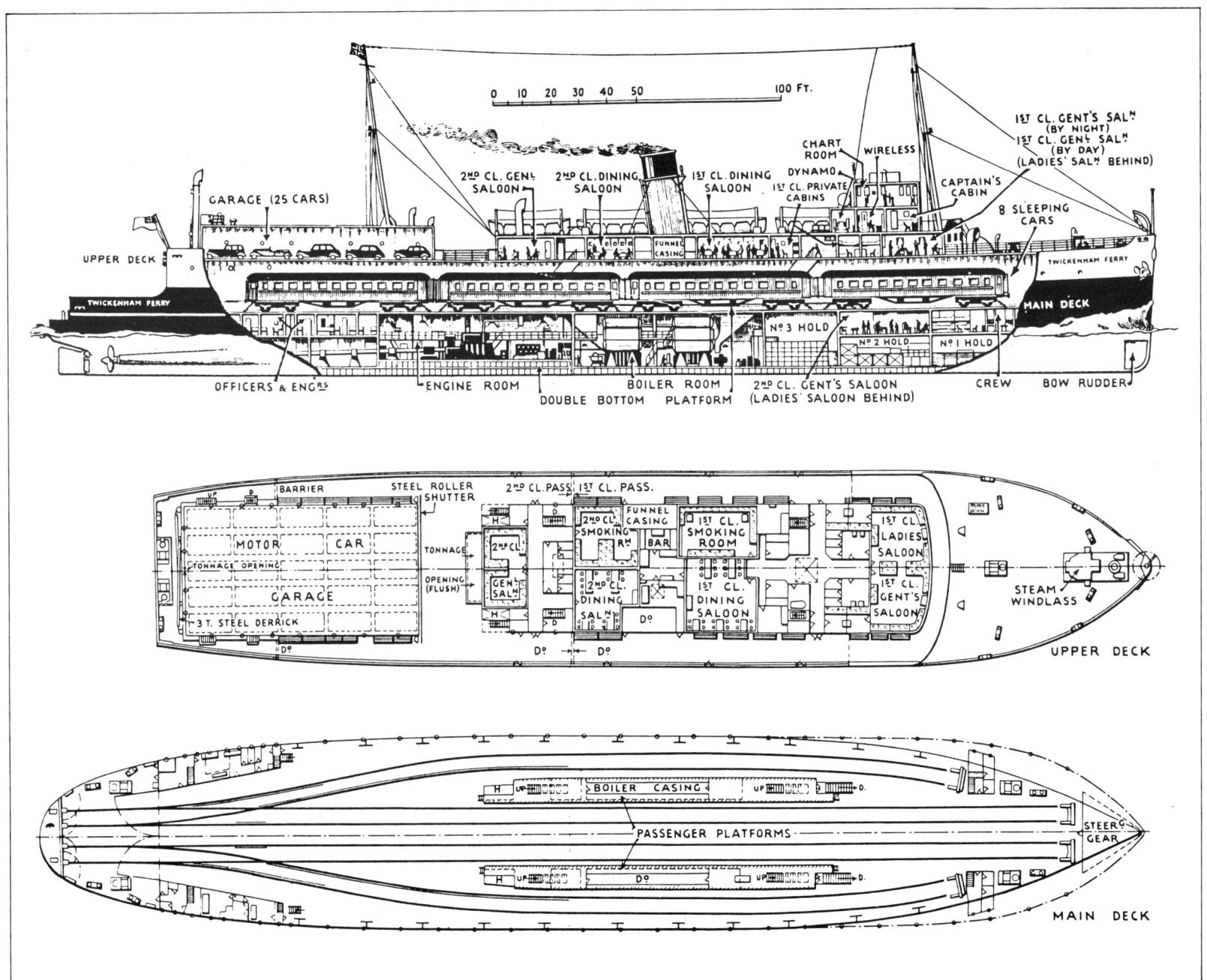

A diagram showing the layout of Southern Railway's first train ferry Twickenham Ferry, *which with her two sisters inaugurated the Dover–Dunkirk route in 1936.*

The same could not be said for the English Channel and although many plans had been made for a train ferry service, nothing materialised until the First World War. The tremendous demand for vehicles and supplies to be shipped across to the front resulted in the British Government building three train ferries, *Train Ferry No 1, 2* and *3*, to run between Southampton and a specially constructed tidal terminal at Richborough in Kent to Dieppe, Calais and Dunkirk. They were distinctly functional looking vessels with a broad hull containing four sets of rails and two flat funnels placed on either beam and joined by a gantry. In 1924 they were bought by the Great Eastern Train Ferry Co Ltd and placed in service carrying freight wagons only between Harwich, where a long hinged ramp was built, and Zeebrugge.

This service attracted the attention of Southern Railway and in 1933 it began looking into the possibility of a commercial train ferry service across the Dover Strait. The first stage of its plan came to fruition in 1934–35 with the delivery from Swan Hunter of three striking new vessels, the 2839grt *Twickenham Ferry, Hampton Ferry* and *Shepperton Ferry*. With their enclosed four-track train decks, built up superstructures containing comfortable passenger accommodation and twin thwartship funnels, they represented a marked advance on the earlier ships and in addition to twelve railway carriages or forty goods wagons, could also carry twenty-five cars in a special garage at the after end of the boat deck. The second stage of the plan was to build an enclosed train ferry dock at Dover, to overcome the 25ft tidal range, but this was delayed by serious construction problems and was not completed until 1936. No such problem existed at Dunkirk, where vessels had to lock in anyway. The famous 'Night Ferry' through passenger rail service between London and Paris was inaugurated in October 1936, with departures in either direction. In addition there were daily freight sailings.

In the meantime diesel propulsion had

Train ferries designed solely for freight traffic lacked the glamour of the passenger carrying variety and were decidedly functional in appearance. Norfolk Ferry *built by John Brown at Clydebank in 1951 was the second of two such vessels commissioned for the Harwich–Zeebrugge route to replace earlier vessels lost in the war. This view gives a good indication of the construction of train ferries, showing the extension of the hull plating upwards around the low train deck, which in this case comprised four lengths of track.* (Ambrose Greenway collection)

been adopted for several European train ferries. First fitted to the small Netherlands three-wagon ferry *Spoorpont I* in 1914, it was taken up ten years later by Italian state Railways for their *Messina* and by Danish State Railways for their *Korsor* of 1927. Another development of the inter-war years was the bow visor which allowed ships to load or discharge at either end, one of the first to be so fitted being German State Railways' 3133grt *Schwerin*, built for the Warnemünde–Gedser service in 1926. On the other side of the world Japanese National Railways built four 3484grt steam ferries in 1924–25 to carry rail traffic across the Tsugaru Strait between Aomori and Hakodate.

The Second World War caused great disruption to European rail systems and consequently to train ferries. The British ships undertook valuable war work, often being used as vehicle ferries, and the *Twickenham Ferry* class ships were later fitted with large gantries aft in order to offload heavy vehicles and rolling stock in near continental ports where no special facilities existed. They were joined in 1951 on the Dover–Dunkirk service by French Railways' first train ferry, the Danish-built *Saint-Germain* (3094grt), a motor driven vessel of more streamlined appearance with only a single funnel. The Harwich route had lost two of its original vessels in the war but the reconstructed survivor was joined by two larger diesel-propelled freight ferries led by *Suffolk Ferry* in 1947.

Other new train ferries to appear in the 1950s were German State Railway's motor-

Completed by Neptunwerft, Rostock in 1959 for East German railways, the 7000grt train ferry Sassnitz *was a companion of Swedish State Railways'* Trelleborg, *which joined the Trelleborg–Sassnitz route in the previous year. The streamlined appearance of these two ships, which ranked amongst the largest of their type, was in marked contrast to earlier train ferries. As an aid to berthing,* Sassnitz *was fitted with a bow rudder as well as a thwartship thruster and could carry 36 rail wagons, 40 cars and around 900 passengers at a speed of 18kts provided by twin Halberstadt diesels.* (Ambrose Greenway)

ship *Deutschland* and diesel-electric *Theodor Heuss* for the Gedser route, both switching in 1963 to the new and much shorter route between Puttgarden and Rødby, the so-called 'Bird Flight' route. No new ships had appeared on the Trelleborg–Sassnitz route since 1910 but this position was rectified in 1958 with Swedish State Railways' Elsinore-built *Trelleborg*, at 6476grt the largest train ferry in Europe. She could carry forty large wagons on about 1300ft of track and over thirty cars in a promenade deck garage; in addition buses and lorries could also be carried on the train deck. Twin turbo-charged B&W diesels developing 10,500bhp gave her a speed of 19kts and she was also fitted with a Voith-Schneider bow thrust and stabilisers.

After the war eight new train ferries – conspicuous in having two pairs of funnels abreast – were built by Japanese National Railways to replace war losses but before long these began to be superseded by a more modern type of motor vessel, starting with *Hiyama Maru* in 1956. In Canada, the government took delivery of the 6654grt icebreaker *Abegweit*, a diesel-electric vessel with propellers at either end, in 1947 for the Prince Edward Island service, and eight years later Alexander Stephen & Son delivered the 5554grt *Princess of Vancouver* to Canadian Pacific for its Vancouver–Nanaimo route. The year 1961 witnessed the inauguration of Italian Railways' 137 mile train ferry service, Europe's longest, between Civitavecchia near Rome and Golfo d'Aranci in Sardinia.

Car ferries

The twentieth century has been marked by a phenomenal increase in motor vehicles, both for the movement of passengers and goods. Ways had to be found of transporting these vehicles across rivers too large to bridge or wider straits separating islands from mainland or one country from another. In all cases a ship was the only answer and for the longer passages vehicles had to be laboriously craned in and out of ordinary cargo holds. For the shorter crossings, however, pontoon type ferries evolved, some being

Examples of the smaller type of ferry used to transport road vehicles across sheltered waters were those which ran to the Isle of Wight. Southern Railway's Lymington, *built by Denny in 1938 for Lymington–Yarmouth service, was a development of similar double-ended ships built for the Portsmouth–Fishbourne route in the late 1920s. She was, however, of special interest in being the first British ferry to be fitted with Voith Schneider cycloidal propellers, which provided omnidirectional thrust and were considered to be particularly suitable for navigating the tortuous Lymington river.* (Ambrose Greenway collection)

self-propelled, others drawing themselves along chains laid across a river bed – the so-called 'floating bridges'. As the years progressed the pontoon type ferry developed into two distinct types: the double ended one on to which cars drove via a ramp at one end, parked during the passage and drove off over another ramp at the other end; and the side-loader where cars drove on and off via side doors. The latter tended to be used to cross more rapid flowing waters.

These early vehicle ferries could all be described by the modern term 'roll-on, roll-off' but they were little short of moving platforms. It was not until 1924 that Canadian Pacific Railway, which was finding it difficult to ship more and more vehicles

from the mainland to Vancouver Island in conventional ferries, ordered a small experimental wooden steamer specifically to carry cars between Bellingham in Washington State and Sidney. Locally built by Yarrows Ltd, the 1243grt *Motor Princess* was only 165ft long but she could accommodate forty-five cars arranged on a full length lower deck and the forward part of the upper deck which had a turntable and was reached by a centreline ramp. Access was by means of doors on either bow or the stern. Not only was she one of the first true car ferries but was also driven by two diesel engines which gave a speed of 14¼kts.

No further move was made until the late 1920s when Townsend Bros, which had started carrying cars across the Dover Strait

in two coasters in 1928, purchased the surplus 'Town' class minesweeper *Ford* from the Admiralty, altered her to carry 29 cars and 307 passengers and placed her in service as *Forde* between Dover and Calais in 1930. Although she had a small stern door ramp, it could only be used in the French port, so cars were generally lifted on and off by crane. The Southern Railway was quick to react and altered one of a class of cargo steamers then building for its account to a car carrying vessel. The aptly named *Auto-carrier* could carry thirty-five cars, also crane-loaded.

In 1936 the Belgian Marine Administration converted the conventional turbine cross-channel ferry *Ville de Liege* into the car ferry *London-Istanbul*. She could carry one hundred cars on two decks linked by a ramp, access being over four ramps fitted to her starboard side, and ran between Dover and Ostend. In the meantime the specialised diesel-driven car ferry was being developed in Scandinavia, initially by Danish State Railways for the comparatively short Great Belt crossing whilst in 1937 Denmark's Aalborg Shipyard delivered the more advanced *Peter Wessel* to Norwegian owners for the open sea route between Larvik and Fredrikshavn.

The first large stern-loading cross-channel car ferry was ordered from Denny by

The Royal Navy's surplus 'Town' class minesweeper Ford *was saved from the breaker's torch by Townsend Bros who converted her into a ferry with the specific purpose of carrying private cars and their passengers across the English Channel. Entering service as* Forde *between Dover and Calais in April 1930, she broke the monopoly of the railway companies on the Dover Strait and was the first dedicated car ferry to operate on an international route. Although fitted with a 9ft × 6ft stern door which hinged down to form a ramp, in practice vehicles were lifted on and off her open after deck by shoreside cranes. However the feasability of the roll-on, roll-off concept, later to be widely adopted in ferry design, was successfully demonstrated in Calais during a strike involving port labour.* (Ambrose Greenway collection)

With her almost completely unobstructed vehicle deck, Norsk-Dansk Turist Co's 1419grt motorship Peter Wessel *of 1937 ranked as one of the first true long distance car ferries to be built. Although fitted with a visor-type bow door, it was only used at Larvik, loading and discharge at Fredrikshavn being directly on to the quay through a side door on the quarter. Sailing overnight, she could carry about 70 cars and 500 passengers, 186 of them in berths, and her twin Polar diesels gave a speed of 15kts. By way of contrast, the first large stern loading car ferry,* Princess Victoria, *built in 1939 for the Stranraer–Larne service, required the building of power operated shore ramps in both ports.* (Ambrose Greenway collection)

London Midland & Scottish Railway for its Stranraer–Larne service in 1938. Named *Princess Victoria* she entered service in July 1939, less than two months before the outbreak of the Second World War. A ship of 2197grt, she resembled an ordinary cross channel steamer in outward appearance, save for a large stern door, but inwardly she had a long open car deck, obstructed only by the engine room casing, which could take eighty cars and was fitted with two turntables. Above the car deck was the main accommodation for 1400 passengers in first and third classes, each being provided with a lounge bar and dining saloon. Driven by twin diesel engines, she was the first British railway-owned channel ship to be so fitted. These were of the Sulzer type and gave a speed of 19kts.

Her design set the pattern for future car ferries and although she became an early war loss, she was replaced by a very similar ship of the same name in 1947 but she too

was lost in a storm with heavy loss of life in 1953. Her stern door had been damaged by heavy seas, allowing water to enter the car deck which had insufficient freeing ports.

Purpose-built car ferries in the shape of the Belgian *Car Ferry* – later renamed *Prinses Josephine-Charlotte* – and British Rail Southern Region's *Lord Warden* (the railways had been nationalised in 1948) appeared on the Dover Strait in 1949 and 1952 respectively. In 1956 Danish State Railways went one step further with the 3195grt *Halsskov*, the first double deck car ferry with a capacity of 200 cars and 1000 passengers. Fitted with both bow and stern doors, she was specially built for the new car ferry route across the Great Belt between Halsskov and Knudshoved. This 'drive-through' principle was to be widely adopted in the new car ferries which began to proliferate after 1960, most of which were fitted with lifting bow visors.

Ambrose Greenway

The port of Dover opened its first purpose-built car ferry terminal in 1953, though initially it had only one ramp. The two stern-loading vessels depicted using it at a later date form an interesting comparison. On the right the former Southern Railway's overnight Southampton–St Malo passenger ferry Dinard *(1769grt), which was converted to carry 70 cars in 1947, though these had to be crane loaded until a stern door was fitted in 1952. Beside her the larger and beamier, 3477grt* Compiegne, *French Railways' first purpose-built car ferry (164 cars) dating from 1958, which was also one of the first to be driven by medium speed SEMT-Pielstick engines, later to be widely adopted for ferry propulsion.* (Ambrose Greenway collection)

Typical Ocean Passenger Vessels 1900–1960

Name	Flag	Built	By	GRT	Length(oa) × breadth × depth × draught Feet-inches Metres	Engines	Speed	Trade Passengers (as built)	Remarks
Liners									
VICTORIAN	UK	1905	Workman Clark, Belfast	10,635	538-3 × 60-5 × 38-0 × 29-6 *164.05 × 18.42 × 11.58 × 8.99*	3 direct drive steam turbines (2 hp, 1 lp) by builders, 15,000shp; 3 shafts	18kts	North Atlantic. 1st 346/2nd 344/3rd c1000	First turbine liner on North Atlantic
MAURETANIA	UK	1907	Swan Hunter & Wigham Richardson, Wallsend upon Tyne	31,938	790-0 × 87-10 × 60-9 × 33-6 *240.78 × 26.77 × 18.5 × 10.21*	4 direct drive steam turbines (2 hp, 2 lp) by Wallsend Slipway, 68,000shp; 4 shafts	25kts	North Atlantic. 1st 560/2nd 475/ 3rd c1300	Held Blue Riband until 1929
GRIPSHOLM	Swe	1925	Armstrong Whitworth, Newcastle upon Tyne	17,993	590-0 × 74-6 × 42-6 × 29-0 *179.82 × 22.73 × 12.95 × 8.84*	2 6-cylinder 4DA oil by B&W, 13,500bhp; 2 shafts	16kts	North Atlantic 1st 127/2nd 482/ 3rd 948	First Atlantic motor liner and notably successful
ASTURIAS	UK	1926	Harland & Wolff, Belfast	22,048	655-9 × 78-6 × 44-9 × 31-1 *199.86 × 23.96 × 13.64 × 9.48*	2 8-cylinder 4DA B&W oil, by builders, 15,000bhp; 2 shafts	17kts	South Atlantic 1st 432/2nd 223/3rd 453	Early vibration and poor speed cured (1934) by lengthening and switch to turbine propulsion
EUROPA	Ger	1930	Blohm & Voss, Hamburg	49,746	936-9 × 102-1 × 48-0 × — *285.51 × 31.12 × 14.63 × —*	12 oil-fired SR geared steam turbines 130,000shp; 4 shafts	27kts	North Atlantic 1st 687/2nd 524/ tourist 306/3rd 507	Consort to record breaking *Bremen*; used catapult and seaplane for express mails
CONTE DI SAVOIA	Ita	1932	Cantieri Riuniti dell' Adriatico, Trieste	48,502	860-0 × 96-1 × 53-4 × 31-2 *262.11 × 29.29 × 16.25 × 9.50*	12 oil-fired SR geared steam turbines by builders, 130,000shp; 4 shafts	27kts	Mediterranean–US 1st 500/2nd 366/ transit 412/3rd 922	Along with *Rex*, Italy's fastest; fitted gyro stabilisers
NORMANDIE	Fra	1935	Chantiers et Ateliers de St Nazaire, St Nazaire	79,280	1029-0 × 117-10 × 57-7 × — *313.62 × 35.69 × 17.56 × —*	4 steam turbines connected to 4 electric motors by Alsthom, 165,000shp; 4 shafts	29kts	North Atlantic. 1st 848/tourist 670/ 3rd 454	Turbo-electric rival to *Queen Mary*; proposed consort never built
ORION	UK	1935	Vickers Armstrong, Barrow-in-Furness	23,371	665-0 × 82-6 × 47-6 × 30-2 *202.68 × 25.17 × 14.48 × 9.20*	6 oil-fired SR geared steam turbines by builders, 24,000shp; 2 shafts	21kts	UK–Australia 1st 486/tourist 653	
QUEEN ELIZABETH	UK	1940	John Brown & Co, Clydebank	83,673	1031-0 × 118-7 × 74-5 × 39-6 *314.23 × 36.15 × 22.69 × 12.04*	16 oil-fired SR geared steam turbines by builders, 200,000shp; 4 shafts	28.5kts	North Atlantic 1st 823/cabin 662/ 3rd 798	World's largest liner Made possible a two ship service
CHUSAN	UK	1950	Vickers Armstrong, Barrow-in-Furness	24,215	672-6 × 85-0 × 38-0 × 29-0 *204.97 × 25.91 × 11.58 × 8.84*	6 oil-fired steam turbines (hp DR geared/ip & lp SR geared) by builders, 42,500shp; 2 shafts	22kts	UK–Far East 1st 758/tourist 401	Notably successful; first liner with fin stabilisers and first (1959) to be fully air-condition
UNITED STATES	US	1952	Newport News SB & DD Co, Newport News, Virginia	53,329	990-0 × 101-7 × 56-0 × 32-3 *301.76 × 30.97 × 17.07 × 9.82*	4 oil-fired Westinghouse DR geared steam turbines, 240,000shp; 4 shafts	31kts	North Atlantic. 1st 871/cabin 508/ tourist 549	World's fastest liner; averaged 35.39kts on maiden voyage
OLYMPIA	Gre	1953	Alexander Stephen, Glasgow	22,979	610-7 × 79-2 × 47-0 × 28-1 *186.10 × 24.14 × 14.32 × 8.56*	4 oil-fired DR geared steam turbines by builders; 25,000shp; 2 shafts	21kts	North Atlantic 1st 138/tourist 1169	Emphasis on high-grade tourist accommodation. First new liner build for Greece since early 1920s
PENDENNIS CASTLE	UK	1958	Harland & Wolff, Belfast	28,582	763-3 × 83-6 × 48-0 × 32-2 *232.63 × 25.48 × 14.63 × 9.81*	2 oil-fired DR geared steam turbines by builders; 46,000shp; 2 shafts	22.5kts	UK–South Africa 1st 197/tourist 473	Upgraded whilst on stocks

Name	Flag	Built	By	GRT	Length(oa) × breadth × depth × draught Feet-inches Metres	Engines	Speed	Trade Passengers (as built)	Remarks
ORIANA	UK	1960	Vickers Armstrong, Barrow-in-Furness	41,915	804-0 × 97-2 × 41-0 × 32-0 245.07 × 29.62 × 12.76 × 9.75	6 oil-fired DR geared steam turbines by builders, 80,000shp; 2 shafts	27.5kts	UK–Australia 1st 548/tourist 1650	Advance from previous 22kts brought North Atlantic speed to Eastern trade

Machinery abbreviations: hp = high pressure; lp = low pressure; SR = single reduction; DR = double reduction.

Typical Short-Sea Passenger Vessels 1900–1960

Name	Flag	Built	By	GRT DWT	Length(oa) (r = registered) × breadth × depth × draught Feet-inches Metres	Engines	Speed	Route	Remarks
Cross-channel vessels									
THE QUEEN	UK	1903	Wm Denny & Bros, Dumbarton	1676	309-9(r) × 40-0 × 15-7 × 13-8 94.4 × 12.19 × 4.75 × 4.16	3 direct drive Parsons steam turbines (1 hp/2 lp); 7500ihp	21kts	Dover–Calais Folkestone–Boulogne	First turbine cross-channel ship; 2 screws each on outer shafts
NORMANNIA	UK	1912	Fairfield SB & Eng Co, Govan, Glasgow	1567	290-3(r) × 36-1 × 15-3 × 12-3 88.48 × 11.0 × 4.66 × 3.73	2 sets Parsons oil-fired SR geared turbines by builders, 6000shp; 2 shafts	19.5kts	Southampton–Le Havre (night)	Pioneer geared turbine merchant ship
ISLE OF THANET	UK	1925	Wm Denny & Bros, Dumbarton	2664	342-0 × 45-0 × 17-6 × 12-10 104.24 × 13.71 × 5.33 × 3.91	2 sets Parsons oil-fired SR steam turbines by builders, 8500shp; 2 shafts	22kts	Dover/Folkestone–Calais	Passengers: 1000 1st class, 400 2nd
ULSTER MONARCH	UK	1929	Harland & Wolff, Belfast	3735 828	358-9 × 46-2 × 19-0 × 15-2 109.39 × 14.08 × 5.79 × 4.63	2 10-cylinder 4SA Sulzer/B&W oil engines by builders, 7500bhp; 2 shafts	17kts	Liverpool–Belfast (night)	Pioneer diesel cross-channel ship; passengers: 418 1st class, 86 3rd
PRINCE BAUDOUIN	Bel	1934	John Cockerill, Hoboken	3050 480	371-0 × 46-0 × 16-7 × 11-1 113.08 × 14.02 × 5.06 × 3.38	2 12-cylinder 2SA Cockerill/Sulzer oil engines, 17,000bhp; 2 shafts	23.5kts	Ostend–Dover	Fastest motor ship in world when built; passengers: 1691
AMSTERDAM	UK	1950	John Brown & Co, Clydebank	5092 1113	377-1 × 52-0 × 27-1 × 15-2 114.94 × 15.85 × 8.26 × 4.63	2 sets Parsons oil-fired SR geared turbines by builders, 12,000shp; 2 shafts	21kts	Harwich–Hook of Holland	Passengers: 321 1st class, 236 2nd
Train ferries									
DEUTSCHLAND	Ger	1908	Stettiner Vulkan, Stettin	2972	354-2 × 53-6 × 22-1 × 16-1 107.96 × 16.3 × 6.74 × 4.9	2 3-cylinder triple-expansion steam by builders, 476nhp; 2 shafts	16.5kts	Gedser–Warnemünde	Stern-loader, 2 tracks
TWICKENHAM FERRY	UK	1934	Swan Hunter & Wigham Richardson, Wallsend	2839 1780	366-0 × 60-5 × 18-2 × 12-6 111.56 × 18.41 × 5.55 × 3.81	2 sets Parsons coal-fired SR geared turbines, 4500ihp; 2 shafts	16.5kts	Dover–Dunkirk (day/night service)	Stern-loader, 4 tracks; transferred French flag 1936
TRELLEBORG	Swe	1958	Helsingør Skibs, Elsinore	6476 1746	451-10 × 61-9 × 25-7 × 17-9 137.71 × 18.29 × 7.80 × 5.41	2 8-cylinder 2SA turbo-charged B&W oil engines by builders, 10,000bhp; 2 shafts	19kts	Trelleborg–Sassnitz	Stern-loader, 4 tracks; bow thrust, cp propellers
Car ferries									
PRINCESS VICTORIA	UK	1939	Wm Denny & Bros, Dumbarton	2197 590	322-0 × 48-1 × 16-8 × 11-6 98.15 × 14.66 × 5.09 × 3.5	2 7-cylinder 2SA Denny/Sulzer oil engines, 5000bhp; 2 shafts	19kts	Stranraer–Larne	First UK stern-loader; passengers: 1400, cars: 80
HALSSKOV	Den	1956	Helsingør Skibs, Elsinore	3195 1025	348-3 × 56-5 × 23-3 × 14-9 106.15 × 17.23 × 7.09 × 4.5	2 6-cylinder 2SA Helsingør/B&W oil engines, 6600bhp; 2 shafts	18kts	Halsskov–Knudshoved (Great Belt)	First double-deck car ferry; bow/stern doors; Passengers: 1000, cars: 200

2

Cargo Ships

The Cargo Liner

By the end of the nineteenth century the cargo liner, as a distinctive type, was already firmly established and many liner companies, particularly those based in Europe, were using it to perform regular services to all corners of the globe. Its origins can be traced back to the early steamers in the Europe–Far East trade and it can best be described as a cross between the cargo-carrying passenger liner and the tramp steamer. Unlike the latter, however, which moved around at random to wherever a paying cargo could be found, the cargo 'liner', by definition, offered advertised sailings on fixed dates from several ports in a particular trade, regardless of the amount of cargo to be loaded or discharged. It had to be capable of carrying almost anything that could be produced in the newly industrialised nations ranging from motor cars to the smallest household items, from heavy products such as steel and railway equipment to pipes, and chemicals in drums. Having distributed these around the world, generally to the less developed nations, it would return with many of the raw materials needed by industry; for example cotton, wool, hides, hemp, rubber and timber as well as foodstuffs such as meat, dairy products, fruit, sugar, coffee and tea with which to sustain the rapidly growing industrial populations. In addition, liquids such as palm or vegetable oil and later tallow were also car-

ried in special deeptanks. Cargo liners could also carry grain when needed but in general all bulk commodities, which did not derive any particular benefit from speedy shipment, were left to the tramp. Not for nothing were these 'maids of all work' sometimes referred to as the backbone of maritime trade.

Cargo liners came in many different shapes and sizes but generally they can be divided into three different types: the general cargo liner (in which can be included the specialist heavy-lift vessel), the refrigerated cargo liner for the carriage of frozen meat and dairy products and the specialised fruit ship, initially for bananas but later for other kinds of fruit.

The general cargo liner

By 1900 the general cargo liner was a ship of between 4000 and 8000grt and some 350–500ft in length. It was built of steel and its hull was subdivided into different compartments by transverse watertight bulkheads. Unlike the tramp, it was fitted with extra decks to form 'tween decks in the holds for cargo stowage. Above the upper deck were placed various combinations of raised forecastle, bridge deck and poop, which contained accommodation for the crew and generally up to twelve passengers (some ships carried more, though special regulations applied if

this occurred). In time these erections were combined to form a light extra deck with closeable tonnage openings, known as a shelter deck. Most cargo liners conformed to this type and could be operated in either the open or closed shelterdeck condition, depending on how deep they needed to be laden, for instance in wartime all shelter decks were closed. Raised forecastles etc were also added above the shelter deck.

Cargo liners had between four and six cargo holds served by an array of booms or 'derricks' – up to twenty or more in larger ships – mounted on the masts as well as on shorter posts known as 'kingposts' or 'samson posts'. These allowed the ship to load and discharge her own cargo, an important consideration as shore cranes were generally only available in the larger European ports. Cargo access was by way of fairly narrow centreline hatches on the weather deck, which were protected at sea by timber hatchboards placed over steel beams and sealed by tarpaulins and wooden chocks to make them watertight. Propulsion at that time was almost entirely by coal-fired triple-expansion plant arranged amidships, driving either single or twin screws for a conservative speed range of 10 to 12kts.

As far as overall design was concerned, four-masters, a hangover from the days of sail, were still very much in evidence, typical

One of the largest shipping groups was that controlled by Sir John Ellerman. It owned many cargo liners and was amongst the first to adopt cruiser sterns, typified by Hall Line's City of Norwich, *built by Wm Gray & Co in 1913. She survived both world wars and was sold for further trading in 1955, finally being broken up four years later. The rather unusual single well aft was a common feature in Ellerman tonnage built up to 1930. The change over to cruiser sterns was a gradual process, the old-fashioned counter stern being retained by a number of well-known companies such as Alfred Holt, Hamburg-America and Wilhelmsen well into the 1930s. (FotoFlite)*

The four-masted profile was one particularly favoured by German liner companies, especially Hamburg-Amerika and Norddeutscher Lloyd, and the 11,800dwt Gera *of 1915 was one of several similar ships delivered to the latter during the First World War. Surrendered to the British Shipping Controller in 1919 she was renamed* Orsino, *as shown here, in 1921 when briefly owned by the David Steamship Co, a temporary British company set up by the Dutch KNSM and United Netherlands Shipping companies to circumvent a ban forbidding resale of surrendered ships abroad. This was lifted in 1922 and she joined United's fleet as* Ouderkerk, *trading mainly to Australia. Sold to Italy in 1934, she became* Gianfranco *but was taken over by Argentina's Flota Mercante Del Estado in 1940 and as* Rio Salado *remained in service until 1955 when scrapped in Venice.* (CMP)

examples being the short bridge deck type developed from cargo–passenger liners for the North Atlantic livestock trade but amongst the most impressive were the twenty-two similar ships built for T & J Harrison Ltd, a Liverpool company trading mainly to Africa and the West Indies, between 1895 and 1921. Four masts were also favoured in German vessels whose merchant fleet ranked second to that of Britain at that time, though many of the fine cargo liners belonging to Hamburg-Amerika-Linie, Norddeutscher Lloyd, Deutsch-Australische and others were either sunk or fell into allied hands after the First World War. Germany continued to produce this type during the 1920s, including Norddeutscher Lloyd's ten-ship, 14kt *Aller* class of 1927–29, whilst the United Netherlands Steamship Co built the 17kt *Aagtekerk* and *Almkerk* in 1934. It fell to Belgium to operate the last and possibly finest ships of this type, the 18kt, triple screw *Stavelot* class. Measuring 8000grt and 546ft overall, the three ships were laid down by Cockerill at Hoboken for German account during the Second World War but completed in 1946–47 for Compagnie Maritime Belge (CMB), eventually passing to Norddeutscher Lloyd ownership in 1955.

To revert to the first decade of this century, brief mention should also be made of a design which in a way anticipated future trends but which in view of the its shortish lifespan was probably not entirely successful. This was the five-ship *Pera* class built for Peninsular & Oriental Steam Navigation Co (P&O) in 1903–05, developed from the company's first cargo liner *Candia* built some eight years earlier. Their main interest lay in

the cargo gear which consisted entirely of steam cranes except for a single derrick on each mast. Cranes were widely used in the coastal trade and were later to be found in many passenger liners, but apart from some used by Nederland Line in the 1920s, they were not really taken up again for cargo liners until after the Second World War.

The depressed trading conditions that had set in after the end of the Boer War began to improve by 1910, leading to a rush of new orders for larger and faster ships. Anticipating the trend, one or two far-sighted owners had acted whilst prices were still low, one such being the well-known Liverpool ship-owner Alfred Holt & Co Ltd (Blue Funnel Line), which had pioneered the introduction of the steamer on to the Far Eastern route in the previous century and had subsequently built up a large fleet of cargo liners. In 1908 it introduced the 6728grt *Perseus*, a slightly smaller development of its earlier four-ship *Peleus* type, and forerunner of nineteen similar ships to be built over the next nine years. Of typical Holt appearance with 'three island' type hull incorporating a long bridge deck on which was mounted a split superstructure and imposing funnel, she was 443ft long (registered) and 52ft 10in in breadth with two full decks and six cargo holds, including deep tanks in Nos 3 and 4, served by an array of twenty-two derricks and eighteen winches. Propulsion was by means of a triple expansion engine of around 4600ihp, driving a single screw for a comfortable sea speed of 14kts, steam being supplied by two double-ended boilers of 200psi. At full speed these consumed some 65 tons of coal a day from a bunker capacity of 1100 tons. Twelve

passengers were carried in the bridge house above the officers and engineers, with cadets and petty officers housed amidships on either side of the funnel casing in what was known as the 'fiddley' and crew aft in the poop. As with all Blue Funnel ships, *Perseus* was immensely strong, built to well over Lloyd's Register requirements as the company carried its own insurance, and both she and her sisters were certainly amongst the finest of their type in the pre 1914 period.

Also falling into the latter category were the seven ships of the *Cardiganshire* class, built for the Royal Mail group at Belfast and on the Tyne from 1913 to 1915 for its newly acquired Glen and Shire Line subsidiaries. Differing from the Holt ships in their composite superstructure, four were twin screw units of 9400grt and 14kts speed – the largest and fastest on the Far East route – the remaining three being single screw 12kt ships of around 7800 tons.

At the outbreak of the First World War, the world cargo liner fleet totalled some 16 million grt, roughly double the size of the tramp fleet which stood at 8.25 million. Some two years previously, however, an event had occurred that would, in time, change the face of cargo liner operation, namely the placing in service of the first large deep-sea vessel to be driven by an internal combustion engine or diesel, so named after its German inventor Dr Rudolph Diesel. *Selandia* and her two sisters were built for Denmark's Det Ostasiatiske Kompagni (East Asiatic Co), the first two by Burmeister & Wain in Copenhagen, an early licensee for the new engines, and the third by Barclay Curle on the Clyde. Designed to be distinctive, they were given a four-island type hull with three masts and no funnel, engine exhausts from the twin diesels being carried up the mizzen mast in narrow pipes. Electrically driven winches

In general, North Atlantic cargo liners tended to be overshadowed by the numerous passenger liners, many of which also carried considerable amounts of cargo. Canadian Pacific's five-ship 'Beaver' class, built to a Denny design in 1928 and illustrated here by Beaverbrae, *were an exception, and with a speed of 15kts ranked amongst the finest of their day. As coal was plentiful at either end of their route between London and the St Lawrence, they were fitted with coal-fired geared turbines and were amongst the first to employ mechanical stokers.* (CMP)

were another innovation. During her highly successful maiden voyage, *Selandia* was inspected by many important people, greatly impressing Winston Churchill, then First Lord of the Admiralty, during a visit to London. Although capable of carrying twenty-four passengers she and her sisters were to all intents and purposes cargo liners and the obvious potential of their design did not go unnoticed.

Other Scandinavian owners were quick to follow the Danish example, among them the highly innovative Rederi-A/B Nordstjernan (Johnson Line) of Sweden and Norway's Fred Olsen & Co. In Britain, Glen Line was well to the fore and under the guidance of Royal Mail group chairman Sir Owen Philipps, later Lord Kylsant, and Lord Pirrie, chairman of Harland & Wolff who had joined the Glen board in 1916, experimented during the war years with several different designs, applying the knowledge gained to immediate postwar construction, culminating in the four ship *Glenogle* class built by Harland & Wolff in 1920–21. Measuring 9500grt, they were driven at about 13kts by twin eight cylinder Burmeister & Wain diesels making them the most powerful motor ships of their day. Their success was such that a further six

similar ships were built, a fifth modified unit for Glen and the rest for a new North Europe–US and Canada Pacific coast service set up in 1921 by Royal Mail (four ships) and Holland America Line (two).

From the end of the First World War, the geared turbine began to replace the reciprocating engine in some new cargo liner tonnage, whilst many existing steamers were converted to oil-firing. Amongst the most striking examples to appear soon after the *Glenogle* class were the six large ships of the *London Mariner* type, built for the Furness Withy Group in its new Haverton Hill shipyard on the Tees in 1922–23. Of about 8000grt, they were driven by two steam turbines geared to a single shaft, giving a speed of 14kts. They were fitted with four goalpost masts, a device previously used by Blue Funnel for a class of large trans-Pacific lumber carriers and several Netherlands liner companies to provide greater derrick outreach, but their real innovation was a large accommodation block placed amidships and housing the entire crew. A very similar design was adopted some four years later by Canadian Pacific for their Denny built 'Beaver' class, notable as amongst the first to be fitted with mechanical stokers.

Despite brief flirtations with the oil engine in the 1920s, British shipowners – with one or two exceptions – opted to remain with the turbine or more familiar reciprocating engines, fearing uncertainties in the world supply of bunker oil. The competing Scandinavian and Continental owners, however, had no such qualms and adopted the motor ship with increasing enthusiasm. Despite higher initial cost, its advantages lay in

lower fuel consumption, increased range (making it ideal for the longer routes), greater carrying capacity (fuel storage in double bottom tanks did not impinge on valuable cargo space), and reduced engine-room staff.

By 1925, the world cargo liner fleet had increased to 23½ million grt, providing more than 80 per cent of the total maritime capacity and four times that of the tramp fleet which had declined to 7½ million tons. The same year saw Alfred Holt introducing the three ship *Alcinous* class for its Netherlands subsidiary Nederlandsche SM Oceaan, the first cargo liners of note to have their engines in the three-quarters aft position.

It was not long before the impetus of the motor cargo liner led to speeds increasing from 11–12kts to 14–15kts as in Furness Withy's advanced *Chinese Prince* class controversially built in Germany in 1926 for Prince Line's round-the-world service, Holt's *Orestes* (1926) and *Agamemnon* (1929) classes and Nederland Line's three-masted *Poelau Laut* (1928) and *Talisse* (1930) classes. Some owners remained faithful to the same design for many years, in particular Norway's Wilh Wilhelmsen whose twelve-ship *Taronga* class (1927–30) were in the same league as those mentioned above. These formed part of a long programme of similar looking split superstructure motorships, begun in the early 1920s, that eventually totalled over seventy units by the time *Tugela* was delivered in 1954.

Despite the worldwide depression in the early 1930s, the decade witnessed the application of new ideas such as the Maierform bow with its distinctive curve, said to reduce

Cargo liners with two funnels were unusual but the twin-screw motorships Sud Expresso *and* Sud Americano, *built by Deutsche Werke in 1929 for Norway's Linea Sud Americana, were also designed to have the then very high service speed of 16kts. Failing to reach this they were returned to their builders, who briefly chartered them to Blue Star Line. Purchased by a German organisation charged with helping liner companies to re-tonnage, they were given lengthened bows and more powerful machinery (11,000ihp) for a trial speed of over 20kts before passing into Norddeutscher Lloyd's fleet as* Elbe *and* Weser. *(The Motor Ship, January 1930)*

resistance and therefore engine power, part-welded hulls and elementary steel hatch covers. In Germany, Hamburg-Amerika fitted diesel-electric propulsion to several ships, whilst in the East, Japan emerged as a producer of fine motor cargo liners. Up to that time no way had been found of transmitting really high engine powers to a single screw – most fast ships still needing two propellers – but by the end of the decade Japanese owners were fitting diesels developing up to 10,000bhp in single screw cargo liners capable of 17kts sea speed and around

With the aid of government subsidies engendered by resurgent nationalism, Japanese liner companies were able to re-equip their fleets in the 1930s with fast new motorships such as the 9800dwt Noto Maru, *one of a class of six built for Nippon Yusen Kaisha's Japan–New York service between 1934 and 1935. Her Sulzer diesel provided a service speed of 15kts, which resulted in a saving of eight days on the previous schedule. A very similar design with single masts was used for the eleven-ship* Akagi Maru *class built after the Second World War. (CMP)*

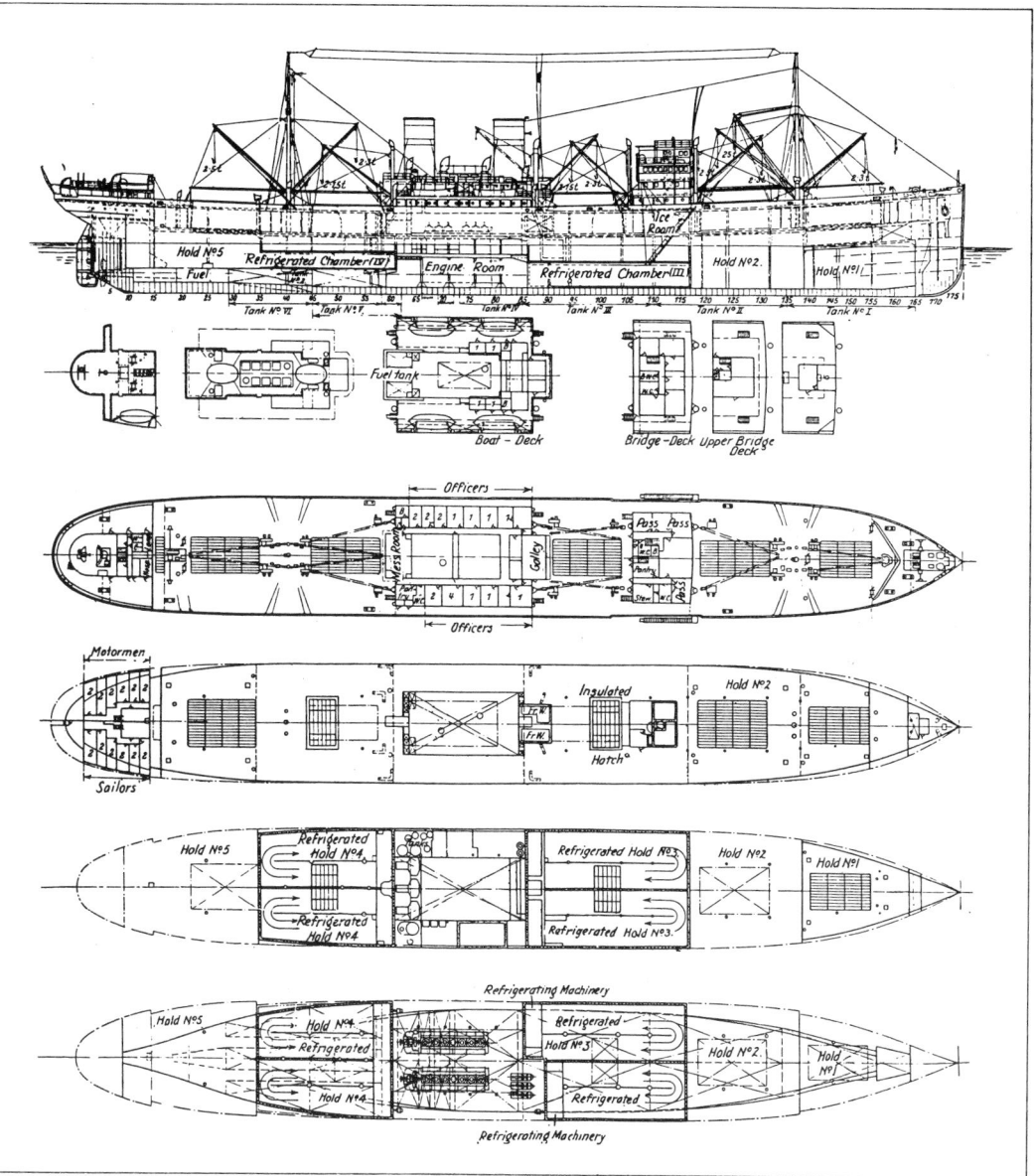

20kts on trials. Perhaps the peak of cargo liner development before the Second World War was reached with the 18kt *Glenearn* class, driven by two powerful B&W diesels totalling 12,000bhp. Built for Glen Line with considerable input from Alfred Holt, which had taken over the company in 1935 following the earlier collapse of the Royal Mail group, their design was to form the basis of numerous ships built for Holt after the war.

Cargo liner losses were again high in the Second World War and to partially compensate for these the British Government had built the *Empire Chieftain* standard type fast cargo liner capable of 15kts, many of which were adapted on the stocks for particular owner's requirements. The United States also produced very large numbers of standard cargo liner types such as the 'Victory' type, the C2s and C3s, most of them welded and all of which proved extremely useful as postwar stopgaps until new tonnage could be built. The larger 17kt C4 type had the bridge placed well forward and engines in the three-quarter aft position.

One of the main problems taxing cargo liner operators and naval architects after the war was the need to find ways of speeding up cargo handling. Ships (and crews) had grown vastly more expensive, yet they still spent as much as half their time tied up in port, so slow was loading and discharge – a problem exacerbated by widespread postwar disruption. Before the war German companies, particularly Hugo Stinnes, had experimented with electric deck cranes but it was Johnson Line of Sweden which finally broke with tradition and opted for a startling design of modern cargo liner in the shape of the eight-ship, twin screw, *Seattle* class, built during 1947–53. These had fourteen electric deck cranes in place of derricks, a single mast, streamlined superstructure and above all high speed, 19kts in service with a maximum of 22kts, produced by twin diesels totalling 14,000bhp. Some were also fitted

with controllable pitch propellers, developed by the company's KaMeWa subsidiary and first fitted to their 1944 built *Suecia*, one of a class of twenty-one similar motor cargo liners built from 1935 to 1948, four of which, from Kockums in Malmö, were the first large all-welded ships to be built in Europe.

Further innovations aimed at simplifying cargo handling and cutting down time in port followed: notably bipod masts and new types of derrick from companies such as Hallen and Stülcken; watertight rolling steel hatchcovers and flush fitting tweendeck hatches, the latter allowing the use of forklift trucks, developed mainly by MacGregor & Co. Large numbers of fine cargo liners in the 15–18kt, 5000–12,000grt range were built in the 1950s as postwar reconstruction accelerated, with many British and most US owners still favouring geared turbine propulsion, whilst continental European, Scandinavian and Japanese owners were firmly wedded to the diesel, these last vying with the United States for speed on the Pacific with fast liners developed from prewar designs. Mention should be made of the remarkable but economically questionable US Maritime Commission order for thirty-five 9200grt cargo liners of the 'Mariner' type, most of which were subsequently 'sold off' cheaply to US liner operators. Dating from 1952–56, they were capable of 20kts in service at an output of around 17,500shp, demonstrating that the earlier problems of absorbing high power in a single screw had finally been overcome.

As the 1950s progressed, Fred Olsen, working closely with MacGregor, experimented with wider hatches, travelling cranes, sideports and palletisation. In 1957, following trial installations in two of their older ships, Johnson Line instigated the use of medium speed diesels, developed from German U-

boat practice, in its seven-ship *Rio de Janeiro* class, thereby saving both space and weight. As in the earlier *Seattle* class, cargo handling was by electric cranes but Nos 3 and 4 holds were divided longitudinally into a large central hold with separate refrigerated holds either side, served in either case by three separate hatches. An idea that later gave rise to the so-called 'open' type ship, where each hold had two or three hatches placed athwartships, greatly facilitating cargo working.

As to overall design, earlier ideas were resuscitated and engines began to be positioned further aft. Some favoured the three-quarters position which retained one hatch abaft the machinery space as in the Norwegian P Meyer's *Havjo* of 1956, Clan Line's *Clan Maciver* and Norddeutscher Lloyd's *Burgenstein* (1958) and British India's *Bulimba* (1959). Others opted for a 'tanker' design with bridge forward of amidships and engines right aft, evidenced by Hansa's heavy-lift ships and East Asiatic's *Bogota* (1956). The latter concept reduced the length of shaft tunnels, giving slightly increased cargo capacity, but sometimes led to vibration problems. From 1962 some designs had both bridge and machinery aft: *vide* Norwegian America Line's *Altafjord* and the French *Ville du Havre*.

Increased competition on the Europe–Far East route led to higher speeds and Ben Line's somewhat secret introduction of the 20kt *Benloyal* in 1959 soon attracted a response from Glen Line and Nippon Yusen Kaisha, forcing other lines to follow suit. This need for speed in turn encouraged the development of advanced underwater forms, including bulbous bows and 'open water' type sterns to increase flow. At the same time engine-room design benefited from advances in automation.

The traditional cargo liner entered its final

Clan Line, which traded mainly to the Indian subcontinent but also to Africa and Australia, lost many of its very large fleet of cargo liners during the Second World War. Its postwar replacement programme included a number of different types, some diesel powered others driven by geared turbines such as the Clan Shaw *class dating from 1950, a design also taken up by Pacific Steam Navigation Co for its South American west coast services. The turbine-driven* Clan Robertson, *built by Greenock Dockyard in 1954, represented a further development on the same theme. As with all 'Clan' ships, she had an extensive derrick outfit including one 105 ton and two 40 ton heavy lifts.* (Ralston)

Cargo liner design began to change during the latter half of the 1950s and a number of new ships had their engines placed nearer the stern in what was known as the three-quarter aft position. Amongst these was French Line's Maryland, first of two 16kt, 7200grt motorships built by Chantiers & Ateliers de Provence for its North Atlantic service. (Ambrose Greenway collection)

stage of evolution in the 1960s, typified by 'open' hatch arrangements and sophisticated mixes of cargo gear, with speeds of 21kts or more, even as high as 25kts in some cases. In a short survey such as this it is difficult to be selective but Union-Castle's 34,720bhp *Good Hope Castle* and *Southampton Castle*, designed to operate alongside the passenger liners in the Cape mail service, must rank amongst the most outstanding. However the container ship was already in being and its widespread adoption on the major trade routes from 1969 onwards led to the speedy displacement of these highly advanced cargo liners, despite a brief twilight interlude when many were lengthened by the insertion of an extra cellular container hold.

Heavy-lift ships

From time to time most cargo liners were required to load awkward or heavy items beyond the limit of their standard derrick outfit. To meet this need, they were generally fitted with at least one or more heavy-lift or 'jumbo' derricks. The tackle required was heavy on manpower and decks were often unsuitable for the task, problems that were of particular interest to a Norwegian naval officer, Captain Christen Smith. Having made his name transporting 200 railway locomotives intact from the UK to Bel-

gium in two specially fitted steamers after the First World War, he went on to design several special types of heavy-lift ship, the so-called 'Belships', the first of which, *Beldis*, was delivered in 1924. With their heavy derricks and winches, long uncluttered decks with large strengthened hatches and special ballasting arrangements, they could carry not only rolling stock but also tugs, barges and even lightvessels.

The liner companies also increased the size of their heavy-lift capabilities, Elder Dempster fitting two 100-ton derricks to *Mary Kingsley*, the eighth and final unit of its 'Explorer' class West African traders, in 1930. Clan Line, and Hansa of Germany both of which served India, were also heavily involved in carrying locomotives and wagons and the latter company fitted 120-ton derricks to its four *Lichtenfels* class ships built in 1929–31.

Both during and immediately after the Second World War, the British Government built eight 15kt heavy-lift vessels with 120-ton derricks similar in design to the 'Belships', some of which were later bought by Ben Line. As soon as restrictions were lifted in Germany however, Hansa, which had lost

its entire fleet in the conflict, set about rebuilding its heavy-lift capability. *Barenfels*, completed in 1951 – the first of three sisters – broke new ground for the company in having bridge well forward and engines aft. At 6974grt she was then the largest ship built in Germany since the Second World War and boasted a derrick capable of lifting 165 tons, mounted on the mainmast at the after end of a very long hatch.

Further heavy-lift designs followed, including one or two built in Japan, but in 1954 Hansa took delivery of a new *Lichtenfels*, forerunner of a class of eight advanced 16kt 120-ton lift ships. Not only was her bridge placed right forward as in Great Lakes steamers but she was also fitted with a revolutionary new type of mast designed by her builder H C Stülcken Sohn, Hamburg, which consisted of two tall tapering masts angled outwards, allowing the derrick mounted between them to serve the hatches both forward and aft of it. Stülcken masts were fitted to all subsequent Hansa cargo liners, as well as many other companies' ships, lifting capacities steadily increasing up to the 300-ton unit fitted to Blue Star Line's 21kt cargo liner *Australia Star* in 1965.

Refrigerated cargo liners

Although refrigeration had been in use on land for a while and the first meat freezing plants had been set up in Sydney and Mel-

Between 1947 and 1956 William Thomson's Ben Line bought four heavy-lift ships that had originally formed part of a ten-ship standard type ordered by the British Government to a Belship design during the Second World War. Benledi – *built as* Empire Admiral *by Vickers-Armstrongs in 1945 – was a 15kt turbine ship, as was* Benalbanach, *but the slightly slower* Benwyvis *and* Benarty *had turbo-electric propulsion. Note her uncluttered decks and extra large hatches, each served by a single 150 ton derrick. In 1962 the company built a new heavy-lift ship,* Benarty, *which was fitted with a 180 ton Stülcken derrick.* (FotoFlite)

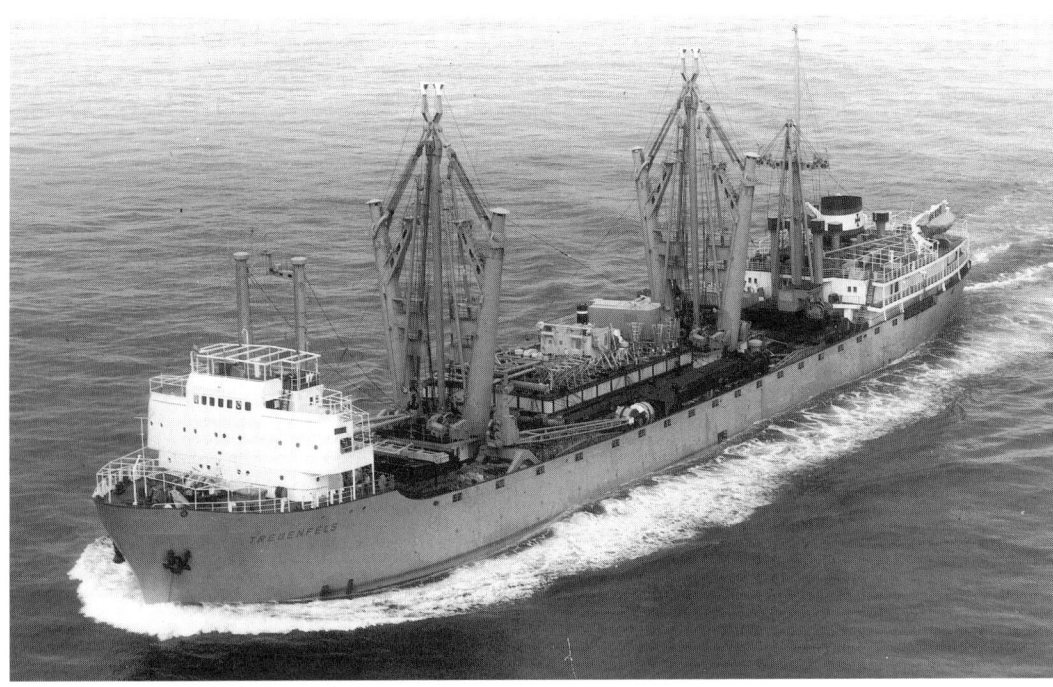

The 12,750dwt Treuenfels *(1960) was one of a number of heavy-lift cargo liners built for Hansa Line by H C Stülcken Sohn in the 1950's and '60s. Fitted with two of their specially designed derricks, each rated at 130 tons, she was capable of lifting 280 tons when they were used in tandem, a record at that time. Her two 5 ton deck cranes were mounted on rails so as to be able to serve all three hatches.* (FotoFlite)

bourne as early as 1861, it was to be another twenty years before a satisfactory means of applying it to ships for the carriage of frozen produce was perfected. The solution was timely, overcoming the alarming shortfall in the UK's home-production of meat and at the same time providing a market for the surplus of livestock produced by Australasia and Argentina, previously wastefully slaughtered for hides and tallow.

Early experiments by two Frenchmen, Ferdinand Carré and Charles Tellier had led to small trial shipments of frozen beef and

Houlder Bros had operated its own refrigerated tonnage in the Australian and South American trades since 1889 but following its sale to Furness Withy in 1911, it sold its Australian interests to concentrate on the River Plate meat trade. El Paraguayo *and her sister* La Correntina, *built for the company by Irvine's of West Hartlepool in 1912, marked the first phase in the reorganisation of Furness Withy's refrigerated shipping. Fitted for the carriage of chilled beef, their long bridge decks were to be a hallmark of the group's meat traders for many years, eventually extending to include the forecastle and all but the final few feet of the stern.* (CMP)

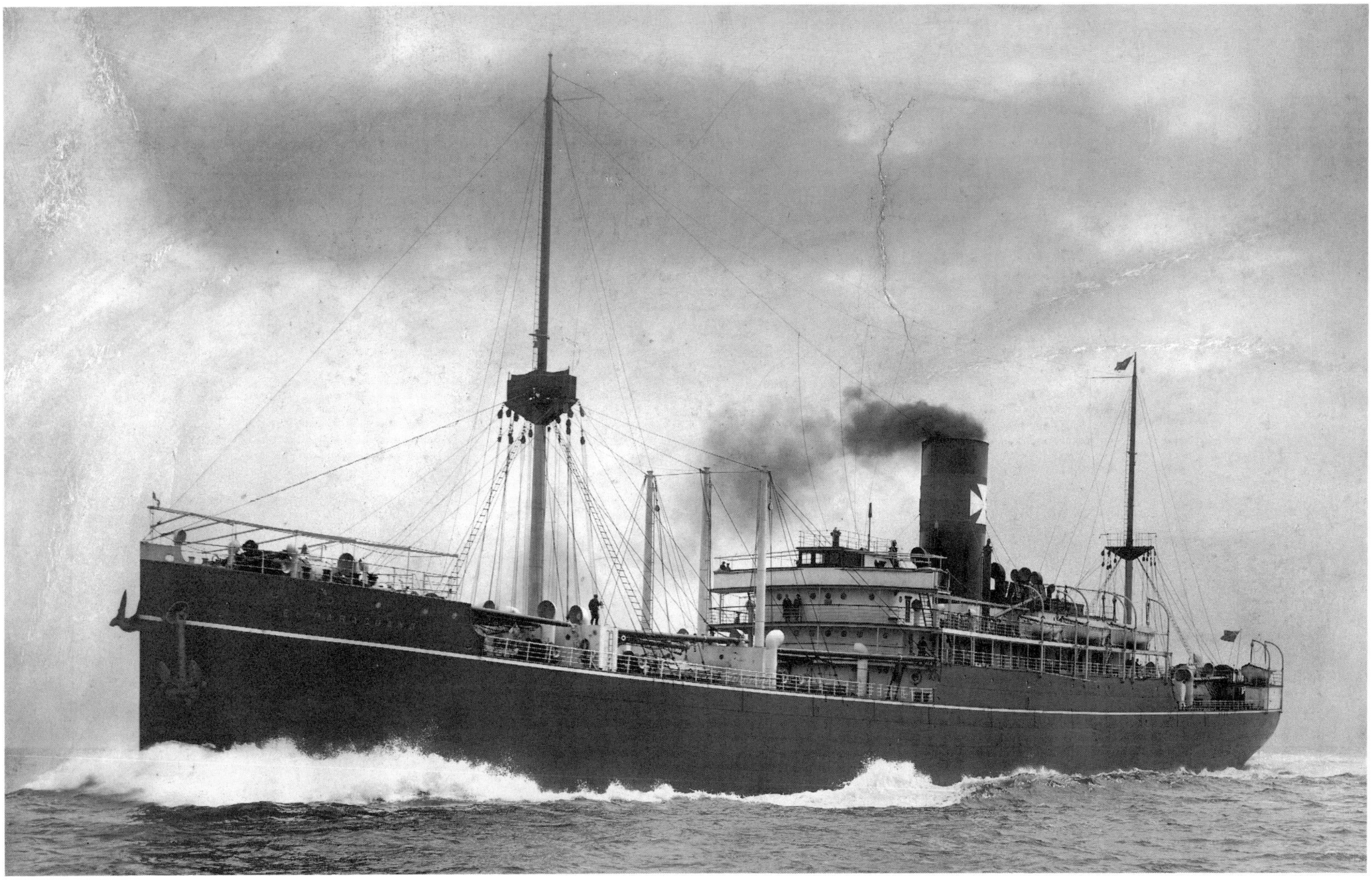

The 11,585dwt Port Gisborne *was typical of the refrigerated cargo liners built for Commonwealth & Dominion (Port Line), part of the Cunard group, during the 1920s. One of five slightly larger versions of the* Port Dunedin/Hobart *pair that introduced diesel propulsion to the Australian trade in 1925, she was built on Tyneside in 1927 and had a loaded speed of 15kts provided by twin Doxford engines. Ships such as this marked the beginning of a whole series of fast refrigerated motorships built for a number of UK owners up to 1939 that came to be known as the Empire Food Fleet.* (CMP)

mutton from Argentina using converted vessels. The latter's first attempt with an ammonia absorbtion freezing plant in *City of Rio de Janeiro* in 1868 failed due to machinery breakdown but his next attempt with an ammonia compression plant in the small steamer *Frigorifique*, resulted in a proportion of meat arriving in Rouen in reasonable condition early in 1877. Real success was only achieved in the winter of 1877–78 when *Paraguay*, fitted with a Carré ammonia compressor, returned to Le Havre from Buenos Aires with 5500 frozen carcasses in good condition.

Future development of marine refrigeration machinery then passed to Britain, where a Glasgow firm called Bell, Coleman & Co, which had invented a cold air machine in 1877, first installed one in the Anchor liner *Circassia* in 1879. In the same year another was fitted to the Burrell steamer *Strathleven*, chartered by the Queenslander Andrew McIlwraith, who had earlier inspected *Paraguay*, and she duly arrived back in London in February 1880 with 40 tons of frozen beef and mutton, the first successful shipment from Australia. Two years later the similarly fitted Albion Line sailing ship *Dunedin* carried the first frozen shipment from New Zealand, leading to other owners quickly converting existing tonnage. The first refrigerated newbuilding for the trade was Turnbull, Martin & Co's *Elderslie* of 1884, the forerunner of many similar ships for Scottish Shire Line.

Other lines active in the Antipodean meat trade by the turn of the century were New Zealand Shipping Co, Federal Steam Navigation Co, Houlder Bros, Shaw Savill & Albion (which had merged in 1882), and two companies that were later to become part of the Commonwealth & Dominion Line (Port Line), Tyser & Co and James P Corry & Co.

Insulation came in many different forms initially such as flake charcoal, silicate cotton and even pumice but in time granulated cork became the most widely used. In cold air machines such as the Bell, Coleman and more widely adopted Haslam types, the air was circulated by means of fans and wooden ducts. In liquid machines such as the compression and absorbtion types, refrigeration was used to cool a non-freezing liquid such as brine which was circulated through pipes arranged in grids either along the sides or ceilings of the insulated chambers.

Ships engaged in the Australasian trade had large proportions of their total cargo capacity insulated for the carriage of frozen meat, dairy products and apples, the remainder being for general cargo. A typical example was *Orari* of 1906, built by Wm Denny for New Zealand Shipping Co. Developed from the 1890s designed *Rakaia* type, many of which had later been completed with four instead of two masts for Federal, she was a flush decker of 7207grt, with about half her total cargo capacity – some 286,650cu ft – being insulated. Two triple expansion en-

gines gave a speed of 14kts but *Otaki*, the third ship of the class, made history by being the first merchant ship to be fitted with a Parsons designed centreline turbine driving a third screw, fed by exhaust steam from the two wing engines. Comparatively high speed was necessary to avoid deterioration of the cargo through unforeseen delays and this, coupled with the high initial cost of fitting refrigerating machinery and the provision of special 'freezer' engineers to run it, made refrigerated ships much more expensive than general cargo liners.

By 1912 well over two hundred refrigerated ships were in commission – almost entirely British-owned – the largest fleets being held by New Zealand Shipping, Federal, Nelson Line and the Furness Withy group. The latter two were heavily engaged in the South American meat trade, which with its shorter voyage time than that from the Antipodes (20 days compared with 30-40) allowed beef to be transported in chilled form,

Delivered late in 1934, Federal Steam Navigation Co's 13,370dwt Durham *with her sister* Dorset *were among the last ships built by the celebrated Belfast shipyard of Workman Clark & Co. Their design was a shelter deck development of the associated New Zealand Shipping Co's* Otaio *class of 1930 and set a style that was still evident in the company's* Somerset *built some eighteen years later. A twin-screw 16kt motorship,* Durham *had a refrigerated capacity of 496,000cu ft (about 70 per cent of the total) and became well known as the training ship for both companies with berths and classrooms for 40 cadets. (B Fielden)*

hung from hooks at between 28½ and 29½°F, which had the advantage of being almost indistinguishable from home-killed produce. By far the greatest proportion of chilled beef was shipped from the United States to Britain, a trade which faded after 1910 due to rapid increases in US home consumption. From 1912, Houlder, in consort with other Furness companies, developed a specific long bridge deck type of meat carrier that evolved through several broadly similar types right up to *Royston Grange* of 1959. Typical was the 14kt *Upwey Grange* of 1925 with some 500,000cu ft of insulated space, the largest outfit at that time, and the first to be fitted with diesel engines.

For strategic reasons, all British refrigerated ships were taken up by the Government during the First World War and all meat was 'frozen down' to enable more to be carried. The ships presented tempting targets and many were sunk, leading to the Government ordering a standard type refrigerated steamer to replace them. Known as the 'G' type, only two were delivered before the Armistice but eventually twenty-three were completed and adapted for use by several companies in the refrigerated trade.

In 1925 – the same year that Commonwealth & Dominion introduced *Port Dunedin* – the first motor ship on the Australasian trade – experiments were again started in the transportation of chilled beef from Australia. Several partially successful attempts had been made in the 1890s but even reasonable success with five trial shipments from Brisbane in *Marathon* in 1910–11 using the Linley sterilising system, which kept beef in good condition for at least seventy days, had failed to elicit support from the graziers. Eventually Government backed research found the answer, which involved injecting small amounts of carbon dioxide into special gastight compartments and this led to the opening up of the Australian chilled beef trade in 1930.

Meanwhile the success of *Port Dunedin* led to orders for other motorships, notably Shaw Savill's *Zealandic* (1928) and New Zealand Shipping Co's *Otaio* (1930). The Ottawa agreements of 1932–33 which guaranteed free entry for British Dominion and Colonial produce in return for UK export preference, led to the ordering of the largest and fastest refrigerated ships yet seen, aptly nicknamed 'Empire Food Ships'. These were all twin screw motorships of 8000 to 12,000grt and 16–17kts speed, with refrigerated capacities up to 600,000cu ft. All the established operators in the Australasian trade, Federal/New Zealand Shipping Co, Shaw Savill, and Port Line produced new designs, some of which lasted with modification right up to 1960, but it was newcomer Blue Star Line, a River Plate trader which extended its services to Australia and New Zealand following the Ottawa decision, that came up with arguably the most conspicuous with its single masted *Imperial Star* class introduced from 1935.

All these ships proved invaluable during the Second World War but many were lost and only four replacements, based on one of Shaw Savill's prewar designs, were ordered before the war ended. After the war developments in insulating materials led to the adoption of fibreglass instead of the compressed cork slabs covered with smooth cement that had come into use before the conflict. Postwar construction followed previous practice but with some elements of streamlining, introduced by Port Line's fine looking flagship *Port Brisbane* in 1949, which also had a deck crane fitted between Nos 4 and 5 hatches. Blue Star produced further impressive ships in the 1950s, starting with the 18kt, 600,000 cu ft *Adelaide Star* class but it was not really until the early 1960s that materially different designs appeared, such as Shaw Savill's *Megantic* and New Zealand Shipping Co's 20kt *Taupo*. The last and largest of this long line of 'reefers', the 21kt sisters *Port Caroline* and *Port Chalmers*, delivered in 1967–68, barely a year before Overseas Containers Ltd and

Shaw Savill & Albion Co's refrigerated motorship Cedric *was the first of two ships, later increased to five, that were built between 1952 and 1956 for the Australasian meat and produce trade, the additional three having greater chilled meat capacity. Her design was a refinement of the fast 'W' class ships of the 1930s, which were themselves based on the company's initial motorship,* Coptic, *built in 1928. Twin 6-cylinder opposed piston diesels provided a service speed of 17.5kts on a consumption of approximately 50 tons of oil a day. The four* Ionic *class ships which followed between 1959 and 1961 were similar save for single-screw turbocharged machinery and pear shaped funnels. (CMP)*

It was still unusual for a UK company to build outside Britain in the mid 1950s when Blue Star Line placed a five-ship order with Germany's Bremer Vulkan shipyard. Gladstone Star and her sister Townsville Star were the last to be delivered in 1957, their longer forecastles marking them out from the other three completed a year earlier. Measuring 10,725 gross with a deadweight of 12,300, they had a refrigerated capacity of 410,000cu ft and were driven at 17kts by a single 10-cylinder diesel. (Ambrose Greenway)

Associated Container Transportation burst upon the Australasian trade, were quickly rendered obsolete as a result of the new containerships being able to carry frozen produce at far less cost.

Banana carriers and fruit ships

The banana was relatively unknown in Europe at the end of the nineteenth century, being mainly carried from the Canary Islands in limited quantities either as deck cargo or in naturally ventilated ships belonging to Elder Dempster, Castle Line and Forwood Brothers. A similar pattern had developed in the United States, leading to the setting up of the Boston Fruit Co in 1885 specifically for the importation of bananas from Central America to the US east coast. This firm merged with other east coast fruit importers in 1899 to form United Fruit Company, a major producer as well as shipper which would grow to a dominant position in both the US and European banana trades.

No serious attempt had yet been made at long distance shipment of the delicate fruit but the issue was forced at the turn of the century when a decline in its traditional cane sugar industry, coupled with United Fruit's decision to set up rival banana plantations in Cuba, led Jamaica to appeal for help

from the British Government. Joseph Chamberlain, then Colonial Secretary, approached Alfred Jones, chairman of Elder Dempster, to look into the feasibility of shipping bananas from Jamaica to Britain. The answer was pessimistic as there seemed to be no way of preventing the fruit ripening *en voyage*. However the Government was well aware of the strides made in marine refrigeration and granted a subsidy to a Captain Lamont, who promptly ordered two clipper-stemmed refrigerated ships but failed to maintain payments on them. With a little arm-twisting Jones was then persuaded to take up both the contract and ships and formed the Imperial Direct West Indies Mail Service in 1900. The subsidy was to last ten years and the ships were required to carry 20,000 stems of bananas in addition to passengers, which puts them beyond the scope of this chapter. Nevertheless the arrival of Imperial Direct's first ship, the 2900grt *Port Morant*, in Avonmouth in March 1901 with a cargo of bananas, some oranges and other fruits, marked the beginning of the refrigerated fruit trade. Two larger ships, *Port Antonio* and *Port Royal*

(4450grt), appeared soon afterwards but Jones soon realised that a separate marketing organisation was needed for bananas and in May 1901 set up another company, Elders & Fyffes Ltd, a joint undertaking between Elder Dempster and Fyffes Hudson & Co – which already had an interest in distributing Canary Islands bananas – but more importantly United Fruit was given a 45 per cent interest in order to guarantee loadings.

It soon became apparent that the trade required weekly instead of fortnightly sailings and Fyffes acquired four second-hand ships from Furness Withy in 1902–3 to run alongside those of Imperial Direct, fitting them with refrigeration machinery. Their first insulated cargo steamers specially designed for banana carriage, the three-ship *Matina* class (3800grt), appeared in 1904 from the Swan Hunter and Barclay Curle shipyards. Their design owed much to *Port Antonio* and they could carry around 60,000 stems of bananas at 13kts. At about the same time United Fruit received three similar ships from Workman Clark, Belfast, the 3300grt, 45,000 stem *San Jose* class. Fyffes followed up with a further nine slightly larger and faster ships completed by 1911, when it switched to building passenger-carrying banana ships.

Built in 1911, the 13kt, 4154grt Aracataca and her sister Manzanares represented the last and largest ships in Elders & Fyffes' initial refrigerated cargo ship programme, begun in 1904 with the pioneering Matina class. With their silver grey hulls and buff funnels they were unmistakable, the same being true of the broadly similar 14kt Chirripo class ships which followed in the 1920s. The same basic design but with a cruiser stern was also evident in Atlantic Fruit Co's faster 15kt Erin and Eros built by Workman Clark in 1932 and 1936, which were unusual in being propelled by a quadruple expansion engine exhausting into a turbo-electric outfit coupled to the shaft for an extra knot of speed. (Ambrose Greenway collection)

The Danish firm of J Lauritzen first became involved in the reefer business in the early 1930s, converting several small steamers for charter to a French company. New refrigerated motorships soon followed, amongst which was the larger 16kt American Reefer *(1936) which was unusual for the time in having five hatches. Similar ships followed and the same basic design was still evident in the more streamlined* Brazilian Reefer *trio of 1954–55.* (CMP)

Bananas were loaded 'green' through doors in the side of the hull, at first by hand and later by conveyors, and were stored in the tweendecks in slatted wooden bins. They were quickly cooled to 12½°C (about 54½°F) and then maintained at this temperature throughout the voyage by the forced circulation of air passed over pipes containing cooled brine. The system also had to be capable of heating the cargo to cope with winter conditions in the northern hemisphere.

Sir Alfred Jones, as he had then become, died in 1909 and the Imperial Direct Line, never a financial success, was sold off when its subsidy expired the following year. In 1913 United Fruit finally acquired the whole of Fyffes' equity and not long afterwards ordered four more banana ships, the 3200 ton *San Andres* class from Workman Clark.

Fyffes had begun to land bananas on the continent of Europe about two years before the start of the First World War and German companies were beginning to show interest in the trade. F Laeisz & Co of Hamburg, known for its famous sailing fleet, built two steamers in 1914 for the Cameroon trade but the war intervened and one achieved notoriety as the raider *Möwe*. Both vessels were ceded to Britain in 1920 as reparations, and

became part of the Elders & Fyffes fleet in 1921.

In 1920 Fyffes embarked on a cargo fleet renewal programme that resulted in the largest group of sister ships ever built for the banana trade, namely the 5350grt, 14kt *Chirripo* class, which numbered nineteen by the time the last was completed in 1930. Built by Workman Clark, Cammell Laird and Alexander Stephen they were slightly larger (100,000 stems) than the prewar ships and differed in having a three island type hull and prominent cooler houses under each mast. The first three of these reciprocating-engined coal-burners were transferred to United Fruit's new German subsidiary, Union Handels, in 1935 along with the older *Manzanares* dating from 1911.

The parent company was also active and successfully pioneered the deep-sea use of turbo-electric machinery in 1921 in *San Benito*, fourth and final unit of a follow up class to the *San Andres*. However, a similar first with diesel-electric propulsion in the first two ships of the Cammell Laird-built *La Playa* class of 1923–24 was a failure and

a third ship was given conventional reciprocating machinery in 1925.

From its early days United Fruit had concentrated on passenger carrying steamers, The Great White Fleet affectionately termed on account of their smart appearance and white hulls, but much of its local banana and fruit trade had been carried in a motley collection of smaller chartered ships known as 'the Mosquito Fleet'. The majority of these were Norwegian owned, one of the largest being the 2826grt *Ellis* built in 1904, and all were ventilated rather than refrigerated. Other shipping companies even converted former US Navy torpedo boats and destroyers to carry bananas. By the mid 1920s this local fleet evolved into a larger type, typical of which was the twin screw 1840grt *Gundersen* delivered to Norwegian owner Chr Gundersen & Co by the Götaverken yard in Gothenburg in 1927. She was notable as the first motor fruit ship and was followed by two improved sisters, *I K Ward* and *Harboe Jensen*, in 1929; both had service speeds of 14kts and three island type hulls. In 1933 Götaverken introduced a new type of citrus carrier which was to set the pattern for many subsequent ships. *Washington Express*, owned by Biorn Biornstad, was much larger at around 3600grt and faster – her twin diesels gave 16kts – but her main feature was a very long raised forecastle that extended to her bridge. Along with sisters *California Express* and *Oregon Express* built in 1934, she inaugu-

Built by Akers in 1930 for Fred Olsen & Co's Canary Islands–North Europe service, Bajamar *was one of the earliest motor fruit carriers. One of four similar ships build in pairs in 1930 and 1933, she represented a particular type of ship engaged in the shorter fruit trades that did not require refrigerating machinery, relying instead on natural draught from numerous large ventilators to cool the holds. Other ships employed mechanical ventilation to achieve the same end.* (FotoFlite)

rated the Pacific Express Line set up by several Norwegian shipowners to carry fruit from British Columbia and the US Pacific coast to Europe. Built in increasing numbers for charter work in the late 1930s – many with forecastle further extended to the after end of the superstructure – such ships gradually took over an increasing proportion of long distance fruit carriage.

The same decade saw France embark upon the creation of a considerable reefer fleet, having previously imported bananas from its West African and Caribbean dependencies by fast passenger ships in the case of the former or in the tween decks of Compagnie Générale Transatlantique (CGT) cargo liners from Martinique and Guadeloupe. Following experiments in 1929 with refrigerating machinery fitted into a second-hand British First World War standard type collier, Compagnie des Chargeurs Reunis of Paris built three flush-decked reefers of the *Kolente* (2000grt) class at Port de Bouc in 1933–34, whilst Louis Martin took delivery of the 2600grt *Alice Robert* from Nakskov, Denmark, in the latter year. She followed the contemporary Norwegian designs but with the addition of a short raised poop. A shorter forecastle on the other hand, extending only to the foremast, identified Compagnie Fraissinet's *Iles de Los* and *Cap des Palmes* built at Elsinore in 1934–35. Compagnie Générale Transatlantique, initially through its subsidiary CGAM, was also very active and by 1939 France had built over twenty new ships, aided by government protectionist measures.

One particular ship, *Francine*, laid down at Odense for a French flag company owned by A P Moller but delivered to the latter in 1936, was unique in having her engines

placed aft. Due to the problems alluded to above, her French charter fell through and she was sold to J Lauritzen in 1937, becoming *Egyptian Reefer*. This Danish company was another comparative newcomer to the reefer trade, having converted several smaller cargo ships before embarking on its own new building programme. In Germany Laeisz had again been active, building its first motor reefer, *Pionier*, in 1933 followed by six similar ships for the Cameroons banana trade by the end of the decade. By the time war came again, Italian owners too had built the *Capitano Bottego* and fast *Ramb* class reefers for the Somali banana trade.

In Britain, meanwhile, a rival to Fyffes had appeared in 1928 in the shape of Jamaica Direct Fruit Line (later Jamaica Banana Producer's Steamship Co Ltd), which commenced operations with the purchase of four vessels from Nelson Line and took delivery of its first new vessel, *Jamaica Pioneer*, in 1931. Two similar ships followed but the diesel-driven *Jamaica Planter* of 1935 was distinctive on account of her single mast and engines placed aft of amidships. However it was Union-Castle Line that built the world's largest refrigerated fruit carriers before the Second World War, starting in 1935 with *Roslin Castle*, one of two 16kt Harland & Wolff-built ships of 7000grt. These were followed by two 7800 ton ships with an extra (fifth) hold in 1937, three more during the war and a further slightly modified pair in 1946.

The Second World War led to the loss of many ships but United Fruit had already embarked on a large newbuilding programme before it had finished, six ships of the twin screw turbine 18½kt *Fra Berlanga* class – large

at over 7000grt – being delivered during 1945–47, with a further group of nine immediately after the war – the 5075grt 16½kt *Yaque* class – during 1947–48. Fyffes acquired some former German tonnage and built one new ship at Alexander Stephen in 1946. Named *Matina*, she was their first turbine vessel with a speed of 17½kts and improved refrigerating machinery, and her design of separate forecastle and bridge deck was continued in their later *Chicanoa* class of 1958.

In Scandinavia, prewar designs were improved upon, and as the 1950s progressed Sven Salen, a Swedish company which had built its first reefer in 1941 and was very much in the ascendancy, built up a fine fleet of 18kt, short raised forecastle type motorships, culminating in the turbine driven *Antigua* (1960) which at 8288grt was the largest of her day. Lauritzen, too, had been renewing its fleet with advanced ships such as the *Brazilian Reefer* and improved *Arabian Reefer* types, the latter having fibreglass and aluminium insulation, whilst for the shorter Canaries/Mediterranean trade Fred Olsen & Co of Oslo built a series of mechanically ventilated ships with engines aft of amidships that were noted for their advanced cargo handling ideas.

From 1951 onwards, following the lifting of restrictions, Germany quickly started to rebuild its reefer fleet, with the result that by 1960 nearly forty fast ships had appeared for owners such as Bruns, Hamburg-Sud, Laeisz, Schuldt and Union, many of them streamlined and all distinguished by very long combined forecastles and bridge decks that extended either to the mainmast or nearly to the stern. Italy's Fassio company built similar ships but in France different ideas evolved, such as the flush-deck *Fort Carillon* class, eleven of which were built for CGT from 1953 to 1962. Other French companies such as Fraissinet, Fabre and Louis Martin favoured designs with engines aft of amidships.

As the decade closed the first 'all-aft' reefer, the free-piston gas turbine propelled *Geestland* (1990grt) was delivered to Geest Industries, a company which had built up the Windward Islands banana trade since

Alsterufer (2683grt), built for Robert M Sloman of Hamburg by Deutsche Werft in 1954, was a typical German reefer ship of the period with her streamlined bridge front, unusual lifeboat positions and drop in upper deck level almost at the stern. Employed in the Ecuador banana trade, she was sold to Greece in 1970. (Real Photographs)

Following the delivery of A P Moller's Francine *in 1937, quite a few years elapsed before engines again began to be moved further aft. The 3677grt* Almirante *was one of three ships built by Bremer Vulkan in 1954–55 for the United Fruit Co subsidiary Empresa Hondurena de Vapores. She could carry 38,000 stems of bananas (later increased to 42,000) and was driven at 15kts by twin MAN diesels geared to a single screw.* (Ambrose Greenway)

1952. The 1960s were to witness the emergence of the more complex multi-temperature reefer, able to carry mixed cargoes of bananas, fruit and meat, whilst speeds quickly increased to over 20kts.

Ambrose Greenway

The Tramp or General Cargo Ship

At the beginning of the twentieth century Great Britain was the accepted shipbuilding centre of the world, one to whom most other nations turned when they needed new tonnage. As for the composition of the British merchant fleet, the passenger liner, despite the publicity it attracted, represented only a small part of the whole. Instead it was the tramp steamer which, in its hundreds, represented the backbone. Not every nation was interested in vessels of this type, most preferring ships with a better turn of speed and the other refinements needed for use on regular services – in other words ships of the cargo liner type. When elderly British tramps came on the market they mainly went to Mediter-

ranean countries, notably Greece and Italy or, in the case of smaller vessels, to Scandinavia.

Lloyd's Register Book for 1904 reveals that Great Britain then owned something over 1600 tramp steamers of 1000 tons net or over (see table). That this figure corresponded to something between 1500 and 1700 tons gross was shown by a comparison of the two tonnages, net and gross, of twenty contemporary ships. Coasters, colliers and the like were thus eliminated, while a study of individual fleets made possible the elimination of all known passenger ships and cargo liners and specialised types such as cable vessels, etc. Even so, the figure can only be accepted as an approximation, possibly slightly on the low side.

With regard to the above, it should be remembered that many large sailing vessels still existed. The Clyde, for instance, was the home of several major fleets, the largest being Thomas Law & Co's Shire Line which owned twenty-one, and Andrew Weir & Co with nineteen. Liverpool had many of note including MacVicar, Marshall & Co which had twelve, Robert Thomas & Co, fifteen and W Thomas & Co, twenty-one. It was

somewhat ironic that for many sailing ships it was the growing number of steamships which provided them with a new form of employment and means of survival – the problems associated with maintenance of coal supplies to a worldwide range of bunkering stations.

Besides the various new designs available at the turn of the century there were many older, well-tried designs still in service. Typical of these rather smaller ships was the elderly but still popular part-awning-deck steamer. This, in essence had two decks (the main and awning) forward of the superstructure, but only one aft. This, the quarter deck, was several feet above the main deck, so compensating for the space occupied by the shaft tunnel. Quite often there was a short well deck forward, this just ahead of the foremast. However, in the early 1900s the type of steamer most popular with tramp shipowners was the single-decker of three-island layout. These generally had two hatches in each well and, depending on size, another between the bridge and funnel. Right aft, on the poop, there might be another smaller hatch served by one or two kingposts.

In older ships the crew was berthed in the

British Tramp Ownership, 1904

Port	Number of companies	Number of vessels	Largest fleets, vessels
London	78	418	Watts, Watts, 26
Newcastle upon Tyne/North Shields	38	278	Runciman, 23
West Hartlepool	30	202	Ropner, 39
Cardiff	39	191	John Cory, 16; Morel, 37
Glasgow	35	163	Maclay & McIntyre, 21
Liverpool	32	138	Larrinaga, 13; Rankin Gilmour, 11
Sunderland	26	100	Westoll, 30
Whitby	11	77	Marwood, 27; T Turnbull, 16
St Ives	3	42	Hain, 28
Totals	292	1609	

The St Ives registered Tregantle *(1903/3091grt) was one of the earlier of the eighty-odd ships built by Readhead of South Shields for the Hain fleet. Her low bridge and absence of crosstrees both give indication of the period in which she was built. A single-decker which measured 323ft bp × 47ft, she had a deadweight tonnage of 5300 and a loaded draught of 21ft 3ins. (Laurence Dunn collection)*

as Moss, MacAndrews, Bruce, Wilson and Papayanni. Given 'tween decks, and three or four hatches, their lack of length resulted in shorter wells and hatches and shorter centre-castle with bridge and funnel close together. Many Scandinavian vessels stood apart by having their masts at the ends of the cargo spaces, this for the easier stowage of deck cargoes, especially timber.

forecastle, but already there was a trend to reposition them aft, in the poop. The officers' quarters were in the bridgehouse and the engineers' normally abreast the engine casing. The length of such ships varied between 320ft and 400ft, their gross tonnage between 2500 and something over 5000, the deadweight capacity seldom exceeding 8000 tons. The Readhead-built *Ilwen* of 1904 was typical of many Cardiff-owned tramps whose normal trade was outward to the River Plate or Black Sea with coal and home with grain. Of 4072grt, she measured 353ft length bp × 50ft breadth, had triple-expansion machinery, three Scotch boilers, a coal bunker capacity of 388 tons and a loaded speed of around 9–10kts. Later sold to London owners and renamed *Kingsbury*, she lasted until the mid-1930s before going to the breakers.

Many three-island type steamers built between the turn of the century and the First World War had two things in common. One was the placing of the third hatch ahead of the bridge, which was repositioned close to the funnel. The other common link was that they had been ordered – usually on spec – by Frank C Strick. With an acute sense of timing, he would order when prices were at their lowest and sell at a profit when confidence returned and freight rates picked up. Many such ships – quite often sold before

completion – went to Germany and Cuba, others to the British India Steam Navigation Co. The constant repetition of certain Strick names could be confusing. For instance in 1912 two brand new ships, *Arabistan* and *Shahristan* were sold to British India which, in the following year, bought another pair similarly named.

With another pre-1914 design the familiar three-island layout was modified by having the bridge deck extended forward and aft to stop just short of the masts. In a later effort to gain yet more cargo space, the bridge deck was extended even further, to beyond the masts which, with the adjacent winches, were repositioned one deck higher. The outcome was the long bridge type, construction of which continued until the mid-1930s.

Mediterranean and Black Sea ports were the venue for many deep sea tramps engaged on the familiar coal–grain/ore trade. However besides these and the many locally-owned tramps (often smaller and bought second-hand) there was a strong element of modern short sea traders, some built as tramps, others with a better turn of speed which operated as cargo liners for firms such

Turret ships and other patent designs

Even though they had been designed in the 1890s, the construction of several well-known types continued well into the twentieth century. By far the best known of these was the Doxford-built turret steamer, the first of which was delivered in 1892 and the last in 1911. During that period over 170 were built by the parent yard at Sunderland, six elsewhere in Britain and one, *Upo Mendi* of 1911, in Spain.

The turret steamer was evolved from the whaleback ship, a type well-known on the Great Lakes, one of which, *Charles H Wetmore* attracted much attention when she visited Liverpool in the early 1890s. Doxford were promptly commissioned to build one like her under licence. This was *Sagamore*, 2140grt, which measured length 311ft and breadth 38ft. Her hull, which sat low in the water, had very curvaceous sides and a snout shaped bow. Completely flush, even to hatch covers, she carried several tall erections or 'turrets', the longest of which was built over the machinery space and contained the accommodation and wheelhouse. It was from

The Greek-owned Fred *(1907/4043grt), a ship of the popular long bridge deck type, had a tonnage of 7200dwt and measured 360ft bp × 50ft, her load draught being 24ft 5ins. Originally J & C Harrison's* Hartington, *she was built by Wm Gray of West Hartlepool. This profile view clearly shows the slim auxiliary funnel – then a quite common feature – which served the auxiliary donkey boiler. (Laurence Dunn collection)*

Turret steamers of various sizes were built – and engined – by Doxford over the period 1892–1911, but the Erika Fritzen *(1905/4136grt) belonged to the most popular size group, her main dimensions being 350ft bp × 51ft × 24ft. Seen while traversing the Kiel Canal with a cargo of ore, she was then bearing her fourth name. Originally the* Ryton, *she was built for the Stephens, Sutton fleet, but was later owned in Norway, Sweden and Germany before being sunk in 1945. (Laurence Dunn collection)*

this that Arthur Havers, Doxford's chief draughtsman developed the turret theme, in which there was one long turret – its width being about half that of the ship. Flanking this turret and not far above the loadline, was the so-called 'harbour deck', the sides of which joined the main vertical plating in large radius curves.

Early turret ships had their engines aft, but by 1900 a larger engine-amidships design had arrived, a ship with four main hatches and a weather deck which was topped by a short forecastle and poop. Over the years there were many repeat orders and no fewer than thirty turrets were given *Clan* names. Excluding the early engines-aft vessels the average turret ship measured between 340ft and 400ft length (bp), the maximum being the 455ft of the 1905-built British India *Queda* and her two sisters. Others with off-beat profiles were those intended for the ore trade, ships with engines aft and many pairs of twin kingposts.

Besides its inherent strength – helped by a cellular double bottom – the turret design was the more popular with owners since its net tonnage was low in relation to deadweight; also that Suez Canal dues were based on the breadth of the upper deck and not on the much wider main (or harbour) deck below. Amended regulations eventually rectified this and so, in 1911, the construction of

turret steamers came to an end. Their success inevitably brought imitations, but the only one to achieve any degree of popularity was the Ropner-designed trunk deck ship.

Ropner, already well-known as a major tramp ship owner, bought a shipyard at Stockton-on-Tees where, in 1896, he built the aptly named *Trunkby* of 2635grt. In addition to outside orders Ropner built twelve of this first design for his own account. Of the familiar three-island layout, they had a vertical sided trunk in each well, so increasing cubic capacity and also raising the hatches to a higher, safer level. In 1904 he introduced a second design of which, as before, a dozen joined his own fleet, the rest being for a variety of other owners. These ships had a continuous trunk which was topped by a short raised forecastle – but no poop. It was the absence of this latter feature and the conspicuous edges to the harbour deck which distinguished these trunk deckers from Doxfords' turrets. Typical of Ropner's later productions, *Stagpool* (built 1905, 4621grt) had a deadweight tonnage of 6000 and measured 356ft length (bp) and 53ft breadth. She was scrapped in 1935, but a longer lasting sister was the Cardiff-owned *Clarissa Radcliffe* of 1904 which was still trading in 1950 while bearing her seventh name, *Antonios K.*

For Sunderland, 1896 was the year of the trunk deck steamer, for besides Ropner's

Trunkby two other yards introduced their own variants, that from Laing being *Oscar II* (3403grt), for the Swedish Johnson Line. Also in that year James Priestman & Co completed what the contemporary shipping press described as 'the first of the Priestman trunk-deck self trimmers'. This was the aptly named *Unique* (2196grt) which, like *Universe* of 1898, was for Norwegian ownership. In common with the next, the Newcastle-owned *Enfield*, the topsides of their hulls were on two planes, the upper part being near-vertical while below, and for the greater part of the length, it sloped sharply outwards – as does the roof of a house. To revert to the Laing shipyard this, in 1901, delivered what was probably the largest trunk decker to date. This was *Hoerde* (5091grt) which, like her sister *Strasbourg*, was for Hamburg-Amerika Linie. Except for the Priestman ships, all these had a three-island layout with trunks in the wells. One other variation could be seen in *Ocland* (built 1907, 3120grt), an engines-aft product of Sunderland Shipbuilding Co. Her long clear trunk deck ran from the tall forecastle to the break of the poop – just under the bridge. Initially fitted with deck cranes, these were later replaced by four masts and conventional derricks.

The corrugated steamer Rio Diamante *(8850dwt) was the last of this type which were built 1921–28 for the Thompson Steamship Co, of Newcastle. The bulges were claimed to improve cubic capacity and also sea kindliness, points which were somewhat offset by the greater cost of repairs should they become damaged. As an indication of prices, the* Rio Diamante *cost £90,000 to build but realised only £33,500 when sold five years later to become the Greek* Chloe. *(Laurence Dunn collection)*

Arch deck ships

Next came the era of the arch deck steamer, of which over two dozen were built during 1912–24, nearly half of them at Blyth. Ships of around 4100dwt, only the first had a counter stern, the rest having the then somewhat novel cruiser stern. Besides the bulge above the waterline the main recognition features were a very slight reverse sheer, a short forecastle and poop and a midship superstructure set between four hatches. Most were for Newcastle upon Tyne owners Sheaf Steam Shipping Co, but two of the later deliveries were for Walter Runciman. In 1923 even the then mighty Swan Hunter organisation was glad to receive orders for two of this type, these being delivered to local owners as the 1742grt *Marjorie S* and *Murie S*. Burntisland also made its contributions with *Sheaf Brook* of 1924 and the sisters *Carlbeath* and *Halbeath*.

The changed tonnage regulations which took away the advantage long held by the turret ship favoured instead a new type. This was the shelter-decker which, over the main deck, had another one with lighter scantlings – the shelter deck. This had 'tonnage openings' which could be opened or closed to suit cargo requirements. In the 'closed' state the extra space could be used for light, bulky cargoes and was then subject to correspondingly higher tonnage dues. For heavy cargoes such as ore, the space was not needed and declared 'open' and was therefore exempt from charges. In 1912 Doxford, having finished with turret ships, delivered the first of many shelter deckers of which the first few measured 440ft length and 58ft breadth. However, the main sequence started a year later with the delivery of *Nordmark* and *Sudmark* – both for Hamburg-Amerika – and the British *Gifford*. Flush deckers with dimensions of 420ft length and 54ft breadth, they had a split superstructure and six hatches, the aftermost being served by a pair of kingposts.

Britain's First World War standard ships

The standard ships built in Britain from 1917 onwards were nearly all of well tried designs, ease of construction being of paramount importance. The emphasis was on three-island type ships, the most numerous being the outwardly similar 'A' and 'B' types which had a length of 400ft bp, but differed internally in having one and two decks respectively – as did the scaled down 'C' and 'E' designs – which had lengths of 331ft and 376ft. All four types had one major recognition feature in common, this being a solid or plated-in bridge-house.

The 'F' and 'F1' types measured 414ft and 400ft in length respectively and were shelter-deckers with split superstructure. Both had a raised forecastle, while those built by Doxford had a cruiser type stern. The most distinctive of all were those of the 'N' type which, designed for easy fabrication, had hull plates with only the minimum of curves. This applied even to the bilge area where, instead of the usual quarter-circle curve, there was a long flat plate set at an angle of about 45 degrees. Between the masts the hull was devoid of sheer, but there was a sudden rise to bow and stern. As for the latter, this was of an entirely new shape – a vee-shaped transom, or 'cheese-cut' as it was sometimes called. Smallest of the general tramp designs, the 303ft-long 'H' type ships repeated the three-island theme but differed in having a cruiser stern. Those of the 'D' type were colliers with a length of 285ft. Ships with engines amidships, and four hatches, the after pair was on a raised quarter-deck. So too was the poop, making it half a deck higher than the forecastle. Outside the scope here in being essentially cargo liners, the 'G' type ships were flush decked save for a short raised forecastle and poop, the latter ending in a cruiser stern.

Doxford continued with its prewar 420ft shelter-deck steamships until well after the First World War. One of especial interest was *Dominion Miller* of 1921 which was instead fitted with the first ever Doxford marine diesel. She was soon joined by the Swedish sisters *Yngaren* and *Eknaren*, and then by a more beamy pair of cargo liners for Furness Withy. It was their performance which gradually won over hesitant shipowners and established the Doxford engine reputation.

Of the several yards which introduced new designs after the war, Doxford can surely claim prior attention, since it is through their products that one can see most clearly the general pattern of development. Their next venture was the Doxford 'Economy' motor tramp. These were headed by *Sutherland*, 9200dwt, which had a length of 412ft (bp) and an 1800bhp diesel which was said to give 11kts on a daily fuel consumption of 6.5 tons. Appearance-wise, she had three of her five hatches forward of a short, compact superstructure. An overall air of neatness was enhanced by a new style conical stern. The Mark-2 version was slightly larger, had a rather more conspicuous superstructure and, optionally, a raised forecastle. In fact they were not dissimilar to various of the 'Empire' standard ships of the Second World War.

Continental designs

A new type of specialist tramp, introduced by Captain Christen Smith, of Oslo in 1921, was designed to carry – and lift – extra heavy loads such as assembled locomotives and rolling stock, also tugs, lightships, etc. In 1926 he commissioned his finest yet, the twin-screw motorships *Belpareil* and *Beljeanne*, both 7203grt. They had specially strength-

The Harland & Wolff built War Shamrock *(1917/ 5174grt) was an A- (single deck) type standard ship which measured 400ft bp × 52ft, her deadweight tonnage of 8175 corresponding to a draught of 25ft. The B-type, similar in both dimensions and appearance, differed in having two decks. The* War Shamrock *had the distinction of being the first of all Britain's First World War standard ships to be completed. (Laurence Dunn collection)*

ened decks and holds and 100-ton derricks which made them independent of shore equipment. Years later their design was repeated for a Second World War standard design. Also from Scandinavia came the 'boilers-on-deck' type steamer, which had its boilers placed high up in the superstructure – instead of being in front of the main engine. An early example was the 1936 Fredriksstad-built, Oslo-owned *Honnor* (1318grt) which had a length of 251ft (bp) and a deadweight of 2490. Flush decked save for a short half-height forecastle, she had a short but tall superstructure placed between four hatches. Bought in 1937 by James Currie & Co, and renamed *Lapland*, she became the first boilers-on-deck ship to be owned in Britain. However the first of this type to be actually built in the UK was the much larger Gray-built *Elmcrest* (4853grt), completed in 1939 which however became a war loss. A longer lasting and therefore better known example was the Metcalfe Shipping-owned *Industria* (built 1940, 4861grt) which, under another name and owner only went to the breakers in 1968.

The German-designed Maierform hull first appeared on cargo ships in the late 1920s, notably on various Neptun Line vessels. Distinguished by its convex lines especially forward, the stem – always raked – was also generally curved. Subsequently the Mid-

dlesbrough firm of Constantine had two of its tramp steamers rebuilt with Maierform bows. Pleased with their performance, the company next ordered three to be built by Hawthorn, Leslie & Co, Newcastle upon Tyne, to Maierform designs, the first of these, *Windsorwood* (5935grt), appearing in 1936. In that same year Short of Sunderland built *Generton* (4781grt), she being the first of a trio built for Newcastle shipowner Chapman. In 1934–35 Blue Star Line had their cargo liners *Doric Star* and *Napier Star* lengthened and given Maierform bows and followed these up by having three of the passenger/cargo liners of the *Almeda Star* class similarly altered.

The mid to late 1930s

The Isherwood system of longitudinal framing had been widely used since its introduction in 1908 on *Paul Paix*, an engines-amidships tanker of 6600dwt. The next Isherwood development, the Arcform type of hull, appeared in the mid-1930s. In this the ship's

topsides were given a considerable amount of tumblehome, the arc of which continued far below the waterline, so eliminating the traditional near-squareness of the bilge area. The first to incorporate this design were the tramp steamers *Arcwear*, *Arctees* and *Arcgow*, all completed in 1936 and 362ft in length. Found to improve sea kindliness and bring a reduction in fuel consumption, it was soon applied to several large Greek tramps, amongst them *Master Elias Kulukundis* of 1938.

By 1939 the British merchant fleet included about 800 tramp ships, totalling just over 3,800,000grt, representing a reduction in numbers of some 1400 since 1914. By this time, however, the average age of vessels was eleven years, helped by disposal of many older vessels during the depression years of the 1930s.

It is also interesting to note that in 1912 an average reciprocating steamer burned about 42 tons of coal; in 1924 this had reduced to about 33 tons for a ship of the same type, and by the start of the Second World War the modern turbine or reciprocating engine tramp only required 22 tons daily.

Such advances are also shown in this comparison:

	1912	1939 (coal)	1939 (diesel)
Gross tonnage	5000	5000	5000
Deadweight tons	8400	8700	9200
Speed	10kts	11kts	10.2kts
Fuel per day	30.5 tons	26 tons	6.75 tons

Certain basic types continued to be built for many years. A product of Armstrong Whitworth's Tyneside yard, the steam-driven Tilsington Court *(1928/6910grt) was one of five sisters built for the Court Line, all in one year. Apart from the addition of a raised forecastle and an extra 2ft in breadth they differed little in layout from the Doxford-built shelter-deckers which were first introduced in 1914.* (CMP)

The Second World War

For Britain's Second World War standard ships, ease of construction was a prime objective, hence the general elimination of sheer between the masts and, less obvious, the simplification of curves in the hull plating. As in the previous war, the emphasis was on general cargo ships (the term tramp was passing out of fashion), most of them being steam driven. Most important were those of some 9000/10,000dwt which had a length of 430–440ft overall. While some were flushed decked, the majority had a short raised forecastle and the traditional split superstructure. However, the later 'C' and 'D' designs had a

composite superstructure with three of the five hatches forward of the bridge. These types differed in having a transom stern and either a half- or full-height poop.

Although small in numbers three standard types deserve mention because of the highly specialised role they had to fulfil. The most important were the ten 'Bel' type heavy-lift ships which, apart from their transom sterns and different machinery, resembled the Norwegian *Belpareil* of 1926. Like her they were designed to carry and off-load extra heavy items of cargo, in this case military equipment. With this in mind they were given derricks capable of lifting loads of well over 100 tons. While very many general cargo ships were used to carry army and other military supplies to northern Russia, only a small proportion were capable of handling very high weights. As a result certain ships

The Empire Crown *(1944/7070grt), seen on trials, was one of the many B-type standard ships built during the Second World War. Although of conventional split superstructure layout with five hatches, they had an extra wide space between the bridge and funnel, this distinguishing them from other standard types. Besides the V-shaped paravane handling fitting this picture also shows the long booms needed for the anti-torpedo nets, also a surprising array of AA gun tubs.* (Laurence Dunn collection)

of the 'Scandinavian' and *Empire Malta* types were fitted with additional extra strong masts and derricks of exceptional length for off-loading the stream of supply ships – so taking the place of non-existant shore cranes.

Intended as general purpose ships, the forty which comprised the 'Scandinavian' type had a deadweight tonnage of around 4700 and an length overall of 328ft. Wm Gray & Co built twenty-four of them, the remainder coming from five other yards. They were of conventional three-island type and steam driven, but those of the *Empire Malta* type had their engines aft and were distinguished by having transom type sterns. Similar in size to the 'Scandinavian' ships, all eight came from the Wm Gray yard.

Nearly 290 'Empire' ships in the 9000–10,000dwt range were built on the North East coast. To name only the major yards, William Gray was responsible for twenty-nine, J L Thompson and Readhead nearly two dozen apiece and Bartram sixteen. Of the sixty-eight 'Empire's of this size built on the Clyde, Lithgows delivered thirty-three. As for the other shipbuilding centres – Belfast, Birkenhead and the River Forth, these collectively delivered another twenty-one. It should be remembered however that these figures exclude the many merchant ships which they built under special licence, and of course, naval vessels.

Postwar reconstruction

The period of postwar reconstruction saw many new ideas come to the fore, some aimed at greater engine-room and hull efficiency. Yet others were concerned with faster cargo handling, through improved forms of steel hatch covers, better derrick control,

electric winches and the use of cranes – these especially for cargo liners. The use of kingposts, single or twin, had long been commonplace but gradually gave way to a new feature. This was the bipod mast which first appeared in 1950, almost simultaneously on the British-registered *Kieldrecht* and on several short sea traders owned by Det Forenede D/S (United Steamship Co), of Denmark. Other eye-catching novelties were the Velle and Hallen type masts and, with them, the use of the single 'swinging' derrick.

Stems, for long vertical or nearly so, had become progressively more raked, something which helped to localise collision damage to areas above the waterline. The clipper stem, last applied to a cargo liner in 1914, lingered on in a very suppressed form as a mere beak, this usually indicating one-time ownership by one of the Pyman family. Treated rather more generously this had become a quite normal feature of ships built at Burntisland. The old style bar stem gradually gave way to a raked and rounded form – a borrowing from Alfred Holt ships – while below the load-line, another feature – the bulbous forefoot or bow – began to show itself.

Some years earlier Watts, Watts & Co of London had realised the value of a knuckle, both forward and aft, as something which made for greater sea-kindliness and drier decks. In their *Wanstead* class cargo liners of 1949–50 the company introduced a completely new crew accommodation arrangement. This comprised two long (port and starboard) side galleries which, on the inboard side, gave access to the crew cabins. In 1958 the company applied this layout to two of their new tramps, the diesel-driven *Weybridge* and *Wimbledon*. Ships of some

10,000dwt and 488ft length overall, they had an unusual profile, the dominant feature being a 243ft long bridge deck which had three hatches amidships. Forward of these, the bridgehouse overlooked a two-hatch well and a short forecastle. Right aft and beyond the engine casing, there was a sixth hatch. Within the bridge deck the side gallery was widened, especially in one area which was laid out for table tennis. Seldom, if ever, had the image of an old style tramp shipping firm been so transformed; all honour to Edmund Watts!

Developments from 1950

How one design can be developed from another was shown in the early 1950s after several North East coast colliers found useful charter work overseas. With this in mind, Readhead of South Shields produced a stretched edition which proved acceptable to the owners of both colliers and deep-sea tramps. In 1953 one of the latter, Stag Line, took delivery of *Camellia*, a bulk carrier of 7800dwt, with a profile conforming to the traditional collier outline, but with a much extended – 278ft long – quarterdeck which had space for three holds/hatches. A ship with five hatches in all and ten derricks, she had a Doxford diesel of 3000bhp which gave a speed of 12kts. Somewhat similar engines-

The Readhead-built long quarterdeck type ships – of which the Hudson Deep *(1952/6198grt) was one – were developed from the traditional Thames–North East coast colliers into something more suited for deep sea trading. Seen in retrospect, they marked an early stage in the development of today's much larger bulk carriers. The* Hudson Deep *which measured 434ft × 56ft had a deadweight tonnage of 7810 and a load draught of only 23ft 5ins. (Laurence Dunn collection)*

In the early 1960s there was a definite trend towards having the engine room placed well aft of the midship point. Among the leaders in this were three Barclay Curle-built sisters, the 15kt, Sulzer-engined Hopecrest, Hopepeak *and* Hopecrag *(built 1961–62–63/all 9858grt), ships of around 14,000 tons deadweight which measured 501ft × 64ft. In their layout one can see the genesis of the more austere SD-14 design which followed a few years later.* (Laurence Dunn collection)

aft themes were developed by other shipyards, so leading to the steady demise of the engines-amidships tramp.

At the other end of the size scale, *River Afton* of 1953 was a more specialised bulker of 16,500dwt built for Ayrshire Navigation Co by Lithgows Ltd. Apart from a pair of kingposts at the break of the forecastle, she was gearless, her long weather deck – which continued to the poop – bearing only a long array of hatches fitted with hinged steel covers. Among British ocean-going bulk carriers two distinct size groups had now evolved. While the smaller ones, gearless and with their bridge either amidships or aft, were designed to fit their relatively small discharge terminals, the others – the true tramps – were designed for worldwide trading. While the former had a top size limit of around 9000dwt, the latter could be of many times that tonnage.

Just occasionally a design achieves a profile so well balanced that, within its idiom, it appears near perfect to the eye. This was so with three motor tramps built in 1961–63 by Barclay Curle. These, *Hopecrest, Hopepeak* and *Hopecrag*, were shelter-deckers of some 14,000dwt which had an length overall of 501ft. The superstructure was well aft of amidships and between it and the forecastle were two masts and four hatches. Another hatch aft was served by a pair of kingposts.

Successful ships, they gave over twenty years of service before being scrapped.

By the mid-1960s the US-built 'Liberty' ship – the most numerous of all war-built types – was coming to the end of its career. Of the several nations which produced their own replacement designs, the Japanese and British proved the most popular. To take the latter first, Austin & Pickersgill's very successful SD-14 design was, in its original form, a 14kt shelter decker of 14,200dwt, hence its name. Introduced in 1967, over 200 were built over the next two decades, both in Britain and under licence abroad. Between the short forecastle and the superstructure were four hatches/holds, these served by derricks worked by the foremast and a pair of kingposts. A fifth hatch aft was served by another pair of kingposts. Each decade has brought its own shapes and styles, and despite its deliberately austere specification, the SD-14 profile bore a marked likeness to the Bartram-built *Avisfaith* of 1962 and to the 'Hope' vessels mentioned above. While the main flow of SD-14s came from Sunderland, some were built under licence at Dundee and many others in Greece and Brazil. In due course more sophisticated specifications were introduced, the main difference lying in their machinery and cargo-handling gear. While the first SD-14 to be delivered was the Greek tramp *Nicola*, British owners included P&O, Australind and Larrinaga.

The Japanese equivalent was the Ishikawajima-Harima HI-designed 'Freedom', an engines-aft design which measured about 470ft in length and 65ft in breadth and had a deadweight tonnage of 14,800. Flush decked, it had all six hatches forward of the superstructure. A Mark 2 version, fractionally shorter but more beamy, had a deadweight

tonnage of 15,600. Its hull, topped by a short forecastle, had five (not six) hatches which were served by gantry type cranes. One unusual feature, common to both, was a short length of bulwark by the stern.

Britain's very last conventional engines-amidships tramp, and the last merchant ship to be registered at Whitby, *Egton* of 1962, was sold for scrap in 1986. Owned throughout her career by Rowland & Marwood's Steamship Co, she had a short forecastle with three of her five hatches forward of the superstructure. This was continued aft to the third of her three stump bipod masts, the fourth hatch being trunked to the deck above. Bartram-built, she had a length of 507ft (154.5m) and a Doxford diesel of 6640bhp. Typical of her period, she had two 5-ton derricks to each hatch.

So, while one era ended, the tramp ship theme continued with very much larger bulk carriers, some of them gearless, others with derricks or cranes. A few continued to be owned in the North East, notably by Ropner, but, for the continuance of the main theme, one needs to switch to Cardiff. There in 1963, Reardon Smith Line took delivery of its last conventionally shaped tramp, the 10,335grt *Houston City*. By the time of her sale in the early 1970s her owners had switched to engines-aft bulkers designed to carry ore and other heavy cargoes. The first of the new generation was *Australian City* (built 1964, 18,461grt), a ship of just over 29,000dwt which had a raised forecastle and poop. Between these were six hatches/holds and three pairs of kingposts, each with its own 5-ton derrick. She was one of two pairs built by Fairfield after which Reardon Smith turned to Upper Clyde Shipbuilders, of Govan which, in 1970, delivered *Vancouver*

City. A 15kt vessel of 14,684grt, she was the first of seven. Known as the 'Cardiff' class, they measured 569ft in length and 84ft breadth and had a deadweight tonnage of just under 29,900 on a draught of 32ft 8ins. Outwardly distinguished by a short forecastle (but no poop) and five 15-ton cranes – one for each hatch – they were powered by Kincaid–B&W machinery of 11,600bhp. After *Vancouver City*, Reardon Smith Line added another eleven ships to its fleet, but in the 1980s, like so many other British firms, it

was forced to withdraw from shipowning. Since then the only Cardiff firm to operate ships of any real size has been Idwal Williams & Co, this through Graig Shipping PLC.

As a tailpiece to this review of tramp shipping, no port could equal the phenomenal rise to greatness of Cardiff, in which Charles E Stallybrass – the author's grandfather – was one of the pioneer shipowners. His career as such started with a financial interest in the 135ft long *Llandaff* which, when delivered in 1865, was the first steam-

ship to be owned and registered at Cardiff. Iron hulled and referred to a little later as being 'engaged in the Bilbao trade', she survived various strandings until finally wrecked in 1899. By 1920 Cardiff had become the world's greatest shipowning centre, yet within a year it was the scene of almost countless bankruptcies, these largely due to the worldwide switch to oil fuel and stiff competition from what had been a war ravaged Europe.

Laurence Dunn

Typical Cargo Liners 1900–1960

Name	Flag	Built	By	GRT DWT	Length(oa) (r = registered) × breadth × depth × draught Feet-inches Metres	Engines	Speed	Cargo gear etc.	Remarks
HUNTSMAN	UK	1904	Charles Connell & Co, Scotstoun	7460 10,825	470.0(r) × 57-2 × 31-10 × 27-4 *143.26 × 17.43 × 9.69 × 8.32*	3-cylinder triple-expansion steam by Dunsmuir & Jackson, Glasgow, 600nhp; 1 shaft	12kts		First of 5 sisters, 4 masts; Europe–South Africa/West Indies
PERSEUS	UK	1908	Workman Clark & Co, Belfast	6728 8600	443.0(r) × 52.9 × 32.0 × — *135.03 × 16.13 × 9.75 × —*	3-cylinder triple-expansion steam by builders, 4600ihp; 1 shaft	14kts	20 derricks + 2 heavy lift 6 holds/2 deep tanks	First of 9 sisters; 12 passengers, Europe–Far East–USA
SELANDIA	Den	1912	Burmeister & Wain, Copenhagen	4964 7400	386-0 × 53-2 × 30-0 × 23-0 *117.65 × 16.22 × 11.89 × 7.00*	2 8-cylinder 4SA oil engines by builders, 2500ihp; 2 shafts	11.25kts	10 derricks + 1 heavy lift electric winches, 4 holds	First deepsea motorship; 2 sisters. Three masts, no funnel; 26 passengers. Europe–Bangkok
CARDIGANSHIRE	UK	1913	Workman Clark & Co, Belfast	9436 13,500	520-0 × 62-5 × 34-7 × 29-10 *158.50 × 19.02 × 10.55 × 9.07*	2 3-cylinder triple-expansion steam by builders, 977nhp; 2 shafts	14kts	20 derricks + 1 heavy lift, 7 holds	First of two; Europe–Far East
LONDON MARINER	UK	1922	Furness SB Co, Haverton Hill-on-Tees	8022 11,200	450.0 × 58-0 × 38-0 × 30-2 *137.16 × 17.68 × 11.58 × 9.20*	2 oil-fired SR steam turbines by builders, 1000nhp; 2 shafts	14kts	18 derricks + 1 heavy lift 7 hatches	Built as *Feliciana*; first of 5. Crew accommodation amidships; London–New York
TAI YANG	Nor	1929	Deutsche Werke AG, Kiel	9307 12,400	481-0 × 60-7 × 29-0 × 30-10 *146.61 × 18.47 × 8.84 × 9.39*	2 8-cylinder 4DA B&W oil engines by builders, 8000ihp; 2 shafts	14.5kts		One of 12 sisters; 8 passengers. US East Coast–Far East via Panama; Europe–South Africa–Australia/Far East
GLENEARN	UK	1938	Caledon SB & Eng Co, Dundee	9784 9500	507-0 × 66-0 × 38-0 × 30-6 *154.53 × 20.12 × 11.58 × 9.30*	2 7-cylinder 2DA B&W oil engines by builders, 12,000bhp; 2 shafts	18kts	24 derricks + 2 heavy lifts. 6 holds/ hatches. Tanks for latex/veg oil	First of 8; 12 passengers (21 from 1947). First Holt group cargo liner with cruiser stern. Europe–Far East
SEATTLE	Swe	1947	Kockums, Malmo	9168	500-4 × 63-11 × 39-10 × 26-8 *152.49 × 19.48 × 12.13 × 8.14*	2 7-cylinder 2DA oil engines by builders, 14,000bhp; 2 shafts	19.5kts	14 electric cranes 1 heavy lift	First of 8, 12 passengers, Europe–NW Pacific; 95,000 cu ft refrigerated
KEYSTONE MARINER	USA	1952	Sun SB&DD Co, Chester, PA	9214 13,399	561-0 × 76-0 × 35-6 × 29-11 *170.99 × 23.16 × 10.82 × 9.11*	2 General Electric oil-fired DR steam turbines, 17,500shp; 1 shaft	20kts	24 derricks 2 heavy lifts (60t) 7 holds/hatches	First of 35 Mariner standard type; folding steel hatch covers, 12 passengers

Name	Flag	Built	By	GRT DWT	Length(oa) (r = registered) × breadth × depth × draught Feet-inches Metres	Engines	Speed	Cargo gear etc.	Remarks
BENLOYAL	UK	1959	Charles Connell & Co, Scotstoun	11,463 11,210	549-6 × 71-0 × 44-5 × 30-0 *167.49 × 21.64 × 13.56 × 9.14*	2 Rowan oil-fired DR steam turbines, 15,500shp; 1 shaft	20kts	20 derricks 2 heavy lifts (70t/ 50t), 6 holds/6 hatches	First 20kt ship on Europe–Far East route; 10 passengers
Heavy lift vessels									
MARY KINGSLEY	UK	1930	Ardrossan Dockyard & SB Co, Ardrossan	4017 5650	382-0 × 51-7 × — × 20-1 *116.43 × 13.55 × — × 6.13*	Kincaid 8-cylinder 4SA B&W oil engine, 650nhp; 1 shaft	12kts	2 100t and 2 smaller h/lifts, 10 derricks, 3 holds	Last of class of 8, specially adapted to carry locomotives and rolling stock for Nigerian Railways
LICHTENFELS	Ger	1954	H C Stülcken Sohn, Hamburg	6800 8514	461-3 × 58-5 × 34-2 × 26-4 *140.59 × 17.80 × 10.41 × 8.03*	2 MAN 6-cylinder 4SA geared oil engines, 5600bhp; 1 shaft	15.75kts	2 Stülcken heavy lifts (120t/30t) + 15 derricks	First of 7 sisters; 12 passengers, Europe–India
Refrigerated vessels									
OTAKI	UK	1908	Wm Denny & Bros, Dumbarton	7421 10,360	465-4(r) × 60-4 × 31-4 × 28-7 *141.85 × 18.38 × 9.54 × 8.72*	2 3-cylinder triple-expansion steam and 1 centreline lp Parsons turbine by builders, 471rhp; 3 shafts	14kts	10 derricks, 2 cranes, 5 holds/ hatches	First merchant ship so propelled 286,180cu ft refrigerated/ 273,200cu ft bale. Europe–New Zealand
GALLIC	UK	1918	Workman Clark & Co, Belfast	7914 10,100	465-0 × 58-4 × 29-1 × — *141.73 × 17.78 × 8.86 × —*	2 3-cylinder triple-expansion steam by builders, 5500shp; 2 shafts	13kts		Built as *War Angus*; First World War standard G type
UPWEY GRANGE	UK	1925	Fairfield SB & Eng Co, Govan, Glasgow	9130 10,100	431-0 × 62-6 × 35-4 × 31-1 *131.36 × 19.05 × 10.76 × 9.48*	2 12-cylinder 2SA oil engines by builders, 1648nhp; 2 shafts	14kts		First motorship in South America meat trade; 12 passengers; 557,000cu ft refrigerated
IMPERIAL STAR	UK	1935	Harland & Wolff, Belfast	12,427 13,100	543-0 × 70-5 × 32-4 × 29-8 *165.51 × 21.46 × 9.84 × 9.05*	2 10-cylinder 4SA B&W oil engines by builders, 12,000bhp; 2 shafts	17kts	20 derricks + 1 50t h/lift, 6 holds	12 passengers. 560,000cu ft refrigerated. Europe–Australia, New Zealand trade
PORT BRISBANE	UK	1949	Swan Hunter & Wigham Richardson, Wallsend	11,942 11,950	559-10 × 70-4 × 30-8 × 29-3 *170.64 × 21.43 × 9.36 × 8.93*	2 6-cylinder 2SA Doxford oil engines by Wallsend Slipway, 13,200bhp; 2 shafts	17kts	16 derricks + 1 60t h/lift, 1 electric crane, 6 holds (5 insulated and lined with sheet alloy)	Designed to be distinctive flagship, 12 passengers. 568,886cu ft refrigerated. Europe–Australia, New Zealand

Typical Fruit Ships 1900–1960

Ship	Flag	Built	By	GRT DWT	Length × breadth × depth × draught Feet-inches Metres	Engines	Speed	Remarks
PORT MORANT	UK	1901	Alexander Stephen & Sons, Glasgow	2831	329.6(r) × 40.1 × — × 17.6 *100.46 × 12.22 × — × 5.36*	3-cylinder coal-fired triple-expansion steam by shipbuilder, 754nhp	14kts	First refrigerated banana ship; 45 passengers
SAN JOSE	US	1904	Workman Clark & Co, Belfast	3296	330.5(r) × 44.1 × 31.6 × 18.0 *100.74 × 13.44 × 9.63 × 5.49*	3-cylinder coal-fired triple-expansion steam by shipbuilder, 320nhp	12.5kts	First US refrigerated banana ship; 45,000 stems
CHIRRIPO	UK	1922	Workman Clark & Co, Belfast	5356 6360	400.0(r) × 51-2 × 32-8 × 26-7 *121.92 × 15.6 × 10.0 × 8.14*	3-cylinder coal-fired triple-expansion steam by shipbuilder, 4000ihp	13.5kts	First of 19 sisters. 12 passengers. 185,000cu ft refrigerated

Ship	Flag	Built	By	GRT DWT	Length × breadth × depth × draught Feet-inches Metres	Engines	Speed	Remarks
WASHINGTON EXPRESS	Nor	1933	Gotaverken, Gothenburg	3643 3200	352-1 × 47-2 × 27-1 × 21-2 107.32 × 14.38 × 8.26 × 6.46	Two 8-cylinder SA Gotaverken/B&W oil; 2 shafts; 3800bhp	16kts	Long forecastle. Shelter deck. 12 passengers. 172,000cu ft refrigerated. Europe–North Pacific trade
ROSLIN CASTLE	UK	1935	Harland & Wolff, Belfast	7017 8510	443-6 × 61-3 × 32-0 × 29-2 135.18 × 18.68 × 9.75 × 8.9	8-cylinder DA B&W oil by shipbuilder, 8000bhp	16kts	First of several large fruit ships for seasonal South Africa trade; 4 passengers
PROTEUS	Ger	1951	Deutsche Werft, Hamburg	2860 3500	413-11 × 49-8 × 16-5 × 20-1 126.17 × 15.18 × 5.02 × 6.49	6-cylinder 2 DA MAN oil, 4800bhp	16.5kts	First German post Second World War reefer. Long forecastle; 12 passengers. 217,852cu ft refrigerated
ANTIGUA	Swe	1960	Oresundsvarvet, Landskrona	8288 8100	493-1 × 62-0 × 39-0 × 27-5 150.3 × 18.9 × 11.89 × 8.38	2 sets De Laval oil-fired DR geared steam turbines, 11,000shp	19kts	12 passengers; 325,000cu ft refrigerated

Typical Tramp Cargo Ships 1900–1960

Name	Flag	Built	By	GRT DWT	Length (r = registered) × breadth × depth × draught Feet–inches Metres	Engines	Speed	Remarks
TRUNKBY	UK	1896	Ropner & Son, Stockton on Tees	2635 —	300–0 (r) × 45–0 × 20–4 ×— 91.46 × 13.72 × 16.20 × —	Triple-expansion steam by Blair & Co, 230nhp; 1 shaft	9kts	Pioneer trunk type steamer
MARIA Z MICHALINOS	Gre	1902	Wm Gray & Co, West Hartlepool	3059 4900	332–0(r) × 48–0 × 21–11 × — 101.22 × 157.44 × 6.69 × —	Triple-expansion steam by Central Marine Eng Works, 300nhp; 1 shaft	10kts	
OTTO SVERDRUP	Nor	1904	J Readhead, South Shields	3526 5400	340–11 (r) × 46–7 × 24–9 ×— 103.94 × 14.22 × 7.54 × —	Triple-expansion steam by J Readhead, 283bhp; 1 shaft	10kts	
HELREDALE	UK	1906	R Craggs, Middlesbrough	3567 6450	346–6 (r) × 50–6 × 23–2 × 22–3 105.63 × 15.39 × 7.07 × 6.78	Triple-expansion steam by Blair & Co, 340nhp; 1 shaft	9kts	
GWENT	UK	1915	Craig, Taylor, Stockton on Tees	5754 —	414–5 (r) × 55–5 × 28–9 × 25–1 126.3 × 16.9 × 8.76 × 7.65	Triple-expansion steam by Blair & Co, 1700ihp; 1 shaft	10kts	
BACKWORTH	UK	1919	Dunlop Bremner, Port Glasgow	2481 3950	302–10(r) × 42–11 × 20–8 × 20–0 92.3 × 12.83 × 6.30 × 6.10	Triple-expansion steam by Dunlop Bremer, 262nhp; 1 shaft	10kts	First World War standard H type
MAASBORG	Ne	1921	Flensburger Schiffsbau Ges., Flensburg	6415 11,450	454–1(r) × 59–10 × 27–8 × — 138.44 × 18.23 × 8. 43 × —	Triple-expansion steam by Flensburger, 399nhp; 1 shaft	11kts	
BARON HAIG	UK	1926	Ayrshire Dockyard, Irvine	3391 5795	342–3 (r) ×48–7 × 22–9 × 21–5 104.34 × 14.80 × 6.94 × 6.53	Triple-expansion steam by D Rowan, 225nhp; 1 shaft	10kts	
KENSINGTON COURT	UK	1927	Napier & Miller, Glasgow	4863 8050	396–6 (r) × 53–3 × 26–6 × 23–8 120.88 × 16.25 × 8.08 × 7.21	Triple-expansion steam by D Rowan, 416nhp; 1 shaft	10kts	
WINDSORWOOD	UK	1936	Hawthorn Leslie, Newcastle-upon-Tyne	5395 8550	454–10 × 55–10 × 28–0 × 25–0 138,67 × 17.03 × 8.54 × 7.62	Triple-expansion steam by NE Marine Eng Co and Götaverken turbocharger, 1550ihp; 1 shaft	10kts	
FORT ST JAMES	UK	1942	Burrard DD Co, North Vancouver, BC	7191 10,551	438–5 × 57–3 × 37–4 × 26–11 133.66 × 17.43 × 11.38 × 8.22	Triple-expansion steam by Dominion Engine Works, 2500ihp; 1 shaft	11kts	Second World War standard Fort type
PANAYIA MOUTSAINA	Gre	1957	Hakodate Dock, Hakodate	10,720 15,875	519–1 × 64–8 × 41–6 × 31–9 158.26 × 19.71 × 12.65 × 9.68	2 Hitachi DR geared steam turbines, 8200shp; 1 shaft	15.5kts	Machinery aft
HOPECREST	UK	1961	Barclay Curle, Glasgow	9919 14,571	501–2 × 63–9 × 41–1 × 31–5 152.81 × 19.43 × 12.53 × 9.60	5-cylinder Barclay Curle/ Sulzer diesel, 7500bhp; 1 shaft	15.5kts	

3

Bulk Cargo Carriers

Oil Tankers

There has always been the requirement to carry some liquids on ships, either as ships' stores or cargo (for example water, oil, tar, wine, etc). A wide variety of containers, such as barrels or jars, has been used for this purpose. Excavated Greek and Phoenician ships have yielded many amphorae while the 'Oseberg' ship, one of the excavated Viking ships, has provided what must be the earliest surviving wooden barrel. In Burma on the Irrawaddy, for centuries large earthenware jars were built into rafts to carry oil from the wells at Yenangyoung. It was inevitable that eventually there would be the need to transport some liquids in bulk. There was no precise date when bulk carriage commenced, the process was gradual and the transition was driven by needs which were different at different times and places. For example we know that some Greek warships had suitable storage for the naphtha in 'Greek Fire' after about AD 660. On the Caspian Sea shortage of timber for barrels caused owners to start loading oil in bulk in the holds of their wooden boats. This trade was already well established when Marco Polo described the scene at Baku in AD 1210 and it continued in much the same form into the 1920s.

On the Atlantic in the nineteenth century the main concerns were to improve the stowage factor, to reduce leakage and to improve

safety. It was obvious that to carry large quantities of liquid in barrels and other containers was inefficient. With some containers, in particular wooden barrels, up to 10 per cent leakage was considered acceptable while as much as 20 per cent was not unusual. It was claimed by some historians that the Chinese had vessels to carry vegetable oils in bulk from around 1650 onwards but more recent study shows that this was not the case.

By 1836 the oil lamp with a circular burner and a chimney had developed into an efficient form of lighting. This created an increasing demand for suitable fuels. Fish, whale and vegetable oils were in use when, in 1848 James Young demonstrated that oil occurring in shale deposits provided an excellent lamp fuel. Meanwhile in 1854 in the United States, a New York lawyer George Bissell and his partners explored the use of naturally occurring 'rock oil' as a lamp fuel, this resulted in the formation of the Pennsylvania Rock Oil Company. Eventually in 1859 the company engaged an unemployed railway conductor, Edwin Drake to drill for oil on their land at Titusville in western Pennsylvania. The

result was that on 28 August 1859 at a depth of 69ft (21m), the world's first oil well began producing eight to ten barrels a day. Other wells rapidly followed in the region and in April 1861 one was producing 3000 barrels a day. In 1860 samples of this oil began arriving in Europe. Orders followed resulting in larger shipments, until on 17 February 1862 the first full cargo of 2888 barrels of oil arrived in London on the US vessel *Nineveh*. The 224 ton brig *Elizabeth Watts*, which had arrived on 9 January, had been chartered by Peter Wright & Sons of Philadelphia to carry a full cargo to London from Philadelphia, but the charterers had to make up about one third of the cargo with coal oil. Shipments of oil then arrived fairly rapidly as demand grew for the new product. At the same time cargoes of petroleum in barrels were also being unloaded in Germany, Belgium, France and other European countries.

In 1862 two iron sailing vessels were constructed at St Peters, Newcastle upon Tyne, with the intention of carrying oil in bulk. On these vessels, named *Atlantic* and *Great Western*, the hold space consisted of four cargo tanks connected in pairs with an

The 2000dwt Lux *was completed by Sir W G Armstrong, Mitchell & Co Ltd in 1888. The* Lux *then delivered one of the earliest bulk oil cargoes to Liverpool, at the time being owned by her builders. Sold to W Dickenson & Co Ltd of London the* Lux *became one of the earliest tanker casualties. In November 1891 while on a voyage from Batoum to Antwerp loaded with kerosene, a fire broke out while the vessel was in the Doro Channel in the Greek Islands. The vessel was abandoned and during the night two explosions were heard. Out of control the* Lux *ran ashore and became a total wreck. (Author's collection)*

The elegance of some of the early tankers is well portrayed in this trial view of Luciline, *built by Craig, Taylor & Co, Stockton-on-Tees in 1893 for Alfred Stuart & Co.* (CMP)

arrangement to allow the oil to expand up the hollow masts! It is unlikely that these vessels ever carried oil in bulk although it is possible they may have carried case oil. A case of oil consisted of two rectangular four gallon cans of oil held in a wooden frame. Case oil was treated as a normal cargo to be carried by all types of general cargo vessel.

As demand for lamp oil and lubricating oil increased so did the search for more efficient methods of transport. Vessels were converted by installing tanks in the cargo holds. In the case of *Charles*, which entered the petroleum trade in 1869, a total of fifty-nine iron tanks were fitted, those in the holds having a capacity of about 30 tons while those in the 'tween decks carried about 12 tons each. No special arrangements were provided to allow for

expansion of the oil cargo. Free surface in the tanks was avoided by topping-up with sea water.

In 1872 the Belgian Red Star Line took delivery of *Vaderland*, the first of three sister vessels, from Palmers Shipbuilding & Iron Co Ltd of Jarrow. She was the first steamship built as a tanker and had a double skin between her oil cargo and the sea with a generous trunk to allow for expansion, alongside which was some passenger accommodation. Unfortunately for the owners the authorities at Antwerp would not allow construction of the storage facility to receive the

The Dunlop-built Lackawanna *(3855grt) was the last of three similar tankers built on the Clyde for the Anglo-American Oil Co in 1893–94, the others being her sisters* Delaware *and* Potomac, *a product of A & J Inglis. Designed to carry around 5000 tons of US petroleum to the UK at a speed of around 12kts, they were regarded as amongst the finest of their day.* Lackawanna *was exchanged for the larger* August Korff *of the German American Petroleum Co in 1910, being renamed* Sirius. *Sold in 1919 she became* Fiamma *and was flying the Italian flag as* Maya *when torpedoed by HM submarine* Perseus *near the Dardanelles in 1941.* (CMP)

From the turn of the century oil tankers began to increase in size and take on a more substantial look, evidenced here by Shell Transport & Trading Co's 8820dwt Pinna built by Armstrong Whitworth in 1901. Sold to Petroleum Steamship Co (one of the Lane & MacAndrew group of companies) in 1907, she was resold ten years later to the comparatively new British Tanker Co, becoming British Earl. In 1929 she changed hands yet again and subsequently bore several other names before being scrapped in 1949. (CMP)

cargo, nor would those in the US allow passengers to be embarked on a vessel that carried oil in bulk. As a result *Vaderland* and her sisters, *Nederland* and *Switzerland*, never carried oil in bulk but they regularly carried case-oil as cargo.

The rapid development of the oil industry in the United States and the ready market for the product aroused interest in the Russian oil industry at Baku. The main difficulty at Baku was communication, there being no railway or pipeline between the oilfields at Baku and the Black Sea at that time. Any exported oil was loaded in bulk into the holds of small wooden sailing vessels on the Caspian Sea for shipment to Astrakhan and other towns on the River Volga. One visitor to the region in 1873 was Robert Nobel, brother of Alfred, the chemist and inventor of dynamite and other explosives, who lived in Paris. Robert and another brother, Ludvig, had a factory in St Petersburg producing small arms and other items but the former persuaded his brothers that they should invest in the oil industry at Baku. After a short negotiation they purchased a refinery and an oil well from the Tiflis Corporation. The Nobels rebuilt the refinery, completing the work in 1876, and continued with further improvements. They then tried to persuade Russian shipowners to improve their vessels and methods of handling the oil. In 1878, having failed in this objective, they ordered to their own account a small cargo steamer from Motala Verkstad, at Norrköping in

Sweden. Delivered later the same year this vessel, *Zoroaster*, negotiated the Russian waterway system and arrived on the Caspian Sea. At first she carried about 240 tons of kerosene in eight tanks installed in the hold. After about a year the tanks were removed allowing her to carry a full cargo of 400 tons. *Zoroaster* was therefore the first tank steamer to enter service and proved an instant success. Other tank vessels quickly followed, Nobels taking delivery of *Buddha* and *Nordenskiöld* the following year, these being combinations of both tanker and dry cargo ship. Cargo tanks were located in the forward and after sections and were separated from the rest of the vessel by cofferdams. Between the cargo tanks there was a dry cargo hold. These vessels had to pass through the Mariniskii Canal locks in three sections. By 1884 over fifty steam tankers were in service on the Caspian Sea and the Russian waterway system was fully exploited for oil distribution, a fleet of impressive river barges being used for this purpose. These served a network of distribution depots that extended from the Caspian to the Ural mountains and to Poland and Finland. By 1900 there were more than 1500 wooden barges engaged in the oil trade and in addition a further 250 constructed of iron or steel. Some of the barges were very large; one, *Martha Poseidnetza* owned by D V Sirotkin, was 504ft (153.66m) in length and was able to carry 9000 tons of oil. It is worth mentioning that it was on the Nobel barges on the River

Volga that diesel engines were first used for propulsion. Only five years after Dr Rudolph Diesel displayed his oil engine at the Munich Exhibition in 1898, a barge named *Vandal* was delivered to Nobel using diesel-electric propulsion. Built at the Sormovo Works in 1903 at Nizhni Novgorod (Gorky) *Vandal* had a length of 244ft 6in (74.54m) and had a cargo deadweight of 650 tons. Her machinery consisted of three 120hp diesels coupled to generators, each generator connected to a propulsion motor driving one of the three propellers.

An interesting development took place in Norway during the winter of 1877–78. Captain Evan Tollefsen had, for a number of years, been in the employ of G C Hansen, a well known Tonsberg shipowner. The main cargo transported by the Hansen sailing fleet at that time was coal. Tollefsen convinced Hansen that they should take advantage of the demand for oil and proposed that some of the Hansen ships could be converted to carry oil in bulk. During the winter of 1877–78 Tollefsen supervised the conversion of

three wooden vessels, the brig *Jan Mayn*, and the barques *Stadt* and *Lindesnæs* to carry oil in bulk. No fires were allowed on board while carrying oil cargoes and despite Tollefsen recording that when carrying oil 'the cabin lamp always burnt with a blue flame' the ships were considered very successful. Four other Hansen ships were later converted in a similar fashion. *Stadt* and *Lindesnæs* were chartered by a French company for fifteen years after their conversion. It was not until 1895 that Hansen had his vessels returned to their old trade, the competition from the new steam tankers making them uneconomical as tankers. Captain Tollefsen was drowned in 1897 off the North American coast when his ship, *Magnhild*, was wrecked after a cargo of coal shifted.

Alfred Suart & Co was one company which built up a substantial fleet of vessels in the early days of the oil trade. After having converted several dry cargo vessels beginning with *Petriana* in 1879, it went on to build five new vessels: *Bakuin*, *Oka*, *Prudentia*, *Wildflower* and *Tankarville* during 1886–89. *Bakuin* was built by Wm Gray & Co of West Hartlepool and her cargo tank section had a double bottom with oil being carried right out to the side shell. Built of iron she had seven transverse bulkheads and in way of the cargo tanks there was a centreline bulkhead. There were also a number of experimental features that do not appear to have been repeated on other vessels. For example the main deck was given a curious reverse camber, it being claimed that this enabled the main tanks to be completely filled and yet at the same time efficiently ventilated, and there was an unusual arrange-

ment of expansion trunks. Of particular interest is that in *Bakuin* there was the first stage in the development of the cargo control room. Liquid level gauges were installed which consisted of a float in each cargo tank attached by a wire and pulley system to a counterweight in the cargo pump room. The counterweight indicated the liquid level on a scale on the pump room bulkhead. The pump controls and all of the master valves had extensions so they could be operated from the upper platform in the pump room.

Prior to 1888 the agent in Germany for the US Standard Oil Co was Heinrich Riedmann of Bremen. In 1884 he had the 1871 ton sailing vessel *Andromeda* converted to carry oil in bulk by building seventy-two steel tanks into the vessel. Two rows of tanks were fitted in each of the holds, orlop deck and 'tween deck. An expansion tank was fitted on each deck. *Andromeda* proved very successful and remained in the oil trade until 22 February 1919, when under the name *Helene*, she was run down and sunk by the steamer *Grangsfjord*.

In 1886 Colonel Henry Swan was naval architect and also a director of Armstrong Mitchell & Co, Wallsend, a firm which had built several Caspian tankers for Nobel and other owners. Swan was very interested in the problems of carrying oil in bulk and produced a design incorporating the best features of existing vessels. Oil was to be carried right out to the shell; provision was made to carry water ballast on the return voyage; cofferdams were fitted at each end of the cargo tank section; the cargo valves could all be operated from the main deck; the cargo main was carried through the cargo

Two-funnelled tankers were a rarity in the early years, only a few examples being built. Buyo Maru, delivered by Armstrong Whitworth to Toyo Kaisen KK in 1908, was also notable as one of the first tankers to fly the Japanese flag. Sold to Britain in 1915 on account of high Japanese petroleum import duties, she was renamed Delphinula by Anglo Saxon Petroleum Co which managed her as a fleet oiler on behalf of the Admiralty. Hulked at Gibraltar in 1938, she was eventually broken up in 1947. (CMP)

tanks, just above the floors; vapour lines were fitted at the top of each expansion tank; cargo pumps for loading and discharging were fitted below main deck level and finally, countersunk riveting was used on all oiltight bulkheads. The shipyard had commenced building this vessel to their own account when Heinrich Riedmann saw her and bought her, naming her *Glückauf* ('Good Luck'), and at the same time ordered several similar vessels. Today we consider *Glückauf* to be the main ancestor of the modern tanker. She was classed with Bureau Veritas, and at the time of construction was considered to be experimental. After five years in service, at her first special survey, only minor additions to the structure were found necessary, notably fitting stiffening angle face bars to some of the stringers. Problems had occurred, however, when *Glückauf* arrived at Philadelphia on her maiden voyage. She was to load 2880 tons of petroleum for Geestemünde but this brought violent protest from the American stevedores when it was found that their services were not needed, the barrel and tinplate manufacturers also objecting. Police had to protect the ship and maintain order while she loaded. It was six or seven weeks before it was possible to bring secretly a couple of coal barges (from Halifax, Nova

Scotia) alongside and top up her bunkers. *Glückauf* then proceeded to Halifax to complete bunkering for the return voyage. After discharging at Geestemünde she returned to her builders and her spar deck was extended forward to the fore mast, increasing the bunker space and enabling her to take on enough fuel for the return voyage. *Glückauf* was lost in 1893 when she stranded during a storm on Fire Island, off Long Island, New York.

The Standard Oil Company formed a British subsidiary in 1888, the Anglo-American Oil Company. Prior to this Standard had been content to charter vessels for its requirements but the new company immediately started purchasing tankers from other companies, in particular the Riedmann fleet which included *Glückauf*. Orders for new vessels were also placed, the first of their new tankers being the 4000dwt *Bayonne*, delivered by A & J Inglis Ltd of Glasgow in 1889. She was soon followed in 1892–93 by three larger ships, the last of which, *Potomac* – one of the finest of her day – measured 5490dwt.

The same period also witnessed the birth of another great tanker owning company, Shell. Marcus Samuel had been born of Jewish parents in 1853 and at the age of sixteen he joined the family trading business, which was mainly concerned with the importation of seashells for decorated products. After extended tours visiting agents in the Far East in 1873 and 1876, Marcus and his brother Sam took over the business in 1882. Some eight years later, Fred Lane of the shipowners and brokers Lane & Macandrew suggested to Marcus that it may be worthwhile selling Russian oil to the Far East, using his well established network of offices

and agents. A railway connecting Baku with Batum on the Black Sea had been completed in April 1883, making Russian oil more accessible. Fred Lane took Marcus on a visit to the Caucasus to see the tankers at Batum and the oil industry at Baku and it became clear to the Samuel brothers that the economics of such an operation were very attractive provided tankers were able to travel to the Far East via the Suez Canal. During the 1880s several loaded tankers had presented themselves at the canal and had been refused passage; the canal authority considering it too dangerous, although no objection had been raised to oil in barrels or cases as part of a general cargo. The Samuels therefore commenced negotiations with the Suez Canal Company to determine what special features and regulations would be required for vessels carrying oil in bulk. Agreement on the requirements was reached by 18 August 1891 and on 28 September an order was placed for three tankers designed to meet them with William Gray & Co Ltd of West Hartlepool. Rumours of tankers being built to transit the Suez Canal with Russian oil began circulating in 1891 and caused considerable alarm, particularly with the Standard Oil Company which regarded the Far East as its private market. It put considerable effort into endeavouring to find out who was behind the scheme and where the vessels were being constructed. Marcus Samuel finally disclosed his hand in a letter to *The Times* on 8 March 1892 and achieved complete surprise. Not only were his vessels, *Murex*, *Conch* and *Clam* (5010dwt), well advanced but so were the necessary storage facilities to receive their cargoes in Batavia, Singapore, Penang, Bangkok, Saigon, Hong

Kong, Shanghai and Kobe. *Murex*, the first Shell tanker, was launched on 27 May 1892 by Mrs Marcus Samuel and on 26 July she left West Hartlepool on her historic voyage, proceeding to Batum to load a cargo of Russian oil. On 24 August she became the first loaded tanker to pass through the Suez Canal.

The desirability of keeping oil tanker cargo tanks together was recognised from the beginning. Unfortunately as tankers increased in size, the methods of ship construction available in the latter part of the nineteenth century did not permit this arrangement. In the light ship condition, concentration of the machinery weight at the after end caused a large trim by the stern, possibly with the bow out of the water. The resulting hull stresses were too high using the normal designs of the period so that when economics demanded larger ships it became necessary to build tankers with machinery located amidships. This arrangement brought with it a number of safety problems. The number of cofferdams isolating the cargo spaces had to be doubled (to four). Worst of all was the necessity of taking the shaft tunnel through the cargo spaces. With riveted construction and the inevitable working of seams it meant that the shaft tunnel was never free of gas. A notable tanker of this type and the largest of her day was the 12,800dwt *Narragansett*, built by Scotts Shipbuilding & Engineering Co Ltd in 1903 for the Anglo-American Oil Co Ltd.

The latter's US parent company was at this time making considerable headway with a new concept, that of tankers towing large tank barges, both on the east and west coasts and also to Hawaii (see *Coastal tankers* below). Encouraged by this, Anglo-American ordered a larger version of the same idea for transatlantic use, delivered by Harland & Wolff in 1907–8 as the tanker *Iroquois* – the first of any size to be propelled by twin screws and the six-masted sail assisted

This interesting vessel was originally completed as the four-masted barque Urania *for Hamburg owner B Wencke Sohne by A McMillan & Sons, Dumbarton in 1902. After several changes of ownership, becoming* Speedonia *in 1914, she was one of a number of sailing ships purchased by Anglo-Saxon for conversion into tankers to alleviate a shortage during the latter stages of the First World War. Renamed* Scala Shell, *her masts and yards were cut down and she was fitted with a pair of triple expansion engines which gave a speed of about 9kts, deadweight capacity being a shade under 5000 tons. In 1931, having outlived her usefulness, she was broken up in Japan.* (CMP)

schooner *Navahoe*. Known to all as 'the Horse and Cart', they had a combined deadweight capacity of over 18,000 tons and, apart from eighteen months during the First World War, traded successfully between the US Gulf and Purfleet on the Thames until 1930, when *Navahoe* became a storage hulk in Venezuela. At the time of their construction the Anglo-American fleet totalled nineteen tankers, four case-oil steamers and sixteen sailing ships. Shell Transport & Trading combined with Royal Dutch Petroleum Co in 1907 to give a combined fleet of thirty-four tankers, the UK arm of which was retitled Anglo-Saxon Petroleum Co Ltd.

Among the engineers interested in the problems of longitudinal strength was a young Lloyd's Register surveyor, Joseph Isherwood. While at Lloyd's Isherwood patented a system of longitudinal framing supported by frequent deep transverses. In 1907 he left Lloyd's to develop his ideas and to devote his time to the commercial development of his patent. The first vessel built according to his system was the tanker *Paul Paix* for Lennards Carrying Co of Middlesbrough, delivered in 1908 by R Craggs & Sons Ltd of Middlesbrough. The 'Isherwood' system proved very successful although some problems still occurred at the bulkheads but these were overcome with the introduction of the 'bracketless' system in 1922.

Several other methods of construction were proposed and tried for tankers, the best known among them being the Foster King system (or FK system) and the Millar system. These were essentially hybrid methods, being a combination of longitudinal and trans-

verse framing, and while successful in their own way, never achieved the domination of the 'Isherwood' system which by 1914 had been adopted in 276 ships. By 1936 over 2000 vessels had been constructed on the 'Isherwood' system, more than half of them being tankers.

At the beginning of the twentieth century the normal tanker had a centreline bulkhead and 'summer' tanks. These were tanks located in what would have been the 'tween deck space had the vessel been a conventional dry cargo ship. The top and bottom of the summer tanks were formed by the weather deck and the deck below, the side shell, and a continuous longitudinal bulkhead which ran through the cargo compartments about one third of the distance from the centreline to the ship's side formed the sides. The space between the inboard side of the summer tank and the centreline bulkhead provided an expansion trunk for the main cargo tank. During winter months when increased freeboard (and hence less deadweight) was required, the summer tanks would be left empty.

While the *Zoroaster* and the other Nobel vessels on the Caspain Sea had burnt oil as fuel in their boilers from the outset, making use of burners that the Nobel brothers had themselves developed, it was a further twenty years before much progress was made in this respect on the North Atlantic. British Admiralty trials in the use of oil fuel, culminating in full scale tests on HMS *Hannibal* on 26 June 1902, were carried out ignoring expert advice and using obsolete burners. The results were such that introduction of

oil fuel into the Royal Navy was delayed for a further eight years. Despite the *Hannibal* trial, the Royal Navy found there was an increasing need for oil and in 1905 purchased the 6100dwt tanker *Petroleum*. The same year, on 3 August, the Admiralty inaugurated the Royal Fleet Auxiliary Service in which the Fleet's tankers would serve. Two years later the 1000dwt Admiralty collier *Karki* was converted into a tanker and the 200dwt *Isla* was purchased, specifically to supply submarines with petroleum spirit. With the decision in 1909 that all future destroyers would burn oil fuel, several more tankers were ordered, the first, *Burma*, being delivered in 1911 by the Greenock & Grangemouth Co.

On 26 May 1908 oil was discovered in the foothills of the Zagros mountains in Persia and a new company, the Anglo-Persian Oil Co Ltd, was formed in 1909 to develop the find. A significant event occurred when this company entered into a long term contract with the British Admiralty for the supply of oil for the Royal Navy. At the same time the British Government invested £2 million in the concern and in 1915 a wholly owned subsidiary, the British Tanker Co Ltd, was formed to operate a fleet of ships to carry Anglo-Persian oil. These were purchases at first but in September 1916 Armstrong, Whitworth & Co Ltd delivered the 3637grt *British Emperor*, the first new tanker built for BP. By the end of the First World War, its fleet totalled twenty-one tankers.

The largest tankers in existence at this time were some of those built for the newly formed Eagle Oil Transport Co set up by Sir Weetman Pearson – later Lord Cowdray – in 1912 to transport Mexican oil overseas. In an unprecedented move, this company ordered ten ships of 15–16,000dwt and a further nine of 9000 tons. Named after Latin American saints, they were built in the UK during 1913–15 and represented some ten per cent of the world's tanker tonnage at

Completed by Whitworths in 1914, the 15,700dwt San Isidoro *was one of an unprecedented class of ten very large tankers built for Eagle Oil Transport Co during 1913–15. Indeed the lead ship* San Fraterno *held the title of the largest tanker in the world when delivered in May 1913. As a result of the outbreak of the First World War,* San Isidoro *was sold to the French Government for service as a naval oiler, being renamed* Dordogne. *She was scuttled by the French navy in Brest Roads in 1940 to prevent her falling into enemy hands.* (CMP)

that time. It is interesting to note that the larger ships carried oil some ten per cent more cheaply than the smaller ones, clearly demonstrating the economies of scale. This was not lost on Pearson, who as soon as the war was over ordered another twenty ships, including six from UK yards that were even larger at 18,000dwt and which adopted steam turbine propulsion as opposed to the quadruple-expansion machinery of the earlier design.

The First World War

In time of war it becomes expedient to produce standard ships in order to rationalise production, to make the most economic use of materials and to facilitate the exchange and replacement of crews. During the First

The War Diwan *was a standard 'Z' type tanker of the 1914–18 War. Forty tankers of this type were ordered but by the end of the war only six had been delivered and six of the contracts were then cancelled. The* War Diwan *was completed by Lithgows Ltd in August 1919 and was taken over by the Admiralty in 1921. On 16 December 1944 she struck a mine in the River Schelde and broke in two.* (CMP)

World War, British shipyards were badly short of manpower and it became necessary to do anything to reduce complexity in order to produce ships quickly. Standard designs for dry cargo ships (Types 'A' and 'B') were produced, the first such vessel, *War Shamrock*, being delivered on 20 August 1917 by Harland & Wolff Ltd of Belfast. By June 1917 it was apparent that unless measures were taken to stem the losses incurred from intensive submarine warfare, UK petroleum stocks would be rapidly depleted. The first step was to adapt the standard dry cargo vessels to carry petroleum by the installation of large vertical, cylindrical cargo tanks in the holds. At the bottom of the cargo tanks the tank top was perforated so that the double bottom became part of each tank. Thus modified these vessels had a cargo deadweight of about 6500 tons. The intention was to produce forty ships and by March 1918, thirty were in the process of being converted. The

first of these so-called 'AO' type was delivered on 28 June 1918 by the Harland & Wolff Govan shipyard and named *War Legate*. The installation of cylindrical tanks, while not an ideal solution, had the advantage of being a quick answer to the problem. A true tanker version of the 'A' and 'B' standard cargo ships was also designed, the 'Z' Type with a length of 400ft (121.95m) and a cargo deadweight of 8000 tons. Forty vessels of this type were ordered but only six had been completed by the end of the war and six were cancelled. Some of these saw service as fleet oilers but most were sold to commercial companies around 1920–21, many going to Shell's Anglo-Saxon fleet. Shell, incidentally, was one of several companies that had converted old sailing ships to tankers during the war to alleviate shortages, an example being the 2603grt *Ortinashell* in 1917, which had been built as the four-masted barque *Oweenee* in 1891.

Attracted by the high rates existing on account of the large demand for oil after the First World War, many Scandinavian owners entered the tanker business in the 1920s. Amongst these was Denmark's A P Møller, who later went on to build up a considerable fleet. Having first obtained charters from the oil companies, he took delivery of five twin screw motor tankers in 1928, two from Burmeister & Wain and three from the Odense Shipyard, one of which was the 7691grt Jane Maersk. *(CMP)*

Simnia was typical of the tall-masted motor tankers built for Shell in the 1930s. A product of Harland & Wolff's Govan shipyard in 1936, she measured 6197grt and could carry around 12,000 tons of oil on a draught of about 30ft. She fell victim to the German battlecruiser Scharnhorst in mid March 1941 when ballasting out to Curacao from the Mersey. (CMP)

design and its variants resulted in lighter construction without any loss of strength, improving deadweight capacity and facilitating tank cleaning.

Another innovation that was to have an even greater influence, not only on the tanker but on all types of vessel, was the gradual introduction of electric welding, first employed in the construction of the coaster *Fullagar* by Cammell Laird & Co Ltd in 1920. Swan Hunter & Wigham Richardson constructed an all-welded tanker in 1933, *Peter G Campbell*, for service on the Great Lakes. The same firm built a larger welded ocean-going tanker, *Moira*, in 1935.

Between the wars numbers of tankers increased steadily, as did both the number of shipowners trading in oil transportation and the number of countries with tanker fleets. At the turn of the century there were just over one hundred tankers of over 2000dwt at sea. By 1920 this figure had increased to over five hundred and the outbreak of the Second World War stood at more than fif-

The 1920s and 1930s

Back in 1916 the 7200dwt tanker *Hamlet* had been delivered by A/B Götaverken, Gothenburg, to Norwegian owners. This vessel is of interest as the first Norwegian motor tanker and the first to be fitted with two longitudinal bulkheads running throughout the cargo section, an arrangement which was later to become standard for many years. Most tankers of the 1920–30s were constructed using a centreline bulkhead with 'summer tanks' but with increasing size and the introduction of twin longitudinal bulkheads, this arrangement gradually became obsolete.

Corrugated bulkheads, patented by the Hogg-Carr Construction Company of Newcastle upon Tyne first appeared in the early 1920s. These consisted of longitudinal bulkheads with a series of horizontal curved corrugations and transverse bulkheads with vertical corrugations. They were supported by stringers and webs but virtually all of the normal stiffeners were eliminated. This

The part-welded Trondheim *was one of many similar tramping tankers built by Norwegian owners for charter work during the 1930s. Delivered by Eriksbergs, Gothenburg, in the same year the Second World War broke out, she was driven by a 6-cylinder diesel and had a deadweight tonnage of 12,648. In 1952 she was sold to Italy's 'Mare Nostrum' Co by her owners Eyvind Matheson, becoming* Punta Ronco *as shown here.* (FotoFlite)

An increasing number of motor tankers were built during the 1920s, amongst which was the twin screw Scottish Minstrel, *second of two sisters delivered to Tankers Ltd in 1921–22 by Vickers Ltd, Barrow-in-Furness. She became one of many war losses when attacked and sunk in July 1940 by the German submarine* U-61 *about 170 miles west of the Scottish island of Colonsay.* (CMP)

teen hundred. In addition there were many smaller tank vessels, river and coastal tankers, bunkering vessels etc.

Diesel propulsion was adopted with enthusiasm by some companies such as Standard Oil but UK owners were on the whole more cautious. The 1930s were marked by a great increase in Norwegian owned tanker tonnage, the majority motor driven, whilst Japanese owners, aided by naval subsidies, produced some extremely fast tankers such as *Tatekawa Maru* of Kawasaki Kisen, which attained over 20kts on trials in 1935 from a single 9000bhp diesel, making her one of the world's most powerful single screw ships.

One of the most successful of the Second World War standard built tanker designs was the 16,800dwt American T2 type, of which 525 were built. The majority of these were of the T2-SE-A1 design which employed turbo-electric machinery of 6000shp for a speed of about 14½kts, the remaining 44 ships of the A2 and A3 designs being given 10,000shp for 16kts. The A1 Esso Manchester, *built as* Santiago *by the Sun Shipbuilding & Drydock Co, Chester, Pennsylvania in 1944, was one of nine surplus T2s purchased by Anglo-American in 1947 and placed under the management of the Esso Transportation Co. Unlike many others of her type, she ended her career as a relatively unmodified vessel, being scrapped at Faslane in 1963.* (FotoFlite)

The Second World War

During the Second World War there was the same requirement to produce ships rapidly as there had been during the First World War. In the UK several classes of standard ocean-going tanker were produced. The first to be delivered were based on the prewar 12,000dwt 'Shell' design. Known as the 'Ocean' class, thirty-four of these vessels were delivered by seven different shipyards from 1941. They were mostly 466ft (142.07m) in length and had a speed of 12kts. A slightly larger class of vessel, also dating from 1941, was the 'Norwegian' class, a design based on the tankers *Sandanger* and *Eidanger* built by Sir James Laing & Sons Ltd, Sunderland for Westfal-Larsen & Co of Oslo in 1938. These had a deadweight of 14,500 tons and a total of twenty-one vessels were constructed. Other standard types built in the UK included the 'Fast Type', thirteen ships of 12,000dwt with a speed of 15kts and the much smaller 'Intermediate' class, ten ships of 5000dwt. Finally four even smaller *Empire Pym* type were built; the latter designed and equipped to enter Continental ports after the Normandy invasion.

In the USA a wide variety of standard types were built in large numbers during the war. A Maritime Commission set up in 1936 had instigated an emergency building programme with the intention of building 500 ships over a ten year period. At that time there were only about twenty tankers under construction in US shipyards. With war be-

coming a possibility, the original programme was doubled in 1939 and again in 1940. One obvious need was for fast fleet tankers to match those being built in Japan. In 1937 several oil companies were approached with the proposition that in return for building tankers incorporating features required by the US Navy, the additional cost would be met by the Maritime Commission. The owners had to agree to operate the ships under the US flag for twenty years and the Maritime Commission agreed to pay the depreciated value to the shipowner should requisition become necessary. Standard Oil of New Jersey placed orders with four shipyards on 5 January 1938 for three vessels each under the scheme. These twelve tankers of 18,300dwt and 17kts speed became the first of the US Second World War standard types and were designated T3-S2-A1. Three of them, *Cimarron*, *Neosho* and *Platte*, were taken over by the US Navy before delivery and four were later converted into escort carriers carrying thirty-five aircraft apiece. The latter took part in 'Operation Torch', the Allied invasion of North Africa on 8 November 1942.

The standard tanker that was produced in the greatest numbers was designated T2-SE-A1 or T2 for short. A total of 481 were built during 1942–45, at four shipyards: the Kaiser Company, Portland, Oregon (147 ships), Alabama Drydock & Shipbuilding Company, Mobile, Alabama (102 ships), Marinship Corporation, Sausalito, California (34 ships) and Sun Shipbuilding & Drydock Company, Chester, Pennsylvania (198 ships). These T2s had a deadweight of 16,628 tons, an overall

length of 524ft (159.7m) and were provided with turbo-electric propulsion developing 6600shp at 93rpm which gave them a speed of 15kts. A further forty-four were given 10,000shp machinery for 16kts. The cargo was carried in one double and eight triple tanks. The T2 was undoubtedly one of the most successful vessels ever designed and long after the cargo tank sections had decayed, new mid bodies were being built and the power plant uprated. The engine rooms proved very reliable and were used on 'jumboised' tankers, bulk carriers, ore carriers, cement carriers, barges, and some ships were even used as floating power stations in Norway, Australia, Vietnam and elsewhere. Some sixty-two of the famous 'Liberty' ships were also completed as tankers.

The postwar years

It was during the Second World War that welding was first used on a large scale for ship construction, particularly in the United States for the standard types. However, several structural hull failures in all-welded vessels caused great concern. Some of these occurred during the war and others immediately after, culminating in the breaking in two of the 31,800dwt tanker *World Concord* in a storm in the Irish Sea on 27 November 1954. Major investigations were commenced in 1944, both in the USA and UK, in the latter case two 12,000dwt tankers, *Neverita* and her sister vessel *Newcombia*, being subjected to detailed strain tests in July and August 1944. *Neverita* was an all-welded vessel while *Newcombia* was mainly riveted.

While much useful information was obtained it was not until after the *World Concord* investigation was under way that the problems of 'brittle fracture' and the need for special steels in highly stressed parts of the hull were fully appreciated. Shipbuilding steels in use at the time became brittle at low temperatures, particularly in the region of a weld, and could easily fracture if highly stressed due to a notch or discontinuity. One outcome of the *World Concord* investigation was the introduction of a number of riveted seams to prevent any crack in the shell plating from running around the hull without interruption.

While oil distribution was mainly in the hands of the major oil companies prior to the Second World War, many independent owners were attracted to the market in the 1950s. Among the names that became more familiar were the Greek shipowners Onassis, Niarchos and Livanos, all of which had very large tanker fleets. Prewar the Scandinavian owners who had been largely involved in dry cargo trades now began turning their attention to the oil trade, Anders Jahre, Leif Hoegh, Hilmar Reksten, Sigval Bergesen and

Rapidly rising demand for oil after the Second World War soon led to the building of larger tankers. Delivered by Swan Hunter & Wigham Richardson in 1950, Shell's 28,330dwt Velutina *was the first of the so-called supertankers under the Red Ensign. Measuring 643ft overall by 81ft, she was propelled at 16kts by three steam turbines geared to a single screw and was followed by three sisterships. Despite being quickly outclassed by much larger tonnage, she lasted until 1971 when her after part was broken up and her forepart converted into the oil rig maintenance barge* Champion. *(FotoFlite)*

Although by no means the largest tanker in the Niarchos fleet, the Liberian-registered World Grace *(32,750dwt) illustrates the significant postwar shift towards far bigger ships associated with the entrance into the market of independent (and particularly Greek) shipowners. Built in 1954 by Kieler Howaldtswerke, she was typical of the streamlined tankers commissioned during the period. Two steam turbines geared to a single shaft gave the ship a maximum speed of 17kts.* (FotoFlite)

A P Møller to name a few. The oil companies made full use of independent tonnage to meet peaks in demand rather than build up their own fleets for this purpose, thus avoiding the need to lay-up excess tonnage from time to time. Notwithstanding, BP, Esso and Shell all embarked on large fleet re-construction programmes, Shell's fifty-ship standard 19,000dwt 'H' and 'K' class deserving particular mention.

Tanker design took a different turn in 1954 when the far-sighted Johnson Line (Rederi-A/B Nordstjernan) of Stockholm took delivery of the bridge and accommodation aft *Oceanus*, 24,500dwt from the Lindholmen shipyard in Gothenburg. Although this concept was widely used in coastal tankers it had only been tried in any larger way in three tankers built by Scotts of Greenock for the Atlantic Refining Co of the US between 1928 and 1931, the first of which, the 8947grt *Brunswick*, was also the first diesel-electric tanker built in Britain. *Oceanus* was the first large tanker so designed but it was three or four years before other owners followed suit, examples being Knut Knutsen's 30,000dwt

The steady growth in tanker size, from the 16,000dwt T2 class of the Second World War culminated at the end of the period covered by this book in the first tanker to pass 100,000dwt. Completed in 1959 by National Bulk Carriers Inc, Kure, Japan, the 72,133grt Universe Apollo *was owned by Universe Tankships Inc, Monrovia, a D K Ludwig company. Changes in freeboard regulations saw her capacity rise to 124,847dwt before she went for scrap at Kaohsiung in the autumn of 1979 after being laid up at Piraeus since April 1977.* (FotoFlite)

Inger Knudsen and Compagnie Navale des Petroles' (CNP) 33,000dwt *Butmah* built in 1958–59. Two ships similar to the latter, *Altair* and *Polaire*, were built for CNP the following year but these started a new trend in having twin funnels. At the same time Shell switched to the all-aft design with its 19,340dwt *Aluco*, the first of a class of medium-size tankers, and by the end of the decade it had become quite widespread, pointing the way to the future.

An event that was to have a considerable effect on another aspect of tanker design occurred in 1956 when Colonel Nasser nationalised the Suez Canal. As a result of the conflict which started in October 1956, involving the UK, France and Israel, the canal was blocked by the Egyptians. Prior to these events the economics of most of the world's tankers had been determined without considering the possibility of closure of the canal. It became necessary to route tankers from the Middle East to Europe via the Cape of Good Hope, nullifying the limitation on size dictated by the canal, with the result that many owners were attracted by the

economic advantages of very large vessels. A number started planning tankers which, if the canal reopened, would be able to pass through in ballast, making the loaded voyage via the Cape. Of course when the canal did reopen on 30 April 1957, a programme to widen and deepen the waterway was soon implemented. The first tanker of over 100,000dwt was ordered by Niarchos from the Bethlehem Steel Company's Quincy yard. However due to a steelworkers strike, her building was delayed for about eighteen months during which time the 104,520dwt *Universe Apollo*, completed in Japan in 1959, entered service for Universe Tankships Inc. Niarchos' *Manhattan* was finally delivered in 1962, and because of her very heavy construction and other special features was later chosen to be specially converted for the historic voyage through the North-West Passage to Alaska in 1969.

Coastal tankers

The first coastal tanker was actually a converted coaster. A small iron cargo vessel,

This small tanker, the Shwedacon *(3391grt) built by Armstrong Whitworth & Co Ltd in 1912 is typical of the small tankers of the period built for service in the Far East. Owned by Indo-Burma Petroleum Ltd, Calcutta, a conspicuous feature is the awning fittings over all the decks. Management of this vessel was transferred to the British Tanker Co Ltd in 1947 and she was scrapped in Sunderland in 1953.* (CMP)

Valeria, built in 1881 by C Keill & Sons (later Charles Hill & Sons) of Bristol, was purchased in 1888 by the Kerosine Company which contracted the Wallsend Slipway to convert her into a tanker. The cargo space was divided into three compartments by transverse bulkheads. When *Valeria* entered service as a tanker in January 1889 there was no network of storage tanks to receive her cargo at ports of call so she carried her own barrelling equipment. On her arrival at a port a team of coopers engaged locally would set to work producing the barrels to receive the cargo being discharged.

Valeria was soon followed by a number of vessels built for the coastal trade. In 1890 Armstrong Mitchell & Co Ltd, built a small tanker, *Ewo*, for W Keswick. *Ewo* was 149ft (45.43m) in length and was only 423grt. In 1892 the same builders delivered the slightly larger *El Gallo* to Spanish owners Desmaris Hermanos. This vessel was 170ft 6in (51.98m) in length with a gross tonnage of 632. The Anglo-American Oil Co Ltd took delivery of a coastal tanker in 1897. This was *Osceola*, built by D J Dunlop & Co of Port Glasgow.

After the first commercial production of oil in the United States in 1859 there was a considerable trade on the rivers in oil in barrels and to a much smaller extent in bulk oil. With the development of the railway system this trade very rapidly diminished. As demand for oil increased so the need for coastal vessels to improve distribution arose. In 1896 Union Iron Works, San Francisco, delivered *George Loomis* to Pacific Coast Oil Company. *George Loomis* had a length of 175ft (53.35m) and carried 800 tons of oil in six cargo tanks. She was in service on the coast and rivers of the US west coast and foundered in a storm in 1918 with the loss of her entire crew. A larger coastal vessel, *Whittier*, delivered by the same builders in 1903, was owned by Union Oil Company of San Francisco. She had a length of 240ft (73.17m) and carried her oil in ten cargo tanks. To enable her to enter the smaller coastal ports her draught was only 16ft (4.88m). Besides operating on the Californian coast *Whittier* also

served the Hawaiian Islands. In this service she would tow *Fullerton*, a four-masted barque equipped to carry oil. At Kibei, in the Hawaiian Islands, *Fullerton* would discharge her cargo using a floating hose as the water was too shallow to allow either vessel to approach the shore closely.

The discovery of oil at Spindletop in Texas in 1901 drew attention to the need for coastal transport on the US eastern and southern coasts. Both the Standard Oil Company and the Sun Oil Company were involved in the development of this trade. The first 5000 barrels of Texas oil were carried to the east coast on a tanker belonging to Standard in March 1901. Sun took delivery of an 1800dwt coastal tanker built by the American Steel Barge Company in 1900. This was *Paraguay* which had a length of 242ft (73.78m) when delivered.

Lake Maracaibo is a very shallow lake on the north coast of South America and it has a very narrow outlet to the sea. In 1918 oil wells in the lake and the surrounding area started production; however, the company owning the concession did not have the capital necessary to develop the oilfield and sold out to Royal Dutch Shell which immediately built a refinery on the coast at nearby Cardon. The problem of finding shallow draught tankers to transport oil from the lake to the refinery was solved by the purchase of eight monitors (*M16–M20, M24, M26* and *M32*) from the Royal Navy and converting them to carry oil cargoes. After conversion these vessels were named *Tiga, Toedjok, Anam, Delapan, Lima, Satoe, Doewa* and *Ampat*

The 2600grt Leonor, *built for N V Curacaosche Scheepvaart Maats in 1928, was one of many shallow-draught tankers in the Shell fleet that were used to ferry oil out of Lake Maracaibo. This task was originally undertaken by a number of small naval monitors purchased by Shell after the First World War and converted into tankers. The twin screw* Leonor *was a development of a series which began in 1923, her long centre trunk deck being a feature of most Maracaibo tonnage.* (CMP)

respectively. They were able to carry 440 tons of cargo on a draught of 7ft (2.13m). By the end of 1921 a tanker of 1320dwt, *Francunion*, was in service. Other vessels followed and from 1925 to 1928 a series of seventeen shallow draught tankers was ordered from Harland & Wolff Ltd, Belfast. The first of these, which all had names using the prefix 'Inver', was delivered on 24 March 1925 and named *Inverlago*. She had a length of 305ft (92.99m) and a draught of only 13ft 3in (4.04m) yet she had a cargo deadweight of 3156 tons. The later ships of the series grew progressively larger as the channel into Lake Maracaibo was dredged. During the Second World War the Maracaibo tankers became easy targets for German submarines. To maintain supplies, seven tankers which were able to carry 5000 tons on a draught of 15ft 1in (4.60m) were ordered from the Barnes-Duluth Shipbuilding Company, Duluth, Minnesota, and entered service in 1943. At the end of the war a pipeline was laid enabling deep-water vessels to load outside the bar. Further dredging was also commenced and by 1953 the need for shallow draught vessels was at an end.

A considerable number of standard coastal tankers were constructed during the Second World War. The most numerous of these were the forty-three diesel-driven 'Chant' type (480dwt) built in the UK at five different shipyards. The name 'Chant' was a contraction of *Chan*nel *T*anker.

The Development of Specialised Tankers

Wine tankers

Wine is one of the most ancient of cargoes. Amphorae at least 3000 years old still containing recognisable wine have been recovered by marine archaeologists from the remains of wrecked Byzantine and Greek ships in the Mediterranean. The large barrels, the tuns,

Built in Germany at A G Weser's Seebeck yard in 1953 for a Palm Line subsidiary, Tema Palm *was an example of a tanker specially designed for the carriage of palm oil from West Africa. Her tonnage measured 6255 gross and 9249 deadweight and she was propelled by an oil-fired triple expansion engine.* (FotoFlite)

in which wine was carried provided the means of measuring a ships capacity for harbour dues and taxation, the (gross) tonnage, which we still use today, although we now use a specified volume rather than loading a new vessel with empty wine tuns to ascertain the vessel's tonnage. Not long after the First World War a Russian tanker is reported to have carried a cargo of wine around many western European ports in an effort to raise foreign capital. It was not until 1935, however, that Soflumar, a French subsidiary of the Netherlands company Van Ommeren, had a vessel converted to carry wine in bulk. The conversion consisted of installing forty tanks in the two cargo holds of a 2500dwt dry cargo ship. The tanks were lined with a material named 'Brauthite' to prevent any contamination of the wine cargo. This vessel, appropriately named *Bacchus*, went into service between Algiers and Rouen carrying up to thirty different wines at any one time. Sunk in the Second World War, she was replaced by a new 3980dwt *Bacchus* built in Holland in 1949.

Chemical cargoes

Ever since the first tankers entered service they have from time to time carried chemical cargoes. In many cases the cargo was caustic soda, or caustic potash for use at a refinery, but often the cargo loaded at the refinery would be a petrochemical produced as a by-product. In 1929 Anglo-Saxon Petroleum took delivery of a conventional tanker of the period, *Murex*, having six pairs of cargo tanks (that is, six cargo compartments subdivided by a centreline bulkhead). In 1931 a sister vessel, *Agnita*, was delivered but she was a very different ship. In each cargo hold was a large 'bottle' the top of which protruded through the upper deck. On her regular voyages, *Agnita* would load concentrated sulphuric acid into the bottles at Rotterdam and transport it to the refinery at Curaçao. There

a cargo of refined products would be loaded into the cargo space surrounding the bottles and the ship would proceed to sea, washing out the bottles as she went, finally calling at Port Arthur, Texas, to load a propane/butane mixture under pressure in the bottles before returning to Rotterdam. Prior to the Second World War there were probably no more than about ten chemical cargoes carried regularly in bulk. Among these were acids carried in small specially constructed tank barges.

After the war two T2 tankers were converted to carry a number of chemical cargoes. They were both built in 1943, *R E Wilson* by the Sun Shipbuilding and Drydock Company as *Monacacy* and converted in 1949 and *Mayflower* built by the Kaiser Company as *Coquille* and converted in 1955. The conversions consisted of providing cargo tanks dedicated to a particular chemical product and the ships operated a liner trade between particular chemical installations. The first purpose-built chemical tanker was *Marine Dow-Chem*, 9936grt, of 1954, built by the Bethlehem Quincy shipyard.

It was not until 1961 that the first multi-cargo chemical tanker appeared, yet another T2 conversion. The aft end of the T2 *Pinnacles* was given a new cargo section and fore end by Rheinstahl Nordseewerke at Emden to become *Alchemist*. In the cargo tank section much mild steel clad with stainless steel was used. Two semi-refrigerated cargo tanks were provided for butadiene while the other tanks were available for up to 18,000 tons of chemicals and solvents.

In the early 1960s several shipowners became interested in the concept of a true multi-cargo chemical tanker. The initiative was taken by Silver Line which started to explore the possibilities and the marine division of the UK Department of Trade formed an advisory committee to advise on any safety measures necessary. The work of this committee was eventually handed over to

Built in 1944 as the cargo ship Cape Nun *by Pennsylvania Shipyards Inc, this vessel was renamed* Beaumont *in 1947. Purchased by Øivind Lorentzen of Oslo in 1953 and renamed* Gasbras Norte *she was converted into a liquefied gas tanker by the installation of sixty-two pressure tanks in the cargo holds with a total capacity of 7475 cubic metres. The maximum cargo pressure was 17.6 kg/m². After conversion she had a dwt of 5150 tons. In 1961 the name was again changed, this time to* Mundogas Norte. (Author's collection)

IMCO (now IMO) and formed the basis for the present IMO regulations for the safety of chemical tankers. Silver Line subsequently built a considerable fleet of versatile chemical tankers, the first being named *Silverkestrel*, *Silvermerlin* and *Silverfalcon*.

Liquefied gas cargoes

We have already learned how *Agnita* built in 1931 was the first vessel to be constructed to carry liquefied gas cargoes. A question often asked is 'why should gas be carried in liquefied form?' The reason is that a liquefied gas occupies far less space than when in the gaseous form. For example one cubic metre of liquefied butane, one of the common fuel gases, produces 229 cu m of butane gas. Another gas regularly transported at the present time is methane. Here the liquid/gas ratio is even more impressive, one cubic metre of liquefied methane producing 625 cu m of gas. While the figure for methane makes it look more attractive as a cargo when compared with butane, methane has to be refrigerated to $-161°C$ before it becomes liquid while butane only has to be refrigerated to $-0.5°C$. Furthermore butane can be liquefied at ambient temperatures by the application of quite modest pressures. Whereas no amount of pressure at the same temperature will liquefy methane. For this

reason *Agnita* was able to carry a propane/butane mixture as a liquid in the gas bottles at readily obtainable pressures.

A small vessel was built for Norwegian owners by D W Kremer Sohn of Elmshorn in Germany in 1939. This ship, *Uniklor*, was only 130ft 3in (39.71m) in length but was designed to carry 225 tons of chlorine gas under pressure.

By the end of the Second World War butane and propane/butane mixtures were regular cargoes on the Mississippi River. As demand for these gases increased, shipowners addressed the subject of their transportation. In 1947 Bethlehem Steel Company converted the wartime standard C1-A type dry cargo vessel *Cape Diamond* to carry liquefied petroleum gas (LPG), installing a total of sixty-eight vertical cylindrical pressure tanks. After conversion the ship was renamed *Natalie O Warren* and handed over to her owners, the Warren Petroleum Corporation. She was later sold to Øivind Lorentzen, the Norwegian shipowner, who renamed her *Mundogas West*. Another Norwegian owner, Hydros Tankskips-A/S, a subsidiary of Norsk Hydro, had two ships constructed in

1949 for the carriage of liquefied ammonia. These were *Herøya* and *Haugvik* which carried their cargo in six horizontal cylindrical tanks. The ammonia was carried under pressure although refrigeration plant was available to cool the cargo to $-10°C$.

The reason why a cargo is sometimes carried under pressure and at other times refrigerated is normally a question of economy. If one compares the cost of a pressure vessel cargo system with a refrigeration system, for gases which can be liquefied at ambient temperatures the break even point is normally between 2000 to 2500 tons of cargo. The result is that smaller vessels carrying gases such as butane, propane, ammonia, butadiene, ethane, etc, keep their cargo liquefied under pressure while vessels over 2500dwt normally carry their cargo refrigerated. Other cargoes such as ethylene, which boils at $-104°C$, could not be liquefied at ambient temperatures no matter how much pressure was applied, and are usually either carried fully refrigerated or partially refrigerated and partially pressurised.

Finally, mention must be made of the large fleet of small liquefied gas carriers owned by A/S Kosangas of Copenhagen. Kosangas owned a substantial and expanding business supplying bottled gas to industry and homes in Denmark and which grew rapidly in the 1950s. Their first vessel was a small cargo

The 2400 dwt Haugvik *and her sister vessel* Herøya *built in 1949 by Marinens Hovedverft of Horten in Norway and owned by Hydros Tankskips A/S of Oslo, (the shipowning company of Norsk Hydro A/S) carried anhydrous ammonia in six horizontal cylindrical cargo tanks. The ammonia cargo was maintained in liquid state partially by pressure and partially by refrigeration (−10° C). These ships were designed to transport ammonia from the company's plant at Bødø on the Norwegian Atlantic coast just inside the Arctic Circle. (Author's collection)*

Delivered in 1957 by A/S Svendborg Skibsværft the Signe Tholstrup *was the sixth new vessel to join the Kosangas fleet. Propane/butane cargoes were carried under pressure in five spherical cargo tanks. The* Signe Tholstrup *had a dwt of 450 tons. Until 1961 the Kosangas vessels were entirely dependant upon pressure to maintain cargo condition. After that date about half of their new vessels had refrigeration plant enabling cargo to be carried in a partial refrigerated condition.* (Author's collection)

ship built in 1947 and converted into a gas tanker by NV Scheepswerft 'Gideon' of Groningen in 1951. This vessel, renamed *Kosangas*, had a cargo deadweight of 70 tons. Other tankers followed in quick succession, *Rasmus Tholstrup*, *Kirsten Tholstrup*, and so on until there were more than thirty vessels in the fleet. With their bright orange-yellow hulls and blue markings they soon became a familiar sight in many ports.

Dry Bulk Carriers

While oil is probably the most important bulk cargo at the present time, this has not always been the case. Large quantities of coal, grain, and later nitrate were required to be shipped around the world, often over considerable distances. At first this was undertaken by sailing vessels but as the nineteenth century progressed and steam propulsion improved, so the task was increasingly given over to steam vessels. The advent of *John Bowes* in 1852, the world's first commercially successful steam collier and the original antecedent of today's bulk carrier, led to the development of the traditional British coaster which gradually took over from sailing ships most of the coastal movement of bulk cargoes.

The deepsea movement of bulk cargo was another matter, however, and the sailing ship held its own for a considerable time, its commercial existence prolonged by the need to ship large quantities of coal at cheap rates to the many new bunkering stations being set up around the world to replenish the rapidly increasing number of steamships. The perfection of the triple expansion marine engine finally gave the steamer the edge over the sailing ship and by the end of

the century the tramp steamer was well established in the bulk trades.

One bulk commodity carried in the early steamers was ore, both copper and iron, which was being demanded in ever larger quantities by the mills and industries of the United Kingdom, Germany and the Netherlands and to a lesser extent by those of Belgium and France. The United States was also rapidly industrialising but in its case ore was shipped across the Great Lakes for onward transportation by rail. It was soon discovered that ore was a difficult cargo. Not only was it extremely heavy, allowing only a portion of a vessel's carrying capacity to be used before it was 'down to its marks' but if the whole cargo was placed in the bottom of a ship, the vessel would roll violently.

Much of the ore destined for northern Europe was shipped from the Spanish port of Bilbao but rising demand led to the development of new deposits in Swedish Lapland in the 1880s. This in turn led to the development of several specially strengthened ships for ore carriage with engines amidships, an example being the British owned *Gellivara* of 3300dwt built by C S Swan & Hunter on the Tyne in 1888. Named after the Swedish Gällivare mine, she was fitted with wing tanks to achieve better stowage of the heavy cargo and at the same time achieve stability.

At the same time developments were taking place on the Great Lakes in North America where a specialised type of bulk carrier was evolving, the first truly dedicated ships of this type. The forerunner of these was the steam barge *R J Hackett* built in 1869 with a length of 210ft (64m) and a capacity of 1000 tons of cargo. By 1882 *Onoko* had been delivered, for some time the largest vessel on the Lakes. In 1885 she is recorded as having carried 3073 tons of iron ore and on another voyage the same year, she arrived in Buffalo with 87,400 bushels of wheat.

Onoko was the first Lakes steamer to be constructed of iron, superseding wood.

Great Lakers have a characteristic appearance with their navigating bridge, a semicircular structure, mounted right forward to provide the best vantage point when piloting the locks and narrows. This arrangement allowed a completely unobstructed cargo space between the machinery space aft, served by many transverse hatches extending for almost the width of the ship. This permitted speedy loading by chute and quick discharge by shore-based grabs. Later ships were fitted with self-discharging apparatus, the first being the 2700dwt *Wyandotte* used to carry coal and limestone to the chemical plant of the Michigan Alkali Co. Her deadweight was increased to 4200 tons in 1910 when she was lengthened by 60ft to 364ft (110m). The self-unloader is a complex vessel. The earliest examples had a hopper bottom to the holds with a single conveyor belt running the length of the hold beneath the hopper. Later vessels were fitted with three conveyor belts giving a better cargo distribution. At the end of the holds an elevating system lifted the cargo to a boom conveyor which carried it ashore. Many different types of elevator boom have been used and some modern elevators actually retract into the hull when not in use. One of the more specialised self-unloading bulk carriers on the Great Lakes was *Samuel Mitchell* (later named *Mel William Selvick*), which was built at Cleveland, Ohio, in 1892. In 1916 she was converted into a self-unloading cement carrier, being still in service in 1981, running between Clarkson and Ashtabula in tow of the tug *John M Selvick*, herself built at Chicago in 1898.

To revert to Europe, two new types of tramp steamer appeared in the 1890s, namely the turret deck and trunk deck ships designed and built respectively by William Doxford & Sons at Sunderland and Ropner, the shipowners, at Stockton on Tees. Both proved to be particularly well-suited to the carriage of bulk cargoes and the inherent strength of their designs, which incorporated cellular

The characteristic form of the Great Lakes steamer, with bridge right forward and engines far aft anticipated many of the features of later sea-going bulk carriers. The W Grant Morden *seen here between the wars was typical: 625ft 0in oa, 59ft 0in breadth, 18ft 0in loaded draught, 8974grt. There were six holds between bridge and engines. (CMP)*

double bottoms, allowed larger ships and the normal tramp to be built with but little increase in the power needed to propel them at the required speed of around 10–11kts. Both types are more fully described in the *Tramp or General Cargo Ship* section of Chapter 2.

The Swedish shipowner Axel Johnson was one of several of his fellow countrymen to enter the iron ore trade in the 1890s, anxious to capitalise on the increasing demand for Swedish ore. In 1896 his company took delivery from the Sunderland yard of James Laing of the 5500dwt *Oscar II*, a trunk deck steamer specially adapted for the carriage of ore. She was soon followed by three other ships from Howaldtswerke at Kiel, the 6540dwt *Oscar Fredrik* in 1900 and the 7740 ton sisters *Drottning Sophia* and *Kronprins Gustaf* a year later. All four were employed in the iron ore trade between Lulea and Oxelosund in the Gulf of Bothnia and either Antwerp or Rotterdam. After 1903 they also sailed from the Norwegian port of Narvik, which had deep water, was ice-free and had been joined to the Swedish mines by a new rail link. This same year also witnessed the delivery of the

engines-aft turret steamer *Grangesberg*, a self-unloading ore carrier of 10,700dwt which at the time was the largest single deck steamer in the world. Built by Doxford to the order of W H Muller's Algemeene Scheepvaart Maats of Rotterdam, she was comprehensively fitted with seven goalpost masts and

twenty-four cargo derricks. In 1916 she became Holland Amerika Line's *Beukelsdijk* but was wrecked off the Norwegian port of Bødo on 28 January 1923.

Amongst other Swedish shipping companies involved in the iron ore trade were A/B Tirfing, one of the founding Brostrom Group concerns, and Rederi A/B Lulea-Ofoten, formed in 1899 and taken over by the Grängesberg mining company in 1903. The latter of the two celebrated its first decade of existence by taking delivery of a new type of engines aft ore carrier from the Tyne yard of Hawthorn Leslie & Co Ltd in 1909. The 8000dwt *Vollrath Tham* was 400ft (122m) in length on a beam of 56ft 6in (17.2m) and was intended for the Narvik–Rotterdam trade. Her interest lay in the fact that she was designed on the Johnson-Welin principle with hopper-like holds which had sloping bottoms and an automatic discharging system. This consisted of separate trunks situated between each of her holds into which ten electric deck cranes lowered 2-ton buckets to be filled from doors placed under each hold.

A general arrangement drawing of the Vollrath Tham *from a contemporary encyclopaedia, emphasising the novel features of the design in the hopper-like holds, the discharging trunks, and the electric cranes, not to mention the engines-aft layout.*

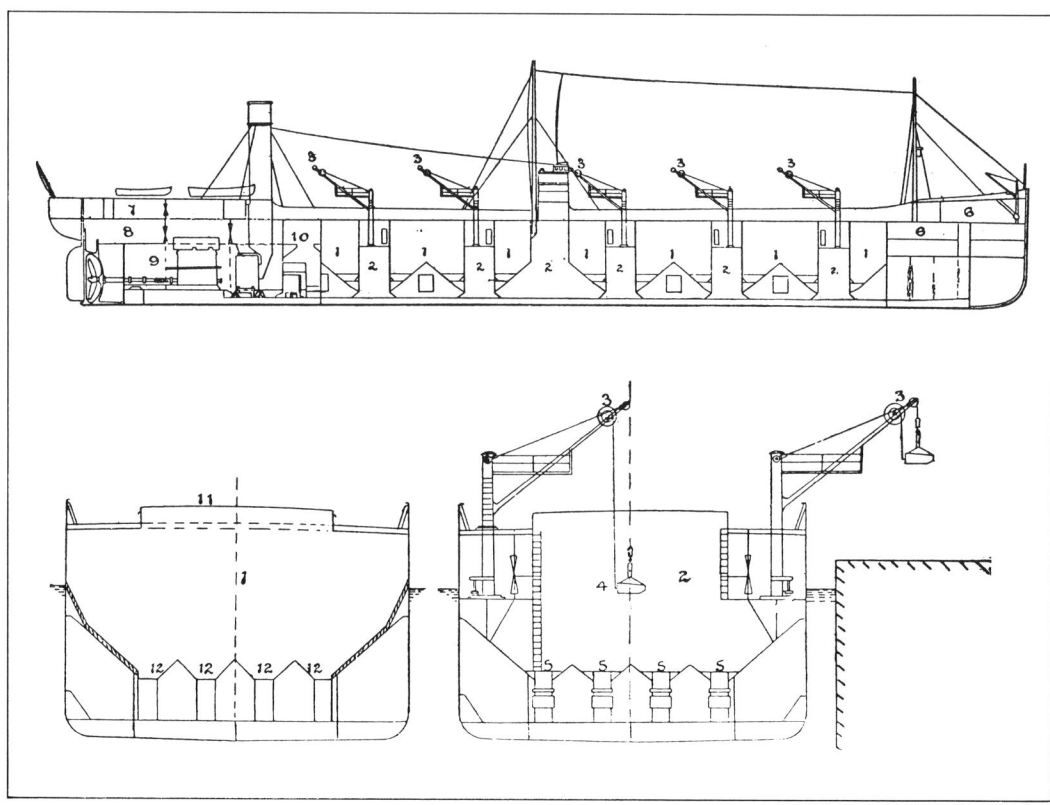

Discharge could be effected in about thirty-six hours, marginally quicker than with the traditional winches and derricks method but more importantly achieved an 80 per cent saving in manpower. A similar but larger ship fitted with twelve deck cranes, the 10,800dwt *Sir Ernest Cassell*, followed in 1910, just eclipsing *Grängesberg* in size. In comparison, the largest Great Lakes bulker some five years later, *James J Hill* was only 8300dwt.

The next development of note came after the First World War when the US-owned Ore Steamship Corporation took delivery in 1922–23 of five twin screw ships of 8300grt and no less than 22,300dwt from the Sparrows Point shipyard of Bethlehem Steel. Apart from the lead ship *Bethore*, which had reciprocating engines, the remaining four were driven by oil-fired steam turbines. It was not long, however, before two even more remarkable ships appeared in 1925. *Svealand* and her sister *Amerikaland* were built in Germany by Deutsche Werft, Hamburg for Angf. A/B Tirfing and measured 15,350grt and 20,600dwt on dimensions of 571ft (174m) overall – some 20ft longer than the US ships – and 72ft (22m) moulded beam on a loaded draught of about 32ft (10m). Driven by twin eight-cylinder B&W diesels at a speed of 11¼kts, they were amongst the first ships to be fitted with wide steel hatch covers and were the largest dry cargo carriers of the time, way ahead of anything else in Europe and indeed could be described as the true forerunners of the modern bulk carrier. They carried iron ore from the open Chilean roadstead of Cruz Grande, where it was loaded in the extremely short time of around two hours (the record was forty-eight minutes), and then proceeded via the Panama Canal to the Bethlehem Steel works at Sparrows

Point, Baltimore, returning in ballast after discharging in about twenty hours. This arduous schedule, involving some 325 days of the year spent at sea, was performed without mishap until 1942 when *Amerikaland* was sunk. Her sister returned to this service in 1946 but traded mainly from Narvik from 1949 onwards. Re-engined in 1951, she was not broken up until 1969, after a remarkably successful career.

There were no further significant developments until the Second World War, with companies including Grängesberg seemingly content to build smallish engines-amidships type ore carriers such as the *Saggat* (5329grt), delivered in 1943. In the same year, however, the Eriksbergs shipyard in Gothenburg launched the first of two 8700grt, 12,600dwt ore carriers for the Brostrom Group. Delivered immediately after the war, *Ferroland* and *Malmland* were in many respects smaller versions of the earlier *Svealand* but designed for the European ore trades. They had a raised forecastle and poop with cruiser stern and a midships placed navigating bridge that was narrow in section with long projecting wings. This design set the pattern for several subsequent ore and ore-oil carriers (see next section) built in Swedish shipyards for Scandinavian owners including Grängesberg, which had become pre-eminent in this type of carriage. It took delivery of a ship of 26,000dwt in 1953 but two years later received the first of five new all-aft self-trimming ore carriers from Götaverken, Gothenburg. The 13,000dwt *Abisko* had four holds which were surrounded by ballast tanks, literally forming a hull within a hull. These were also suitable for carrying coal or grain, the latter being prevented from shifting by a system of hinged flaps, normally secured under the sloping top of the hold for

Morar was one of a class of ore carriers built for charter to BISCO (the British Iron & Steel Corporation) that were specifically designed to enter locks at Port Talbot. Delivered to Scottish Ore Carriers Ltd by Lithgows, Port Glasgow, in 1959, the ship was unusual in being the first cargo vessel fitted with free-piston gas turbine engines geared to a single shaft. The bridge amidships arrangement was then in the process of being replaced by an all-aft superstructure, which is the present standard for bulk carriers. (CMP)

ore carriage, which could be fixed in a vertical position.

Although it had been in use in the Great Lakes for many years, the all-aft profile was introduced elsewhere in the 5500grt ore carriers *Pathfinder* and *Prospector* built by Hawthorn Leslie in 1950 for the Pan-Ore Steamship Co Inc, a Panamanian subsidiary of Aluminum Company of America Inc, Pittsburgh. It was also adopted by Houlder Bros, one of a number of British shipowners that built ore carriers in several different sizes to guidelines laid down by the British Iron & Steel Corporation (BISCO) which took them on long-term charter. The smallest group, which included the Houlder ships, were limited in size to 427ft (130m) in length and 57ft (17.4m) breadth, and about 9000dwt by the entrance lock at Port Talbot, one of their principal ports of call. Others were around 15,000dwt with four hatches if the bridge was amidships and six if engines and all accommodation was aft. Ships of this comparatively small size were ideal for the UK and European steel markets, which due to the proximity of sources of supply, did not need ore in the quantities required by the US and Japan for instance. To serve these markets a number of very large ore carriers were built, led as in the tanker and ore-oil ship fields by the Ludwig Group which took delivery of the 20,900grt, 60,400dwt *Ore Chief*, *Ore Titan* and *Ore Transport* in 1954–55 from its subsidiary shipyard National Bulk Carriers Inc situated in Kure, Japan.

Apart from dedicated ore carriers, other specialised bulk carriers began to appear for commodities such as bauxite (aluminium ore), cement, gypsum, nitrate, phosphate and even sugar. For the carriage of the latter eleven ships were built in the UK for Silvertown Services Shipping Ltd and Sugar Line Ltd during the mid to late 1950s. Typical of these was *Sugar Gem*, built in 1956 by Hawthorn Leslie, a ship of 8674grt and 9820dwt with bridge amidships and engines at the after end of a long poop.

Other bulk cargoes such as coal and grain were still carried mainly in tramp ships, though these had greatly improved in design and some were capable of steaming at 15kts. A change occurred in 1955 when over a dozen bridge and engines aft tramps of about 15,000dwt and 16kts speed were built in Japan for several owners, including Niarchos. Most of these were still fitted with masts and cargo gear but they represented an important interim stage in the move towards today's general purpose tramp bulk carrier. The eventual design of the latter was in some ways anticipated in the same year by two 12,700dwt nitrate carriers, also built in Japan, *John Wilson* and *Chilean Nitrate*, which were all-aft ships fitted with six deck cranes for cargo handling.

The first of the new generation of gearless bulk carriers began to appear from 1958 onwards, early examples in the 14,000-16,000dwt range belonging to Dutch, German and Norwegian owners. Both machinery and accommodation were arranged aft and they were fitted with wide hatches on a long cargo deck to facilitate loading and discharge by shore elevators or gantries.

Their appearance was timely as it gave many break-bulk and tramp operators the opportunity of benefiting from the more attractive cargo rates then applying to the bulk trades. The acceptance of the bulk carrier as a special type of ship was recognised in the 1960 Convention for the Safety of Life at Sea and from then on its proliferation was rapid.

Ore/oil carriers

The tanker has one big disadvantage in that its very design and the trade in which it is engaged makes it suitable to carry cargo only on one leg of its voyage. A tanker will almost always proceed to its loading port in ballast and make the return voyage with cargo. That is not to say that tankers have only carried oil cargoes. At times when the oil trade has been depressed tankers have operated for periods in the grain trades but their small cargo hatches make them suitable for very little else. At the beginning of the century tanker operators occasionally endeavoured to find a cargo for what is normally the ballast voyage; a few enterprising operators did occasionally carry grain on the outward voyage and oil on the homeward voyage and sometimes today tankers will be pressed into service to carry grain cargoes. Perhaps the oddest tanker cargo recorded, on the twin-funnelled *Santa Rita*, was carried in February 1907 and which included a shipment of 800 pianos to replace those destroyed in the San Francisco earthquake. It is not surprising therefore that combination carriers have been developed to try and improve trading possibilities.

The first ore/oil combination carrier was built by Bethlehem Steel for Canadian owners in 1921. The 14,300grt *G Harrison Smith* was designed to carry oil to South

America in her wing tanks and return with ore in her centre holds. Although successful, the concept was not taken up again until after the Second World War, when Grängesberg-Oxelosund of Stockholm ordered *Rautus* and *Raunala* from Götaverken in Gothenburg. These 13kt motorships had a deadweight of 12,100 tons with engines and main accommodation aft and a particularly narrow navigating bridge placed amidships. Ore was carried in two long central holds, around and below which were a number of oil tanks. Grängesberg and other owners followed the same pattern in several later classes of ship in the 15,000–26,000dwt range built up to the mid 1950s but the bridge was moved aft in the 34,200dwt *Malgomaj* built by Götaverken in 1959, which had two ore holds of 240ft (forward) and 195ft served by seven and six hatchways respectively. The covers were of a new design incorporating two hinged sections operated hydraulically by a telescopic unit mounted on the edge of each coaming.

The early 1950s were marked by another group of notable ships, including the *Bomi Hills* type built by the Fairfield Shipbuilding & Engineering Co, Govan, for Norwegian owner Torvald Klaveness to carry iron ore from Liberia to North America and oil on the return voyage. These could also carry latex in deep tanks forward. By far the largest combination carrier of the period was the 56,100dwt *Sinclair Petrolore* built at Kure Shipyard, Japan in 1955 for the Ludwig group's Liberian offshoot Universe Tankships Inc. She had a bridge placed well forward at the after end of the forecastle and was fitted with her own automatic discharging system consisting of underhold conveyors and a 200ft long unloading gantry. The ore/oil carrier would later give rise to another ship type, the ore/bulk/oil vessel or OBO (see *The Shipping Revolution* p21).

Conclusion

To summarise, by 1960 there were about 4500 tankers of all types in service throughout the world. Among these were specialised

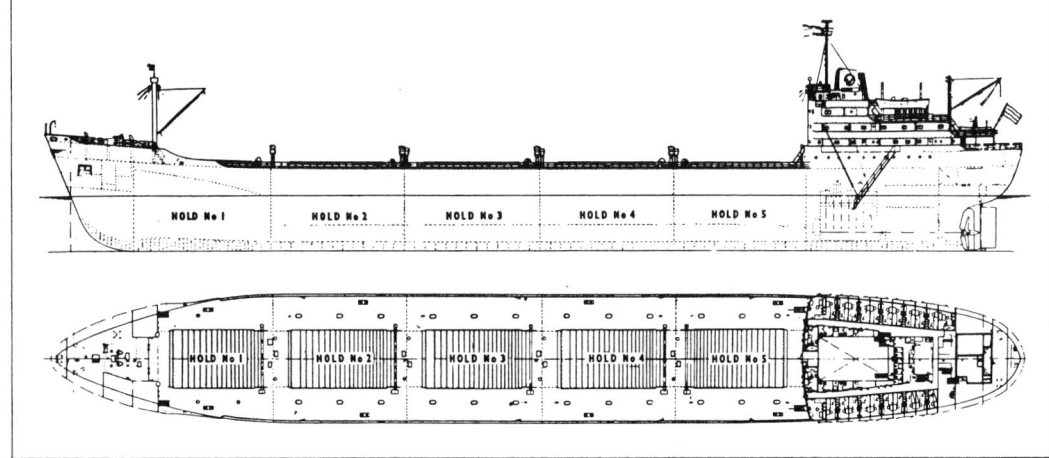

The layout of a typical bulk carrier of about 1960: the Holendrecht *of 11,931grt was the first of a series of single-deck gearless bulkers built by Wilton-Fijenoord, Schiedam and Cantieri del Mediterraneo, Pietra Ligure, Italy. Designed for transporting grain, the class could carry 16,750dwt in five cargo holds (centre and wing holds). The centre holds were self-trimming, under electric hatch covers, and the wing compartments were used for bulk cereals only. Diesel machinery drove the ship at about 14kts.*

M/S »Virtala« 21 900 tons d.w.
Kombinerat malm- och tankfartyg

The 21,900dwt Virtala was one of several ore/oil combination carriers built for the Swedish Grängesberg company in the 1950s. This ship was one of the first of the type with all-aft superstructure and was launched by Kockums of Malmo in 1959. The hydraulic hatch covers for the ore holds are apparent, but the pipework for the tanker role can also be made out just inboard of the deckedge. The ship was propelled by an 8-cylinder MAN diesel of 7300bhp, giving a speed of 14.5kts. (Grängesbergsbolaget, by courtesy of Roger Jordan)

tankers for crude oil, refined products, petrochemicals, many different chemicals (acids, chlorine, alkalis, solvents, etc), wine, edible oils, molasses, liquefied gases, water and many other products. They ranged from small river and harbour bunkering vessels to large supertankers of over 100,000dwt. About 1000 bulk carriers were in service at this time, also in great variety. Specialised vessels were in service for iron ore, bauxite, cement grain, sulphur, phosphate, coal, sand, etc. Among these were the newer types, the ore/oil and OBOs and the distinctive vessels for service on the North American Great Lakes. Some of the more specialised vessels were fitted with self unloading gear making them less dependant on shore equipment for cargo handling. At the same time accommodation had improved almost out of recognition from the vessels built at the turn of the century with most of the crews now being accommodated in single cabins. Radio, radar, echosounding, direction finding systems, were all normally installed while crew numbers on the largest vessels were down to about fifty persons.

P B Watson

Typical Liquid Bulk Cargo Vessels 1900–1960

Ship	Flag	Built	By	GRT DWT	Length (oa) (r = registered) × breadth × depth × draught Feet–inches Metres	Tanks	Engines	Speed	Remarks
Typical tankers									
GLÜCKAUF	Ger	1886	Armstrong, Mitchell & Co, Low Walker	2307 2704	300-6(r) × 37-2 × 23-2 × 19-0 *91.62 × 11.34 × 7.07 × 5.80*		Triple-expansion steam; 1 shaft	11kts	Generally accepted prototype of modern tanker
MUREX	UK	1892	Wm Gray & Co, Hartlepool	3564 4600	338-0(r) × 43-0 × 28-0 × — *103.05 × 13.11 × 8.54 × —*		Triple-expansion steam; 1 shaft	11kts	First tanker to transit Suez Canal loaded
NARRAGANSETT	UK	1903	Scotts SB & Eng Co, Greenock	9196 12,800	512-0(r) × 63-5 × 32-7 × 27-3 *156.10 × 19.33 × 9.94 × 8.31*	20	Triple-expansion steam, 2500hp; 1 shaft	11kts	Engines amidships; largest tanker of her day
PAUL PAIX	UK	1908	R Craggs & Sons, Middlesbrough	4196 6400	355-2(r) × 49-5 × — × — *108.29 × 15-06 × — × —*	16	Quadruple-expansion steam, 2000ihp; 1 shaft	10kts	Engines amidships; first vessel constructed on Isherwood longitudinal framing system
WAR RAJPUT	UK	1918	Armstrong Whitworth, Newcastle upon Tyne	5800 8000	412-0(r) × 52-0 × 31-0 × 25-1 *125.61 × 15.85 × 9.45 × 7.65*		Triple-expansion steam; 1 shaft	11kts	Engines amidships; First World War standard 'Z' type
BRITISH INVENTOR	UK	1926	Palmers SB & Iron Co, Newcastle upon Tyne	7200 11,000	430-0 × 57-0 × 34-3 × 26-9 *131-10 × 17.38 × 10.44 × 8.17*	30	2 Krupp 2-stroke oil engines, 2500bhp; 1 shaft	12kts	First Isherwood bracketless vessel
KROSSFONN	Nor	1935	Odense Shipyard, Odense	9323 14,225	513-0 × 65-0 × 36-0 × 28-9 *156.35 × 19.8 × 10.97 × 8.76*	20	2 7-cylinder oil engines, 4800bhp; 1 shaft	13kts	Typical Scandinavian motor tanker

Ship	Flag	Built	By	GRT DWT	Length (oa) (r = registered) × breadth × depth × draught Feet–inches Metres	Tanks	Engines	Speed	Remarks
ESSO GETTYSBURG	US	1942	Sun SB & DD Co, Chester, Pa	10,448 16,613	523-6 × 68-0 × 39-3 × 30-1 159.60 × 20.73 × 11.97 × 9.17	26	Turbo-electric; 6000shp, 1 shaft	14.6kts	T2-SE-A1 standard tanker
WORLD UNITY	Lib	1952	Vickers, Barrow-in-Furness	20,667 32,813	653-0 × 86-0 × 45-9 × 34-6½ 199.03 × 26.22 × 13.95 × 10.53		Geared steam turbine, 1 shaft	16.5kts	Typical 1950s supertanker
OCEANUS	Swe	1954	Lindholmens Varv, Gothenburg	16,145 24,500	610-8 × 76-3 × 43-3 × 32-9 186.14 × 23.25 × 13.19 × 10.00		2 9-cylinder oil engines, 8150bhp; 1 shaft	14.5kts	First large tanker with engines and accommodation aft
UNIVERSE APOLLO	Lib	1959	National Bulk Carriers, Kure	72,133 114,356	949-9 × 135-5 × 67-6 × 50-9 289.48 × 41.28 × 20.57 × 15.47		2 General Electric steam turbines; 27,500shp, 1 shaft	15.5kts	First tanker over 100,000dwt

Chemical and gas tankers from 1945

Ship	Flag	Built	By	GRT DWT	Length	Tanks	Engines	Speed	Remarks
NATALIE O WARREN (liquefied gas)	US	1944	Pusey & Jones, Wilmington, DE	7298 5308	393-6 × 60-2 × 37-7 × 27-7 119.9 × 18.34 × 11.49 × 8.4	68 vertical cylinders	Geared steam turbines; 1 shaft	15kts	Standard C1-A type dry cargo ship, converted 1947 to liquefied gas tanker. Cargo carried under pressure
HERØYA (liquefied gas)	Nor	1949	Marinens Hovedverft, Horten	1841 2400	254-2 × 37-10 × 26-0 × 24-6 77.48 × 11.54 × 7.93 × 6.55	6 horizontal cylinders	1 5-cylinder Nordberg diesel, 1500bhp; 1 shaft	12.5kts	Partially refrigerated cargo; LPG and ammonia
MARINE DOW-CHEM (chemical)	US	1954	Bethlehem SB Co, Quincy	9936 16,625	551-2 × 68-3 × 37-6 × 30-4 160.98 × 20.82 × 11.43 × 9.24	26	Geared steam turbines; 7700shp; 1 shaft	15kts	First purpose-built multi-cargo chemical tanker
CHEMICAL TRANSPORTER (chemical)	US	1943	Kaiser Co, Portland, Oregon	10,730 16,887	523-7 × 68-3 × 39-3 × 30-2 159.57 × 20.78 × 11.97 × 9.19	26	Steam turbine, 7240shp driving generator connected to electric motor, 6000shp; General Electric Co	14.5kts	T2 type tanker built as *Coquille* converted to liquid chemical carrier 1955
KITTE THOLSTRUP (liquefied gas)	Den	1957	Svendborg Skibsværft, Svendborg	397 330	168-4 × 28-7 × — × 9-10 51.28 × 8.71 × — × 3.00	5	1 4-cylinder Alpha/B&W diesel, 480bhp; 1 shaft	10kts	Cargo carried under pressure

Typical Bulk Ore and Combination Carriers 1900–1960

Ship	Flag	Built	By	GRT DWT	Length × breadth × depth × draught Feet–inches Metres	Engines	Speed	Remarks
GRÄNGESBERG (ore)	Ne	1903	Wm Doxford, Sunderland	6749 10,000	220-2 × 62-0 × 26-0 × – 76.13 × 18.90 × 7.93 × –	Triple-expansion steam, 370nhp	9kts	Turret decker
SIR ERNEST CASSELL (ore)	UK	1910	Hawthorn Leslie, Newcastle upon Tyne	7739 10,800	454-5 × 60-4 × 32-4 × – 138.5 × 18.39 × 9.84 × –	Triple-expansion steam by NE Marine Engineering, 402nhp	10kts	Self-unloader, electric cranes; cruiser stern
G HARRISON SMITH (ore/oil)	Can	1921	Bethlehem Steel Co, Sparrows Point	14,305	550-6 × 72-3 × 44-1 167.79 × 22.02 × 13.44	2 triple-expansion steam, 4100ihp	10.5kts	First ore/oil carrier
SVEALAND (ore)	Swe	1925	Deutsche Werft, Hamburg	15,357 20,600	571-3 × 72-2 × 44-1 × 32-3 174.16 × 22.00 × 13.44 × 9.83	2 8-cylinder B&W diesels, 4800bhp	11.4kts	When new world's largest ocean-going cargo vessel
RAUNALA (ore/oil)	Swe	1946	AB Gotaverken, Gothenburg	8769 12,100	488-10 × 59-5 × 35-6 × 27-9 149.00 × 18.11 × 10.83 × 8.46	2 6-cylinder Gotaverken diesels, 4200bhp	13kts	First post Second World War combination carrier
ORELIA (ore)	UK	1954	Wm Gray & Co, Hartlepool	6848 9258	426-10 × 57-2 × 33-5 × 26-7 130.16 × 17.43 × 10.19 × 8.10	2 5-cylinder CMEW diesels, 3652bhp	11.5kts	'Port Talbot' type; bridge and accommodation aft
NIKITAS ROUSSOS (bulk)	Gre	1960	Mitsubishi HI, Kobe	14,203 20,433	580-8 × 74-6 × 43-0 × 31-6 177.02 × 22.71 × 13.11 × 9.59	2 8-cylinder Mitsubishi/ Sulzer diesels, 10,700bhp	16.5kts	Universal gearless bulk carrier, bridge aft

4

Coastal and Short-Sea Shipping

THE YEARS from 1900 to 1960 saw significant developments in coastal and short-sea shipping, both in the technology of ships and their trading patterns. The century opened with the steam coaster having established a clear lead over the sailing vessel, but the motor coaster then swept from behind to render the steamship itself obsolete. The period also saw the genesis of the specialist ship types which were to do so much to revolutionise shipping in the later decades of the twentieth century.

Much technological development was stimulated by the growing competition which coastal shipping was facing. Coastal shipping retained its big advantages: water transport is the most energy-efficient way of moving goods and people. But rail, road and air offer advantages of speed, passenger comfort, flexibility and door-to-door delivery which give them a competitive edge. In many parts of the world this has meant that purely coastwise shipping has become restricted to cargoes such as coal, stone and petroleum products which can be moved in very large quantities. Although nominally coasters, the ships carrying these cargoes have often been indistinguishable from ocean-going vessels. In contrast, short-sea shipping has flourished as international trade has grown, so that by 1960 the small ships described in this chapter were more likely to be employed making a

sea crossing than running between two points on the same coastline.

Rigorously defining a coastal or short-sea ship is all but impossible. From around the world examples can be found of every size of ship running coastwise, whilst vessels of as little as 500 tons regularly cross oceans. This chapter concentrates on the smaller ships which have developed largely to suit conditions around Europe, where during our period a coaster has usually been regarded as a vessel less than 250ft (76m) in length.

A European bias in this chapter is inevitable for other reasons. Europe has always provided the biggest market for coastal and short-sea shipping, and in conjunction with early industrialisation in northern Europe this meant that yards in these countries took the lead in coaster design and building. If an owner in Australia, Asia or even southern Europe wanted a steam or motor coaster, he came to a British, Dutch, German or Scandinavian yard, or bought one of their products

second-hand. The other major industrial nation to use coastal shipping was the United States, but here distances were so great that coastal routes often required ocean-going ships. During the period under review, ship construction in the US had little influence on coaster design elsewhere, and neither did that in the other great shipbuilding nation, Japan.

In 1900 the typical powered coaster anywhere outside the US was most probably built to a British design; by 1960 its parentage was just as likely to be Dutch. As this chapter will show, this change reflected the major technological development in coastal and short-sea shipping in the period, the replacement of the steam engine by the diesel.

Steam at its zenith

Steam ships were first used in coastal and short-sea liner trades where their ability to maintain a regular service outweighed their

Tiny steamers such as the Clyde puffer Chindit *(1945, 74grt) regularly made short sea crossings, to the Scottish islands and to Ireland. Like many puffers the* Chindit *was built to a restricted length of 66ft to fit the locks on the Forth and Clyde Canal, on which owner and builder J Hay & Sons Ltd had their shipyard.* Chindit *was constructed to a design which had not appreciably changed since the Hay family began building coasting-type puffers in the 1880s. By 1945, however, it was all but obsolete and the* Chindit *lasted only until 1960, not being given the diesel engine which extended the life of several older puffers. An unusual and slightly impractical feature of most puffers was the placing of the wheelhouse behind the funnel. Note also the boat, inconveniently stowed on the hatch.* (John Clarkson)

extra capital and fuel costs. As efficiency improved, particularly with the development of compound and triple expansion engines, steam moved increasingly into the bulk trades which had remained the preserve of the coastal sailing ship. The latter had no fuel bills, but dependence on wind and weather meant that they could not make as many voyages in a given period as a steamer, nor guarantee such reliable deliveries of cargo. Sailing coasters were built in some numbers in the twentieth century, and the fitting of auxiliary engines allowed some of them to potter on through to 1960 and beyond. However, by the first decade of the century, the steam coaster represented the state of the art in small ship design. British shipyards had done most of the development work, and were the largest constructors of the type, although Dutch, German and Scandinavian yards also built coastal steamers. Indeed, a certain complacency amongst British builders and owners meant that development of the steam coaster after 1900 was limited, leaving it vulnerable when more efficient vessels appeared in the 1920s and 1930s.

The simplest powered cargo carrier is the single-hold vessel with a one- or two-cylinder steam engine. Usually referred to as steam lighters, such craft were widely used in estuaries, around large ports and on inland waterways. Modifications to improve their

seaworthiness produced the simplest steam coaster. Freeboard was increased, whilst the combination of pronounced sheer with higher bulwarks helped keep the vessel dry in a seaway. Use on salt water required more sophisticated engines with condensers: when employed inland feedwater for the boiler could be drawn straight from the canal or river. Clyde 'puffers' such as the 66ft *Druid* (built 1906, 89grt) were quite capable of surviving the exposed waters off the west coast of Scotland, and similar types were built for use in the Baltic and elsewhere.

The smallest cargo vessels capable of routinely undertaking voyages in open waters are a size larger at 90ft to 140ft (27m to 43m). Like the schooners and ketches they replaced, these single-hold steamers were designed for trading to the smaller harbours and jetties which, at least until the First World War, were important sources or destinations of cargo. The ability to use these outweighed their limited cargo capacity of 250 to 300 tons.

The design features of these small coasters were well established by 1900 and changed remarkably little over the next quarter century. Forward, a forecastle raised one deck or half a deck above main deck level gave extra buoyancy forward where it was needed, and provided basic accommodation for seamen and firemen. The raised deck aft gave some protection against seas breaking over the stern, and

also had the benefit of increasing the height of the machinery space to accommodate the tall, two-cylinder compound steam engine which was usually fitted. This deck was referred to as a poop if it was a full deck high, otherwise the term quarterdeck was used.

Smaller ports could not be depended upon to have their own cranes and these coasters had at least one derrick on the fore mast and sometimes another rigged on a full height or stump mast at the after end of the hold. There was often a third mast right aft which had no cargo handling function, and early photographs of ships such as *Admiral* (built 1906, 263grt) show that they carried a gaff and boom to rig a steadying sail. *Admiral* was equipped with a full suit of sails when new, and her crew – who would have had experience in pure sailing ships – would set them whenever the wind served, not only to save coal but also to give an easier motion.

This was the first type of steam coaster to become obsolete, and its construction virtually ceased during the trade depression of the late 1920s. Having itself displaced the coastal sailing ship, the small steam coaster found its coastwise cargoes being diverted to the railway and the motor lorry. Nevertheless, and despite serious competition from the small motor coaster, *Admiral* and similar ships steamed on as late as the 1960s in areas where they filled a niche, for instance carrying coal to small ports around the Irish Sea.

For coasters over about 140ft (43m) in length, the raised deck above the machinery was extended forward to about half the length of the ship, and the navigating bridge was placed at its forward end. In many of these ships the cargo capacity was divided into two holds, usually by means of a bulkhead positioned below the bridge.

This design, known as the long raised quarterdeck type, was so popular that it deserves a little explanation. One factor encouraging this design was loadline regulations which allowed the freeboard to be reduced to two inches below a notional main deck: the main deck in these vessels being consid-

Steam coasters such as the Glenmona *(1917, 217grt) were amongst the smallest cargo ships regularly used to cross open seas. Despite this the unenclosed wheelhouse was a typical feature, the only protection for the helmsman being a canvas dodger, the supports for which can just be discerned. A small sail can also be seen, furled to the foremast. At the age of thirty* Glenmona *disappeared in the Irish Sea where, apart from a spell under the Belgian flag, she had spent her life.* (John Clarkson)

Although completed slightly before our period, the Fluor *(built 1898, 884grt) illustrates splendidly all the features of the long raised quarterdeck coaster, for so long the backbone of the British coaster fleet. Like* Glenmona, *she has a full set of sails; indeed the mizzen mast has little purpose other than to set a steadying sail. The light gangway between forecastle and bridge was fitted to several ships built for her owners, William Robertson of Glasgow, probably in anticipation of ocean voyages, as his larger ships like* Fluor *were occasionally employed on the North American coast. Embroiled in the Russian civil war,* Fluor *was scuttled at Leningrad in 1918, although she was later raised and broken up. Ships like her survived in some numbers until well after the Second World War, and indeed were still being built in the late 1940s.* (R S Fenton collection)

small coaster. When the hold is filled with cargo most of the weight is therefore forward, and the ship tends to trim by the head, especially as the bunker coal is burnt. Being down by the head makes steering less certain, allows the screw to come out of the water in a rough sea, and may cause draught problems when a loaded ship has to use a port with a restricted depth of water. The raised quarter-

deck helps overcome this by allowing proportionally more cargo, and hence more weight, to be placed in the deeper hold aft.

Placing the bridge at the forward end of the quarterdeck was almost a trademark of British-built coasters of this size, although similar ships were built elsewhere in Europe. This bridge position gave better visibility, and also benefited captain and mate by isolat-

ered as that in the well forward. Another consideration was how level the vessel sat in the water, in other words its trim. The engine room occupies almost half the after end of a

The short-sea cargo liner usually had to load and unload small parcels of cargo, and do so quickly in order to maintain a schedule. To speed cargo handling, the old-established General Steam Navigation Co Ltd of London fitted many of its ships with electric deck cranes. These are seen clearly in this aerial view of Cormorant *(1927, 1220grt), which also shows that her second and third holds were well served by derricks, including one for heavy lifts.* Cormorant *served her owners for thirty years, being broken up in 1957.* (FotoFlite)

In contrast to colliers employed on the East Coast of the UK, those running on the Australian coast had a full quota of cargo gear. Oorama *(built 1921, 1051grt) is essentially a larger version of* Fluor, *with four hatches instead of two and extra derricks. Until Australia established its own shipbuilding industry most of its coastal ships came from UK yards,* Oorama *being completed at Paisley for the Adelaide Steamship Co Ltd. In 1949 she was sold to the Wallarah Coal Co Ltd who ran her in the busy coal trade to Sydney.* (Warwick Foote)

ing their cabins from the engine room. The engineers were accommodated above the machinery in the deckhouse aft, with the seamen and firemen in the forecastle.

Ships of this layout were very commonly built for both the tramp and the coastal liner trades, an example of the latter being *Suffolk Coast* (built 1917, 870grt). The tramp picked up cargo wherever it could get the best rate, and almost invariably lifted bulk goods, such as coal, coke, stone, iron ore, grain or timber. The liner had a set schedule between certain ports. Her cargoes often comprised small parcels of goods, frequently transhipped from ocean-going ships, although many lifted bulk cargoes when there was nothing better on offer. Built for similar ports and similar conditions, tramp and liner were often alike in appearance, and often the only external difference was the cargo gear. To expedite loading and unloading the liner would usually have extra masts at the after end of the hold, or – as in the case of *Suffolk Coast* – two derricks to each mast. Extra speed was also desirable to maintain schedules in the face of adverse weather or loading delays. But speed at sea is bought at a very high price in terms of fuel consumption. When, as happened with *Suffolk Coast*, the liner was downgraded to a tramp its usual speed was just nine knots. Speed was rarely an important consideration

in the coastal bulk trades, as there was little point in reaching a port early and then having to sit at anchor awaiting high water before the ship could berth.

These larger steamers survived the competition from motor vessels better than smaller coasters. Hulls almost identical to that of *Suffolk Coast* were built from the 1890s to the late 1940s, by when steam was truly obsolete. In the 1930s the counter stern was gradually replaced by the cruiser stern, which was easier to build and gave improved fuel economy. This was an innovation introduced to the coaster by the Belgian owner and builder John Cockerill with ships such as *Rubis* (built 1897, 630grt). In later designs the bridge was moved to the after end of the main hold, making construction more economical. Adoption of forced draught fans to supply air to the furnaces meant that funnels did not need to be as tall as in the early part of the century. Oil firing, however, was adopted only slowly, and on their voyages to the breakers in the 1950s and 1960s the last coasters of this type still burnt coal.

The size of a ship is usually constrained by the dimensions of ports served – especi-

ally the depth of water available and the dimensions of locks – and by the amounts of cargo offering. Steamers the size of *Suffolk Coast* proved a good compromise for European waters, able to enter most important ports yet carry an economic quantity of cargo over relatively short distances. Elsewhere distances were much greater, and Australian inter-state steamers, for example, were essentially ocean-going ships in coastal trades. Australia did have small coasters, but they were usually confined to specialised, short-distance work, such as the thriving coal trade out of the Hunter River ports to Sydney. *William McArthur* (built 1924, 2392grt) was completed in Scotland for this trade, and was essentially a larger version of *Suffolk Coast*, with three rather than two hatches and masts positioned accordingly. The ability to discharge their own cargoes was usual amongst the 'sixty milers', so called because of the distance from Newcastle to Sydney, and *William McArthur* had a generous provision of derricks, plus gaffs rigged high up each mast. To expedite discharge two gangs of 'wharfies' would work at every hatch, each using one derrick.

Larger coasters built during the first two decades of the twentieth century often had engines, bridge and accommodation positioned more or less amidships. Placing the superstructure here meant there was more metal-

The Swedish steamer Alstern *(built 1917, 964grt) in the Thames in 1954. The upright supports for deck cargo in the forward well deck suggest that she had been employed in the Baltic timber trade. Timber is relatively light, and the* Alstern *would only be down to her marks with a full deck cargo. Raised quarterdeck steamers like this were popular with Scandinavian owners, who often bought ships which had been built in the United Kingdom for the coal trade, although* Alstern *was completed at Helsingborg. She lasted until 1966, latterly under the Lebanese flag.* (R S Fenton collection)

The sailing ship origins of the early Dutch motor coaster was often apparent from its extreme sheer and counter stern. A noteworthy feature of Start *(1933, 203grt) is the hinged mast to suit her for inland navigation, and which requires the derricks to be offset vertically. Such was the pace of development of the Dutch coaster in the 1930s that* Start *was something of an anachronism when completed, as hull forms like that of the* Henrica *were soon the norm. Nevertheless,* Start *motored on until the 1970s, retaining both her Lloyd's 100A1 classification and her original German diesel. Despite her diminutive size, she was permitted to trade as far afield as the Red Sea, the Black Sea, the African coast and the Azores.* (Roger Sherlock)

work amidships, improving the longitudinal strength of the ship at a point where bending stresses were greatest. Compared with an engines-aft ship, the amidships design also trimmed better when light. This was an important factor when a port had draught restrictions, or when a ship had to use a berth which dried out at low water: the ship which trimmed evenly could get off or on to such a berth with the minimum of water. A disadvantage with this design was the longer shafting needed to drive the propeller. The shaft tunnel took up space in the after hold which could have been devoted to cargo carrying, and this also made the vessel trim by the head when loaded. A frequent answer to this problem was, once again, a raised quarterdeck. There was a remarkable degree of international consensus about the usefulness of this design, and similar steamers came from most of the European shipbuilding countries. One of the last of the smaller engines-amidships steamers was *Lady Dorothy* (built 1916, 578grt), slightly smaller than the contemporary *Suffolk Coast*.

Difficulties with trim could be largely overcome by providing adequate water ballast capacity in the double bottom, and many later and larger engines-amidships vessels had a three island hull form, comprising a fo'c'sle forward, a bridge deck amidships and a short poop aft. Typical of these was the Norwegian-owned and built *Bruse Jarl* (built 1923, 1890grt). Cargo gear was placed at the extremities of the holds to give the longest possible clear space for stowing timber on deck, and derricks were rigged high up the masts to clear the deck cargo. This profile became known as the 'Scandinavian', or 'Fredrikstad' type after the Norwegian yard

which developed the design. Much of Europe's timber came from the Baltic, and Scandinavian builders and owners specialised in this type of ship. Similar ships were also built in North America, as part of the massive emergency programme of the Second World War. These N3 type short-sea traders were intended largely for use in European waters, and were amongst the last steamers built with engines amidships. By the end of the war the writing was on the wall for the marine steam engine, although there were still a few owners unable or unwilling to read it.

The challenge of the diesel engine

The design of the coastal motor vessel owes as much to the sailing ship as it does to the steam coaster. Many features of the steam coaster were later incorporated, but the design which did so much to establish the superiority of the motor coaster in the 1920s and 1930s evolved largely from sailing craft, and shared their advantage of a shallow draught.

By 1900 the internal combustion engine was beyond the experimental stage, and its advantages over steam were becoming apparent. As its name implies, fuel is burnt inside the engine, where its energy is used directly to generate power in a cylinder. In contrast, a steam engine can only convert the energy in oil or coal to power by first using it to boil water, a process which involves unavoidable energy losses. The steam engine also requires boilers, expensive to build and maintain, which add weight and take up space which could be used more profitably for cargo.

The coaster powered by an internal com-

bustion engine, universally known as a motor coaster, was slow to reach maturity, but when it did in the decade after the First World War it quickly rendered the small steam coaster obsolescent. For larger vessels, the advantages of this type of engine were not so marked, but by 1945 it was the machinery of choice even for these ships.

There are essentially three ways of igniting the mixture of vapourised fuel and air in the cylinders of an internal combustion engine. Ignition by an electrical spark, as in the petrol engine, has been little used at sea. More popular in the first decades of this century was the hot bulb engine, in which a heated filament or bulb caused the explosion. But the type which was eventually most successful was that devised by Rudolf Diesel, in which heat generated by compression of the vapour produced ignition.

Early internal combustion engines were not considered reliable enough to be used as the sole means of propulsion at sea. They were first employed on inland waters, where a breakdown was less likely to have serious consequences. It is claimed that the Sulzer-engined *Venoge* (built 1905, 125 tons) for use on Lake Geneva was the world's first diesel-engined vessel. The development of a practical marine diesel was the major, and perhaps the only, Swiss contribution to coastal navigation; although Denmark's Burmeister & Wain can also claim some credit for this.

The internal combustion engine was also adopted for use as an auxiliary in sailing coasters, where it was found useful to assist manoeuvring in harbour, and might be used when the wind was unfavourable. For this purpose it had a number of advantages. It was compact, and could usually be installed even in a wooden vessel without major modifications, although this was often at the expense of the crew's accommodation. Early models, especially the Swedish Bolinder hot bulb engines, were uncomplicated machines

This design of Dutch coaster – with counter stern, raised quarterdeck and two masts – became established in the 1930s and continued to be built right through our period. Henrica (1948, 461grt) was part of the enormous rebuilding programme undertaken by Dutch owners in postwar years, and which led to their domination of European coasting trades. Second-hand Dutch motor vessels readily found owners outside northern Europe, just as British steam coasters had done a generation earlier, and in 1960 Henrica was sold to Pakistan. (World Ship Photo Library)

which could be operated without specialised engineering skills.

The Dutch adopted the auxiliary motor with alacrity. For the small ships which were suited to navigate their many canals and rivers the steam engine and its boilers were too cumbersome, and even the smallest models would have significantly reduced cargo capacity. The internal combustion engine, however, was to give their almost obsolete sailing ships a new lease of life.

Early British attempts to develop a true motor coaster did not meet with outstanding success. A number were built in the years just prior to the First World War, but the boldest venture was that of Glasgow shipowner John M Paton. In 1912 he ordered no less than eighteen motor vessels, the largest of which was *Innishowen* (built 1913, 118grt) and whose design was based on that of the Clyde 'puffer'. A variety of engines of British, Dutch and Swedish manufacture was installed. But the combination of relatively new technology and inexperienced engineering personnel seems not to have proved reliable enough for short-sea voyages, and several of the ships were wrecked following engine failures. The outbreak of the First World War prevented the necessary develop-

ment work being carried out and the fleet was dispersed.

As so often happens, military requirements accelerated technical development. Although the race to build dreadnoughts might have helped precipitate the First World War, the naval weapon which came closest to deciding it was the submarine. For cruising on the surface a reliable engine was essential, and both Britain and Germany developed diesel engines which were quite capable of taking submarines from the North Sea to the far end of the Mediterranean. Although something of a military sideshow, the campaign at Gallipoli also made a contribution to the acceptance of the internal combustion engine for marine use. Anticipating the need to land troops and equipment on beaches here and elsewhere, the British Admiralty ordered large numbers of small landing craft. To ensure a shallow draught, these X-lighters

were fitted with lightweight motors, many being hot-bulb engines. After the war, these X-lighters were sold off and many were converted for commercial use, giving some British coastal shipowners their first experience of the motor vessel.

Ironically, neither combatant exploited the internal combustion engine to the full during peacetime; this fell to the neutral Netherlands. The Dutch had profited during the war in the time-honoured fashion of serving both sides: their inland ships trading to Germany, their coasters working for Britain and France. As many Dutch ships were owned by their masters, profits were ploughed back into the ships, so that sailing vessels acquired engines, and new and better ships replaced older ones. This stimulated a remarkable period of technical development amongst Netherlands coaster builders, and by 1924 a ship was completed which set the pattern for the future development of the motor coaster. The motor sailer had evolved into a type of vessel which was to have a profound influence on coastal and short-sea shipping throughout the world.

The seminal vessel was *Gideona* (built 1924, 139grt) from the Koster yard at Gronin-

During the 1930s British owners began to show enthusiasm for the motor coaster, a decade after their Dutch competitors. British shipyards rose to the challenge, and several produced successful designs, although often with a strong hint of Dutch practice. Brockley Combe (1938, 662grt) was completed at Bristol for the locally-based Ald Shipping Co Ltd, an early British exponent of the grey hull – another hallmark of Dutch coasters. Brockley Combe frequently traded to the Channel Islands, and was wrecked there in December 1953. (R S Fenton collection)

After a slow start caused by parlous economic circumstances between the wars, Germany built up a considerable fleet of motor coasters after the Second World War. Estebrugge *(1958, 499grt), seen in her natural habitat of the Kiel Canal, claims to have the same tonnage as many contemporary Dutch coasters, but is considerably longer and has more extensive cargo gear with four derricks serving her two hatches. Her builders were soon offering the option of cranes rather than derricks. The goalpost mast forward of the superstructure which carries navigational equipment was also a feature of many contemporary German coasters. Coasters usually have longer lives than deep-sea ships, and after swapping the German flag for the Greek in 1975,* Estebrugge *survived into the 1990s.* (Roger Sherlock)

gen. She was powered by a Netherlands-made two-cylinder diesel, although many of her successors had machinery built in Germany which became available relatively cheaply thanks to the parlous economic situation in that country. The 'Koster' type had all the features which were to make the motor coaster so successful. The shallow draught which the lightweight diesel made possible allowed her to run to ports which might well be inaccessible to a steamer carrying an equivalent tonnage. A single mast which could readily be lowered allowed her to penetrate far inland up rivers and canals. Firemen were unnecessary, and many masters further reduced crew costs by acting as their own engineers, often assisted by a deckhand known as a 'motordriver' who would double as a greaser. The captain–owner's family often made up all or part of the crew, keeping wage costs to a minimum. The coaster was often the family's home and – with the minimum of shoreside overheads – as long as it could earn enough to pay interest on its mortgage and meet running costs it could keep sailing when low freight rates drove other ships into lay-up.

Social factors contributed to the success of the Dutch motor coaster, but it was the efficiency of the diesel engine that told in the long run. As the 1920s progressed and the gloom of a deepening recession replaced the optimism of peace, these little coasters used their advantages to make inroads into trades which the British steam coaster owners, in particular, had called their own. Unlike those of some European countries such as Germany, British trades were open to all owners, and Dutch owners exploited this enthusiastically.

Many British owners stayed faithful to the steam engine they had grown up with, and remained so until they went out of business. Others embraced the motor coaster, particu-larly owners on the Thames who were both vulnerable to competition from the nearby Netherlands and remote from coal supplies. Some, such as T J Metcalf, bought Netherlands-built vessels such as *Ellen M* (built 1930, 264grt). Others built in British yards, including F T Everard & Sons Ltd, which were early users of wooden motor vessels, and whose first modern motor coaster was *Ability* from Great Yarmouth (built 1928, 262grt).

After Everard, Coast Lines Ltd was one of the most influential owners to adopt the diesel, with *Fife Coast* (built 1933, 367grt) from their own Ardrossan yard. James Pollock, Sons & Co Ltd at Faversham had been fitting their small craft with Bolinder engines since 1910, and their later output included a series of successful motor colliers beginning with *Camroux I* (built 1934, 323grt). The Goole Shipbuilding & Repairing Co Ltd built some larger motor coasters, for instance *Benguela* (built 1936, 534grt), which was to give 43 years of service.

In Germany the economic situation in the 1920s did not encourage owners or shipbuilders to experiment with new technology. For the small coastwise cargoes on offer, auxiliary sailing ships usually sufficed, often those sold by Dutch owners as they traded-up to fully fledged motor coasters. Owners wanting something more sophisticated ordered motor coasters from Netherlands yards. Despite the success enjoyed by German engine builders such as Deutz, Motorenwerke Mannheim and Krupp in supplying diesels to the Netherlands, relatively few motor coasters were built in Germany and even these were often modelled on contemporary Dutch vessels. An honourable exception was the Nobiskrug yard at Rendsburg, whose *Marie Mathilde* (built 1926, 117grt) and others had rather severe lines in contrast to the graceful curves of Netherlands-built vessels. One notable German innovation came in 1931: a liner service between Copenhagen and Berlin which exploited the ability of the shallow draught motor coaster to trade far inland.

From *Gideona* the Dutch motor coaster continued evolving. Some larger ships had their bridges amidships, such as *Reality* (built 1936, 347grt). From 1935 the Koster yard attempted to repeat its earlier success with the 'New Koster' type, which had engines amidships and a shelter deck. The latter feature exploited loopholes in the tonnage regulations which meant that a deck which technically was not totally enclosed did not count towards the tonnage on which harbour and other dues were paid. Shelter-deckers were popular with liner companies, whose cargoes often came in light but bulky bundles, and the General Steam Navigation Co Ltd of London bought two from Koster, *Alouette* (built 1938, 276grt) and *Drake* (built 1938, 531grt). However, the 'New Koster' did not have the success of its predecessor in setting the direction of Dutch coaster design.

By the outbreak of the Second World War, two Dutch designs had emerged which between them set the agenda for coaster construction for the next two decades. A typical example of the more popular type with a long raised quarterdeck was the delightfully named *Mr Linthorst Homan* (built 1939, 400grt) which had engines aft and two hatches served by a single mast amidships. The break in deck height amidships in these ships made them less efficient at carrying a full deck cargo of timber, and Dutch owners and builders increasingly favoured the flush-decked design known to them as the 'gladdekker'. Stowage of a deck cargo was simplified by placing masts at either end of the well deck, an arrangement adopted quite early, as for the Rotterdam-built and owned *Birmingham* (built 1934, 399grt).

These Dutch motor coasters and the

bigger motor vessels from British yards meant that the larger steam coaster was now obsolescent, just as in the 1920s the smaller steamers had been eclipsed by the *Gideona* type. The outbreak of war gave the steam coaster a reprieve, however, at least in Britain. An emergency ship construction programme was begun which concentrated on series production of established types in order to minimise design and construction time. The split between steam and diesel was influenced more by the capacity of the marine engineering industry and by the availability of home-produced coal than by economic considerations. Nevertheless, it is significant that of some 400 coastal cargo ships built, less than a third were steamers, and these were mostly larger coasters and colliers. In postwar years, steam machinery was only considered for coastal vessels when there were overriding considerations, such as the desire to burn locally-mined coal. The diesel engine had conquered the coast.

In postwar years, it seemed that the Dutch were reaping the harvest of their success in exploiting the motor coaster. Their fleet of coasters had suffered heavy losses during hostilities, and they set to work to rebuild it with energy, not to mention financial help from a government which recognised the economic importance of shipping. By 1950 the prewar total of 500 coasters had been passed and by the mid 1950s over 700 were trading. But it is hard to escape the conclusion that design had ossified. Apart from a minor increase in size, slightly more powerful engines and gentle but ineffectual 'stream-

lining' of the bridge and the funnel casing, ships similar to those built in the late 1930s were turned out until 1960 and beyond. One of the reasons for this was that the regulations on such matters as certification of officers and inspection of safety equipment were often less onerous in coasters under 500grt, and Dutch-owned vessels rarely exceeded this size.

But if owners in the Netherlands were losing their lead, their country's influence on coaster building worldwide was undiminished. Dutch designs were widely imitated and, as postwar reconstruction got underway, yards in many European countries turned out their own versions. German owners and builders more than made up for their prewar inertia, and were followed closely by the Swedish and Danish shipping industries. The effect was less marked in British yards, which had a long and honourable tradition of coaster building. In addition, and partly as a result of Dutch competition, the typical British postwar coaster was a larger vessel. *Sandringham Queen* (built 1955, 1308grt), ordered from Goole by one of the tramping companies in the Coast Lines group, had dimensions very similar to the large steam coasters built a quarter of a century earlier.

By the 1950s, owners outside Europe and the US had a wide choice of builders open to them. Motor coasters built in British, Dutch and other European yards could be found trading around Australia, running between New Zealand and the Pacific Islands, serving ports along the coast of South Africa, conveying cargo and passengers in the Red

Sea and the South China Sea, carrying sugar in the Caribbean, coasting around South America and avoiding the ice in the Gulf of St Lawrence. In a few countries, including Australia, Canada and notably Japan, a domestic shipbuilding industry was developing, but in coaster construction European – and particularly Dutch – influence remained strong until the end of the period under review.

Specialised coasters

A specialised coaster is designed for one particular type of cargo, or to run between particular ports. It will carry more and will load and discharge it faster than a ship designed for more general trading. Its drawback is its lack of flexibility: a ship designed to carry coal efficiently may not be able to stow a full load of a less dense cargo such as timber, and will not be able to switch trades so readily if demand for coal falls off.

For this reason, specialised vessels are frequently built for organisations which have some control over the supply of or demand for the product carried. For instance, collieries, coal merchants, electricity or gas undertakings may own just sufficient specialist colliers to handle the amount of coal they produce or need all the year round, and charter general traders when demand peaks during the winter.

Coastal colliers were amongst the most numerous of specialised coasters. Often intended to serve a limited number of berths, they were built to the maximum size these could handle. The very busy coal trade on the east coast of the United Kingdom produced vessels such as *Sir William Walker* (built 1954, 2901grt), completed for the nationalised electricity industry. Discharging equipment at a power station or gas works could unload a ship far faster than its own gear, and so the collier had the bare mini-

Firth Fisher *(1950, 979grt) is clearly a direct descendent of the* Fluor, *built half a century previously.* Firth Fisher *has a diesel engine and improved accommodation and navigational equipment, but retains the long raised quarter-deck layout with bridge amidships. Three derricks serve the holds, and she still has traditional wood and canvas hatch covers. Within a few years, vast changes to shipping would make this type of coaster redundant, nowhere more obviously than in the fleet of her owners James Fisher & Sons Ltd of Barrow, which was to include cellular container vessels, specialist heavy lift ships, and even nuclear fuel carriers. Making way for these new types, the* Firth Fisher *was sold to Greek owners in 1971. (John Clarkson)*

mum of masts, usually just poles to carry navigation lights and radio aerials, plus a light derrick for stores. The postwar ships had mechanical hatch covers which helped reduce the size of crew and speeded turnround. Holds were usually hopper-shaped so that during discharge the remaining coal slid down to where it could be readily picked up by the grabs. In vessels with the square section hold better suited to carrying a variety of cargoes, trimmers would be needed to shovel the coal to and from the sides and corners, adding to costs and slowing discharge.

Sir William Walker represented what was probably the last new design of steamer to be built anywhere. She was oil fired, but her predecessors in the fleet had burned coal. An abundant supply of coal at loading ports was a factor in this choice of machinery, but so strongly was the economic tide flowing against coal that most of these colliers were converted to oil firing before their demise in the 1980s.

An interesting variation of the coastal collier was designed to trade to power stations and gas works far up the River Thames. To carry the maximum amount of cargo, they needed to reach their discharge berths round about high water. This meant they were passing under the large number of fixed bridges when there was least clearance. Vessels such as *Wandle* (built 1909, 889grt) were

therefore built with the lowest possible superstructure, and with masts and funnels hinged so that they could be folded on to the deck when proceeding up and down the river. In consequence, they were colloquially known as 'Flatirons'.

The period 1900 to 1960 saw spectacular growth in the oil and petrochemical industries. Oil largely took the place of coal as a fuel, whilst products derived from it stimulated the expansion of the chemical industry. Liquids can always be conveyed in barrels in dry cargo ships, but it is much more efficient to carry them in tanks built into the hold, and this is the principle behind the oceangoing crude carrier which originated in the late nineteenth century. Coastal tankers were slower to develop, not becoming familiar until after the First World War, when owners began to order steamers such as *Pass of Melfort* (built 1926, 757grt) for charter to oil companies. Again, development was stimulated by military needs, the British Admiralty

building a number of small tankers to supply bunker oil to warships. A few of these 'oilers' later entered commercial service.

Although sharing many features of its ocean-going counterpart, the coastal tanker was intended not to carry crude oil but to distribute products from the refinery to depots or to customers such as power stations. In the oil trade, cargoes included motor spirit, bunker oil, lubricating oil and bitumen for road-making, the last-named requiring tanks with heating coils to ensure this viscous cargo could be pumped out. Small numbers of other specialised tankers were built or converted, for instance to carry wine across the Mediterranean or molasses around the Caribbean. The 1950s saw the first tankers adapted for carrying chemicals, such as acids or caustic soda, which required tanks made of specially coated or treated steel to resist the chemical's corrosive properties. Another type pioneered in this period but which became more familiar in later decades was the liquefied gas tanker, whose holds were fitted with circular tanks to hold propane or butane under pressure.

Whatever its cargo, the coastal tanker had engines and accommodation placed aft, whilst larger examples had a separate bridge

Brunswick Wharf (1951, 1782grt) displays the low profile that gave rise to the nickname 'flatirons' for these up-river colliers. All fittings above the low wheelhouse were hinged to allow passage under the Thames bridges. A squat appearance disguises the fact that she is in reality a sizeable collier, her 270ft being about the maximum length possible to serve Battersea Power Station. After twenty years with the British nationalised electricity undertakings, Brunswick Wharf was sold to Norway to begin a new career as a cement storage hulk. (World Ship Photo Library)

Transiting the Manchester Ship Canal, the Pass of Balmaha *(1942, 784grt) clearly shows the low freeboard typical of a coastal tanker in loaded condition. She was one of a group of twenty-three steamers built during the Second World War to a standard design and known as the* Empire Cadet *type. These were based on an earlier ship built for the Bulk Oil Steamship Co Ltd,* Pass of Balmaha's *owners. She served refineries and distribution depots around the UK until 1967.* (R S Fenton collection)

amidships. Because the low freeboard of a tanker made the deck an unsafe place to walk in a seaway, a raised gangway connected the superstructure forecastle and pump room. The low freeboard also meant the superstructure was much more enclosed than in a dry cargo vessel. A light derrick sufficed for handling stores and hoses, the real cargo gear being the pumps housed deep in the hull in a space between the tanks.

Just as developments in coastal tankers presaged many of the special types which contributed to the shipping revolution of the 1970s and 1980s, and the up-river collier anticipated the low air draught coaster, so examples of other pioneering specialist vessels can be picked out.

Short-sea and coastal reefers were rather a speciality of the Dutch. *Nellie* (built 1937, 500grt) had a standard motor coaster hull which was insulated and painted white, with refrigeration equipment accommodated in a small house on deck. She was an example of a Dutch coaster sold to owners in the southern hemisphere, becoming *Zeehaan* to run

between South Africa and the Congo with frozen meat and fish.

Many short-sea traders were equipped to carry livestock, for instance those bringing Irish cattle to the English market. Adaptations included stalls for the animals in the holds and shell door openings in the ship's sides so that the livestock could be driven on and off.

Some coasters were adapted to load particularly heavy items. An example was *Sea Fisher* (built 1940, 2991grt), an ordinary British collier which had its hatches enlarged to carry the gun turrets of the *King George V* class battleships from the manufacturer to the yards where the warships were fitting out. During the Second World War several British colliers were equipped with heavy-lift derricks to facilitate the unloading of

tanks and heavy military equipment at the Normandy beachhead.

Although the container coaster is generally regarded as a child of the 1970s, hints of things to come were apparent much earlier. In the 1930s, short-sea cargo liners began to carry small containers on deck. In the 1950s a number of owners involved in Irish Sea trades modified coasters to improve their ability to handle unit loads, the most visible change being the removal of cargo gear. Perhaps the oddest example was the elderly steamer *Loch Linnhe* (built 1928, 753grt), which traded between Preston and Belfast with deckloads of containers and road trailers.

The years from 1900 to 1960 were particularly interesting ones in coastal and short-sea shipping. They saw the survival of much technology from the beginning of the steam age, yet witnessed the relatively rapid eclipse of steam reciprocating machinery by the diesel engine. Design innovations also appeared, the widespread application of which were to so change the face of coastal shipping in later decades. These years also saw some of the most attractive powered vessels ever built. For the observer, if not always for the owners and crew, it was indeed a golden age.

Roy Fenton

Tiny derricks indicate that the Ulster Drover *(1930, 891grt) is no conventional cargo steamer, and the open door in her side confirms that she is a specialised livestock carrier. She is seen arriving in the River Mersey, ready to discharge her cargo of Irish cattle to the lairage at Birkenhead. Like other ships owned by Coast Lines companies, she changed names and colours on several occasions when switched between the group's different services. The appropriate name* Ulster Drover *was her last, and she carried it from 1954 until broken up in 1959.* (A Duncan)

From 1864 the Tyne Steam Shipping Company operated passenger cargo ships in the London and Continental trades, many of which had their engines placed aft. Following a merger with the Tees Union Co and Furness Withy's coastal passenger interests in 1903 to form the Tyne-Tees Steam Shipping Co, new designs began to appear such as the 1712grt Stephen Furness, *built by Irvine of West Hartlepool in 1910 to be the flagship of its London service. A triple expansion engine gave her a speed of about 15kts and she could accommodate about 250 first and 120 second class passengers. Taken up as an armed boarding steamer in the First World War, she was sunk by submarine in the Irish Sea in December 1917. (Ambrose Greenway collection)*

Coastal Passenger Vessels

In the days when travel on land involved the use of horse and coach, the only alternative was the coastal sailing vessel. Typical of these were the fast sailing smacks which maintained a regular service down the east coast of the United Kingdom, especially to London, and some of these were owned by the antecedents of companies that were later to become well known in the coastal trade. In time schooners replaced the smacks in order to combat the early steamships but the great efficiency of the latter led to their gradual adoption from the 1820s, one of the pioneers being General Steam Navigation Co (GSN), of London.

By 1900 the UK was served by a considerable network of coastal services carrying both passengers and cargo. The ships maintaining these ranged from relatively large and fast steamers running down the east coast to small vessels serving the western islands of Scotland. The majority of the services linked the large northern port cities with London and some of the best-known on the east

coast were run by Aberdeen Steam Navigation Co, Dundee, Perth & London Shipping Co, Carron Company (Grangemouth), London & Edinburgh Shipping Co (Leith), GSN (Granton), Tyne Steam Shipping Co (later Tyne-Tees) and Thos Wilson Sons & Co (Hull).

On the west coast, Glasgow was a hub for many local services to the islands and to Irish ports, whilst Clyde Shipping Co also provided a link with London. Liverpool was connected to the capital by the ships of F H Powell & Co and Samuel Hough, two concerns which merged with John Bacon Ltd in 1913 to form the nucleus of what was to become Coast Lines, and Dublin and Cork were served by the British & Irish Steam Packet Co with its 'Lady' boats and the City of Cork Steam Packet Co respectively. Not all services traded to London, examples being Wm Sloan & Co which linked Glas-

gow with the Bristol Channel and the self evident Aberdeen, Newcastle & Hull Steamship Co. Messrs Langlands & Sons sailed northabout from Liverpool to Leith and in the summer months ran cruises to the Western Isles in addition to offering a complete round Britain trip once a fortnight. Save for the last example, most of these coastal journeys involved at least one and in many cases two nights at sea and the steamers were fitted with saloon accommodation, first class passengers being carried aft following the normal practice of the day. Cheap fares were also available for deck passengers on some shorter routes, such as Newcastle to London. In general speed was not a consideration in order to time arrivals to suit the tides, 12–14kts being regarded as sufficient, but those serving the Firth of Forth tended to be slightly faster at 15–16kts. Considerable amounts of cargo were carried and the use of hydraulic deck cranes was widespread.

The early years of the century up to the time of the First World War in many ways marked the peak of the British coastal passenger trade with over fifty new ships being placed in service, the largest of which was

Glasgow-based Clyde Shipping Co began running a service to London in 1882, regular calls being made at Belfast, Plymouth, Southampton and Newhaven. Its 1550grt Eddystone, *built by D & W Henderson in 1927, was typical of the later versions of a long line of similar ships that maintained both this and other services around the Irish Sea. Cabin accommodation was generally provided for around 80 passengers prior to the First World War but this was reduced to less than 50 in subsequent ships. (F W Hawks)*

Bergen Line's Midnatsol, *built locally in 1910, was a typical example of the early flush-decked passenger steamers that maintained the Norwegian Coastal Express service. Although most of the route northwards from Bergen lay in sheltered waters, occasional passages had to be made across open water and her elegance belied her ruggedness. She was the first of these steamers to carry her navigating bridge one deck higher than usual, allowing an observation lounge to be installed below it.* (Ambrose Greenway collection)

Carron Company's *Carron* of 1910, a 16kt ship of 2354grt. Others of note were London & Edinburgh's *Royal Scot* (1726grt/17kts) and Tyne-Tees' *Stephen Furness* (1712grt/14kts). Typical of the smaller ships was the diminutive 22-berth *London Queen* (599grt/10½kts) of London & Channel Islands Shipping Co Ltd, which was later joined by two larger ships carrying forty and sixty passengers.

Designwise, the majority of these coastal steamers were of the well-deck type but this was often masked by high-sided bulwarks, giving the impression of a flush hull. Passengers by this time were generally carried amidships, upward of 300 in some of the east coast ships which sailed to London twice a week (three times in the case of Leith) and between forty and sixty in the west coast ships which sailed at least once a week. Great play was made of the tourist potential of these services and many different combinations of voyage were possible, an example being from London up the east coast to Edinburgh, across to Glasgow by train and back to London via the west and south coasts.

Many ships were taken up for war duties and quite a number were lost but the general upheaval caused by the war resulted in the coastal passenger trade never being quite the same again. Faced with stiff competition from

improved rail and road connections and the increase in private vehicle ownership, some companies persevered and built what turned out to be the last generation of traditional coastal passenger steamships. Amongst these were Tyne-Tees' *Bernicia* and *Hadrian* of 1923, London & Edinburgh's *Royal Fusilier* (1924) and *Royal Archer* (1928) and finally Clyde Shipping' *Rathlin* and *Beachy* of 1936. The Depression did not help matters but the final blow really came with the proliferation of the long-distance motor coach and by the time war came again in 1939 the battle was all but over. After the war a few ships continued to carry up to a dozen passengers, Coast Lines' *Caledonian Coast* and *Hibernian Coast*, twin screw, engines-aft motorships of about 1260grt dating from 1947–8, being the last to do so until the mid 1960s.

Outside the UK, one of the best known coastal passenger services is the Hurtigruten or Norwegian Coastal Express Service, which since 1893 has linked Bergen with the main ports and settlements on the west

coast and around the North Cape to Kirkenes, a few miles short of the Russian border. Its steamers, which belonged to several different companies, have literally been the lifeline to many of these places over the years and their daily arrival has nearly always been an eagerly awaited event. At first the ships were flush-deckers of 700–1000grt with engines amidships but they increased in size in the 1920s, culminating in the 1570 ton *Lofoten*. This pattern changed with the next steamer, Bergen Line's *Nordstjernen* ('North Star') built by Fredriksstad Mek Verk in 1937, which had a raised forecastle extending to just below her bridge, an innovation that was to be continued in no less than fourteen subsequent motorships built in Italian, Danish, German and Norwegian shipyards up to 1964. These changed subtly over the years with different masting arrangements and from 1950 the after hold was dropped and all cargo handling concentrated in a forward hold served by deck cranes. Starting with *Finnmarken* in 1956, machinery was moved well aft but the final two ships were given dummy funnels amidships.

Elsewhere in the world, especially where natural features made land communication difficult, the coastal passenger steamer provided the easiest and cheapest alternative. This was especially true in the Adriatic

Following the Second World War the several shipping companies involved in running the Norwegian Coastal Express service agreed to build a new standard type of motorship in order to cut down on costs. Det Stavangerske's Sanct Svithun *was the last of four ships built in Italian shipyards in 1949–50, four broadly similar vessels subsequently being built in Denmark. Propelled at 16kts by a Fiat diesel of 2500bhp, she was lost by stranding in October 1962.* (Ambrose Greenway collection)

The old-established Bombay Steam Navigation Co operated several coastal passenger services southwards from Bombay. From 1920 these had been maintained by four converted 'Town' class minesweepers and a number of older vessels, but these began to be replaced in the 1930s with several new ships built in Britain. Amongst these was Prabhavati, an twin-screw steamer 14kt steamer built in 1933 for the crack Goa mail run. (CMP)

where many ships maintained links along the coasts of Italy and Yugoslavia, the latter island-strewn and mountainous. Both Greece and Turkey made good use of former British channel and coastal steamers for their many local coastal and island services.

Going further east we come to India, a large country which despite an extensive British-built railway system, also needed coastal communication by steamer. For many years this was supplied by the famous British India Steam Navigation Co but a few Indian companies managed to enter the trade, notably Bombay Steam Navigation Co, which ran coastal services to Goa and beyond.

Malaya and the East Indies was another region where the coastal passenger steamer held sway for many years, run in the main by either the Straits Steamship Co, associated with Alfred Holt, or the Netherlands-owned Koninklijke Paketvaart Maats. Straits ran regular passenger services out of Singapore, its premier route being a weekly service to Penang, some 350 miles to the northeast. From early on this was served by unusual looking ships with bridge placed well forward and engines aft but in 1927 *Kedah*, a new 2499grt express turbine steamer built by Vickers Ltd, Barrow-in-Furness, joined the route. In looks she closely resembled some of the earlier UK coastal steamers but with more open promenade decks and fixed awn-

ings. Her speed of 19kts was, however, considerably faster. She had accommodation for 80 first class passengers and could carry 960 'deck' passengers on the 21-hour trip from Singapore to Penang. The only variation to this was at weekends when she would include Belawan, Sumatra, in her itinerary. The Philippines, is another country that has relied heavily on coastal passenger ships. These were usually purchased second-hand but a number of new motorships were commissioned in the 1930s, such as the 1200 ton *Legazpi* built in Hong Kong and the yachtlike *Don Esteban* and *Don Isidro* built in Germany. Both China and mountainous Japan also made much use of coastal passenger steamers.

In Australasia, the United States and South America, distances were so great that coastal passenger steamers were large enough to be treated as passenger liners in their own right. There were however smaller steamers such as those which operated in the northwest USA around Puget Sound and on overnight services on the east coast. At first these were developments of the 'Sound' type paddle steamers which had low narrow hulls sponsoned out to carry several wider passenger decks above them and notable examples were the 3830grt *Yale* and *Harvard*, built in Chester, Pennsylvania, in 1907 to plans prepared by Wm Denny. Amongst the very first turbine steamers to be built in the US, they

were driven at 23kts by triple screws and carried nearly 1000 overnight passengers between Boston and New York, later transferring to the west coast. A new group of larger express steamers with normal hulls designed by Theodore Ferris were introduced in the 1920s, reaching a peak with Clyde Line's 6200grt New York–Miami sisters *Iroquois* and *Shawnee* of 1927 and Eastern Steamship Co's similar sized *Arcadia* and *St John* of 1932. All had very long superstructures and side-loading facilities for the carriage of cars, whilst the former pair pioneered the use of a bulbous forefoot to cut down water resistance. Increasing competition from road and air and the coming of war killed off these coastal services for good.

To the north of the USA, Canada was another country to make great use of the coastal passenger steamer, the best known being the elegant ships belonging to Canadian Pacific Railway. The pattern for many of these was set by the three-funnelled steamer *Princess Victoria*, whose hull and ma-

chinery was completed by C S Swan & Hunter, Newcastle upon Tyne early in 1903. Her wooden superstructure and accommodation were fitted in Vancouver and she entered service between that port and Victoria, Vancouver Island. The following year an overnight round trip to Seattle was included in her schedule, adding up to a rigorous daily steaming total of 325 miles. Measuring 1943grt she could make more than 20kts

from two triple-expansion engines. Over the years Canadian Pacific ships increased to over 5000grt with speeds up to 23kts but from time to time were briefly rivalled by ships of the Grand Trunk Pacific Railroad and later Canadian National Railways, notably the latter's three fine *Prince Henry* class ships built by Cammell Laird & Co in 1931. These measured nearly 7000grt and were capable of 24kts.

The 5875grt Princess Kathleen *was a typical example of Canadian Pacific's large coastal passenger steamers. The first of two ships built by John Brown at Clydebank in 1925 for the triangle route linking Vancouver, Victoria and Seattle, she was originally licensed to carry 1500 passengers (290 in overnight berths) and 30 cars. Four steam turbines geared to twin screws gave a speed of 22kts.* (CMP)

The last of the traditional Canadian Pacific type were the twin-funnelled turbo-electric *Princess Patricia* and *Princess Marguerite* built by Fairfield in 1949 but by then the huge increase in vehicular traffic was demanding a different type of ship and the expensive side-loading *Princess of Nanaimo*, which followed from Fairfield three years later and could carry a mix of 150 cars and 1500 passengers in traditional Canadian Pacific comfort, suffered from being neither one thing nor the other.

The giant Hamburg-Amerika Line built its first turbine steamer Kaiser *for the local Hamburg–Heligoland summer excursion service in 1905. A further turbine ship* Cobra *followed in 1926 but a switch was made to diesel propulsion for the Howaldtswerke-built* Konigin Luise *of 1934, seen here arriving at Cuxhaven. To enhance manoeuvrability, her twin screws were placed immediately in front of two fully balanced rudders and she was capable of carrying 2000 passengers at 17kts. Note the squared off transom stern, a feature that was even more marked in the subsequent Voith-Schneider propelled* Helgoland *of 1939. Both became war losses.* (Ambrose Greenway collection)

Before leaving this subject, a final brief mention should be made of the many coastal excursion steamers. The majority of these were paddle steamers and the best known were probably those on the Clyde, which also gave birth to the world's first commercial turbine steamer, *King Edward*, built by Wm Denny & Bros in 1901. Her performance revolutionised the world of excursion steamers but the superior manoeuvrability of the paddle steamer, which was also better suited to working in shallow water, led to the latter type being retained right up to the Second World War and beyond. One of the companies to do so was General Steam Navigation Co which built the 1500grt paddler *Royal Eagle* for its London–Kent Coast run in 1932 but by then the diesel driven excursion ship was beginning to make its appearance. The New Medway Steam Packet Co's Denny-built *Queen of the Channel* of 1935 introduced a new pattern and the larger 1500 ton *Royal Sovereign* which followed two years later, was given a sponsored hull, much as in the old US 'Sound' steamers, and this feature was retained by GSN, the company's new owners, in their final excursion ships built soon after the Second World War.

Among the last of the traditional coastal excursion type steamers to be built were those for the summer services from Hamburg, Bremerhaven and Wilhelmshaven to Heligoland, the so-called 'seebäderschiffe'. Turbine ships had begun to replace the early paddlers on these routes in 1905 with the delivery of *Kaiser* but diesel propulsion took over in the 1930s, an example being the 2400grt *Konigin Luise*, which was fitted with a flat transom stern of the type so popular today. The 4438grt, 21kt *Wappen von Hamburg* built in 1965 was the last and largest ship of this type.

Ambrose Greenway

Typical Coastal and Short-Sea Cargo Vessels 1900–1960

Ship	Flag	Built	By	GRT	Length × breadth × draught Feet–inches Metres	Engines	Remarks
ADMIRAL	UK	1906	W Walker, Maryport	263	12.2 × 22.1 × 9.51 36.9 × 6.7 × 2.9	2-cylinder compound steam engine (45rhp) by J Ritchie	Single-hatch steam coaster designed for use in the stone and coal trades around the Irish Sea
DRUID	UK	1906	J & J Hay, Kirkintilloch	68	66.5 × 17.9 × 8.6 20.25 × 5.45 × 2.6	2-cylinder compound steam engine (17hp)	Clyde puffer built to navigate the Forth and Clyde Canal but also suitable for trading on the west coast of Scotland
WANDLE (collier)	UK	1909	Wm Dobson & Co, Newcastle	889	205.2 × 32.1 × 14.4 62.55 × 9.8 × 4.4	Triple-expansion steam engine (155nhp) by J P Rennoldson	Low air draught collier for working under Thames bridges to the gasworks at Wandsworth
INNISHOWEN	UK	1913	P McGregor & Sons, Kirkintilloch	183	74.7 × 18.3 × 8.7 22.8 × 5.6 × 2.65	2-cylinder Kromhout oil engine by D Goedkoop	Pioneer British motor coaster based on design of Clyde puffer
SUFFOLK COAST	UK	1917	W Harkess & Son, Middlesbrough	870	198.0 × 30.7 × 12.5 60.35 × 9.4 × 3.8	Triple-expansion steam engine (97rhp) by McColl & Pollock	Long raised quarterdeck steamer built for owner's regular cargo services around the British Isles
BRUSE JARL	Nor	1923	Trondhjems MV, Trondheim	1890	265.8 × 42.2 × 17.9 81.0 × 12.9 × 5.45	Triple-expansion steam engine (118nhp) by builders	Engines-amidships steamer for the Baltic coal, coke and timber trades
GIDEONA	Ne	1924	J Koster Hzn, Groningen	139	98.4 × 17.7 × 7.0 30.0 × 5.4 × 2.1	2-cylinder oil engine by Mfbk de Industrie	Early Dutch motor coaster whose design did much to establish the success of these vessels
WILLIAM McARTHUR	Aus	1924	J Lewis & Sons, Aberdeen	2393	284.0 × 40.61 × 19.1 86.6 × 12.4 × 5.8	Triple-expansion steam engine (270nhp) by builders	Scottish-built steamer for the Australian coastal coal trade

Ship	Flag	Built	By	GRT	Length × breadth × draught Feet–inches Metres	Engines	Remarks
PASS OF MELFORT (tanker)	UK	1926	Blythswood SB Co, Glasgow	757	181.8 × 29.7 × 13.5 55.4 × 9.05 × 4.1	Triple-expansion steam engine (125nhp) by J G Kincaid & Co	An early purpose-built coastal tank steamer
ALOUETTE	UK	1938	J Koster Hzn, Groningen	276	157.7 × 25.8 × 6.9 48.1 × 7.9 × 2.1	6-cylinder oil engine (71nhp) by Humboldt-Deutzmotoren	Small engines-amidships motorship with shelter deck for near-Continental liner trades
MR LINTHORST HOMAN	Ne	1939	van der Werff's Scheepsw, Westerbroek	400	156.0 × 26.4 × 8.6 47.55 × 8.0 × 2.6	6-cylinder oil engine by Motorenwerke Mannheim	Dutch coaster of the raised quarterdeck design which was built in large numbers for over 20 years
SIR WILLIAM WALKER (collier)	UK	1954	Austin & Pickersgill, Sunderland	2901	340.2 × 44.6 × 18.0 103.7 × 13,6 × 5.5	Triple-expansion steam engine (1475ihp) by North Eastern Marine Engineering Co (1939) Ltd	Large oil-fired steamer to carry coal to power stations mainly on the south coast of the UK
SANDRINGHAM QUEEN	UK	1955	Goole SB & R Co, Goole	1308	232.8 × 36.0 × 15.3 71.0 × 11.0 × 4.7	7-cylinder oil engine (1120bhp) by British Polar Engines	Typical British postwar motorship for the coastal bulk cargo trades

Typical Coastal Passenger Vessels 1900–1960

Name	Flag	Built	By	GRT DWT	Length(oa) (r) = registered) × breadth × depth × draught Feet-inches Metres	Engines	Speed	Route	Remarks
Coastal passenger vessels									
SHEERNESS	UK	1903	Caledon SB & Eng Co, Dundee	1274	250-0(r) × 35-2 × 16-7 × 17-4 76.20 × 10.73 × 5.06 × 5.27	1 3-cylinder triple-expansion steam by builders, 293ihp	12kts	Glasgow–London	Passengers: 90 1st class
PRINCESS VICTORIA	Can	1903	C & S Swan & Hunter, Newcastle upon Tyne	1943	300-0(r) × 40-6 × 15-5 × — 91.44 × 12.34 × 4.69 × —	2 triple-expansion steam by Hawthorn Leslie, 434nhp	20kts	Vancouver–Victoria–Seattle	
ROYAL SCOT	UK	1910	Caledon SB & Eng Co, Dundee	1726	290-2(r) × 38-2 × 18-1 × 17-6 88.45 × 11.64 × 5.52 × 5.33	3-cylinder triple-expansion steam by builders	17kts	Leith (Edinburgh)–London	Passengers: 100 1st class, 120 2nd
BERNICIA	UK	1923	Hawthorn Leslie, Hebburn	1839	282-4(r) × 40-0 × 17-6 × — 86.04 × 12.19 × 5.33 × —	3-cylinder triple-expansion steam by builders	15kts	Newcastle–London	Passengers: 136 1st class, 100 2nd
KEDAH	UK	1927	Vickers Ltd, Barrow-in-Furness	2499 1170	330-0 × 50-4 × 17-8 × 14-8 100.58 × 15.31 × 5.38 × 4.47	2 sets oil-fired SR geared turbines by builders, 5800shp; 2 shafts	19kts	Singapore–Penang–Belawan	Passengers: 80 1st class, 960 deck
LOCHEARN	UK	1930	Ardrossan Dockyard, Ardrossan	542	155-8 × 29-1 × 9-4 × — 47.46 × 8.87 × 2.83 × —	2 12-cylinder Gardner oil engines, 500bhp	10kts	West coast of Scotland	MacBrayne's first motorship
RAGNVALD JARL	Nor	1956	Blohm & Voss, Hamburg	2196 652	266-7 × 41-6 × 21-5 × 14-10 81.26 × 12.62 × 6.52 × 4.51	MAN 10-cylinder 4SA oil engine, 2960bhp	15kts	Bergen–Kirkenes	Engines aft, C-p propeller. Passengers: 63 1st class, 242 2nd
Excursion vessels									
KING EDWARD	UK	1901	Wm Denny & Bros, Dumbarton	502	250-6 × 30-1 × 10-6 × 7-0 76.35 × 9.17 × 3.20 × 2.13	3 Parsons direct drive steam turbines, 399nhp; 3 shafts	20kts	Clyde estuary	First turbine merchant ship; 2 screws on outer shafts
ROYAL SOVEREIGN	UK	1937	Wm Denny & Bros, Dumbarton	1627 228	277-3 × 47-0 × 11-9 × 8-7 84.52 × 14.32 × 3.58 × 2.62	2 12-cylinder 2SA Sulzer oil engines, 840nhp; 2 shafts	19kts	Thames estuary and near continent (summer only)	Sponsored hull; passengers: 1600

5

The World's Fishing Fleets

FISHING and whaling vessels are merchant ships which go to sea with empty holds and rely on the sea to fill them. They hunt to earn. By 1900 the steam trawler, the whale catcher, the steam drifter and the steam long-liner were all established, but not to the extinction of sail. Although by 1903 there were no smacks left at Hull, 34 remained at Grimsby, 356 at Lowestoft, 138 at Ramsgate and 193 at Brixham. They survived at Lowestoft and Brixham up to the Second World War, some being built in the 1920s including the well-known *Master Hand* of 1920. Sailing drifters, a widespread breed, lasted just as long, the last Scottish zulu under sail fishing until 1939, although not broken up until 1947. Worldwide fishing in 1900 was still dominated by sail, notably on the Grand Banks off Newfoundland where Gloucester schooners and St Malo barquentines were mothers to fleets of dories, as is still the case except that both mother ships and dories are now all powered vessels.

in the smacks to keep the catch alive date from the seventeenth century, while salt still remains the preservative on the Grand Banks and fish are dried in the open air in Newfoundland and Norway. Ice was introduced to British fishing in the 1840s, at first from local ponds, then from the 1870s brought from Scandinavia, finally being made at the fishing ports from the 1890s. Hull, for instance, could produce 50 tons a day, starting from 1891.

Apart from keeping the fish edible there was the economic incentive to spend as much time as possible catching. A smack working by herself took days on passage to and from the fishing grounds but by the 1840s there was a solution to this in the North Sea, the 'fleeting' or boxing fleet system, whereby the trawlers stayed at sea but transferred their

catch in boxes packed with ice to carriers which took it to Billingsgate in London, or to Hull or Grimsby when the railways came. Steam fish carriers were introduced in 1865 and were fitted with trawling gear, as fishing vessels were exempt from London port dues. The use of carriers allowed the sailing smacks to remain at sea for six to eight weeks for they could be provisioned by the carriers. When steam trawlers came they could stay out longer, up to twelve weeks, only needing to return for coal and refits. Ice, mail, provisions and water, were brought out by the carriers.

Ice gave smacks working alone the chance to go further afield, under sail to the Shetlands and Norway, under steam, as they grew in size and power, to the Faroes, Iceland, Spitsbergen and the White Sea, the

The development of large fishing vessels

Wherever it takes place fishing is dominated by one overriding problem, the need to keep the catch edible. In the days before fast internal transport, fish were locally caught and locally eaten, although there were devices to widen the market. The use of wells

At the turn of the century much fishing was carried out by sail-powered vessels, and this carried on for some decades. Among those still fishing under sail between the wars was the Brixham fleet of ketch rigged trawlers, some of which are seen here in August 1931. In the foreground is the well known Valerian, *built at Brixham in 1923; she measured 78ft 10in overall by 18ft 7in beam, for a registered tonnage of 39 tons.* (CMP)

A typical Hull steam trawler from the early part of the twentieth century was Caesar *(311grt), owned by Hellyer's Steam Fishing Co Ltd. Built by Earle's Co, Hull, and completed in March 1906, she was fitted with a triple-expansion steam engine made by Amos & Smith. She was employed as a fish carrier and was notable as the first fishing vessel to have wireless equipment installed, this being supplied by the Marconi Marine Co in June 1913. Another Hellyer trawler,* Othello, *had similar equipment installed shortly afterwards.* (Laurence Dunn collection)

reliability of steam allowing trawlers to return with fish in saleable condition. Near water fishing referred to the North Sea, the Irish Sea, the English Channel; middle water to the Bay of Biscay, the Faroes, the Norwegian coast; distant water to Iceland, Spitsbergen, Bear Island, the White Sea and even Greenland. By the late 1880s Hull steam trawlers were off the Faroes, by 1891 off Iceland and by 1905 in the White Sea.

In 1900 the steam trawler with the otter trawl was of established design, fishing from the side as was the way under sail, turning across the wind to shoot and haul the 36ft (11m) wide beam trawl over the side bulwarks, the only way such an unwieldy piece of timber could be handled and the best method of bringing the heavy trawl doors alongside. In shape the side fishing screw trawler, the sidewinder, followed the sailing smack, although initial experiments took a different turn. Paddle tugs had been used to tow smacks to sea and it occurred to the tug owner William Purdy of North Shields, to try trawling from his tug *Messenger*. This November 1877 experiment proved successful, not only on Tyneside but later at Scarborough and in the 1880s at Cardiff. However paddles were vulnerable in heavy weather and got in the way of handling a trawl. The screw however could fit neatly into a hull built on smack lines and the first steam trawlers were smacks, complete with a full set of sails. Steam had come to power smack capstans in the late 1870s and orders for the first screw trawlers soon followed, starting with the iron *Zodiac*, built for Grimsby owners in 1881 by Earle's of Hull. In 1882 the iron *Aries* appeared (95.4ft long, 20.3ft breadth) with a compound engine which gave a speed of just under 10kts. These early

steam trawlers doubled as fish carriers, already well established under steam. Another pioneer, preserved in model form at the Science Museum, London, was the wooden Leith-built *Hawk*, 87.2ft long, schooner rigged with a beam trawl. There had been an earlier attempt at trawling under steam with the iron *Corkscrew* of 1844, a pioneer of the screw propeller and believed to have been tried as a fishing vessel in 1858. But she proved unprofitable and was soon sold.

As steam enabled trawlers to go further afield greater attention had to be paid to their seaworthiness. The open foredeck of the earlier flush decked trawlers, following smack design, was replaced by a raised fo'c'sle and turtle- or whaleback to keep the seas off the fish pounds where the men were working. At the same time the fine bows were replaced by stems with more flare to ride up and over approaching waves. In 1906 the Hull trawler *Macduff* was built with a flush deck, contrasting with *Myton* of the same year complete with a whaleback fo'c'sle. A good sheer forward became standard with a low freeboard but a deep draught aft to accommodate a large diameter but slowly revolving propeller which would never lift clear of the water. Counter sterns were standard but during the 1920s the cruiser stern was introduced, spoon shaped to give a better flow of water past the rudder. Early trawlers were noticeably narrow beamed to gain speed from not so powerful engines.

Narrow gutted too were the steam longliners built for Grimsby owners. They had the same hull form and deck layout as the trawler but were without the gallows fore and aft which distinguished the sidewinder using the otter trawl. Early gallows were level topped with splayed legs but during

the 1900s the standard and stronger inverted 'U' was generally adopted. Their need arose because, whereas the beam trawl was towed by a single warp, the otter boards needed a warp each, one forward and one aft, running through sheaves and blocks from the winch. The gallows were designed to pass the warps outboard and take the strain of the tow; they had of necessity to be strong.

The warps dictated the deck layout of the trawler demanding an amidships position for the all important winch, mid-way between the fore and aft gallows with the engine and boiler casing behind it. Deck space to handle the catch could only be forward, hampered by the warps but necessarily here because the fish room could only be forward too, ahead of the machinery space. It is difficult to think of a more exposed place to gut fish in the Arctic winter but there was no alternative. Once established the design remained for some sixty years, altering only in size and shaping, along with navigational refinements, better accommodation and changing from coal to oil firing steam to diesel and diesel electric. Small hatches led to the cork insulated fishroom where the catch was laid in rows between crushed ice.

Command was centred on the wheelhouse which was roofed and glazed, in most cases by 1900, for distant water craft, although the small boxing fleet trawlers made do with an open bridge. Some of these had this placed abaft the funnel which gave the skipper a good view of the gear but poor visibility ahead as the 'Woodbine' smokestack got in the way. A few bridge aft trawlers remained into the 1940s but placing the bridge forward of the funnel was pretty well standard for new ships after 1914.

Steam trawlers still clung to sails during the early years of this century using both fore and main trysails and headsails before 1914, but by the 1930s these had reduced to a main trysail only to steady the ship when shooting and hauling across the wind whilst drifting to leeward, thus allowing the net to

An example of the residual canvas still carried by steam trawlers can be seen in the main trysail of the Fleetwood-registered Dorothy Lambert; however, she also has a furled headsail forward. Built in 1923 as the Oyama, the ship was one of a Smith's Dock type that was popular just after the First World War. (CMP)

stream away from the ship with no risk of fouling the propeller.

Mechanical aids to work the gear were few in the early days. Shooting and hauling of the trawl were dependent on manpower helped only by the foremast gilson, a lightish tackle for heaving the gear overside and inboard, while the the heavier foremast fish tackle lifted the cod end inboard, weighing several tons in the case of a good haul. Later refinements included the foremast derrick, used for heaving the cod end overside and for unloading at the fish dock, the gill guy amidships for heaving the belly of the net inboard and the after gilson worked in conjunction with the foremast gilson.

Crew's quarters in the early trawlers were in the fo'c'sle with the galley aft above the cabins of the skipper, mate and engineers. Washing and toilet facilities were either basic or non existant, as in the smacks. Most spartan of all were the 110ft long trawlers of the boxing fleets which had changed over to steam as early as 1882 when the Great Northern Steam Fishing Co of Hull built *Onward* and *Vigilant*. Transferring the ice packed fish boxes to the carrier was an every morning hazard undertaken by 17ft open boats working to a rotational system whereby the boarding trawlers steamed to windward of the carrier, dropping off their fish laden boats which returned piled high with empty fish boxes as their parent ships worked down to

leeward. The two man boarding boat was a stout craft fitted with buoyancy tanks and an oil tank for calming the sea. A lifeline was secured along the keel, as capsizes and swampings were commonplace with many drowned during each May to September season.

Whereas boxing fleet trawler design remained static, the distant-water ships improved. Use of the space under the whaleback forward as a net store gave the crew added shelter but by the 1950s their accommodation had been moved aft, handier to the galley and messroom. Sizes grew steadily from 109ft in *Macduff* of 1906 to 131ft in *Nodzu* of 1929, 156ft in the *Scalby Wyke* of 1935 and, in the latter days of the sidewinder, up to 178ft in the case of *Boston Seafire* built at Beverley in 1948. Middle water trawlers exemplified by the 'Castle' class built from 1917 stayed at around 125ft (38m). There

has been no handsomer ship than the latter day side fishing trawler, with its pronounced forward sheer, sweeping flare of the stem, low run aft to a modified cruiser stern, curved wheelhouse front with its many windows (intentionally small to minimise the risk of breakage), powerful tapered funnel, and raked masts, latterly only a single foremast in some ships. They were the products of specialist yards at Aberdeen, Beverley, Selby, Middlesbrough. One final improvement was the limiting of the fishing gear to the starboard side only. Starboard side fishing balanced the torque of the propeller and for long had been the usual practice, with the port side for emergency use only. With the port fittings taken out there was more accommodation and storage space.

New navigational and fish finding aids were rapidly accepted; radio direction finding from the 1920s then radar and Decca; the echo sounder soon after the First World War which led on to asdic and sonar. Radio itself came just before the First World War, distinguished in the early days by abnormally high masts like those fitted to the Hellyers of Hull trawler *Othello* of 1907 and fish carrier *Caesar* of 1906. One permanent feature has been the pole mounted compass forward of the wheelhouse, so placed to clear magnetic interference. As a standby it has lasted into the age of the stern trawler.

In the engine room triple-expansion

Delivered in May 1937 by Cochrane & Sons, Selby, was the steam trawler Fighter, *built for Earl Steam Fishing Co Ltd, Grimsby. She was a relatively large distant-water ship, with an overall length of 188.4ft (57.4m) and was powered by a triple-expansion steam engine made by Amos & Smith. (Laurence Dunn collection)*

For many types of smaller fishing vessel design continued
to be based on the practices of the days of sail, but the
advent of the economical and compact oil engine made the
addition of mechanical power relatively simple. These
Swedish fishing ketches, photographed about 1930,
represent the transitional phase. They have engines and
wheelhouses, but retain a substantial rig on a hull derived
from their sailing predecessors – note the counter stern of
the inboard vessel. (CMP)

machinery followed compound in the 1890s
and a low pressure turbine was added in
some ships from the mid 1930s. Steam was
raised in coal-fired Scotch boilers, although
oil-firing was fitted in a Cardiff trawler in
1939. Nevertheless coal burners continued
to be built, the last, *Cayton Bay*, in 1949. One
of the last steam trawlers at Hull was *Arctic
Ranger* built in 1957 for Boyd Line and there
were two Grimsby steam trawlers built in
1958. The oil engine pioneered in trawlers
by the Japanese in the 1920s had obvious
advantages, especially for smaller vessels, but
British distant water owners were slow to
adopt it. An early example was the Grimsby-
owned *British Guiana* of 1936 for the North
Sea while *Princess Elizabeth* of 1952 was the
first in Hull. A further refinement was
diesel-electric propulsion, locally led by Hellyer's *Portia* of 1956, which gave more flexible control of speed and direction.

Among smaller fishing craft worldwide,
the oil engine took over directly from sail. It
was not difficult to find space to fit a motor,
nor was it too expensive. The Swedish
Bolinder and the Glasgow-made Kelvin were
aimed at the smaller fishing vessel and were
widely adopted before 1914 but larger boats

The French ocean-going Marcella, *built in 1933 by
Chantiers & Ateliers de St Nazaire (Penhoët) SA, Grand
Quevilly, was a pioneer diesel-engined trawler. She has a
cruiser stern, and low profile with funnel placed well aft.
She was 1152grt, and equipped with a St Nazaire
6-cylinder engine; her dimensions were 218.6ft
(66.6m) registered length, 34.5ft (10.5m) breadth and
16.6ft (5.06m) depth.* (Laurence Dunn collection)

waited until the 1920s with Japanese and
Continental owners leading the way. They
took the British distant water trawler as their
model but improved on it, notably in size. A
late example was the German *Carl Kampf I* of
1940, 180ft (54.9m) long, a steamer with a
sharply raked Maierform stem and a long
bridge structure. Her fish hold could also be
used for extra bunkers. A contemporary Italian trawler measured 170ft and was diesel
powered with refrigerating plant aboard. In
fact her eight cylinder engine took up almost
as much space as a steam engine and boiler
but the bunker space was less. The French
built very large trawlers for the Grand Banks,
salting their catch like the line fishermen.
With 700 tons of salt aboard they made six
month round trips to Newfoundland. Between 1905 and 1925 French trawlers doubled in tonnage and their length increased to
over 200ft; the steam *Islande* of 1926 was
210ft long and the diesel powered *Victoria* of

1927, 197ft (60m). However, she stuck to
steam for her winch and auxiliaries, although
the French introduced an electric trawl
winch in 1929. French trawlers of the 1950s
went over to starboard side fishing and contrived an undercover foredeck for gutting
and sorting.

Equally large were the Spanish and Portuguese trawlers on the Grand Banks, up to
250ft (76m) long, but the Spanish were better
known for their small pair trawlers, only 80ft
(24m) long, such as the steam *Libana* and
Berdin Cabea built at Aberdeen in 1931, as
was the diesel *Ala-Izan* of 1936. Nova Scotian
and US Eastern Seaboard trawlers remained
at 135ft (41m). Their appearance tended to
be more streamlined with the trawl winch
concealed in the superstructure. This was
possible because the winches were electric in
a diesel powered ship. The Japanese embarked on an ambitious distant water fishing
fleet during the 1930s. They learned trawling
from the Cardiff trawler firm Neale & West
during the 1900s and from 1929 started to
build 1056bhp motor trawlers such as the
203ft (61.9m) long *Suruga Maru*, regarded as
an experimental vessel with generous accommodation aft for a large crew.

Refrigeration

An Arctic fishing trip from a British port
took three weeks with fishing starting five or
six days after setting out. This meant the

Christian Salvesen's experimental trawler/factory ship
Fairfree, *outwardly an obvious warship conversion, but incorporating a number of innovations, including freezing equipment. The ship also used a variable depth trawl and was fitted with a prototype stern ramp – its gantry and control room is visible aft in this photo. The ship experienced many problems but the company was sufficiently encouraged to design a series of purpose-built follow-ups.* (CMP)

first fish caught were over two weeks old when they reached the market, at the limit or beyond saleable condition despite the layers of ice. If at least the early catch could be frozen, the trawler could fish longer and take more. There had been fish freezing experiments since the nineteenth century and freezing at sea since the 1920s, largely the work of the French using brine freezers, in one case in a mother ship which could freeze 12 tons of fish a day. British experiments followed in the trawler *Ben Meidie* in 1926–27 and Hellyer of Hull tried mother ships to process line caught halibut but the real impetus to market frozen fish to the public came at the end of the Second World War when austerity reigned and alternative foods were in demand.

The initiative came from the whaling firm Christian Salvesen of Leith in association with the inventive Sir Dennistoun Burney of airship fame. He had been experimenting

with a variable depth trawl using an ex-*Algerine* class minesweeper, *Felicity*, which was renamed *Fairfree* and fitted with freezing equipment. The use of a stern slip in whale factory ships suggested a similiar application in a trawler with the trawl hauled up the slip and the bag emptied on the stern deck. Stern trawling was not new; there had been small American stern draggers, and tuna clippers and small trawlers out of Haifa had tried it, but none had used a slipway. *Fairfree* was given one but this was not very successful, yet Salvesen pressed on to build a trawler and fish factory ship, which in the whaling industry was a role played by two types of vessel although there had been attempts at catcher factories, though one of these was limited to walrus hunting. Use of a slip was vital for the success of the factory, as whaling

methods were to be followed with fillets rather than oil as the end product. Rudolf Baader of Lübeck had by the early 1950s put a fish filleting machine on the market, the first of a series which was to be much improved. Multi-plate freezing equipment to handle fillets in quantity had been pioneered in the 1920s by frozen foods innovator Clarence Birdseye and the US Bureau of Fisheries so it was now feasible to produce a workable fish factory. She had to be big to be economic and the result was the diesel *Fairtry* launched in 1954 by John Lewis of Aberdeen; 2605grt, 280ft (85.3m) length overall with a proposed crew of eighty compared with the twenty of the 145ft (44.2m) overall 700grt sidewinder. Three ideas came together in *Fairtry*, a factory catcher, trawling from the stern via a slipway, and using a big ship to achieve a profitable catch. She was successful on the Grand Banks, well out of range of the British side fishing trawler and two more *Fairtry*s followed, *Fairtry II* in 1959 and *Fairtry III* in 1960. All three produced frozen fillets at sea.

However the British fishing industry did not respond, although much interest was shown by the USSR, Germany and Japan. Having obtained the plans from Lewis's the Russians produced copies in their twenty-four unit *Pushkin* class of 1954–57, the first generation of a vast fleet, followed in 1958 by the East German-built *Mayakovsky* class

The stern trawler factory ship Fairtry II *was completed in April 1959 for Christian Salvesen Ltd of Leith. The building of* Fairtry II *and* III *came about following the successful operation of the pioneer fish factory* Fairtry I *which had been fitted with freezing and processing plant which was associated with the rapidly increasing importance of the frozen fish market which had been emerging since the early 1950s.* Fairtry II *was built by W Simons & Co, Renfrew, and was of 2857grt, and her three insulated holds had a capacity of 46,554cu ft. She was equipped with three Ruston & Hornsby 6-cylinder diesel engines of 4230bhp connected to electric motors giving 2000shp.* (Laurence Dunn collection)

Following the success of the Christian Salvesen factory trawler Fairtry I *in 1954, the Soviet Union adopted the concept for its own needs and embarked on a building programme which was to result in the world's largest fleet of stern trawling fish factory vessels, built mainly in the Soviet Union, Poland and East Germany. The lead ship of the* Tropik *class,* Tropik, *was delivered by Volkswerft Stralsund, East Germany, in 1960, was of 2435grt, and fitted with two 8-cylinder diesels of 1650bhp, and had a speed of 12kts. By the end of 1966 no less than ninety of this class had entered service, and another class of vessel which commenced building in the Soviet Union in 1957 was even more numerous.* Tropik *is shown here with a fleet of nearly a hundred Eastern Bloc trawlers in the English Channel in November 1962.* (CMP)

and many more. In 1957 West Germany built *Heinrich Meins*, a whole-fish freezer – not a factory but with plant that froze the complete fish after gutting. Initially she had Voith-Schneider propellers but these were removed because of their complexity. Another German pioneer, *Sagitta* of 1958 was propelled by gas turbines. Japan also copied *Fairtry* with *Umitaka Maru* of 1956, likewise a factory, and other nations followed; Poland, East Germany, Romania, Spain, Portugal, France with factory trawlers; the Netherlands, Belgium, Iceland and Denmark with freezers. With their established side-fishing fleet Britain did not follow suit until 1961 with the West German-built *Lord Nelson* which could freeze the early part of her catch. However *Junella* of 1962 could freeze the whole catch, this being the result of experiments with the sidewinder *Marbella* in 1958. These earlier stern trawlers had their funnels and engine room casings amidships, which limited deck area, but the twin exhaust uptake arrangement soon followed. Some feared the catch would become too heavy to haul up the stern slip or that the net would burst, as it was not feasible to bring in the cod end in stages as on a sidewinder. On the other hand the stern trawler could fish in heavier weather and indeed keep moving

head to wind as the net was shot and hauled. Above all the crew could work under deck.

Other types

Turning to other types of fishing vessels, herring drifters followed a more modest course of development with a wide variety of sailing craft in use well into the twentieth century. Lying head to wind with two miles of nets before them demanded beamy stable hulls, deep draughted aft to grip the water. British sailing drifters varied from the Scottish scaffies, fifies and zulus, to Manx nickies and nobbies, all lug-rigged, to the gaff-rigged

ketches of Great Yarmouth and Lowestoft and the luggers of Penzance. Steam came at about the turn of the century, with *Lowestoft* an early example, built in 1900 and rigged as a ketch with the engine in an almost auxiliary role. Early steam drifters were mostly underpowered but by 1914 the wooden hulled, flush-decked 75ft (23m) vessel was established. This had a graceful forward sheer with vertical stem, a generous beam and deep draught aft to make sure the propeller was always immersed. Tug-shaped counter sterns were favoured because they were less liable to collision damage and wood construction continued into the 1930s parallel with steel, with lengths increasing to just over one hundred feet. For a full description of a wooden steam drifter Ted Frost's *Tree to Sea* (Terence Dalton, Lavenham 1985), an account of the building of *Formidable* by Chambers of Lowestoft in 1917, cannot be beaten, while the steel *Lydia Eva* of 1930 has been preserved. Many drifters could double

At one time a common sight around the coasts of the North Sea, a fleet of steam drifters from the port of Buckie. The fleet is returning to port, deploying the fenders that allowed them to moor up alongside one another without hull damage. (CMP)

as trawlers which allowed them to work all the year round and not just limited to the autumn and winter herring seasons. A typical Dutch drifter trawler of the 1950s, diesel powered and steel hulled, measured around 90ft (27m) in length. Forward sheer was reduced to cut down on windage when riding to her nets. A bow rudder took over the steering as the drifter dropped astern whilst shooting her nets and the vessel was designed to carry home her salted catch in barrels, which meant gutting on the foredeck.

More certain of success among pelagic or surface fish such as the herring, as well as demersal or bottom feeding fish, is the purse seine net which is employed world-wide and because of the variety of catch it is worked from a variety of craft. While the Danish seine (snurrevaad), a type of trawl, was shot and hauled in an encircling sweep by a small wooden motor vessel of 60ft (18m), purse seiners on the Pacific coast of North America were in the 1940s being built up to 85ft (26m), while one, *Falcon*, had a 900hp engine and a 600 ton refrigerated fish hold capacity. These boats were built up forward with a streamlined superstructure similar to the rod and line tuna clipper, the idea being to have plenty of space aft to handle the seine. The menhaden fishing on the east coast of the United States used the two boat purse seining system, introduced in the late nineteenth century, with two purse boats carried in davits aboard a mother 'steamer'. They loaded their catch aboard the

'steamer' which grew after 1945 into a 600-ton capacity ship employing two 36ft (11m) purse boats, built of aluminium and since 1953 fitted with the Puretic power block which reduced the purse boat crew from twelve to six. To empty the seine, US vessels installed centrifugal pumps to fill the midships fish hold. This put the pilot house and accommodation forward and the engines aft. The two boat system spread as early as 1900 to the Icelandic and Norwegian herring fishing employing smaller purse boats modelled on whalers and carried aft in davits aboard their parent.

Single boat purse seining needs a skiff to set the net but all the hauling is done by the ship, aided latterly by the power block which replaced the seine table and was mounted on a boom. Net drums have also been used in the British Columbia and Puget Sound salmon fisheries. Deck layout became similar in Alaskan and Canadian boats whether they were fishing for salmon, herring, sardines, anchovy, mackerel or tuna, namely a transom stern and wide aft deck with both the engine and superstructure forward. Length limits of 50ft (15m) for Alaskan craft caused them to be built as wide as 17ft with 16–18ft skiffs fitted with motors up to 165hp. By 1960 there were large tuna seiners working off the Californian coast, such as the 136ft long, 350 ton capacity *Santa Helena*, with a twelve man crew and a crow's nest for tuna spotting.

Before mechanical handling, purse seiners in the Portuguese sardine fishing shared with

The Italian ocean-going motor trawler Genepesca-I *was built in 1949 by Cantieri Riuniti dell'Adriatico, Trieste, for Compania Generale Italiana Della Grande Pesca. Of 1650grt, she was fitted with two 6-cylinder diesel engines of 1200bhp, and was capable of about 11kts. Clearly seen here is the tripod foremast with backswept arms for hoisting the catch. Also notable are the long forecastle, and short poop which extends to a large bridge structure.* (Laurence Dunn collection)

France and Spain employed twenty-five to forty men to haul. Because shoals were small large nets were needed to gather as much as possible, in contrast to South Africa where 60ft (18m) purse seiners used the smaller lampara type of net, with the fish bag in the middle to work the dense shoals of pilchard and mackerel. Large crews of thirty or more were also the rule among the Japanese one boat seiners; wood or steel with fish hold forward, accommodation aft and engine room, deckhouse and bridge amidships, the purse winch forward of the deckhouse and the nets stowed in the stern. Their two boat seiners were smaller versions of these but the single boat seiner was the mother ship to a small flotilla, light boats to attract the fish, fish finding boats and fish carriers. Fish hold capacity was now up to 85 tons.

Line fishing vessels were equally diverse. While British steam long liners resembled trawlers much line fishing was done from small craft, notably the Grand Banks dories, attached to a mother ship, for long under sail, such as the schooners of Nova Scotia and the US Eastern Seaboard, the barquentines of St Malo and the varied rigs of the Portuguese. Powered vessels took over, either auxiliary or full power; a notable auxiliary was the Portuguese four-masted gaff rigged schooner *Argus*, steel built in 1939 in Holland, 209ft long overall with a 600 ton capacity for salted cod. She had a 400bhp Sulzer diesel and refrigerating plant for the bait. A larger sailing ship on the Banks was the 1920 built French four-masted steel barquentine *Zazpiakbat*, likewise an auxiliary. She could freeze her catch, which saved carrying salt, and her dories went after halibut as well as cod. Portugal built auxiliary ships during the Second World War such as *Maria Frederico* in 1944 along with full motor ships like *Santa Maria Madalena* of 1939, which looked like a trawler but was home to forty to fifty dories nested on the upper deck. At 202.8ft (61.8m) long and 1043grt, she needed a crew of seventy to man her fleet. Japanese line fishing mother ships went up to a thousand gross tons and carried their one or more catching boats on deck or towed astern. Smaller vessels worked as catchers themselves, either with drift lines or pole and line combination boats.

Pole and line fishing was shared between the Americans and their Pacific coast tuna clippers, the British Columbia salmon trollers, the tunnymen of the Bay of Biscay and the Japanese. British Columbia salmon trollers were quite small, such as the 45ft 10in *Cecilie C* with a 12 ton capacity and the French and Spanish cutters and ketches with their 50ft rods either side of the mainmast went up to 85ft in length. Pacific tuna clippers were larger, pioneered by *Northwestern* of 1930, the first to keep bait alive for long periods. The wooden *Pan American*, just under 150ft long with a 1200bhp diesel was built in 1945 at San Francisco. As in the purse seiners the superstructure was well forward; the low stern area being taken up by bait tanks and their circulating pumps low because of the men fishing on the platforms. She had twenty-two crew, although

The motor trawler Boston Weelsby, *registered at Grimsby, was typical of the vessels of this type produced in the United Kingdom from the mid 1950s. Completed in September 1961 by leading trawler builders Cook, Welton & Gemmell, of Beverley, she was 412grt, and fitted with a 6-cylinder C D Holmes/Werkspoor diesel engine of 1050bhp. With the decline of the UK fishing fleet, many vessels were sold to overseas interests;* Boston Weelsby, *which was built for Boston Deep Sea Fisheries, was sold to Irvin & Johnson of Cape Town, owners and operators of South Africa's largest fleet of fishing vessels. (Laurence Dunn collection)*

fourteen was more usual as in the 1941 built *St George*, 102ft long with a 300hp engine. The tuna catch could be frozen, as for example in the 1938 built *The Prospect* of San Diego, wood with a clipper bow and an unusual fine stern, unlike the normal transom. Freezing the catch gave a 6000 mile radius of operation. Tuna clippers could convert to purse seining or trawling. The crow's nest was needed for tuna shoal spotting.

Japanese vessels angling for skipjack and albacore had a long low bow platform over the clipper stem and fishing platforms either side. As many as fifty-five men would be on the bow and leeward platform in a boat over 100grt. Bait was kept in a well open to the sea while ice was stored in the hold. Accommodation was cramped in a typical larger vessel such as the wooden 1949 built *Kaio Maru No 11* (length 81.36ft, breadth 18.04ft), powered by a 210hp engine and with a crew of fifty-seven. Japanese pole and line fishing mackerel boats working at night with fish luring lamps were even more cramped for they needed a larger crew – as many as sixty in the wooden *Kyowa Maru No 8* of 1958 (88.9ft in length, 19.03ft breadth with a 380bhp engine). Mackerel bait is frozen sardine or herring, as opposed to the live bait, generally sardine, needed to entice the skipjack. Squid jigging was done from smaller boats at around 68ft in length and by 14ft breadth with a 115hp engine and a crew of fifteen. Fish luring lights were rigged from poles running the length of the deck and fishing platforms built outboard right round the hull.

Fishing methods

Trawlers have become ever more efficient catchers of demersal or bottom feeding fish such as cod, hake, haddock, coley, halibut, plaice and sole, while the evolution of the pelagic or mid water trawl has allowed mid water or surface feeding fish such as herring to be caught by the new generation of stern trawlers, while the purse seine has been employed in the herring, tuna, salmon, mackerel and sardine fisheries with success, to the extinction of the drift net which was for long the North Sea method. Line fishing, of prehistoric origin and the most efficient means until the trawl was perfected, remains of value when the bottom is rough and when quality is all important, despite the complexity of baiting up and unhooking the catch. Bottom or just off the bottom line fishing has proved the best way to catch halibut and other flatfish in prime condition, while by trolling the baited line, tuna or tunny may be caught in commercial quantities. Oysters and shellfish are taken by various forms of dredge, lobsters and crabs by traps, while whales and swordfish are shot by harpoon.

Between 1890 and 1900 the bottom trawl was revolutionised. Up to the 1890s it was limited in width and therefore catching power by the length of the beam which kept it open, an average of 36ft and a maximum of 52ft. A smack could manage no more but steam opened up new possibilities with the introduction of the otter board or door which acted like a kite when towed at an angle,

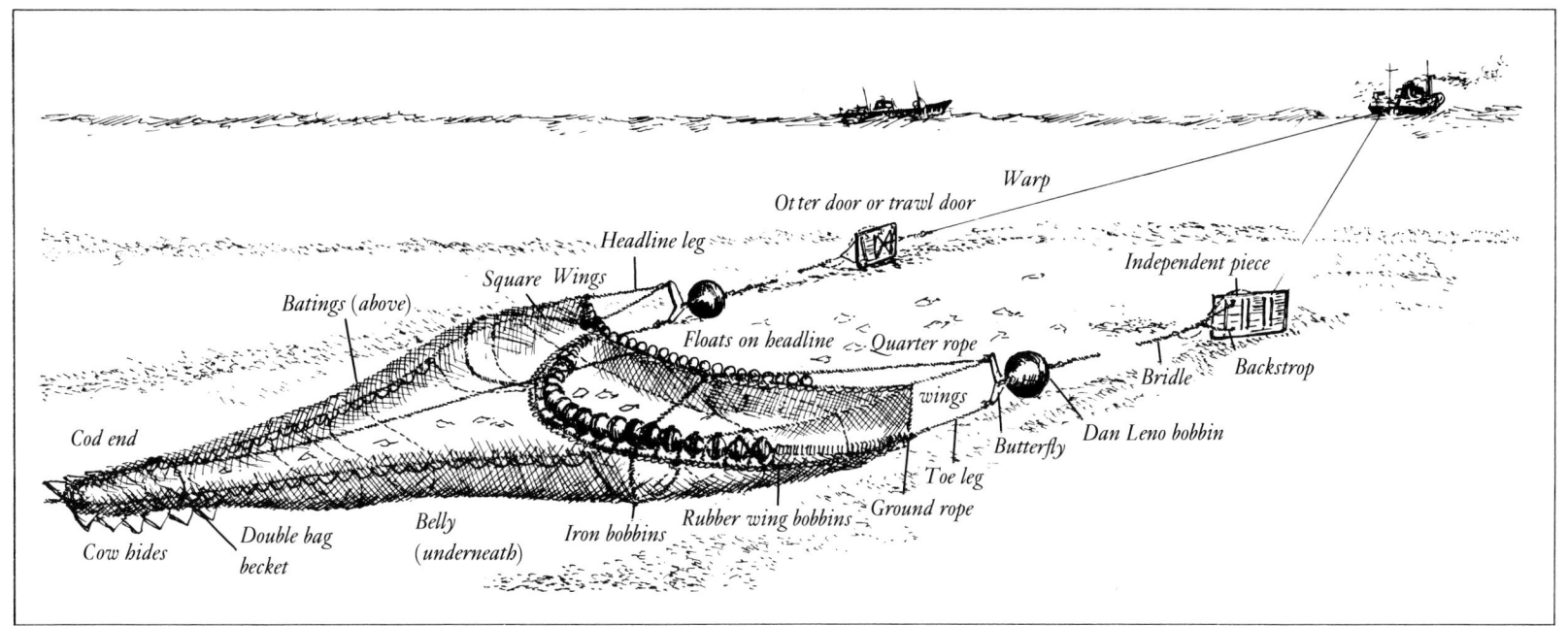

Batings (above)
Square Wings
Headline leg
Otter door or trawl door
Warp
Independent piece
Floats on headline
Quarter rope
Cod end
wings
Backstrop
Bridle
Dan Leno bobbin
Butterfly
Toe leg
Double bag becket
Belly (underneath)
Iron bobbins
Rubber wing bobbins
Ground rope
Cow hides

Types of fishing: the Vigneron-Dahl trawl. Not to scale.
(Drawing by the author)

converting a longways pull into a sideways one and so keeping the mouth of the net open. Work had been done in Ireland by a person called Musgrave as early as the 1860s, possibly for illegal salmon netting, but no seagoing application was attempted until 1885 and then unsuccessfully with the new steam screw trawler *Irrawaddy*. Otter boards incidentally were never very successful with sailing smacks, although tried, for example, by Brixham men, because they could not tow at the constant speed needed to keep the boards or doors open. Further trials with steam took place off Shields in 1892 with greater success and some of the pioneer paddle tug trawlers used them. In 1894 Scott of Granton patented the trawl which bears the name of that port in the Firth of Forth and which later became standard gear for British owners. Early otter trawls (the name is believed to have come from a Scarborough trawler called *Otter*) had a width of some 60ft increasing to 80ft and by the mid 1890s, along with the gallows for the warps, they were in general use by British, Netherlands, German and French fishermen, with Japan following in 1905. At first the doors were attached directly to the wings of the net, which was kept open vertically by means of floats secured to the headline and which travelled over the bottom on wooden rollers or bobbins spaced along the ground rope. Modifications followed in size and shape of floats and bobbins but the major advance was the separation of the doors from the wings by the tow and headline legs, so broadening the effective width. Movement of doors and warps stirred up the bottom and fright-

ened the fish into the path of the net, also achieved by stretching chains loosely in front of the ground rope. Once engulfed by the wings, with the bobbins rolling towards them there was no escape for the fish, only an inexorable progression towards the cod end, some 120ft (36m) away. Eventually the distance between doors and wings became some 600ft of bridle and tow and headline legs, with 300ft across between the doors in the case of the Engel 250ft (76m) long ground-rope net which could hold up to 60 tons of fish. Spread of the tow and headline legs had been achieved by the French Vigneron–Dahl patent of 1922 which introduced the danleno bobbin and butterfly to effect this; the butterfly did the spreading while the danleno stopped the net wings from being caught up on obstacles. Danleno was the British way of saying *gandineaux*, the French for the the bobbins, and recalled the music hall star as an anglicised equivalent. A variant of the danleno and butterfly was a small otter or pony board to spread the legs and maintain width. Bottom trawl headline heights increased from the 6ft or so of the Granton trawl to the 14ft of the Fécamp high headline trawl of the 1960s. This was done by using kites like small otter boards which acted in the same way, a modification tried as early as the mid 1920s by the Germans for a herring trawl and developed during the 1930s using more kites. It was the precursor of the pelagic trawl aimed at mid water fish which from the 1960s was to be used with devasting effect.

The length of time the net was down depended on the quantity of fish around, but

averaged 1 to 4 hours at a speed of 3–4kts, with six to eight hauls every 24 hours. In a 'single boater', speed and time were at the discretion of the skipper but no such independence was granted his colleagues in the North Sea boxing fleets who fished under the orders of an 'admiral' who signalled both course and speed, when to shoot and when to haul. Such control was essential in a fleet of twenty or thirty close spaced boats and no 'naval' signals were obeyed with greater alacrity. In the same way the morning transfers of full fish boxes from trawler to carrier and the return of empties were done according to a plan. It was for the benefit of the men of the boxing fleets, isolated for up to three months at a time, that the Royal National Mission to Deep Sea Fishermen was founded in 1881 by Ebenezer J Mather. His aim was to provide alternatives to the cheap spirits of the 'coopers' (pronounced copers) which were endangering men's lives; along with tobacco the mission ships dispensed medical care, reading matter, a chance to socialise, and of course the Gospel. The subsequent activities of the Mission have been of incalculable benefit to the fishing profession, notably in times of loss and despite the decline of distant water fishing, its work continues.

Heavy coal consumption measured against the price of fish spelt the end of the boxing fleets in 1936. The last two, both from Hull, *Gamecock* (Kelsall, Lane & Beeching) and *Red Cross* (Hull Steam Fishing & Ice Co) had in the end merged to make economies but to

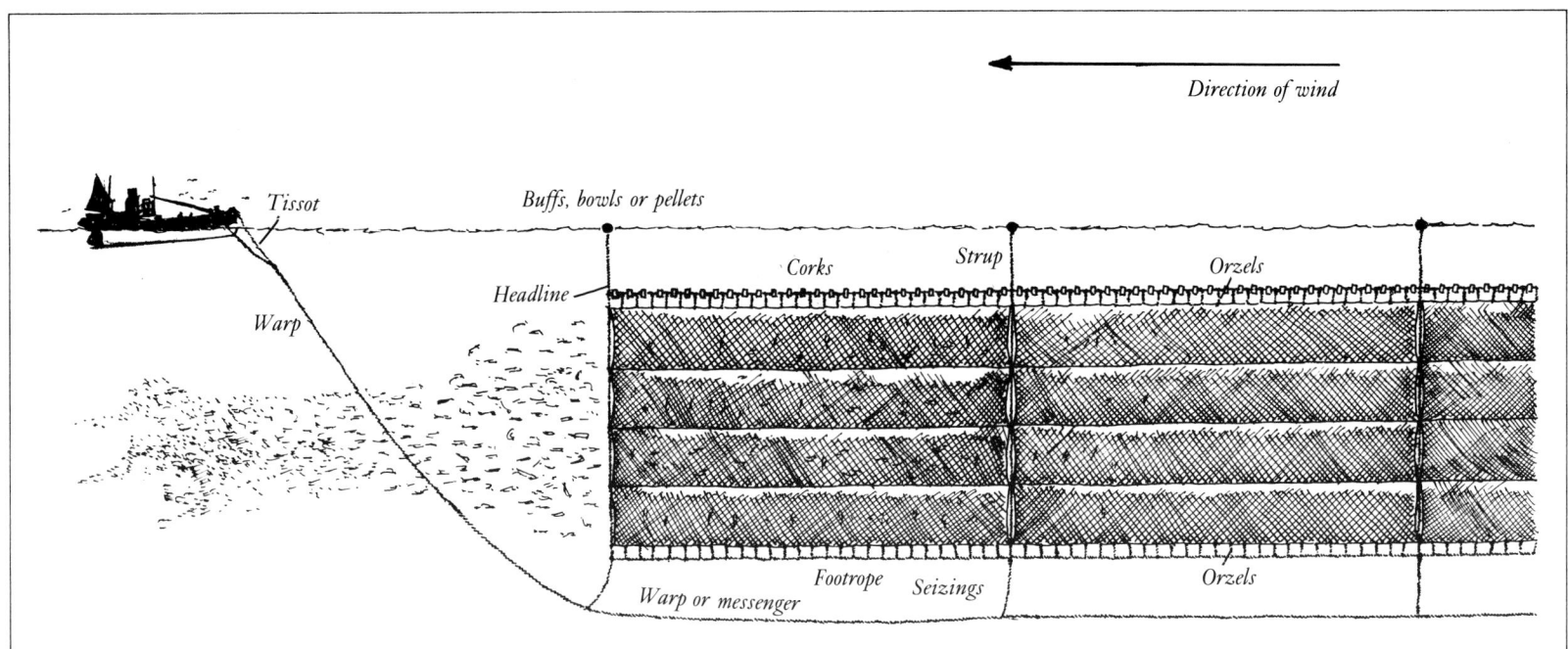

Direction of wind

Tissot

Buffs, bowls or pellets

Corks *Strup* *Orzels*

Headline

Warp

Warp or messenger *Footrope* *Seizings* *Orzels*

no avail. In another form the fleeting system has been revived with the mother factory ship and her attendant trawlers which transfer their catch for processing aboard, a development of the 1960s. A variant has been the practice of 'klondyking' whereby local fishermen sell their catches to a foreign factory. Pelagic whaling was akin to the fleeting system as is the Grand Banks line fishing from dories.

Bottom trawling between two vessels has been the Spanish method since the 1890s, under sail, steam and motor. This pair, or 'pareja', trawling became even more efficient as ships increased in power and nets in size. The trawlers work from between a quarter to half a mile apart and tow for up to ten hours. The warps are from two to three thousand feet long and have the effect of funnelling the fish towards the mouth of the net. Hauls of 180 tons have been known, sufficient to clear whole grounds. The trawlers are generally exact sisters with associated names such as *Terra* and *Nova* or *Virgen de Lourdes* and *Virgen de la Almudena*. One of the pair is the command boat with the 'capitan nautico primero' and the 'patrón de pesca primero', or fishing captain, the other vessel has both ranks but subordinate. They haul in turn and so fill their holds equally.

An early design of mid water trawl was introduced in 1948 by the Dane Robert Larsen. It was worked between two boats and kept up by floats and down by sinkers. Used for herring it could measure up to 130ft (39m) wide and 180ft (55m) long. Subsequently mid water design was angled towards

one boat operation with the Germans in the forefront of development. Nets 200ft (61m) wide and 130ft (39m) high were made with floats along the headline and sinkers at each end of the ground rope. By adjustment of speed and length of warp the net could work at any depth – a genuine pelagic trawl. In the late 1950s came the added refinement of the netzonde, a sonar device mounted on the headline to spot the concentration of fish ahead of the net, which facilitated aimed trawling. This coupled with sonar or asdic equipment ranging ahead of a ship and with echo-sounders, echograms and cathode ray fish finders giving a picture below the keel, granted every assistance to the skipper but little hope to the fish.

Before the advent of the mid water trawl the British herring fishing industry depended on the drift net and the seine type, either the ring net or purse seine. The drift net was simply a two mile curtain of loose mesh which entrapped fish by the gills; if the curtain was long enough they had to hit it. This was passive fishing, not seeking but waiting for the shoal to appear. Each net was some 180ft long and 30ft deep and a drifter would shoot a hundred in just over an hour, then laying up to 120 fathoms of warp along with the 'tissot' or guy rope by which she swung head to wind. Shooting was at dusk and hauling by use of the capstan at daybreak. Because of the short trips processing was done ashore except in the case of those salted and packed in barrels aboard.

More effective for surface and shoal fish was the purse seine introduced as early as

the 1880s in Sweden for herring, in 1904 in California for tuna. The net is indeed a purse with the purse line threaded through rings along the foot of the net to gather it into a bag. Some nets have been as much as 900ft deep but 300ft is more normal with a length ten times the depth. Catches grew so large that hauling became a problem, solved by the Puretic power block, invented in 1953 by Mario Puretic, a Californian of Yugoslav descent. Generally the block is hydraulically powered. The net drum was another innovation of the same date, spreading from the Pacific coast salmon fishery to mid water trawls and anchored gill nets.

Commercial line-fishing survives in spite of purse seines and pelagic trawls. Lines are multi-hooked, each hook depending from a branch or snood of varied length, spaced at intervals exceeding the combined length of two snoods so that entanglement is avoided. 'Great' lines had 4680 hooks to a 'string' of 180 lines, or 6240 hooks to a string of 240 lines. 'Small' lines with 800–1000 were made up into 40–50 fathom lengths. Lines may be set on or off the bottom for demersal fish like halibut, buoyed and anchored at one or both ends, at one end if the boat pays out the line and then works back to recover it. Again they may be set for mid water or surface fish like tuna, the Japanese specialising in drift lines, buoyed but drifting with the tide and current. They date from the early eighteenth century, modern ones for tuna stretching for up to 75 miles. A Japanese line boat takes four hours to set 2000 hooks, baiting as the line is paid out, and ten hours to haul immediately after casting, using a line coiler.

A North Sea long liner of the years between the wars set thirty baskets with 480 fathoms of line in each, with a snood and hook every three fathoms, totalling 15 miles of line and over 5000 hooks. Cod, haddock and flatfish were the principal catch, with the halibut the most prized. Search for halibut took the steam long liners to the Hebrides, Rockall, the Faroes and Iceland and the Norwegian coast. They used steam line haulers and packed the catch in ice. Halibut off Greenland prompted Hellyers of Hull to fit out summer expeditions of mother ships and dories with the intention of freezing the catch aboard these early fish factory ships. *Helder*, renamed *Arctic Prince*, was the first to be despatched in 1926, while *Arctic Queen*, formerly the Lamport & Holt *Vasari*, went out in 1929. Both ships continued to be used until 1935, doubling as floating cold stores, but were then sold as competition was developing and halibut were becoming scarce.

Grand Banks line fishing from dories from May to October predates Grand Banks trawling by many decades and survives because so much of the ground is foul. Small lines have been used with 5ft snoods, 2.5 fathoms (15ft) apart, which are baited before shooting. Motor dories have replaced sail and oar and the use of radio and radar has lessened the dangers of fog, icebergs and collision. *Arctic*

Queen had to be fitted with a gigantic foghorn to meet these problems.

Rod fishing for tuna has been undertaken commercially in the Pacific since before the 1920s, the rods hand held but two or more (up to four) may be linked to a single line. Success depends on ground baiting or 'chumming' with live bait. The men sit round aft on special racks or platforms with the chummer behind them by the bait boxes above the bait wells. Refrigeration of the catch has replaced crushed ice.

The tunny, the European tuna, is caught by trolling with the 50ft rods angled at 45 degrees so keeping the lines clear of the wake. Each rod trails six to eight lines weighted to keep them apart and each baited with imitation horse hair. Because tunny shoal the boats work in groups, although for this reason the purse seine has largely taken over both in European and Pacific waters. Spanish tunnymen mounted four rods, two forward, two aft.

British Columbia salmon fishermen trolled with four to six lines each weighted and fitted with a swivel for the three hooked and spoon baited branch lines. Each of the lines could be reeled in separately by a small winch or gurdie driven off the main engine. Skipjack and albacore can only be caught by rods and the Japanese angle for them with 15ft to 20ft rods, ground baiting and spraying the sea surface with water to attract the fish, the albacore needing two rods per line.

Squid are caught commercially by jigging

with grapnel type hooks which snag the squid, the jigging up and down attracting them so that they either take the hook or are impaled. One thousand to fifteen hundred a night may be caught by one man using two or more lines but the Japanese have devised a machine which will work the line by quick/slow motion using oval drums. With fifty hooks on, the weighted line goes to the sea bed and is hauled up in jerks.

Development of the whale factory ship

In a sense the catching and processing of whales has always been pelagic or carried out at sea, with a mother ship, the whaler herself and a fleet of open, oared catchers. Once harpooned and dead the whale was towed back to the ship for flensing and cooking of the blubber. Apart from the baleen the rest of the carcass was waste. Flensing had to be done alongside and only whales which remained afloat when dead could be handled, these being 'right' whales, the right ones to hunt. Whale processing at sea faced problems of space and unsteadiness but processing ashore had fewer obstacles and shore stations became widespread when new whaling methods were introduced. Although old style whaling with rowing boat, hand harpoon and try works aboard a sailing ship, or latterly a steamer with sail assistance, persisted to the late nineteenth century and in the case of the Americans until 1928, and the hand harpoon was still used in the Azores until recently, Svend Foyn's methods took over the bulk of the industry; the steam whale catcher, the harpoon gun and harpoon with explosive head. There had been harpoon guns since 1737 and Foyn's use of accumulator gear to 'play' the whale derived from the work of the American Thomas Roys who was operating in a similar fashion, establishing a shore station in Iceland in 1865. But Svend Foyn (1809–95), a citizen of Tøsberg on the Oslofjord, who mounted his first expedition in 1864 and who was awarded his

The factory ship Sir James Clark Ross *was a converted cargo ship without the benefit of a slipway so flensing was carried on alongside – the catch is visible around the ship in this photograph – as had been done since the days of sail.* (CMP)

Mechanised whaling: the early factory ship
Thorshammer *with her attendant fleet of 'catchers', at*
Simonstown about 1932. The factory was a tanker
conversion, the built-up flensing deck being visible
amidships. (CMP)

first whale catching patent in 1873, gave Norway that ascendancy in the industry which she maintained almost to the end. The old methods had hunted the right whale to near extinction but the new could pursue the larger and faster rorquals. Although these sank when dead a pump from the catcher, first employed in the 1880s, could inflate them for towage to the station.

Early factory vessels

Shore stations employing the new methods were set up in Iceland, the Faroes, Spitsbergen, Newfoundland, Finnmark in northern Norway from where Foyn himself operated, and the Shetlands, where the Scottish firm of Christian Salvesen established a station in 1904. They worked well enough but were restricted by the range of their small coal burning catchers which could not manage a return steaming distance of more than 200 miles. The answer lay in a ship with the processing equipment on board, not to attend the catchers at sea but to moor in a bay or fjord handy to the catching area. The cooking processes needed plenty of fresh water and plenty of steam; the water could be pumped from the shore whilst the ship's boilers could produce the steam, provided the engines were stopped. Roys tried to process oil aboard two steamers in 1865, while Foyn had an experimental floating factory off Spitsbergen and Bear Island in 1890, but Christen

Christensen (d 1923) of Sandefjord, also on the Oslofjord (nearby Larvik is the other whaling port of Norway) was the true pioneer of the factory ship. His Framnaes shipyard specialised in the conversion of merchant ships into whale factories by installing tanks for bulk carriage of whale oil and by setting the cooking equipment in the hull above the tanks and not on deck as in the sailing whalers. In 1903 Christensen fitted out the steamer *Telegraf* of 737grt to work off Spitsbergen but she was too small and more success attended *Admiralen*, equipped at Framnaes for a more rewarding Spitsbergen expedition the following year. She was an iron steamer built at Sunderland in 1869 as *Ariadne* of 1517grt and latterly owned in Hartlepool. Christensen gave her four open-topped cookers, one pressure cooker, a blubber chopper, evaporators to distill fresh water and settling tanks for refining the oil. In 1905 *Admiralen* went to the Antarctic with two catchers and, based on the Falklands, had some success but insufficient to make a profit. Yet Christensen was undeterred although his second factory, *Fridtjof Nansen*, 2563grt, was lost off South Georgia in November 1906.

By this time South Georgia was established as a whaling centre, entirely due to the energy of Carl Anton Larsen (1860–1924). Larsen had in 1892–93 and 1893–94 been sent to the Weddell Sea by Christensen to look for whales and he had subsequently been again to the Antarctic in 1901–3 with the Swedish explorer Otto Nordenskjöld. Their ship *Antarctica* was lost but the expedition was rescued by the Argentinian gunboat *Uruguay*. Whales were seen in such numbers that Larsen persuaded Argentinian capital to

establish the whaling station at Grytviken (Cauldron Bay) in 1904, the first of the eight stations on this inhospitable island, including Salvesen's Leith Harbour, started in 1909.

Meanwhile whaling continued in the north, notably in the northern Pacific, with Russia and Japan active, the latter with steam catchers from 1899, the former with a factory ship, the steamer *Michail*, 3643grt, from 1903. She had been bought in 1899 with a view to conversion into a floating factory, so predated *Telegraf* and *Admiralen*. The work was done at Danzig and all would have been well were it not for the Russo-Japanese War which broke out in February 1904. For Japan, whale meat for home consumption was the principal need but for Norway, Britain and other nations, oil from rorquals, so abundant in the Antarctic, was the overriding demand. Although mineral oils had replaced whale oil for lighting and lubrication, indeed in the early 1900s the demand for whale oil had dropped, the advent by 1906 of a new process, hydrogenation, gave the oil a more assured future. By hydrogenation the oil could be converted to odourless and tasteless solid fat, a possible ingredient of soap and margarine, and by way of glycerine, a component of explosives. If whale oil could be produced cheaply in large quantities, a ready market was available. The whaling industry was not slow to take advantage of this and large scale Antarctic expeditions began, to the alarm, as early as 1911, of those who feared for the future of whale stocks.

Floating factories were an essential part of operations; apart from South Georgia there was one other shore establishment at Deception Island in the South Shetlands, but ships came south in greater numbers. All were conversions: Salvesen had *Neko*, 3576grt, built in 1891 and the clipper bowed *Horatio*, 3239grt, formerly *Horsley Tower* of 1892; A/S Hektor of Tønsberg with *Hektoria* (5003grt) and Thor Dahl of Sandefjord started with an old sailing ship of 1042grt as an anchored factory. Because of this continued dependence on the shore, whaling became subject to licences from Britain, which claimed sovereignty over the sector of the Antarctic continent on the Falklands side, the Falkland Islands Dependencies, the South Shetlands, South Orkney and South Georgia. Licensing meant restriction and this the whaling companies sought to avoid. The answer was to take the factory ship to sea, in other words pelagic whaling. A start had been made in the 1912–13 season (the Antarctic summer bridges the New Year), when off South Orkney the factories had been forced by ice conditions to flense and process amid the pack. This semipelagic whaling worked and it was here that the harpoon gunner Petter Sørlle first had the idea of a stern slipway.

Munitions and food demands during the First World War gave an impetus to the industry, although the Norwegians were deterred by the British from selling whale oil to the Central Powers. On the other hand licences were cancelled and whaling became unrestricted. Although restrictions were reimposed after the war, the possibilities of unlicensed whaling were not lost on the Norwegians, among them C A Larsen. The Ross Sea, on the New Zealand side of the continent, was found to carry large stocks and it was there, although risking his expedition in the ice, that Larsen went for the 1923–24 season, armed with a licence from the British

who also claimed this sector. His ship was a former Brocklebank cargo steamer, *Mahronda* built in 1905 of 8223grt, which was appropriately renamed *Sir James Clark Ross*. She had no slipway, so flensing continued alongside, making use of the ice as a working platform where possible. With fourteen pressure cookers, ten open cookers and two Hartmann rotary cookers, the ship was well equipped and achieved great success. The pressure cookers had been an early improvement of the late 1880s but the Hartmann rotary digesters spread the pressure more evenly, resulting in greater oil extraction. They were the 1911 patent of the German August Sommermeyer and were made by the Berlin engineers R A Hartmann. Separators were to follow in 1924, cutting out the settling tanks, but the slipway problem remained.

There had been many ideas for lifting the whale carcass aboard where it could be handled faster, more safely and above all more completely. Before and during the First World War the waste had been excessive in the rush for oil. Only the belly blubber had been taken, leaving 6000 carcasses rotting away on Deception Island with 80 per cent of their oil content abandoned. Henceforward the accent was on full use of the whale and only processing it aboard could achieve this. In 1897 the schooner *Herald* had managed to heave whales over the counter by a winch. They were flensed on deck but taken ashore for processing. Ideas included lifting a whale aboard in a net and floating it in through a hatch, but a slip was the realistic answer, either at the bow, amidships, or at the stern. An amidships slip was tried but proved unsuccessful; however a bow slip was fitted to *C A Larsen*, 13,246grt, a 1925 conver-

sion from the Eagle Oil tanker *San Gregorio*. The ship had a successful career but her slip had to be sealed by a heavy bow door. A stern ramp was the solution fitted to another 1925 conversion, the single screw *Lancing* 7866grt, built in 1898 as *Knight Errant*. On 14 July 1925 the first whale, a humpback, was hauled on deck off the Congo (whaling was not confined to the polar regions). The slipway on *Lancing* was the work of Petter Sørlle who had proposed and patented two slips, one on each side of the rudder post for single screw ships, as in the *Lancing*, and a central slip for twin screw ships. They became the standard design for purpose built factory ships, most of which were twin screw, although it was also fitted to the single screw *Kosmos* of 1929, water ballast bringing it down to sea level.

Up to 1920 no ship had been designed and built as a factory, all had been conversions from tankers, which already had the tanks, from cargo ships, or from passenger liners which had plenty of space. In 1929 Salvesen acquired two 'Shire' cargo liners from Royal Mail, *Carmarthenshire* and *Cardiganshire* which became respectively *Sourabaya*, 10,107 grt and *Salvestria*, 11,938grt. In 1932 they converted the twin screw, former White Star liner *Runic* into *New Sevilla*, 13,801grt. She was the only large factory to have worked in the Arctic. Another White Star liner, the twin screw *Suevic* became *Skytteren* (12,358grt) in 1929, operated by a consortium of gunners with success, while *Athenic* of 1904 became *Pelagos*, 12,100grt, associated with Anders Jahre. All were given central stern slipways and no longer resembled passenger ships. Tanker conversions included *Thorshammer*, 12,200grt for Thor Dahl, formerly the Eagle Oil *San Nazario* of 1914. She was single screw and the slip had to be 'humped' over the engines.

Purpose-built vessels

But the era of conversions was finishing apart from some latter day examples. The first new factory ship was built for A/S Hektor in

Before the introduction of the purpose-built whale factory ship in 1925, owners and operators relied on conversions from cargo ships, passenger ships or tankers. One such vessel was Southern Princess *(12,092grt), which had been built in 1915 by Armstrong Whitworth as the Eagle Oil tanker* San Patricio. *She was sold to Southern Whaling & Sealing Co of London, converted to a whale factory, and renamed. In the peak years of the mid to late 1930s Southern Whaling also owned the factory vessel* Southern Empress *and sixteen whale catchers.*

1920 at Port Glasgow. She was *Ronald*, 6249grt, with twelve open cookers for blubber, six pressure cookers for meat and a tank capacity of 36,000 barrels, or 41,000 barrels if the double bottom was used. There are six barrels to a ton, so she could carry 6800 tons.

Ronald had no stern slip but this milestone was reached in 1929 with *Kosmos*, 17,801grt, built by Workman Clark of Belfast to the order of Anders Jahre for the Pelagos Company of Tønsberg. She and Rasmussen's *Vikingen* of 1929, 12,801grt, set the pattern for whale factory design; central stern slipway, a pair of funnels athwartships and the maximum deck area possible with the bridge placed right forward. Initially there were slipway problems; the friction of the carcass made it stick, overcome by runners, and the winches were too weak but more powerful ones were designed, while the final perfection was Gjelstad's whale claw to grip round the flukes, saving men having to go down the ramp.

Steam-raising power was essential to success for the cookers, the winches, the evaporators, the bone saws, which from the early 1920s replaced the 8–10ft hand crosscuts, and for the generators. The main engines were triple expansion but more steam would be available if they were diesel, which in any case needed less bunker space. The *Haugar*, 2243grt and *Pioner*, 1721grt, both of 1929,

were small factories with oil engines designed for work in the north and off the Congo but the second *Sir James Clark Ross* (14,363grt) was built for the Antarctic with Burmeister & Wain diesels. By this time, 1930, boilers were turning over to oil firing both in factories and catchers and there was a return to steam reciprocating propulsion despite problems of keeping on the move and cooking at the same time, necessary when whales became scarce. Meanwhile factories were growing in size and sophistication and the Germans led the way in both. Their *Walter Rau*, 14,867grt, built in 1937 with two four-cylinder compound engines was among the best equipped, with a canning factory, a meat meal plant, a blood meal plant, meat refrigeration, and a plant for meat extract and for vitamin preparation. She did well in her first season, her products including 21.5 tons of blubber fibre for synthetic wool and 11 tons of glands for medical experiments. Before 1939 the largest cargo ship afloat was the Unilever owned, German built and German flag *Unitas* of 1937, at 21,845grt. With an extra deck her displacement totalled 45,000 tons. Propulsion was by a pair of triple-expansion engines coupled to low pressure turbines. Eventually she became Union Whaling of Durban's *Abraham Larsen*, was sold to the Japanese in 1957 and made her last Antarctic expedition in 1964–65.

To make up for wartime losses several whale factory ships were ordered in 1944–45. These included Norhval *(13,830grt), which was a product of the Furness Shipbuilding Co shipyard at Haverton Hill on Tees. She was delivered in November 1945 to Norwegian owner Melsom & Melsom, of Larvik, a well-established whaling industry operator. The twin-screw* Norhval *was 555.4ft (169.3m) in length overall.* (CMP)

tankers and vehicle and plane carriers, the Japanese vessels even carrying midget submarines. Slow and high sided, they were excellent U-boat targets. Britain and Japan lost all theirs and the three surviving German vessels were handed over as reparations. New building started in 1945 by Salvesen with *Southern Venturer*, 14,493grt, and in 1946 *Southern Harvester*, 15,448grt, both built by Furness at Haverton Hill, where in 1945 the same builders had also launched *Norhval*, 13,830grt, for Norway's Melsom & Melsom. Anders Jahre's 19,000grt *Kosmos V*, built by Furness in 1948, never became a factory ship, a fate which was to befall the Argentinian *Juan Peron*, 24,570grt built by Harland & Wolff at Belfast in 1951. In a period of declining whale stocks and a more severe imposition of quotas, begun in 1932 but, after the establishment of the International Whaling Commission in 1945, restricting not only the number of whales caught but the length of season and the hunting area, factories were not needed and both *Kosmos V* and *Juan Peron* lived out their lives as tankers.

After an absence from whaling of some 150 years the Netherlands re-entered the scene in 1946 with a state supported venture and the four-funnelled factory ship *Willem Barendsz* (10,647grt) converted from the motor tanker *Pan Gothia* of 1931. Another four-funneller was the former T2 type tanker *Olympic Challenger*, a maverick factory ship flying the Panamanian flag but owned by an Uruguayan company under the beneficial control of Aristotle Onassis. Between 1950 and 1955, this vessel and her twelve ex-corvette catchers went on the rampage, ignoring

In 1930–31 41 factories and over 200 catchers were working in the Antarctic and they caught 28,325 blue whales out of a total of 37,438. But 1937–38 was the record season with a total of 43,328 baleen whales, helped by the addition of fifteen new factory ships. By the 1930s with the perfection of hydrogenation, margarine was 100 per cent whale oil, hence the Unilever participation which had started in 1919 with Lever Brothers buying the Southern Whaling & Sealing Co. Japanese whaling became established in the Antarctic from 1934. They started by buying the factory *Antarctic* from Norway which they renamed *Tonan Maru*. Of 9839grt, she had been built in 1906 as *Opawa* for the New Zealand Shipping Co. But the Japanese were not slow to build their own. They bought the plans of the second motor driven *Sir James Clark Ross* from the Furness Shipbuilding Co of Haverton Hill on Tees. The result was *Nisshin Maru* ('Always New') of 1936, 16,764grt, similarly diesel powered as was

her sister the 17,600 ton *Nisshin Maru No 2*. Many more Japanese factories followed, again with the use of plans from the Furness Shipbuilding Co. The Soviet Union on the other hand was slower to take up pelagic whaling and only had *Aleut*, 5106grt, a conversion from a US ship. She worked in the Bering Sea and did not move down to the Antarctic until 1946–47 by which time the Soviets also had *Vikengen* which had been sold in 1938 to Germany and renamed *Wikinger*. After the Second World War she was awarded to the Soviets in reparation and renamed *Slava*.

The Second World War and after

For the whaling industry the Second World War brought disruption with heavy losses among the factories, most of which became

Kosmos III *was built for Norwegian owner Anders Jahre of Sandeford, and delivered by Gotaverken of Gothenburg in November 1947. She was of 18,047grt and equipped with a 9-cylinder Gotaverken oil engine of 6750bhp giving a speed of 13kts. With the decrease in whaling activity by Anders Jahre* Kosmos III *was sold to a Japanese owner in 1961 and under their ownership has seen many more years service.* (CPL)

all regulations and only ending her piratical career when the crew went on strike. The Netherlands continued with a second *Willem Barendsz*, 26,839grt, purpose-built as a factory in 1955, sold to Japan in 1964, but back to the Netherlands in 1966, becoming a fish-oil factory in South Africa a year later. By this time the industry was left to Japan, which acquired factories from other nations and also built them, confusingly perpetuating the old names *Tonan Maru* and *Nisshin Maru*, for instance there was a new *Nisshin Maru* (16,811grt) in 1951. The Soviet Union how-ever had the distinction of building the last and largest whale factories, the 35,000grt *Sovietskaya Ukraina* of 1959 and the *Sovietskaya Rossiya* of 1961.

At the time of her building the British flag factory *Balaena* (15,760grt) of United Whal-ers, completed in 1946 by Harland & Wolff of Belfast, commanded much attention. A description of her could stand for the last flowering of pelagic whaling. Her 321ft 6in (98m) long whaling decks had a width of 77ft (23.5m) and a new feature aft was a hangar, catapult and crane for two Walrus flying boats. Aircraft had been tried as early as 1919 from a shore station and one was carried by the first *Kosmos* in 1929, only to be lost. The Walrus was useful for prospecting ice conditions but not so much for whale spotting as the whales kept moving; Salvesen used helicopters which could stay with the whales and report their intentions.

The after deck or after plan was the blubber stripping deck, the forward plan was the dismemberment area. To speed this *Balaena* was equipped with nine 10-ton and four 5-ton derricks, sixteen steam winches, nine electric winches, ten warping capstans and two 40-ton winches for hauling carcasses up the stern slipway. There were also four steam bone saws. The factory deck was 375ft long, 77ft wide and 22ft high with an intermediate 7ft high deck as a mounting for the factory equipment. This comprised twenty-two pres-sure cookers for the bones, ten for the blub-ber, eight rotary cookers, a liver extraction plant, a meat meal plant and separators. There was a freezing plant for the best meat and a refrigerated hold. However, meat was

In her day the British Balaena *was the ultimate whale factory ship. With an integral slipway, well laid out processing decks, and an unprecedented degree of mechanisation, the factory was capable of using almost every part of the whale carcass. A novel feature of the ship was the hangar, and one of the two Walrus flying boats carried for reconnaissance can be seen aft.* (CMP)

normally transferred to a transport ship along with oil and other products, the normal prac-tice since pelagic whaling started. *Balaena* had an elaborate system of conveyor belts and elevators to speed delivery to ships along-side. The whale oil tank capacity was 19,150 tons. They were filled with fuel oil for the outward journey and as this was used up, the tanks were cleaned ready for the whale oil; 2240 tons of fresh water were carried in tanks fore and aft. As in all purpose built factory ships the bridge was well forward containing the officers' and management ac-commodation, along with the chemists and the gunners. Below this in the hull was the crew space, with the engineers and air crew aft, plus a hospital and operating theatre. The meat plant included pressing and drying equipment with uptakes inside the derrick posts. Once dried the meat was ground and bagged, as was the bone meal after the extrac-tion of oil. Little was wasted.

Whale catchers

Svend Foyn's steam whale catchers were small and underpowered; the pioneer *Spes et Fides* of 1864 was 94ft 9in long with a 50ihp engine and a speed of 7kts. At first she had seven guns but six were soon removed. With a quiet steam engine its aim was to stalk the whale – it could not possibly chase it – but once the harpoon had struck, the catcher would be towed at up to 14kts despite check boards used as water brakes until the whale tired. Foyn's second catcher was smaller but a little more powerful and power and speed continued to increase. Early steam catchers set the characteristics which remained, the harpoon gun mounted on the stemhead with

a good arc of fire and the accumulator gear to play the whale, the equivalent of the angler's rod and reel, comprising the whale winch, the whale line blocks and the springs. This accumulator gear was first patented by the American Thomas Roys in 1866 but underwent much modification. For the search a crow's nest was essential, a legacy from the sailing whaleship. Early hull design was conventional, not unlike a contemporary trawler with a flush deck and less of a sheer than was later developed for seaworthiness, as happened in trawler design. To illustrate whale power, in 1903 a Newfoundland catcher was towed ahead at 6kts with her engines half speed astern, a tug of war fol-lowed with the catcher's stem almost pulled under water. The struggle went on for twenty-eight hours.

Although Norway remained pre-eminent in the whaling industry, Japan soon adopted Svend Foyn's methods. In 1899 they built a steam catcher *Dai-Chi Chosu Maru*, lost in 1901. Subsequent Japanese catchers were chartered from Norway, or Norwegian built such as *Togo* of 1906, and although Norwe-gian gunners were hired, the Norwegians trained Japanese for this exacting role, the gunner, on whom success depended, being the commander of the catcher. In 1907 Japan started to build catchers again, while Salvesen ordered their first new vessel in 1910 from a local yard, Hawthorn of Leith, named *Scapa*, of 400ihp and capable of 11.5kts. Smith's Dock of South Bank on Tees, Middlesbrough, also delivered their first catcher in 1910, *Hananui II* for New Zealand. Six more catchers followed in 1911 and the yard became specialists in their design.

Early catchers had compound machin-

One of the most prolific builders of whalers (catchers) was Smith's Dock of Middlesbrough, which delivered in 1928 the steam catcher Southern Flower *(328grt). She transferred from Southern Whaling to Christian Salvesen and was requisitioned by the Admiralty during the Second World War, becoming the victim of a U-boat torpedo in 1945.* (CMP)

ery but in 1892 the first triple expansion engines were installed in *Glückauf* built by Akers of Oslo and this type, some with two low pressure cylinders, soon became the most widely adopted, British whale catchers using no other type of steam engine. Steam turbines were tried once by the Japanese just before the Second World War and a gas turbine catcher was built too, but the simplicity, flexibility and strength of the steam reciprocating engine proved ideal for the work. Nevertheless as early as 1911, when the marine oil engine was in its infancy and had hardly been tried in an ocean going ship, the Dundee whaling firm of Irvin & Johnson, by then established at Capetown, ordered three diesel driven catchers from Smith's Dock. These pioneers were not a success and it was many years before a diesel was again tried. A popular engine with the Norwegians was the Fredriksstad 'steam motor' made by their works on the Oslofjord, a back to back four cylinder compound using superheated steam at 220psi. Working on the uniflow principle it was as, if not more, economical than a triple and the four cranks gave a good balance. The first catcher to have it fitted was *H J Bull*, built in 1935 for Anders Jahre, and it remained in production, also built under licence, into the 1950s. The *H J Bull* had many firsts; she had two Scotch boilers, Wilson-Pirrie steam steering gear, refrigeration for provisions and she was the first of a larger type of 'scout' or whale seeking catcher, the inspiration for the corvettes of the Second World War.

Smith's Dock had been responsible for earlier design innovations when in 1925 they introduced the cruiser stern and detached balanced rudder, detached that is from the stern frame and propeller, as a means of achieving greater manoeuvrability – sometimes too manoeuvrable, as instanced by the capsize of the catchers *Scapa* in 1928 and *Simbra* in 1947. These refinements were first applied to *Southern Spray* and *Southern Wave* owned by Lever Brothers, which had been the first to introduce oil firing with their *Southern Floe* of 1923, the first catcher to be designed to burn oil after earlier experiments. Norway's first oil-burner also appeared in 1923. This was a big advance on coal and essential for successful pelagic whaling which started that same year since catchers could so easily be refuelled by tankers or by an oil burning factory ship. While Scotch boilers were standard in catchers, some were fitted with water tube patterns, installed by British, Norwegian and German builders from 1936.

Harpoon guns became available as breech loaders from 1925, a quicker and safer operation for loading the propellant, although the harpoon could only be handled at the muzzle. An earlier improvement dating from 1911 had been a recoil system which gave the gunner a steadier weapon and so greater accuracy. By the 1930s design had advanced to a wider gun platform which gave more room for training the piece, and by this time too the walkway from the hunting bridge above the wheelhouse to the gun platform was an accepted feature. This had been suggested by gunner Ole Iversen and it allowed the gunner last minute control of the ship. In later catchers greatly increased forward sheer meant that the walkway was almost horizontal.

Wireless telegraphy links had been estab-

lished as early as 1911–12 between catcher and factory and in 1912 wireless telegraphy was also possible between Port Stanley and Montevideo so that factories could communicate with their head offices by relay. Direct communication by wireless telegraphy with Tønsberg, Sandefjord or London had to wait until 1927. By this time radio telephony was also available as was radio direction finding, which aided the return of catchers to their factory. Radar was a post-Second World War benefit; shot whales could be marked by reflectors, while the asdic or sonar used to hunt submarines was fitted to catchers in a dome beneath the keel to search for whales. Another sonar device, the 'whale scarer', appeared in the early 1950s, designed to frighten and tire the whale so that it would surface more frequently.

By 1935 catcher size and power had become established at around 600grt and 2700ihp. Almost all catchers were commandeered for naval service by both sides in the Second World War and their design was developed into the corvette and elongated into the frigate, both with four-cylinder triple expansion engines. Catchers were the basis too of German patrol boat design. After 1945 many corvettes became catchers and whale towing boats, Onassis' *Olympic Challenger* expedition relying on ex-corvette catchers.

Catchers remained steam driven, apart from the 1911 oil-engined craft, until 1937 when the Japanese built the 297grt *Seki Maru* for their Taiyo Hogei KK with a 900hp two stroke diesel. Although noisy she was successful because catchers were no longer stalking but chasing the whale. The latter had no chance with a 14kt catcher which could keep up with it but not tire. Catchers of the 1940s and '50s exceeded this speed, and over 18kts was achieved when the Japanese built *Kos 55*, 735grt and 3600bhp, was completed in 1964 for Anders Jahre, while the many Russian diesel-electric catchers of the same period, of 843grt and also 3600bhp, reached 19kts. *Seki Maru 18* of 1957, 647grt, 203.2ft (62m) long and 3000bhp is an example of the later whale catcher, with faired ends to her bilge keels so that the whale line would not catch, with twin electric whale winches (all-electric auxiliaries had been introduced a few years

The main features of the typical catcher can be seen in this close-up of Thor Dahl's Thorarinn: *the harpoon gun mounted right forward with catwalk access from the hunting bridge (the gunner conned the ship as close to the target as possible before going forward); the lookout position at the masthead; part of the accumulator gear that absorbed shocks and allowed the whale to be 'played' runs over blocks at the crosstrees just below the crowsnest; and the casting with integral sheaves at the stemhead. The hull form, with steep sheer forward and little freeboard aft, was standard, but* Thorarinn *and her sisters, built in 1928–29 by the great Norwegian specialist firm of Akers Mek Verksted, were among the first to replace the overhanging counter sterns with the more modern cruiser form.* (CMP)

previously), and with an air operated brake for the propeller. This last had been introduced before the Second World War; it was essential to stop the propeller revolving once the harpoon had struck and the forerunner and whale line had begun to run. Later propellers had controllable pitch which allowed the engine to run at its most efficient revolutions, the boat's speed being controlled by altering the pitch of the blades. The 60 fathom forerunner, coiled in a steel basket at the foot of the gun, was by this time of nylon, first introduced by Salvesen in 1945. It had more stretch than hemp or manilla which meant it was kinder on the accumulator gear as well as being stronger with a longer life, able to handle fourteen to sixteen whales, whereas manilla could only manage eight or nine before renewal.

Edward W Paget-Tomlinson

Acknowledgement

I must acknowledge with gratitude the help of Arthur G Credland, Keeper of Maritime History at the Town Docks Museum, Hull, in the preparation of this chapter.

Typical Fishing Vessels 1900–1960

Ship	Flag	Built	By	GRT	Length (bp) × breadth × depth Feet–inches Metres	Engines	Remarks
Trawlers							
MINO	UK	1903	Goole SB & Rep Co, Goole	168	110–4 × 20–10 × 11–1 *33.6 × 6.4 × 3.4*	1 C D Holmes triple-expansion steam; 1 shaft	North Sea boxing fleet trawler
MARGARET DUNCAN	UK	1913	Cochrane & Sons, Selby	224	120–1 × 22–0 × 11–6 *36.6 × 6.7 × 3.5*	1 C D Holmes triple-expansion steam; 1 shaft	Middle and distant water trawler
MASTER HAND	UK	1920	George & Thomas Smith, Rye	46	70–0 × 18–6 × 9–0 *21.3 × 5.6 × 2.7*	Wooden-hulled sailing ketch	Lowestoft near-water
VICTORIA	Fra	1927	Burmeister & Wain, Copenhagen	849	197–3 × 32–11 × 16–4 *60.1 × 10.0 × 5.0*	1 4-stroke single acting B&W 6-cylinder diesel; 1 shaft	Grand Banks trawler
SCALBY WYKE	UK	1935	Cochrane & Sons, Selby	443	156–0 × 26–1 × 14–2 *47.5 × 8.0 × 4.3*	1 C D Holmes triple-expansion steam; 1 shaft	Hull distant water trawler

Ship	Flag	Built	By	GRT	Length (bp) × breadth × depth Feet–inches Metres	Engines	Remarks
CARL STANGEN	Ger	1937	Norderwerft Köser & Meyer, Hamburg	433	162–8 × 26–10 × 12–11 49.6 × 8.2 × 3.9	1 triple-expansion and low pressure turbine, double reduction gearing and hydraulic coupling; Deutsche Schiff & Masch Seebeck, Wesermünde; 1 shaft	Hamburg distant water trawler
BOSTON SEAFIRE	UK	1948	Cook, Welton & Gemmell, Beverley	689	178–0 × 30–7 × 16–0 54.3 × 9.3 × 4.9	1 C D Holmes triple-expansion; 1 shaft	Hull distant water trawler
LORD NELSON	UK	1961	Rickmers Werft, Bremerhaven	1226	221–9 × 36–6 × 23–4 67.6 × 11.1 × 7.12	1 4-stroke single acting Mirrlees 6-cylinder diesel (2000bhp); 1 shaft; 16 kts	Stern trawler, part freezer, part fresh; 12,000cu ft frozen fish capacity
Other fishing vessels							
FORMIDABLE	UK	1917	John Chambers, Lowestoft	40 net	88–0(oa) × 19–0 × 10–4 26.8 (oa) × 5.8 × 3.1	1 compound steam; Crabtree & Co; 1 shaft	Wooden-hulled North Sea herring drifter
ZAZPIAKBAT ex-*Anneliese Rathfen*, ex-*Georg Kimme*	Fra	1920	AG Weser, Bremen	786	201–5 × 29–10 × 15–4 61.4 × 9.1 × 4.7	Four-masted auxiliary barquentine; 2-stroke single acting Callesen 4-cylinder diesel; 1 shaft	Grand Banks; registered St Pierre and Miquelon (converted 1929)
PAN AMERICAN	US	1945	Martinolich SB Co, San Francisco	514	149–10 × 32–8 × — 45.7 × 10.0 × —	1 4-stroke single acting 8-cylinder diesel; Enterprise Engine & Foundry Co; 1 shaft	Wooden-hulled Pacific coast tuna clipper
Whale factory vessels							
ADMIRALEN ex-*Gibraltar*, ex-*Ariadne*	Nor	1869 (converted 1904)	W Pile & Co, Sunderland	1517	254–0 × 32–3 × 17–9 77.4 × 9.8 × 5.4	1 compound steam; Blair & Co; 1 shaft	Iron-hulled; early floating factory vessel, non-pelagic whaling
SIR JAMES CLARK ROSS ex-*Mahronda*	Nor	1905 (converted 1923)	Harland & Wolff, Belfast	8223	470–4 × 58–5 × 31–4 143.4 × 17.8 × 9.6	1 quadruple-expansion steam; Harland & Wolff; 1 shaft	Pioneer pelagic factory vessel; no stern slipway
LANCING ex-*Flackwell*, ex-*Calanda*, ex-*Omsk*, ex-*Rio Tete*, ex-*Knight Errant*	Nor	1898 (converted 1925)	Charles Connell & Co, Glasgow	7991	470–0 × 57–3 × 31–11 143.2 × 17.5 × 9.7	1 triple-expansion steam; Dunsmuir & Jackson; 1 shaft	First factory vessel with stern slipway
KOSMOS	Nor	1929	Workman Clark, Belfast	17,801	554–1 × 77–3 × 49–7 168.9 × 23.6 × 15.1	1 quadruple-expansion steam; Workman Clark; 1 shaft	Pioneer purpose-built factory vessel with stern slipway
WALTER RAU	Ger	1937	Deutsche Werft, Hamburg	14,869	554–1 × 74–6 × 33–6 168.9 × 22.7 × 10.2	Four-cylinder compound steam; Deutsche Werft; 2 shafts	Very complete processing plant
BALAENA	UK	1946	Harland & Wolff, Belfast	15,760	539–8 × 77–5 × 34–1 164.5 × 23.6 × 10.4	Triple-expansion steam; Harland & Wolff; 2 shafts	Last British-built factory vessel for British owner
SOVIETSKAYA ROSSIYA	SU	1961	Nosenko SY, Nikolayev	33,154	713–0 (oa) × 91–8 × 62–5 217.33 × 27.94 × 19.05	2 B&W diesels, 15,000bhp; 2 shafts, 16kts	Insulated space 3980cu m, oil capacity 21,652cu m
Whalers (whale catchers)							
ØRNEN	Nor	1902	Framnaes Mek Verk, Sandefjord	103	91–2 × 18–1 × 10–8 27.8 × 5.5 × 3.2	1 Akers triple-expansion steam; 1 shaft, 12 kts	First catcher built by Framnaes
H J BULL	Nor	1935	Fredriksstad Mek Verk, Fredrikstad	570	151–0 × 30–8 × 16–11 46.0 × 9.3 × 5.1	1 4-cylinder compound steam; Fredriksstad Mek Verk; 1 shaft, 16kts	Pioneer larger catcher
SEKI MARU	Jap	1937	Hayashikane SB, Shimonoseki	297	129–0 × 24–0 × 13–9 39.3 × 7.3 × 4.19	1 2-stroke single acting 6-cylinder Niigata Tekkosho diesel; 1 shaft, 14kts	First successful diesel catcher
KOS 50	Nor	1951	AS Stord Verft, Stord	608	169–4(oa) × 29–6 × 18-1 51.6 (oa) × 9.0 × 5.5	4 cylinder compound; 1900 hp; 1 shaft, 15kts	
SEKI MARU NO 17	Jap	1956	Hayashikane Zosen, Shimonoseki	641	203–1 (oa) × 31–10 × 16–8 62.0 × 9.7 × 5.0	1 2-stroke single acting 10-cylinder Hayashikane diesel; 3000bhp, 1 shaft, 15kts	

6

Service Vessels

Tugs

Ocean-going and salvage tugs

By the end of the nineteenth century deep-sea towing had become established. One famous late nineteenth-century tow which caught the public eye was undertaken by the paddle tug *Anglia*, owned by Wm Watkins and nicknamed 'three-fingered Jack' because of her three funnels. Cleopatra's Needle which now stands on the Victoria Embankment in London was given to Britain by the Ruler of Egypt and encased in an iron tube for towing to Britain in 1878. Halfway home it broke away, ending up in the Spanish port of Ferroll where *Anglia* was sent to bring it the rest of the way. She accomplished this despite the idiosyncrasies of a tube which refused to be pulled in a straight line.

That was by no means the only noteworthy deep sea tow before 1900 but proves that it had been done and by a paddle tug at that.

This era had seen huge steps forwards both in engineering and in trade all around the

world. The industrial nations were spreading their wings and sending their goods to remote places in ever larger ships which tended to break down. Large pieces of equipment had to be shipped to new ports in, for example, Africa and India. How did one get a floating dock to the Far East? – there was only one way and that was to tow it.

Tugs also were getting larger and more powerful, which made them suitable for the long ocean voyages and ferocious weather conditions, which in their turn brought about changes in their design.

Governments used tugs for a great many purposes, and by the time the First World War started the British Government had amassed a considerable fleet. They were badly needed to salvage the vessels mined or damaged in U-boat attacks. Very often valuable cargoes were saved by damaged vessels being run ashore to prevent them foundering, then being salved.

Admiralty tugs also made long passages with barges or monitors to distant theatres of war and it has to be remembered that these were not sophisticated ships. Conditions on

board must have been very primitive, as was communications equipment. They also had to carry vast quantities of coal for boilers which were voracious consumers of the precious fuel.

By the end of the First World War, the British Admiralty was building much larger vessels such as the 'Saint' class. For example *St Fergus* built in 1919 by Fleming & Ferguson on the Clyde was 135ft long with twin boilers and a steam reciprocating engine producing 1250ihp. She had a high forecastle which housed most of the crew, although the forecastle deck ran back to midships forming the boat deck. Even so, her wheelhouse was small and her equipment minimal.

The Netherlands had come into the busi-

An early combined ocean-going tug and salvage steamer was the London registered Warren Hastings, *built in 1886 by R Duncan & Co, of Port Glasgow.* Warren Hastings *was owned by V S E Grech & Co which owned several large tugs and salvage ships around the turn of the century.* Warren Hastings *was 616grt and equipped with two compound steam engines of 2000ihp giving a speed of 14kts, and her salvage pumps could pump water at the rate of 4000 tons per hour.* (CMP)

The Smit tugs Witte Zee (left) and Zwarte Zee arriving at Wellington, New Zealand, with a floating dry dock in tow. Witte Zee was built in 1914 by J & K Smit of Kinderdijk, Netherlands, for the Rotterdam firm. Of 465grt, she was equipped with a triple-expansion steam engine producing 1000ihp. The 604grt Zwarte Zee, also built at Kinderdijk, was fitted with a triple-expansion engine developing 1500ihp. (CMP)

ness before 1900 and rapidly attained its dominant position in the salvage and ocean-towing industry. Their names are household words – Smit and later Wijsmuller, as are the names of some of their vessels, for example *Noordzee* (750hp, built 1892), *Zwarte Zee* (1500hp, built 1896). Building on their experience gained through towing dredging equipment around the world, the Dutch worked hard and succeeded in taking much of the business which the British had secured in the past. Most of the towing of floating docks was undertaken by companies such as Smit. *Zwarte Zee* mentioned above was only the first of her name. The third appeared in 1933 and had twin diesels which produced a total of 4200bhp. She was something of a 'first', being the largest tug of her time, Smit's first diesel tug and it was also the first time so much horsepower had been put into such a small hull. She had Vulcan hydraulic couplings which could combine the two engines on to the one shaft, so that one engine gave her 13kts and two engines 17kts. With 300 tons of fuel on board she could cruise at full speed for twenty-five days or if necessary stay at sea under normal conditions for as long as five weeks. A later *Zwarte Zee* (1963) had 9000bhp and could attain at 20kts. Germany, too, had an interest in the salvage business and the firm of Bugsier built the large twin screw motor tug *Seefalke* (3000ihp) as early as 1924.

The tug/salvage steamer Fritiof *owned by the long-established Gothenburg Towage & Salvage Co A/B, of Sweden. Built in 1920 and of 672grt,* Fritiof, *equipped more as a salvage steamer than a tug, was one of a large fleet owned by the company which provided handling and general towing in the Gothenburg area, and coastal and short-sea towing services. (CMP)*

Among the owners of high horsepower tugs there was great rivalry and for many years the word 'horsepower' became suspect. Some owners referred to their tugs' horsepower as the total amount on board, including not only the main engines but the auxiliary machinery as well. This, of course, gave a false impression of the tug's capability, as only the main engines should have been included. It lead to the adoption of the 'static bollard pull' as the criterion of a tug's performance, which indicated how much force the vessel could exert with her engines when standing still.

It was after the First World War that Smit first started to put salvage ships 'on station', near the Western Approaches, acting rather as ambulances waiting for an accident to happen. This was facilitated by wireless telegraphy which enabled them to keep in contact with their owners and also listen out for any SOS or Mayday call. The practice spread and soon tugs were stationed near many of the world's major trade routes.

However it must be remembered that this type of operation was very cost consuming. It was all very well to have a tug on the spot or within calling distance, but the investment in the ship, its equipment and crew was enormous. As the century progressed the cost of all these increased to crippling proportions until the practice had to cease. However during the years while it lasted, the 'on-station' salvage tug gave sterling service.

Other countries were not slow to follow the Netherlands' example – the United States, Germany, France, Japan, Sweden, Greece, Denmark, Russia and, of course, many others. An example was the American *Relief* which was owned by Merritt & Chapman; 185ft long, she was built at Wilmington, Delaware in 1907, had a 1600hp steam engine, a crew of twenty-six and operated worldwide. She

The German owned Seefalke, built in 1924 by J C
Tecklenborg of Bremerhaven, survived the Second World
War, and gave much useful postwar service prior to the
introduction of a later namesake in 1970. This twin-
screw deepsea tug was fitted with two 6-cylinder Klöckner
Humboldt Deutz diesel engines giving 3000ihp. She was
owned by Bugsier-, Reederei- und Bergungs-, AG,
Hamburg, formed in 1889, which over the years has
maintained a fleet of large tugs for worldwide operations,
and has been the leading German company in the deepsea
towage and salvage field. (John Mannering; Laurence
Dunn collection)

house was extended out to the ship's side, though strangely her bridge was open to the elements. She survived until 1978 when she went to the shipbreakers.

As the century progressed so the equipment carried on board increased in scope and complexity. A dedicated salvage tug had to be self sufficient and could be expected to have on board spare generators, pumps and compressors for transfer to a casualty; ejectors, hoses, welding gear, wires, diving gear and a host of other equipment that may be needed in an emergency. These ships were often far from home and had to have everything they were likely to need at hand.

The crew also had to be dedicated men with a wealth of experience in the often unrewarding business of 'no cure – no pay': a phrase that meant just that – if at the end of the salvage venture nothing was saved, the salvage company and the crew received no reward. In the 1990s that no longer applies in every case.

The diesel engine was fairly well established by the time shipping was engulfed by the Second World War. Large ocean-going tugs took their place on convoys across the Atlantic and in the Mediterranean. Many were lost. Amongst others, the British Admi-

The 1924-built twin-screw Seaman, *was one of a fleet of harbour and deepsea tugs owned by United Towing Ltd, of Hull. A product of the Selby shipyard of Cochrane & Son, she was 369grt, and equipped with an Earle's triple-expansion steam engine giving 1200ihp and a speed of 12.5kts. Her coal bunker capacity was 214 tons and she had a range of 4000nm. Like other tugs of her era which survived the Second World War,* Seaman *had a long career and was not broken up until 1964. United Towing, her owners throughout* Seaman's *forty-year career, was an amalgamation in 1921 of several River Humber tug operators.* (CMP)

The 3000ihp ocean-going tug Thames *(601grt) was built in the Netherlands by P Smit Jr of Rotterdam in 1938 and saw worldwide service throughout her career. She was fitted with 3in–6in centrifugal pumps and a carbolic acid fire-extinguishing plant. Her owners, Smit of Rotterdam, transferred her in 1960 to its London-based associate company Overseas Towage & Salvage, and she was renamed* Salvonia. *She stranded and became a total loss on the Philippines coast in 1964 when undertaking salvage operations.* (Laurence Dunn collection)

had tall masts to carry her radio equipment and the heavy derricks so useful in salvage work. The US salvage fleet was to do much good work, especially in the Second World War.

The South African Railways & Harbours Board have always had some fine salvage tugs, which also doubled as harbour tugs. Their eastern seaboard produces some extremely inclement weather and as Cape Town is half way between Europe and the Far East it sits on several important trade routes. Because of its large reserves of coal, South Africa tended to keep steam tugs longer than other countries. In 1934, the above concern took delivery of the 154ft *John Dock*. She had twin screws driven by steam engines and, although she did not have a forecastle, her solid-looking deck-

Built as ATA 238, one of a large group of standard design tugs, and purchased from the US Government in 1947, the 2500ihp Noord-Holland was owned by the Netherlands firm of Bureau Wijsmuller, based at Ijmuiden. Built by Gulfport Boiler & Welding Works, Port Arthur, Texas, she was of 548grt and fitted with a 12-cylinder General Motors diesel engine. Taking delivery of its first tug in 1913, and becoming well-known in towage and salvage, Wijsmuller operated very much in the shadow of its larger Rotterdam competitor Smit. In fact, its then four largest tugs were sold to Smit in 1927. (FotoFlite)

ralty produced the *Bustler* class, which were Britain's answer to the Smit and Bugsier tugs. They were 205ft long, were powered by twin Atlas Polar diesels producing 3020bhp in total, and had a range of 5000 miles at 12kts – three quarters of their full speed.

This class produced the famous *Turmoil*. In 1952 she was working for the Overseas Towage & Salvage Company and went to the aid of the US freighter *Flying Enterprise*, a journey which took her into the history books. For five and a half days her crew fought to bring the crippled ship into port only to see her finally sink off Falmouth. It was 'no cure–no pay', so there was no salvage fee for the owners, master or crew, only notoriety – not because of their skill and dedication, but because the master of the *Enterprise* refused to leave his ship!

The United States Navy also built numerous tugs for service in the Second World War. They were designated by letters and numbers, for example the ATRs, ATAs, ARSs and ATFs and saw service in every theatre of the war. Another class, the V-4s,

were large and were the first US tugs to be fitted with Kort nozzles. They were operated for the Government by the Moran Towing & Transportation Company and saw service off the Normandy beaches. They were 194ft long and had twin diesels each developing 2250hp driving a single propeller. The forecastle deck ran aft of midships with another two layers of deckhouse above that and they were well armed. Too big for commercial companies most were scrapped, though a few were sold for further use.

Obviously, not all salvage relates to aid of a vessel in distress; some of it can involve archaeological sites. One of the best known of these was the royal warship *Vasa*, the pride of the Swedish nation, which sailed in August 1628 from Stockholm, and, having reached open water, gently turned over and sank. Some cannons were brought up in 1664 but it was not until 1957, when the wreck was relocated by coring, that serious consideration was given to lifting her.

The Neptun Salvage Company became involved and in May 1961 after much trial and tribulation, *Vasa* was finally brought into her own dock. She had been preserved by the mud into which she had gradually sunk and was lifted from it by cables passed underneath her and attached on either side to pontoons. *Atlas*, a 120ft, 1000ihp tug built by Cochrane & Son, of Selby, England and *Ajax* a 119ft, 2500ihp tug built by Kramer & Booy of Kootstertille, Netherlands and two other salvage vessels from Neptun were involved.

By the late 1950s, the Soviet Union, too, was building large ocean-going tugs with icebreaking bows as a great deal of their

Owners of the 3000bhp Jean-Bart were Societé de Remorquage et de Sauvetage du Nord, of Dunkirk, France, which with associate companies owned and operated a large fleet of ship-handling and deepsea tugs. Jean-Bart was built in 1956 by Ateliers & Chantiers de France at Dunkirk, and was of 717grt, had a length of 162.5ft (49.5m), breadth 33.5ft (10.2m) and draught 16.4ft (5m), and was fitted with two 8-cylinder Werkspoor diesel engines. The size contrast with the harbour tugs in the background is apparent. (Laurence Dunn collection)

A leading Far East deepsea tug and salvage operator is Nippon Salvage, which introduced in 1960 the tug/salvage vessel Hayashio Maru, *built by Mitsubishi Zosen of Shimonoseki. Of 1156grt, she was fitted with a Uraga/ Sulzer 8-cylinder diesel engine developing 3200bhp, and was capable of 13.5kts. She was fitted with two 15-ton derricks for use in salvage operations.* (Laurence Dunn collection)

coastline is icebound in winter. In 1959 they built *Diomid* one of the *Atlant* class, which was diesel-electric and 172ft in length. She had a raised forecastle which ran aft of midships and two tiers of deckhouses above that.

As the cost of the big tugs escalated, labour costs and fuel did likewise. It became obvious that salvage tugs had to find alternative employment so they turned to long distance towing, taking an ever increasing number of vessels to the shipbreakers in the Far East. Eventually the offshore industry would require powerful tugs to tow installations out to deep water sites and with that would come the super tugs of 10,000hp or more.

Ship-handling tugs

Tugs have been around a long time. Three thousand years ago the Egyptians used oar propelled vessels as tugs to pull vast barges on the Nile and up to the nineteenth century oared vessels were used to haul sailing ships out of harbour to catch a breeze. Every movement in harbour was similarly achieved.

An example of a nineteenth century tug was the paddle vessel *Monarch* of 1833 made famous in Turner's *The Fighting Temeraire*. As her paddle wheels acted in unison, she couldn't make a turn without iron ballast

being moved from side to side on rails to lift one paddle out of the water. Furthermore her 20hp was scarcely impressive!

By the turn of the century, engineers had transformed the boiler and the steam engine to the point where horsepower was more in the order of 600 or 1000, possibly a little more.

In Europe, tug shape had become recognisable – narrow gutted, fine lined with a pointed bow. The deckhouse was well forward, above that an open bridge (a favoured few had a tiny caboose), a tall funnel, and a

Upon arrival at Port Said on its voyage from Italy to Japan, part of the 50,000 ton Admiralty Floating Dock 35 *in tow of Smit's 4000ihp sister tugs* Mississippi *and* Thames. Mississippi *(built 1960) and* Thames *(1961), were products of the J & K Smit shipyard at Kinderdijk, and measured 674grt; they were equipped with two Smit/ MAN diesel engines, were capable of 15kts, and carried a crew of twenty. With the decline of the salvage station tug in the 1950s and '60s, operators of large tugs sought new business and became very much involved in the towage of vessels to breakers, particularly from Europe and North America to the Far East, and the worldwide movement of rigs and barges for the offshore oil and gas exploration industries.* (Laurence Dunn collection)

A typical Thames river and London dock ship-handling tug was Doria, *built by Philip & Son, Dartmouth, in 1909, for William Watkins Ltd, an old-established London tug owner. Of 96.2ft registered length, and 20.6ft breadth, she was fitted with triple-expansion steam engines developing 550ihp.* Doria *is pictured here with another Watkins tug assisting the Newcastle steamer* Mill Hill *(built 1930, 4318grt) through the cutting between the Royal Victoria Dock and the Royal Albert Dock, London. (CMP)*

tow hook just forward of midships attached to the after end of the casing. The profile was very flat with very little rise at the forward end.

American tugs, however, looked different. Their hulls were long, slender and low, but the front of the bridge was circular and the deckhouse, aft of which was a heavy towing bollard, extended almost to the stern.

Both these shapes were to remain for fifty years or so, but what did alter was the power and style of the machinery, the sophistication of the equipment and design characteristics to improve stability. The latter was a particular problem, as many a tug was lost by being pulled over sideways or 'girted', when the tow wire accidentally came round on to the beam. Much thought and ingenuity went into the development of swivelling tow hooks which prevented this from happening.

The paddle tug began to disappear around 1900. The paddles were unwieldy, greatly increased the beam of the vessel and, in spite of the manoeuvrablity afforded by turning one paddle astern and one ahead, were quickly superseded by developments in the design of the screw propeller. Paddle tugs did however survive in several places, notably in the Royal Navy which was still building them as late as 1958. Elsewhere very few were in service by the start of the Second World War.

Typical vessels of the early part of the century were the famous 'Sun' tugs owned by W H J Alexander of London. They worked the Thames, handling the multitude of craft so familiar on the river. *Sun IV* was built in Hull in 1915 and was 105ft long with a gross tonnage of 200. She had a closed

bridge above the main deckhouse which gave the skipper a good all-round view, blocked only by the funnel. They were smart, attractive vessels and followed a style which was to be around for many years.

Equipment was minimal. Two lifeboats on radial davits, a simple tow hook aft of the casing, towing bows fitted over the casing and a festoon of old motor tyres round the bulwarks as protection. Accommodation was

A typical US tug of the between the wars period was Eleu *(built 1929 by Bethlehem Shipbuilding Corp, San Francisco, 335grt) owned by Inter-Island Steam Navigation Co of Honolulu. Unlike European tugs where the superstructure is cut down as much as possible and the towing hook is placed as near to midships as can be achieved, the design of US tugs differs in that they usually have a long superstructure and the towing hook, usually backed by a towing engine, is much further aft. (CMP)*

William Watkins Ltd, tug owners in London since the mid nineteenth century, owned a substantial fleet of Thames river and dock tugs. Typical of these was Gondia, *200grt, built by Cochrane & Sons, Selby, in 1927, and fitted with an 850ihp triple-expansion steam engine made by Crabtree & Co, of Great Yarmouth. Throughout her peacetime career she was employed in ship-handling in the port of London.* (CMP)

simple, as were navigation systems. Their coal-fired boilers and triple expansion engines were typical of the age.

It took time for any real developments to change the design of harbour tugs. The First World War had come and gone and it was not until the 1930s before diesel engines were considered in Europe, following US developments in the previous decade. Tug owners liked the big, slow turning propellers needed for steam engines and which took a 'grip' on the water. The faster turning diesels with their smaller screws posed a problem which was overcome by the introduction of a gearbox to lower the revolutions, also by the arrival of the big, slow-running, direct reversing diesel such as the British Polar type.

The same period witnessed the first of two new inventions that would later have far-reaching effects on the use and operation of tugs, both originating in Germany. The Kort nozzle of 1932 was literally a tube fitted round the propeller. It was carefully shaped to control the flow of water and produced a substantial increase in 'thrust' or the pulling power of a vessel. Despite its success, it was twenty years before it came to be generally accepted. Originally a fixed

Middle: *A typical United States harbour and coastal towage tug was* Turecamo Boys, *operated by B Turecamo Towing Corp of Brooklyn, New York. Built by Jakobson Shipyard Inc, of Oyster Bay, Long Island, in 1945, the 75ft (22.9m) long* Turecamo Boys *was fitted with an 8-cylinder General Motors diesel engine of 800bhp for main propulsion, and had a maximum speed of 11.4kts at 750rpm. On her trials a crash stop from full speed ahead to dead in water was made in 28 seconds.* (General Motors)

Bottom: *One of many large harbour and salvage tugs built for the Railways and Harbours Administration of South Africa, was the twin-screw* Sir William Hoy, *a product of the Armstrong Whitworth shipyard at Newcastle upon Tyne in 1929. Of 786grt, and fitted with two triple-expansion steam engines she was the most powerful (3577ihp) tug based as Durban, and was the forerunner of nine similar tugs built up to 1940.* Sir William Hoy *had a career spanning fifty years, being finally scrapped in 1979.* (CMP)

The first British-owned diesel-electric tug was Acklam Cross, *built for Tees Towing Co, Middlesbrough, in 1933 by Hall Russell & Co, Aberdeen. The 725ihp diesel-electric machinery fitted to the 150grt* Acklam Cross *was made by Peter Brotherhood of Peterborough. Dimensions of* Acklam Cross *were 90.5ft (27.6m) registered length, 22.1ft (6.7m) breadth and 11ft (3.35m) draught. (Laurence Dunn collection)*

tube, it eventually became part of the rudder and turned with it, increasing efficiency even more.

The second invention was the Voith-Schneider propeller which was quite revolutionary and consisted of a series of blades hanging vertically from a tube, the whole unit revolving rather like an egg-beater. By adjusting the pitch of the blades the water flow could produce thrust in any direction through 360 degrees. Although the idea had

These tugs of Moran Towing Corp of New York are pictured upon the arrival of the Cunard liner Queen Elizabeth *on 21 October 1946 following her first peacetime commercial transatlantic crossing. Moran tugs, with their black funnels and large white M had been a familiar sight in the port of New York for many years, but with the decline of the passenger liner so did the tug fleet of Moran, which adjusted its operations to additionally provide coastal and offshore towage services. (CPL)*

been applied to ferries in the 1930s, it was not until 1955, through the efforts of Wolfgang Baer, that it was first fitted to a tug – HAPAG's *Stier* – where the 'propeller', instead of pushing from the stern, pulled from a position well forward giving rise to the term 'tractor tug'. The concept completely altered ship handling, but while it was accepted on the continent of Europe, it was slow to be taken up in Britain and even slower in the United States.

Another invention was the straight hull line which was also widely adopted. Instead of hull plates being furnaced and shaped, a design was produced to mimic the curve of a ship's hull using straight, flat plates. A particular example of this type of construction was patented in the 'Hydroconic' hull by UK naval architects Burness, Corlett & Partners. A number of designers used 'chine' hulls as these were termed but the Hydroconic patent followed a clearly defined pattern.

As time progressed through two world wars and with the increasing pace of technical advance, the design of ships' hulls rapidly improved. Vessels became more squat, the breadth increased, the fore deck was swept upwards and extra tiers of deckhouses appeared. Sleeping and messing facilities were modernised, navigational and communication equipment were taken over by the electronics industry, towing wires came into the plastics era and machinery became more and more powerful. More than ever the tug became a large engine wrapped up in the smallest possible parcel.

A development of the harbour tug, but one occurring only in limited numbers, was the tug/tender – a combination of a ship-handling tug and small passenger ship – which was used to ferry passengers and their baggage to and from ocean liners anchored in the stream or in open roadsteads. This practice started in the later half of the nineteenth century, when ordinary tugs were granted a passenger certificate for the purpose.

Later a specific design of around 600 tons evolved incorporating a tug hull with a greatly enlarged superstructure; Cunard Line's *Skirmisher* (1884) and White Star Line's *Magnetic* (1891) being early twin screw examples capable of carrying up to 1200

Built in 1959, Stranton *is typical of numerous tugs built in the 1940s and '50s for ship-handling in UK docks and harbours. Constructed at the Appledore shipyard of P K Harris & Sons,* Stranton *was owned by Tees Conservancy Commission, Middlesbrough, which later became Tees & Hartlepool Port Authority.* Stranton, *which had two identical sister tugs, was 145grt, twin screw, and equipped with two 8-cylinder Blackstone oil engines giving 1200bhp. (Alan Sparrow)*

Cable ships

After the first successful underwater telegraph cable had been laid in 1851 (between St Margaret's Bay near Dover and Sangatte, France), the following decade and a half saw the completion of many similar projects in different parts of the world. The first transatlantic telegraph cable had been laid in 1858 but had failed within a very short time. In the meantime considerable improvements had been made in the construction, insulation and manufacture of underwater cable, and in 1866 the steamship *Great Eastern* laid what was in reality the first successful transatlantic underwater telegraphic cable. The success of the venture aroused public interest in this form of communication, and the years up to, and beyond, the turn of the century saw a progressive increase in many parts of the world in the numbers of new cable routes planned and laid.

In those early years the ships engaged in the task were conversions of ordinary commercial vessels which had the power, capacity, stability and seaworthiness for the work. Gradually these came to be replaced by custom-built ships designed specifically to meet the variety of conditions encountered by the cable laying companies. At that time the laying of cables was entirely in the hands of the cable manufacturers, who were thus in a position to offer customers a complete package, from surveying the proposed route

passengers. Apart from the liner companies, the idea was also taken up by some of the railway companies as well as a number of tug-owning companies such as Alexandra Towing of Liverpool, Clyde Shipping Co of Glasgow and Red Funnel of Southampton. The latter concerns built or converted several vessels up to the 1930s, many of which had promenade decks extending to the stern, an example being Alexandra's *Romsey* built in 1930. After the Second World War the decline of traditional passenger liner shipping, as air travel increased, hastened the tender's demise.

One other type must be mentioned: the US river towboat which developed in quite a different way. A typical Mississippi towboat is absolutely rectangular, could well be 150ft long, have engines developing 5000 or 6000hp and be able to push forty or fifty loaded barges in front of it. Push tows have

been adopted in many parts of the world, but none look so impressive as those on the Mississippi.

No story of tugs would be complete without a mention of what is perhaps one of the most remarkable feats of towing ever carried out. During the Second World War the invasion of Normandy was planned to take place on open beaches, as attacking a port was far too dangerous. To supply the invasion force an entire port had to be built. There were two big towing jobs to be done, first to send a veritable armada under tow across the Atlantic from the United States, and then to tow everything across the English Channel. Something like two hundred tugs, half of them American, were pressed into service for the assault and an entire port was assembled. Without the humble tug and the skill of their crews it could not have been done.

Ken Troup

Typical of a turn-of-the-century cable ship, the 7981grt Colonia *was built in 1902 by Wigham Richardson & Co Ltd, Newcastle upon Tyne for the Telegraph Construction & Maintenance Co Ltd, London. With triple-expansion machinery driving twin screws, she was the largest cable ship afloat at the time of her completion, and her four tanks could hold some 3000 miles of cable. In 1928 she was sold to Norwegian interests in Sandefjord and converted into a floating whaling factory, being named* Torodd. *After two seasons in the Antarctic, she was laid up, but sold in 1934 to an Oslo-based whaling company. After three Antarctic seasons with this company she was sold to German interests, renamed* Sudmeer, *and made three more visits to the Antarctic, before she was lost during the Second World War. (CMP)*

to making and laying the cable. The cable operators became responsible for the maintenance and repair of their cables, which led to the conversion or construction of vessels specifically for this work and suited to local conditions. However as time passed, and especially in the post First World War years, the situation gradually changed, with operating companies undertaking the laying of their own cables, and the cable manufacturers concentrating on that side of the work only. This led to the construction of ships which, as well as being able to undertake maintenance and repair, were capable of laying considerable lengths of cable.

Although Marconi had carried out successful experiments in wireless telegraphy in 1896, this new form of communication did not prove to be as detrimental to what had become a well established part of commercial life as was feared. In fact, though competitive, the two systems grew to become complementary to one another, rather than the reverse.

It was inevitable that after the invention of the telephone by Bell in 1876 attention would be given to developing submarine cables to accommodate this new form of communication. Successful experiments were carried out, but for a number of technical reasons only comparatively short routes were possible. However, with the introduction of

the repeater or relay, and its successful incorporation in a submarine telephone cable in 1943, the way was opened for the further progress. By the 1950s major changes in cable laying techniques began to take place. The introduction of larger diameter cables, underwater rigid repeater/amplifiers in the telephone cables, better means of recovery and improved navigation systems all meant that the laying of long distance underwater telephone links was now possible. These changes were reflected in the design and equipping of the ships, and led to the construction of some very sophisticated dual purpose vessels.

Operations

Survey

Before any cable could be laid the proposed route had to be surveyed. Until comparatively recently there was not a great deal of information available on charts concerning ocean depths, so not only did soundings have to be taken – the ships were fitted with special sounding machines – but much additional data obtained concerning the nature and composition of the sea bed, and the temperature of the sea water on and in the vicinity of the route. A rough sea bottom could chafe the cable, while temperature

could affect its performance and that of the repeaters.

Cable

The telegraph cable comprised a central copper conductor round which were wound sequential layers of gutta percha insulation, brass tape, bituminous wax tape, jute, wire armouring, and two more protective coverings. Weight varied according to the make up of the cable. Where cables were liable to damage by chafing or abrasion due to tidal movement, or mechanical damage by anchors or fishing nets, the degree of armouring was increased. Shore ends, too, had to have an increase in the degree of armouring. A reasonable average figure for the weight of a nautical mile of deep sea cable was about $2\frac{1}{2}$ tons, which increased when the above criteria were present.

Stowage

On board ship the cable, fed from the shore establishment, was stowed in large cylindrical tanks, their diameter depending upon their location within the hull. In the centre of each was a cylindrical tapered core or cone, the depth of the tank in height. This was necessary to prevent coils collapsing into the centre. Also in the tank was a movable (vertically) shaped horizontal framework known as a 'crinoline', designed to prevent several turns of cable rising at the same time when laying was in progress.

When loading, the cable was laid from the outside of the tank to the centre, at which point thin battens were placed across the coils and the cable was taken back to the outside of the tank and the process repeated. When a tank was full the cable was taken over to the next one and loading continued in the same way.

With the advent of telephone cable fitted with repeaters, new arrangements had to be made to cope with the latter. The part of the cable in which a repeater had been fitted was stowed in one of a series of special cradles on deck adjacent to the tank. This led to a complicated arrangement of bights of cable in that deck area before the cable could continue to be fed into the tank.

A large proportion of the internal volume of a cable ship was devoted to the cable tanks. Workmen are shown here carefully stowing the cables in the 40ft diameter tanks of the Ocean Layer *in 1957. The ship carried about 1000 nautical miles of cable in four tanks, and was being prepared for renewal and replacement work in the Indian Ocean.* (CMP)

The forecastle deck of the Retriever, *showing the cable engine and the drums leading to the bow sheaves. The photograph was taken in May 1961 in London's Surrey Commercial Docks as the ship was about to sail to Bermuda to lay the shore ends of a new cable connection with the United States.* (CMP)

Laying

The key piece of equipment in laying and recovering cable is the specially designed winch, or cable engine. Generally two of these winches were fitted either on the fore deck or on the deck below, in which case their drums projected through the deck over in a hatchway. Several turns of cable were taken round the drum before being led to or from the bow sheaves. For telegraph cable these were of about 3ft 6in diameter, but latterly, following the arrival of repeaters, their size was increased twofold or threefold; the winch drums were also made larger. In addition, monorail gantries were erected over the bow sheaves to handle repeaters. Steam, because of its ease and flexibility of control, has long been the ideal prime mover for the winches, but recently modern technology has enabled similar characteristics to be applied to electric or electro-hydraulic cable winches.

When laying cable over the stern a different system was employed. As the ship moved forward the cable was paid out via a large braked drum, which controlled the rate of lay. Before reaching the drum the cable passed through a series of braked jockey pulleys which kept the cable in tension. However, for telephone cable fitted with repeaters a different system had to be adopted. The cable passed over the series of jockey sheaves as with a telegraph cable, but when a repeater came along, the cable was removed from the sheaves, a rope was attached to it and fed through the sheaves while the repeater was placed in a trolley which passed alongside the sheaves as paying out continued. When the repeater had passed the sheaves, the rope was removed and the cable fed back over the sheaves. (The process was reminiscent of the way in which the anchor of a 'wooden wall' was weighed by attaching a rope messenger to the cable and leading this to the capstan, the cable itself being too large for turns to be taken round the capstan barrel.)

Later this method was replaced by an improved system, in which the cable and repeaters passed along and between, and were gripped by, a series of pairs of rubber-tyred wheels in two rows, the wheels being able to move apart vertically to accommodate changing diameters as the repeaters approached and passed between them.

From the braked drum the cable ran over a single sheave at the stern, but when repeaters were present it was passed along a chute fitted on deck and of a curvature over the stern to take the rigid repeaters (usually some 10ft long) next to the sheave.

To ensure that the cable turns on the drum of the winch were always under tension, whether laying or hauling in, a device, usually referred to as the 'hauling off and holding back gear' was fitted adjacent to the winch. Originally of a mechanical type driven from the winch, it has been superseded by a smaller (that is, with fewer pairs of wheels) version of the rubber-tyred apparatus used when stern laying.

Dynamometers

A very important element in cable work, whether laying or recovering, was the tension in the cable. Knowledge of this at all times was essential in order to control the speed of laying and to be certain that the cable was following the contours of the sea bed and not being stretched between high points. It was equally important when recovering a cable, to avoid exceeding its braking strain. The data was obtained by fitting a dynamometer between winch and sheaves. This was a machine which, either by mechanical or, more recently, electrical means, registered the precise tension in the cable at all times.

The ships

Cable ships, whether layers, repairers, or repairer/layers are through the exigencies of their work sophisticated vessels. They conform to the requirements of the classification societies so far as construction and standard outfit is concerned. In appearance they have an almost unique silhouette, which has changed little over the years – a clipper stem surmounted by a sheave assembly with, more recently, a monorail gantry above, machinery and thus the funnel placed aft of midships, a long flush, open forward deck for handling and working on cables, and an outfit of boats considerably in excess of those required under statutory regulations. Some operators, however, found that the conventional poop, bridge and forecastle design was more suitable for ships which spent much of their time in areas subject to heavy weather, since it offered better sea-keeping qualities and gave more protection for cable work.

Cable laying was complicated by the inclusion of repeaters at intervals along the length of the cable itself. Not only did they require special handling during laying, but also needed careful checking, work being carried out by two engineers in this photograph taken aboard Mercury in 1964. (CMP)

forward of the foremost tank and in some cases in the wings alongside them. Unlike almost all other vessels, cable ships discharge their cargo while at sea, so they have enhanced water ballast capacity and systems which can be brought into use to compensate for the weight of the cable as it is used, and so maintain a suitable trim condition, thus avoiding problems with the work in hand. Since the ships can spend long periods at sea, they carry adequate quantities of stores, fresh water and bunkers. Much attention is always given to the comfort and amenities of the crew and specialists on board. Workshop and cable testing facilities are provided.

In the early years it was the practice to lay the designated cable in one continuous length. In order to be able to complete a number of very long lays of this kind, several vessels were built with sufficient stowage capacity to meet this requirement. One such was the Telegraph Construction & Maintenance Company's *Dominia*, built in 1926 on Tyneside. Her four tanks had a total capacity of almost 180,000 cubic feet (5097 cubic metres), in which could be carried the whole of the 3627 nautical miles of telegraph cable (weighing some 8592 tons) required for the link across the Pacific between British Columbia and Fanning Island, a small atoll roughly midway between Hawaii and Tahiti. This was, in fact, a replacement of the original cable, which had been laid in 1902 in one length by the same company's *Colonia*, also built specially for that purpose.

Until the arrival of the diesel engine steam, and in particular the triple expansion engine, had been the means of propulsion, and it continued to be so for many years. Its great advantage lay in the ability to operate at very low speeds for long periods, coupled with extreme flexibility of movement. In more recent times, thanks to the introduction of a means of simulating the advantages of steam propulsion, some turbo- or diesel-electric installations have been fitted in several vessels.

The nature of the work carried out by these ships influenced their design. The bulk and weight of the cable required that its containers (tanks) be fitted in that part of the ship best suited to the purpose: that is, the main body of the hull. So doing brought the machinery spaces aft of midships, yet allowed one more tank, if needed, to be fitted abaft the engine room over the shaft tunnels. Ancillary equipment connected with the work, such as buoys, grapnels, etc, and many other items and stores, were stowed in a hold

Governments, government departments, and in some cases the armed forces, of most of the leading maritime nations own and operate cable ships, in addition to the cable manufacturers and cable companies. As well as the principal deep sea routes an increasingly complex system of telegraph and telephone cables has been laid, and con-

An example of the smaller type of cable ship, the Ariel was built by Swan, Hunter & Wigham Richardson Ltd, Newcastle upon Tyne in 1939 for the General Post Office, London. Length overall was 250ft 6in, breadth 35ft 3in, draught 16ft 4in (76.4m × 10.7m × 4.9m) and gross tonnage 1479. Triple expansion machinery of 1400ihp, driving twin screws, gave a speed of 12kts. (J Bowen collection)

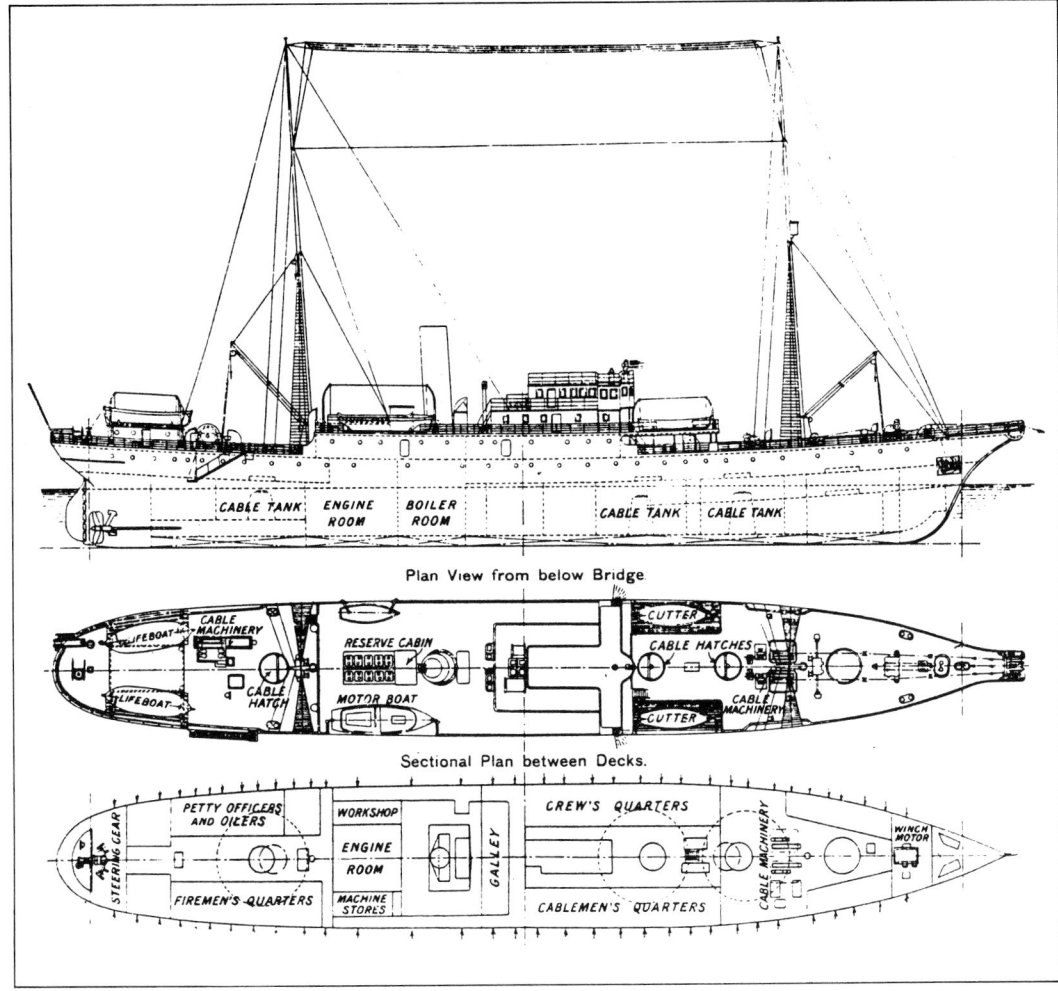

CABLE TANK | ENGINE ROOM | BOILER ROOM | | CABLE TANK | CABLE TANK

Plan View from below Bridge

CABLE MACHINERY | CUTTER | CABLE HATCHES | LIFEBOAT | RESERVE CABIN | CABLE HATCH | CABLE HATCH | MOTOR BOAT | CUTTER | CABLE MACHINERY | LIFEBOAT

Sectional Plan between Decks.

STEERING GEAR | PETTY OFFICERS AND OILERS | WORKSHOP | ENGINE ROOM | GALLEY | CREW'S QUARTERS | WINCH MOTOR | FIREMEN'S QUARTERS | MACHINE STORES | CABLEMEN'S QUARTERS | CABLE MACHINERY

The Edouard Jeramac *was built 1914 by Forges & Chantiers de la Méditerranée, Graville, near Havre, France for cable repair work in the North Atlantic. Sold to All America Cables in 1929, she reverted to French ownership after the Second World War and was renamed* Pierre Picard. *From* The Electrician, *3 July 1914.*

1946 was bought by the French Government. She sank in the harbour at Brest, France in December 1952.

Faraday was the second ship to bear this name, and was built in 1923 for Siemens Brothers, London, by Palmers Shipbuilding & Iron Company at Jarrow on Tyneside. Her dimensions were, length 394.3ft between perpendiculars, breadth 48.3ft, depth 34.5ft (120.2m × 14.7m × 10.5m), gross tonnage 5533. The triple expansion steam machinery, driving twin screws, developed 2960ihp, and gave a speed of 12 knots. The line of four cable tanks amidships, with a total capacity of 91,000 cubic feet (2577 cubic metres) brought the boiler and engine rooms well aft. The position of the four tanks led to an interesting layout of the upper and shelter decks. The central area of each was clear except for the boiler and engine casings, with accommodation arranged down each side of each deck. On the shelter deck a trough linked all tank hatches, and was extended aft to the stern working deck, where there was a paying out machine. Two cable engines were fitted on the upper deck forward, with hatches on the shelter deck in way of their drums. There was the usual outfit of dynamometers and other ancillary equipment associated with cable work, with a well equipped test room forward on the port side of the large central deckhouse. A three sheave assembly was fitted over the clipper stem, and two sheaves were fitted at the stern on the starboard side. Forward, aft of the fore peak, was a hold for the stowage of buoys and other stores and gear. The ship carried a very comprehensive outfit of boats.

After a full working life, the ship was laid up at the beginning of the war, but was later bombed and sunk off Cornwall whilst on a passage to Milford Haven.

The diesel-electric *Alert* was built for the Post Office's Deep Sea Cables Service in 1961 by the Fairfield Shipbuilding & Engineering Co Ltd, Glasgow. The extreme overall length is 418.0ft, breadth 54.5ft, depth 33.25ft (127.4m × 16.6m × 10.13m), and deadweight tonnage 4600. The hull is strengthened for navigation in ice. The three cable tanks have a capacity of 57,960 cubic feet (1641 cubic metres). All picking up and

tinues to be laid, over short-sea and inter-island routes, and between places in neighbouring countries. In addition to the specially designed and custom-built ships constructed in many countries to service and maintain this web of submarine cables, a variety of small commercial craft such as coasters, coastal cargo ships, colliers and the like at one time or another have been fitted out for specific tasks. A number of very interesting conversions have taken place, such as the transformation of a large steam yacht, built in 1898, into a cable laying and repair ship in 1921, or the conversion of a 5360 tons deadweight cargo ship into a layer/repair ship.

The following three examples of layer/repair ships show how, whilst the basic design has remained, it has been able to accommodate the technological and operational changes which have taken place during the first five decades of this century.

Edouard Jeramac was built in 1914 for the Compagnie Française de Cables Télégraphiques by Forges et Chantiers de la Méditerranée, Graville, near Havre, France. Her primary role was the maintenance and

repair of the country's north Atlantic cable system. As the plan shows she was conventional in appearance, with dimensions 269.0ft × 1.0ft × 17.55ft draught, (82m × 12.5m × 5.35m) and a displacement of 3800 tons. The two triple expansion steam engines driving twin screws gave a speed of 11 knots. Water ballast was carried in the double bottom and the hull was strengthened for navigation in ice. Comfortable accommodation was provided for the crew of about eighty, and she was equipped with workshops, an infirmary and pharmacy. In addition to the two lifeboats and a dinghy, she carried two cutters and a motor launch for use in cable operations. The two cable tanks, one forward and one aft, had a total cable capacity of 885 tons. Buoys, grapnels, and other equipment were stowed in the hold forward, being handled by a derrick on the foremast in conjunction with a steam winch. The cable gear was fitted on the main deck, with the drums projecting through hatches on the spar deck, where the control gear was also sited.

The ship was sold to All America Cables in 1929, without a change of name, and in

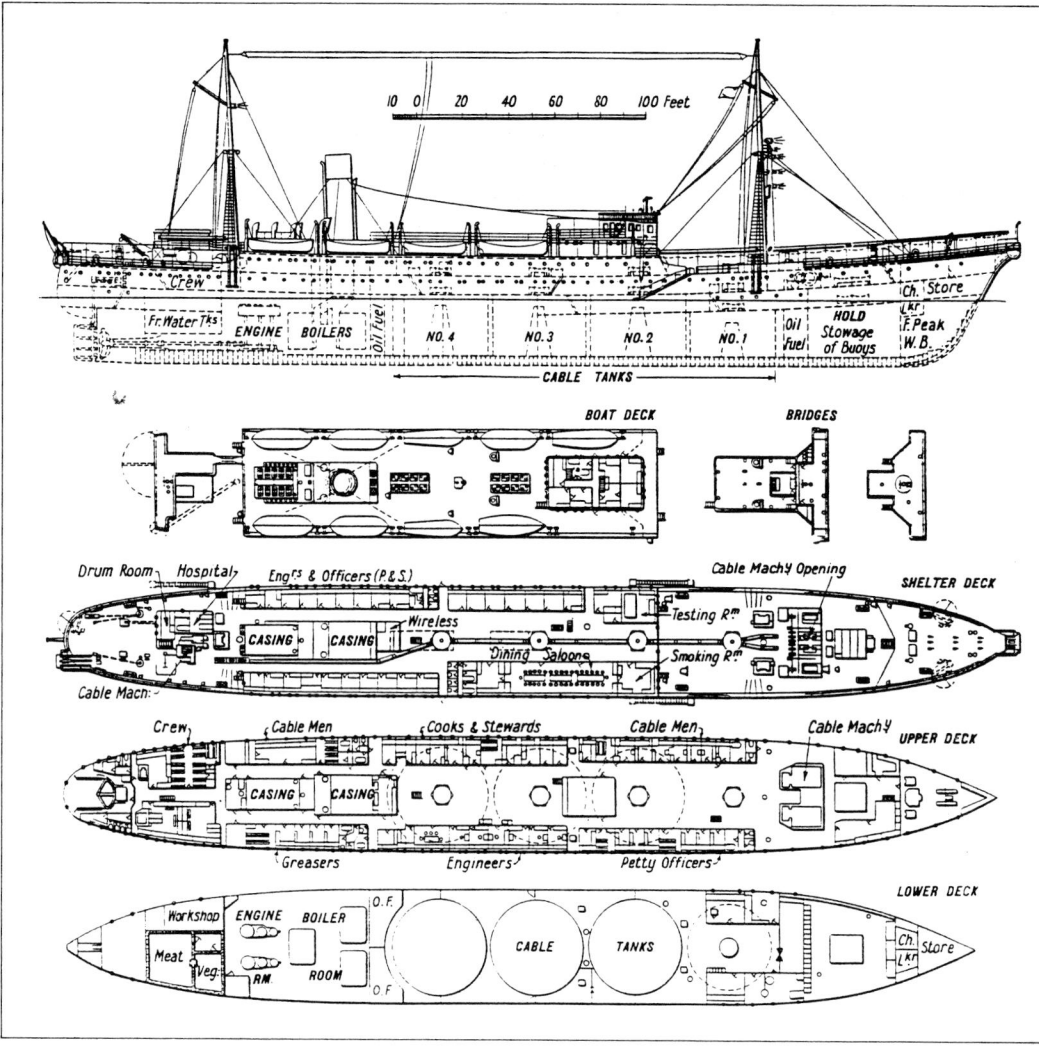

Built 1923 by Palmer's Shipbuilding Co Ltd, Newcastle for Siemens Brothers, London, Faraday *measured 394.3ft, by 48.3ft, by a depth of 34.6ft (120.2m × 14.7m × 10.5m), for 5533grt. Triple expansion machinery of 2960ihp drove twin screws, the engine room being three-quarters aft, in a pattern that became common for cable ships. Laid up in September 1939, but recommissioned by the Admiralty in December 1939, the ship was bombed and set on fire by a lone German aircraft on passage from Falmouth to Milford Haven on 25 March 1941, abandoned, and drifted ashore near St Anne's Head. Illustration from* Shipping Wonders of the World.

paying out operations on repairs are carried out over the bow, and three sheaves 8ft (2.44m) diameter are fitted at the top of the curved stem. To handle the repeaters, each of which is a rigid unit some 10ft (3.05m) long and 12in (0.3m) in diameter, fitted to modern telephone cables a monorail gantry, complete with lifting and transporter gear, is fitted over, and extended some way ahead of, the bow sheaves. Two picking up and paying out machines are fitted forward on the main deck, with the drums projecting through a hatch in the upper deck. One of these is used when laying cable over the stern. Dynamometers and hauling off and holding back gear are located adjacent to the machines. The paying out gear at the stern is suitable for laying long lengths of cable complete with repeaters. For this operation the cable is fed along a trough running along the centre of the upper deck from the vicinity of the forward tank to the stern sheave. A well-equipped test room, with operations control room next to it, are sited on the upper deck amidships.

Alert was the first Post Office ship to have diesel-electric machinery. Four Mirrlees eight-cylinder turbo-charged four-stroke engines, each with a maximum continuous output of 1860bhp are each coupled to an AEI 895kW main generator. Power from the generators goes to two main propulsion motors, each of 2200shp, driving two screws to give a service speed of 15 knots. Equipment is fitted to provide the very fine speed

Although not radically different in appearance from the Faraday *of a generation earlier, the* Monarch *was actually completed in 1946 for the General Post Office by Swan, Hunter & Wigham Richardson Ltd, Newcastle upon Tyne. Dimensions were: length overall 483ft 7in, breadth 55ft 8in, draught 27ft 10in (147.4m × 16.9m × 8.5m), measuring 8056grt. Triple expansion machinery of 4500ihp, via twin screws, drove the ship at 14½kts. Cable machinery was electrically driven, and she could carry some 1900 nautical miles of lightweight cable and repeaters. She was sold to Cable & Wireless, London in 1970, being renamed* Sentinel. *(CMP)*

An example of a ship from the end of the period covered by this book, the Alert *was built in 1961 by the Fairfield Shipbuilding & Engineering Co Ltd, Govan, Glasgow for the Post Office, London. Length extreme over sheaves was 418ft 0in, breadth 54ft 6in, draught 22ft 5½in (127.4m × 16.6m × 6.84m) for 6413grt. Diesel-electric machinery drove twin screws giving the ship a service speed of 15kts. From* The Motor Ship, *June 1961.*

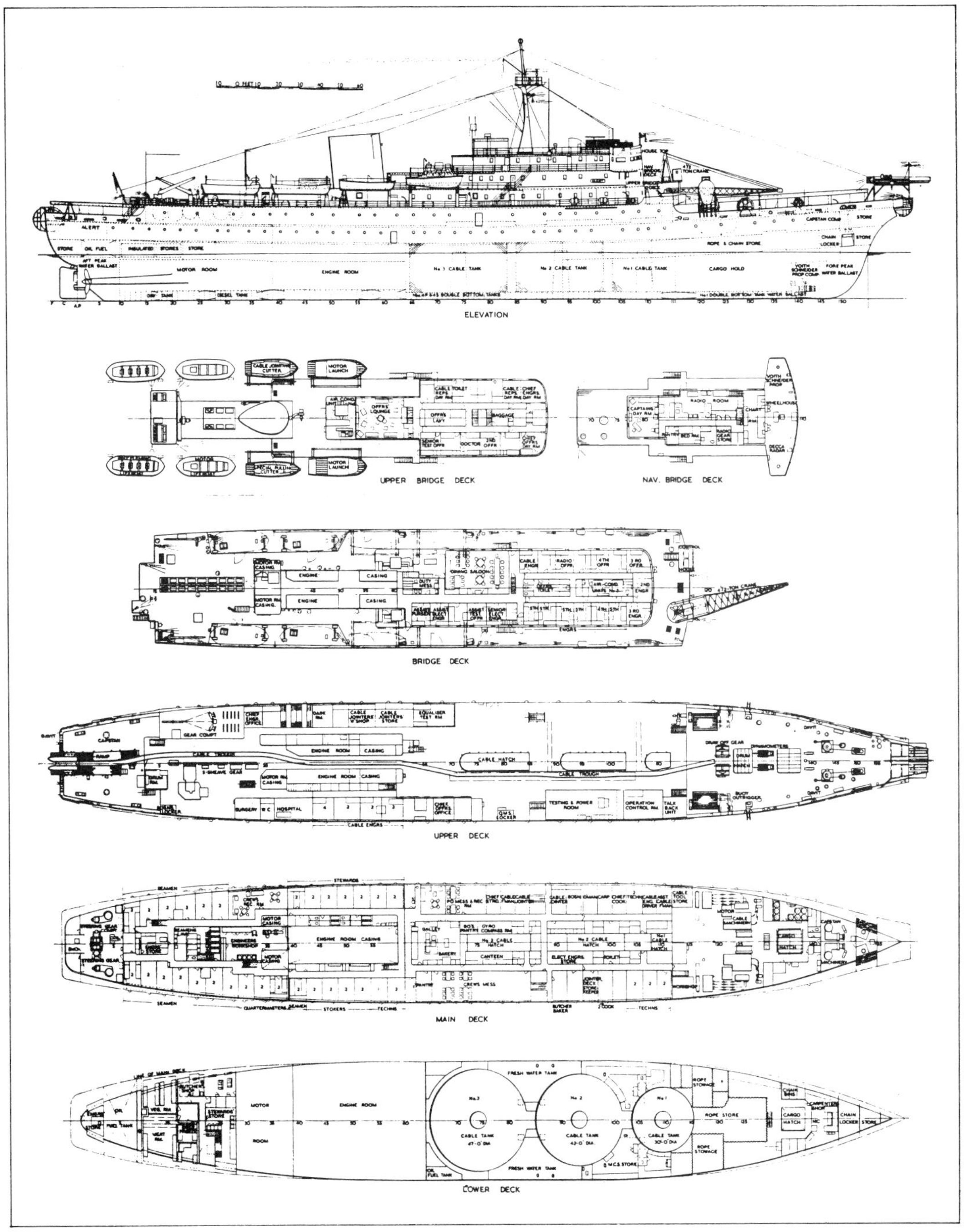

control demanded by cable operations to be readily available.

To facilitate precise manoeuvring of the vessel over a cable track the ship is fitted with a Voith Schneider cycloidal propeller, placed between the fore end of the cable working gear store situated forward of the foremost tank and the after end of the fore peak water ballast tank. The vessel carries a comprehensive set of navigational and communication equipment. Accommodation for officers, crew and cable personnel is to a high standard and is air conditioned.

Power cables

Whenever cable ships are mentioned, a general reaction is that this is a reference to those vessels concerned with submarine telegraph and telephone cables. However there is a growing network of fairly short runs of electric power cables. Whilst their composition and the shore terminals differ from those of the submarine communication cables, much of the work associated with laying them is similar to that of the latter. Because of their length in many cases it has been found possible to use or adapt smaller vessels for the purpose. Indeed it was not unknown for a set of the necessary gear to be kept in store, and for it to be fitted to a small coastal cargo ship when a laying job was scheduled. In between times the ship was able to continue in the owner's normal trading activities.

John Bowen

The 4534grt Ocean Layer *was under construction by Flensburger Schiffsbau-Gesellschaft and still on the stocks at the end of the Second World War. She was taken as a prize and completed as the* Empire Frome *for the Ministry of Transport in 1948. Powered by double compound steam machinery with an exhaust turbine, the ship was single screw. In 1953 she was acquired by Submarine Cables Ltd, London and converted to a cable layer by R S Hayes (Pembroke Dock) Ltd. On 15 June 1959 whilst engaged in cable laying work in the Atlantic, she caught fire and had to be abandoned, the crew being saved. She was towed to Falmouth by a German salvage tug, but was later declared a constructive total loss. She was sold to Dutch shipbreakers and scrapped in Holland.* (CMP)

Icebreaker Development to the 1960s

The icebreaker is one of the more unusual types of specialised vessel not designed to carry cargo or passengers.

With the onset of winter several northern countries have in the past found it necessary to change their trading patterns or be cut off from the rest of the world. Finland, in a severe winter, can have no ice-free ports and in normal years can have only limited trade through some of its southern ports. The Swedish iron ore ports in the Gulf of Bothnia had to close down in winter and cargoes were shipped across Norway to the ice-free port of Narvik. Russia also had difficulty in keeping her trade routes open to the west due to a large coastline that is never free of ice even in summer. With the winter closure of the Great Lakes, Montreal and Quebec, cargoes had to be transferred to Halifax, Nova Scotia, or directed through the United States to ensure trade continued. In each case the alternative to the cost of trade lost was the icebreaker.

Icebreakers work through a combination of power and weight, using their power to force their bows up onto the ice and then crushing it with their weight. To achieve this satisfactorily a basic icebreaker design evolved which included the following: a cut away forefoot under the stem to allow it to lift onto the ice; a specially strengthened hull with additional frames forward and thicker plating around the waterline; pronounced tumblehome to avoid damage from pressure ice; high installed power and a length/breadth ratio of about 4:1.

From quite early on an extra propeller was incorporated under the bow of some of the larger icebreakers, a feature which worked well in the Baltic but had to be removed from the later Arctic icebreakers due to constant damage from the greater thickness of ice.

Back in 1870 Russia had strengthened a tug, *Pilot*, and used her as an icebreaker to extend the season at Kronstad. Of limited success due to her light weight and insufficient power, she was the forerunner of this specialised type of vessel. Although there had been many ice-strengthened vessels before, mainly sealers and whalers, it was *Pilot* that set the scene and during the next twenty-five years numerous small icebreakers were built to keep Baltic ports open longer.

Russia/Soviet Union

The real development of icebreakers was to come from a British shipyard following an order placed by Imperial Russia. At the end of the nineteenth century that country was eager to increase its international trade and also spread its empire eastwards. To achieve this it needed to open up its sea routes, normally closed for much of the year. The first large Russian icebreaker, *Yermak*, was built by Sir W G Armstrong, Whitworth & Co, Newcastle upon Tyne, in 1898. At 8730 tons full load displacement and with three triple-expansion steam engines producing a total 9390ihp driving triple screws, she was to last for over sixty years, remaining one of the largest icebreakers and setting the pattern for many others. Built for Baltic service, she had a long and busy life in the Arctic, finally being broken up in 1964.

The Russians had always desired to open up the North-East passage to commercial traffic and their large fleet of icebreakers developed during the early part of this cen-

The Lazar Kaganovitch *was one of four 'Stalin' class icebreakers, the first such vessels designed and built by the Soviets. The ship was launched in April 1937 from the Marti Yard at Nikolayev and served in the Arctic during the war. She is shown in May 1947, when she still had a quarter of a century to serve.* (Author's collection)

Moskva, *the first of a class of five Arctic icebreakers built by Wärtsilä Sandvikens shipyard, Helsinki in 1960. The first diesel-electric Polar icebreaker built by Wärtsilä, producing 22,000shp, when built she was the most powerful conventional icebreaker.* (Author's collection)

tury was part of this plan. During the First World War they built several more in Britain, including *Sviatogor*, also by Armstrong, Whitworth. She spent many years in the White Sea and rescued the crew of the Soviet merchant vessel *Chelyuskin* during her ill-fated voyage to test the viability of making a trip from west to east in a single season.

The First World War caused the closure of the Baltic and in order to keep an alternative trade route through the White Sea, several icebreakers and ice-breaking vessels were purchased from Britain and Canada. These were followed by new icebreakers from Russian shipyards.

During the 1920s and early 1930s the Soviet Union relied on older vessels but appreciating that a war in Europe was likely to occur and would place a strain on Soviet shipping, it made an appraisal of its icebreaker fleet. The result was the construction of the four 'Stalin' class ships, large and very powerful, stationed in the White Sea. They were *Yosef Stalin*, *Vyacheslav Molotov*, *Otto Schmidt* and *Lazar Kaganovich*. With a displacement of 11,000 tons, three shafts delivering 10,050shp, and carrying three aircraft, they were completed at Leningrad and Nikolayev during 1937–39, and added considerably not only to the Soviet Union's icebreaker strength but also to her prestige. Even so, the Second World War necessitated the loan of US and Canadian icebreakers for service in Arctic waters.

The Soviet icebreaker fleet was in a poor condition in the immediate postwar years, however some of the older vessels such as *Krasin* (ex-*Sviatogor*) were re-engined and modernised, their exceptional strength and thickness of plating allowing them to give further adequate service, depending on the severity of the ice in which they worked.

To fill the gaps until new vessels could be built the USSR borrowed three of the US Navy 'Wind' class breakers and also received several German and Finnish breakers as war reparations in 1945–47. However, the postwar surge to develop and people the Arctic

regions prompted the USSR to build a new generation of icebreakers. An order was placed for three vessels with Wärtsilä Koncernen AB Sandvikens Skeppsdocka, Helsinki, and in January 1955 the first of these, known as the 'Kapitan' class was delivered. These vessels, *Kapitan Belousov*, *Kapitan Voronin* and *Kapitan Melekhov*, of dimensions and power similar to the Finnish *Voima* (see below), were to be the forerunners of many icebreakers to be built by Wärtsilä for the Soviet Union.

With the success of the 'Kapitan' class in the Baltic, orders were placed in 1957 for a series of five Polar icebreakers, designed to work off Siberia. The first of these, named *Moskva*, was completed in 1960 by Wärtsilä.

The vessels of this series are powered by eight nine-cylinder Wärtsilä/Sulzer diesels with electric drive, producing a total 22,000shp and making them the most powerful conventional icebreakers ever built. They do not have bow propellers due to the likelihood of damage in the hard Arctic ice.

In 1959 the Baltic Shipbuilding & Engineering Works, Leningrad, stole a march on the rest of the world by completing the first nuclear powered vessel, *Lenin*. With three Kirov nuclear reactors driving four steam turbines producing 39,200shp, she was the most powerful icebreaker then in existence. Nuclear power gave her greater range without the need to refuel in inhospitable conditions, allowing her to stay in service longer

Lenin, *the world's first nuclear surface ship, with 39,200shp she is capable of moving continually through pack ice 8ft thick at 3 to 4kts. Withdrawn from service in December 1989 she was used as a floating power station.* (Author's collection)

Voima seen here in drift ice was the first ship in a programme to renew Finland's obsolete icebreaker fleet. She was the first icebreaker to have twin bow screws and a heeling system to help 'roll' her way out of pressure ridges. Modernised in 1979, she is still in service. (Author's collection)

during the summer months. In 1966–67 she suffered a nuclear accident in which thirty of her crew died of radiation poisoning and many others were injured. Abandoned for several months, she was later taken to an Arctic shipyard and rebuilt with two new reactors and an increase in power to 44,000shp; she continued in service until 1989. The success of nuclear power led to the Soviet Union building six more of an improved and larger type in their own shipyards and two at Wärtsilä.

Finland

The ice-breaking season in Finland begins in November and ends in May. During this period an icebreaker can be in constant use day and night without a break and with minimal time for maintenance. As Finland's trade grew, so did the need for year-round navigation and ports that were once closed every winter were being kept open in all but the worst winters. This placed heavy demands on the Baltic icebreaker fleet and explains why icebreaker design has developed of late in Finland, particularly from the time of their replacement programme initiated after the Second World War.

Finland's early fleet consisted of two late nineteenth century icebreakers built in Britain, of a design similar to *Yermak*. In 1926 the Finns went to the Rotterdam firm of Smit

for the building of the 4825 tons standard displacement *Jäärkarhu* (9200ihp). She was taken over by the Soviet Union in 1945 and continued to operate in the Gulf of Finland as *Sibiryakov* until 1972. In 1939 *Sisu* (2000 tons std displ) became the first in a long line of diesel-electric icebreakers built at Sandviken's shipyard, Helsinki, later to become better known as part of the Wärtsilä group.

After the Second World War the Finnish government sought to replace its ageing fleet of icebreakers, including those taken by the Soviet Union as war reparations. In 1954 Wärtsilä delivered *Voima*, a ship that was to be the start of a new generation of icebreakers.

Voima had all the standard icebreaker design features but with less pronounced tumblehome. Power was provided by six eight-cylinder Atlas diesels driving four generators, one for each propeller, giving a total

10,500bhp. With twin screws fore and aft, the forward ones drew the water from under the ice ahead of the vessel and fed it down the side of the hull to reduce friction. In addition she was provided with heeling tanks with high-speed pumps which could transfer 300 tons of water in 45 seconds. This enabled the vessel to literally wriggle out of tight situations. Modernised and re-engined in 1977–78 with Wärtsilä diesels, her power was increased to 17,460bhp. The *Karhu* class of twin-screw diesel-electric Baltic icebreakers followed; these were smaller (2721grt) and less powerful (7500bhp) but equally successful.

Sweden

Sweden had many small harbour icebreakers but, faced with a growing need to keep open its eastern ports open in the Gulf of Bothnia, as long as possible during the winter, it built the larger *Ymer* at Kockums in 1932. Her novel diesel-electric propulsion, the first to be fitted to an icebreaker, gave greater control over the amount of power transmitted to the screws and proved to be extremely successful, becoming almost standard in subsequent ships.

Following the lead given by the Soviet Union, Sweden went to Wärtsilä for its postwar tonnage, *Oden* of 1957 being a sister of

Sisu, built in 1939, was the first of a long line of diesel electric icebreakers built by Sandvikens Shipyard, Helsinki, later to become Wärtsilä. Withdrawn from service in 1975, she was converted to an army headquarters ship in 1975 renamed *Louhi* until sold to Finnish breakers in 1985. (Author's collection)

The Canadian N B McLean, *seen here in the St Lawrence, was involved in escorting shipping in Hudson Bay. Built in 1930 and powered with two triple expansion engines she was severely damaged by fire and sold to Taiwan breakers in 1989.*
(Canadian Department of Transport)

the Finnish *Voima*, likewise *Tor* (1964) a sister to the 1963-built 3955grt *Tarmo*.

Canada

Canada needed to increase its icebreaker fleet with the development of the St Lawrence Seaway and to cope with enlarged winter trade to Montreal and Quebec. In addition to this commercial work icebreakers were also used for flood control during the spring thaw. Many large ice floes leave the Great Lakes and upper reaches of the St Lawrence, jam in the bottlenecks of the river, and create large dams. If not continually cleared, there is a high risk of flooding in the low lying lands behind the jams, and many icebreakers are involved in this work when not assisting other vessels.

The Canadian icebreaker fleet initially consisted of sealers and ice-breaking mail vessels, but in 1904 Canada turned to British shipyards for its first purpose-built vessel, *Montrose*, from Napier & Miller, Glasgow. Sold to the Soviet Union in 1942, she operated in the Far East until 1955 when she was broken up. The order for *Montrose* was followed by orders for two more vessels (*Lady Grey* of 1906 and *Earl Grey* of 1909) from Vickers Sons & Maxim Ltd, Barrow-in-Furness. Although not built solely for ice-breaking, they gave many years service in this role. *Lady Grey* remained in service until 1956 when she was sunk off Dartmouth, Nova Scotia, following a collision with a Quebec ferry. *Earl Grey* was originally built as an ice-breaking passenger mail ship and vice regal yacht. Sold to Russia in 1914 for $493,000 and renamed *Kanada*, she was used purely as an icebreaker on the Northern Sea route between Murmansk and Vladivostok. Withdrawn from service in 1960 and broken up at Murmansk in 1964, her wheelhouse and radio cabin are now on exhibition at Moscow's maritime museum.

In 1929 the first icebreaker to be built in

Canada, *Saurel*, was delivered by Canadian Vickers yard. This was followed in 1930 by *N B McLean*, of 6500ihp, a product of Halifax Shipyards, Halifax, Nova Scotia; both were powered by triple-expansion engines. They were built for operation in the St Lawrence River, Maritime Provinces and northern waters, and in addition to carrying supplies to distant Arctic outposts *N B McLean* was very much involved in escorting ocean shipping using the Hudson Bay-Hudson Strait route to the port of Churchill. It was not until 1953 that the first of the Canadian postwar icebreakers, *d'Iberville*, was built – unusual in having 10,800ihp steam turbines.

She was followed in 1954 by the diesel-electric *Labrador* (10,000shp), built by Marine Industries, Sorel.

The Canadian replacement programme continued in 1960 with the 18,000bhp *John A MacDonald*, which in autumn 1969 assisted the US icebreaker *Northwind* in the tanker *Manhattan*'s experimental voyages in the North-West Passage. At the time of her delivery she was the most powerful icebreaker under Canadian registry and cost $10 million to build. She was designed to provide adequate stability under the worst possible operating conditions, including accumulation of ice on her topsides.

The John A Macdonald *seen here assisting in the experiments with the US tanker* Manhattan. *At 15,000shp and an open water speed of 15.5kts, she was Canada's most powerful icebreaker when built.* (Author's collection)

Northwind, *one of the seven American 'Wind' class icebreakers built between 1944 and 1947. This view shows the reconnaissance helicopter returning after searching for open leads while escorting the American tanker* Manhattan *on her trip around the North of Canada in 1969. During the passage she encountered 10ft to 15ft thick ice.* (US Coast Guard)

United States

The United States was a relative newcomer with regard to icebreakers and with little need for them commercially, up to the introduction of the 'Wind' class, relied on ice-strengthened cutters. Designed to supply US bases established in Greenland in 1941, these seven vessels – reputed to have cost $10 million each – were built during the Second World War for the US Navy and were powered by diesel-electric engines driving three screws, the bow propeller being removed later because of several incidents of damage in Arctic ice. Designed to break ice 9ft thick and not used for commercial work, they spent much of their working lives in the Antarctic, supplying scientific bases, although they did take part in the 1969 trials by the tanker *Manhattan* on the feasibility of tanker navigation through the North-West Passage. Three were transferred to the Soviet Union under Lend-Lease in 1945 and saw service in the Arctic until their return in 1950–51.

The only true US 'commercial' icebreaker, although operated by the US Coast Guard, was *Mackinaw* (5252 tons full load displ), completed by Toledo Shipbuilding Co, Ohio, in January 1945 as *Manitowoc*. Built for Great Lakes service to open the shipping lanes in late March, she had many of the features of the 'Wind' class vessels but was longer and wider with significantly less draught. Diesel-electric drive producing 10,000hp, enabled her to break through 4ft of solid ice. Too large to enter the locks of the canals, she has spent her whole life on Lake Michigan and Lake Superior.

The US Navy icebreaker *Glacier* was the most modern and most powerful under the US flag when she entered service in 1955. Displacing 5100 tons (8449 tons full load), her ten Fairbanks Morse diesels and two Westinghouse 10,500hp electric motors, give 16,900shp and a speed of 17.5kts. Designed for breaking ice more than 20ft thick, she was transferred to the US Coast Guard in 1966.

Despite the fact that steam has given way to diesel-electric propulsion and nuclear power has been widely employed in the Russian icebreaker fleet since 1959, the basic lessons of *Yermak* are still applied today – weight, power, strength.

Ian Stockbridge

Typical Tugs 1900–1960

Ship	Flag	Built	By	GRT	Length (r = registered) × breadth × depth × draught Feet–inches Metres	Engines	Horsepower (bollard pull, tons)	Speed	Remarks
Ocean-going and salvage tugs									
ROODE ZEE	Ne	1898	L Smit & Zoon, Kinderdijk	540	164–0(r) × 30–0 × 18–0 × — 50.0 × 9.15 × 5.49 × —	Triple expansion by De Schelde	1500ihp	11kts	
WILLEM BARENDSZ	Ne	1921	Jonker & Stans, Hendrik Ido Ambacht	515	157–10 × 30–2 × 15–4 × 14–9 48.10 × 9.2 × 4.68 × 4.50	Alblasserdam triple-expansion coal fired (412 tons); 1 shaft	1000ihp	12kts	
ZWARTE ZEE	Ne	1933	L Smit & Zoon, Kinderdijk	836	198–4 × 32–2 × 19–9 × 15–4 60.46 × 9.81 × 6.0 × 4.67	2 Werkspoor 6-cylinder diesel engines SR geared with hydraulic couplings; 2 shafts	4200bhp	17kts	World's largest salvage tug when built
TURMOIL	UK	1945	Henry Robb, Leith	1136	204–11 × 38–8 × 19–0 × 17–8 62.46 × 11.79 × 5.8 × 5.37	2 British Auxiliaries 8-cylinder diesel engines SR geared with hydraulic couplings; 1 shaft	3020bhp (40)	14.5kts	One of 8 *Bustler* class built for Admiralty; range 5000nm
ABEILLE 26	Fra	1952	Ch & At de St Nazaire, St Nazaire	719	178–9 × 32–9 × 16–0 × 15–3 54.51 × 9.96 × 4.88 × 4.65	2 6-cylinder SGCM/MAN diesels; 1 shaft	3450bhp (32)	15kts	Salvage
HERKULES	Nor	1960	Mjellum & Karlsen, Bergen	799	176–8 × 32–9 × 18–7 × — 53.83 × 9.99 × 5.67 × —	4 Klockner Humboldt Deutz diesel engines; 1 shaft	4600bhp (31)	12kts	Ocean, ice-breaking and salvage tug, range 12,000nm

Typical ship-handling tugs

Ship	Flag	Built	By	GRT	Length (r = registered) × breadth × depth × draught Feet–inches Metres	Engines	Horsepower (bollard pull, tons)	Speed	Remarks
COLLINGWOOD	UK	1905	J Cran & Co, Leith	149	96–9 × 21–7 × 12–6 × — 29.49 × 6.58 × 3.80 × —	Compound steam by J Cran; 1 shaft	600ihp	10kts	River Mersey
SUN IV	UK	1915	Earles SB & Eng Co, Hull	200	116–6 × 25–8 × 13–0 ×12–5 35.51 × 7.83 × 3.97 × 3.73	Triple-expansion steam by Earles; 1 shaft	750ihp	10kts	River Thames
DITTO	UK	1930	Cochrane & Sons, Selby	109	83–7(r) × 21–6 × — × 12–9 25.48 × 6.58 × — × 3.89	Triple-expansion steam by C D Holmes; 1 shaft	600ihp	10kts	River Humber
T H WATERMEYER	SA	1939	A & J Inglis, Glasgow	620	155–7 × 33–1 × 15–6 × — 47.43 × 10.09 × 4.72 × —	2 Lobnitz triple-expansion steam; 2 shafts	3000ihp	12kts	Coal burner; Capetown
MOIRA MORAN	US	1949	Levingston SB Co, Orange, Texas	238	100–0 × 27–0 × 14–9 × 13–2 30.48 × 8.23 × 4.49 × 4.00	16-cylinder General Motors diesel; 1 shaft	1747bhp	13kts	US coastal
CENTAUR	Ger	1958	Jadewerft, Wilhelmshaven	160	97–0 × 26–0 × 12–5 ×10–0 29.57 × 7.93 × 3.81 × 3.05	8-cylinder Klockner Humboldt Deutz diesel; 1 shaft	1400bhp	12kts	Kort nozzle; Bremen

Tug/tender

Ship	Flag	Built	By	GRT	Length × breadth × depth × draught	Engines	Horsepower	Speed	Remarks
FLYING BREEZE	UK	1913	J T Eltringham, South Shields	387	133–8 × 28–7 × 14–11 × 13–5 40.73 × 8.74 × 4.54 × 4.04	Triple-expansion by Shields Eng. Co; 1 shaft	750ihp	11kts	River Mersey

Typical Cable Ships 1900–1960

Name	Flag	Built	By	GRT	Length (oa) × breadth × depth Feet / Metres	Tank capacity cu ft/cu m	Machinery	Owner	Remarks
VIKING	UK	1901	Armstrong Whitworth, Newcastle upon Tyne	929	207.0 × 36.0 × 13.7 63.1 × 10.9 × 4.2	—	SS TE	Amazon Telegraph Co	To Fundaçao Brasil Central 1945. Sunk off Para 1950
RECORDER	UK	1902	Dunlop & Co, Glasgow	2253	295.0 × 40.7 × 15.1 89.9 × 12.4 × 4.6	—	TS TE 2120ihp	Imperial & International Communications Ltd	Built as *Iris* for Pacific Cable Board. To Imperial & International 1929, renamed *Recorder*. Broken up Rosyth 1952
LADY DENISON-PENDER	UK	1920	Fairfield, Glasgow	1995	282.6 × 38.1 × 23.8 86.2 × 11.61 × 7.2	20,830 589	TS TE —	Eastern Telegraph Co	Transferred to Imperial & International Communications Co. 1929. Broken up Antwerp 1963
ALL AMERICA	US	1921	Swan Hunter & Wigham Richardson, Newcastle upon Tyne	1819	293.4 × 37.0 × 24.7 89.3 × 11.3 × 7.5	14,000 396	TS TE —	All America Cables	Broken up Charleston, VA 1961
EDOUARD SVENSON	Den	1922	Orlogsvaertet Copenhagen	1560	260.0 × 35.0 × 16.1 79.2 ×10.7 × 4.9	16,000 453	TS TE 1900ihp	Great Northern Telegraph Co	Broken up 1968
PATRICK STEWART	Ind	1925	Wm Simons Ltd, Renfrew	1572	226.0† × 37.5 × 25.0 68.9 × 11.4 × 7.6	— —	TS TE 1200ihp	Indian Government	To Royal Indian Navy 1932. Converted to survey ship, renamed *Investigator*
DOMINIA	UK	1926	Swan Hunter & Wigham Richardson, Newcastle upon Tyne	9250	509.0 × 59.0 × 40.7 155.1 × 18.0 × 12.4	179,670 5088	TS TE —	The Telegraph Construction & Maintenance Co Ltd	Sold USSR 1937, renamed *Nikolai Ejov*
TOYO MARU	Jap	1937	Kawasaki DY, Kobe	3718	347.4 × 48.4 × 25.4 105.9 ×14.7 × 7.7	47,456 1344	TS impulse geared turb 3600shp	Japanese Government	Fitted with Voith Schneider bow propulsion unit
MONARCH	UK	1946	Swan Hunter & Wigham Richardson, Newcastle upon Tyne	8056	483.7 × 55.7 ×27.9* 147.4 × 16.9 × 8.5	125,000 3539	TS TE 4500ihp	General Post Office (GPO)	Sold Cable & Wireless 1970, renamed *Sentinel*
STANLEY ANGWIN	UK	1952	Swan Hunter & Wigham Richardson, Newcastle upon Tyne	2553	314.6 × 41.0 × 25.9 95.9 × 12.5 × 7.9	18,850 534	TS TE 1450ihp	Cable & Wireless Ltd	Broken up Antwerp 1972

Name	Flag	Built	By	GRT	Length (oa) × breadth × depth Feet / Metres	Tank capacity cu ft/cu m	Machinery	Owner	Remarks
SALERNUM	Ita	1954	Navalmechanicca Castellammare di Stabia, Naples	2834	339.6 × 41.4 × 18.5* *103.5 × 12.6 × 5.6*	22,354 *633*	TS diesel + diesel-electric 3500hp	Compagnia Italiana Navi Cablografiche	
MARCEL BAYARD	Fra	1961	C & A Augustin Normand, Le Havre	4502	387.1 × 51.2 × 30.2 *118.0 × 15.6 × 9.2*	80,507 *2280*	TS diesel-electric	French Government	Constructive total loss following fire 1981
RETRIEVER	UK	1961	Cammell Laird, Birkenhead	4218	366.0 × 47.5 × 29.5 *111.6 × 14.5 × 9.0*	21,000 *595*	TS diesel-electric 3800shp	Cable & Wireless Ltd	

Abbreviations
SS   Single screw   TE   Triple expansion steam engine   *   Draught
TS   Twin screw   D/E   Diesel electric   †   Length between perpendiculars

Typical Icebreakers 1900–1960

Name	Flag	Built	Builder	GRT Disp	Length × breadth × depth × draught Feet/Metres	Engines	Power	Remarks
YERMAK	Rus	1898	Armstrong, Whitworth & Co, Newcastle upon Tyne	4955 8730	320.0 × 71.5 × 35.6 × 25.0 *97.54 × 21.79 × 10.85 × 7.62*	3 triple-expansion, Wallsend Slipway; 3 shafts, 12kts	9390ihp	First large Russian icebreaker; BU Murmansk 1964
EARL GREY	Can	1909	Vickers, Sons & Maxim Ltd, Barrow-in-Furness	2356 3400	265.0 × 47.5 × 23.0 × 17.8 *80.1 × 14.49 × 7.01 × 5.42*	2 triple-expansion; 2 shafts, 17kts	6000ihp	Sold Russia 1915, renamed *Kanada*, and used on Northern Sea route between Murmansk and Vladivostok; renamed *Tretiy Internatsional* 1920, *Fedor Litke* 1921, BU 1960
SVIATOGOR	Rus	1917	Armstrong Whitworth & Co, Newcastle upon Tyne	4902 9300	318.0 × 71.5 × 42.2 × 25.9 *96.92 × 21.79 × 12.80 × 7.9*	3 triple-expansion, Richardson Westgarth & Co, 3 shafts, 16kts	10,000ihp	Renamed *Krasin* 1921. Re-engined and rebuilt 1958; proposed to use as musuem
N B MCLEAN	Can	1930	Halifax Shipyards, Halifax, NS	3254 5034	277.0 × 60.0 × 24.0 × 19.6 *84.42 × 18.28 × 7.31 × 5.94*	2 3-cylinder triple-expansion; 2 shafts	6500ihp	Officially rated as 'medium icebreaker'. Severely damaged by fire; BU 1989
YMER	Swe	1932	Kockums Mekaniska Verkstad, Malmo	3053 4545	257.9 × 63.3 × — × 21.0 *78.65 × 19.26 × — × 6.40*	6 6-cylinder diesels with electric drive; 15.9kts	9900ihp	World's first diesel-electric icebreaker
EASTWIND	US	1944	Western Pipe & Steel Co, San Pedro, Cal	— 6515	269.0 × 63.5 × — × 29.0 *81.99 × 19.35 × — × 8.83*	6 Fairbanks Morse diesels with electric drive; 2 shafts, 16kts	12,000bhp	Completed for US Navy, transferred US Coast Guard 1965
MACKINAW	US	1945	Toledo SB Co, Ohio	— 5252	290.0 × 74.3 × — × 19.0 *88.44 × 22.66 × — × 5.79*	3 Fairbanks Morse diesels with electric drive; 2 shafts aft, 1 forward, 18kts	10,000shp	Used in fresh water of Great Lakes for extending season
D'IBERVILLE	Can	1953	Davie SB & Rep, Lauzon, Levis, PQ	5678	310.3 × 66.5 × 40.2 × 30.4 *94.65 × 20.27 × 12.27 × 9.27*	Canadian Vickers/Unaflow steam turbine; 2 shafts, 16kts	10,800ihp	
VOIMA	Fin	1954	Wärtsilä/Sandvikens, Helsinki	3481	274.0 × 63.8 × — × 22.2 *83.52 × 19.45 × — × 6.77*	6 8-cylinder Atlas diesels with electric drive; 4 shafts (2 fwd, 2 aft), 15kts	10,500bhp	Modernised 1978–79. Re-engined (Wärtsilä 17,460 bhp) and accommodation moved out of hull
LABRADOR	Can	1954	Marine Industries, Sorel	3823	269.0 × 63.5 × 37.8 × 29.1 *82.00 × 19.46 × 11.54 × 9.18*	6 10-cylinder Fairbanks Morse diesels with electric drive; 2 shafts, 16kts	10,000shp	
LENIN	SU	1959	Baltic SB & Eng Works, Leningrad	14,067 16,000	440.0 × 90.6 × 52.9 × 34.5 *134.02 × 27.60 × 16.13 × 10.52*	3 Kirov nuclear reactors with 4 steam turbines; 18kts	39,200shp	Worlds first nuclear icebreaker; re-engined 1967–72 (44,000shp) after nuclear accident
MOSKVA	SU	1960	Wärtsilä/Sandvikens Helsinki Helsinki	9427 15,360	400.6 × 80.4 × 45.9 × 35.4 *122.10 × 24.51 × 14.00 × 10.79*	8 9-cylinder Wärtsilä/Sulzer diesels with electric drive; 3 shafts, 19kts	22,000shp	First of class of five Polar icebreakers – largest conventionally powered type
JOHN A MACDONALD	Can	1960	Davie SB & Rep, Lauzon	6186 9307	315.0 × 70.0 × 41.1 × 28.1 *96.01 × 21.32 × 12.53 × 8.58*	9 Canadian Locomotive Fairbanks Morse diesels with electric drive; 3 shafts	18,000bhp	Assisted with *Manhattan* voyages through North-West Passage

7

Ship Design and Construction

THE TURN of the century was something of a watershed in ship design and construction. Steel had become established as a strong, cheap and reliable material, which not only permitted larger and lighter hulls but higher boiler pressures. The triple expansion steam reciprocating engine was likewise a cheap and reliable prime mover, albeit of limited power output and modest fuel efficiency. Statutory load lines had been established, discouraging overloaded and unseaworthy vessels. Seawater ballast in double bottom tanks was widely used in place of expensive and inconvenient sand or gravel, improving seaworthiness on empty voyages and speeding loading and discharging. Electricity was being applied not only in ships themselves, where lighting and safety standards were much improved by eliminating naked lights, but for powering equipment on board, on the dockside and in shipyards. Ashore, mechanical handling of

cargo was speeding up port turn-rounds, particularly for bulk cargoes such as grain, making the use of ever larger ships economic.

The tanker had emerged as the first real specialist cargo vessel type in the late 1880s, opening up new trades such as to the East Indies. Mechanical refrigeration permitted the transport of meat and dairy products from the southern hemisphere, offering cheap food for the fast growing urban populations of Europe. Emigration was in full flood, particularly to the United States, demanding more passenger-cargo ships.

In the 1890s the first steam turbine had been demonstrated by Charles Parsons, offering the prospect of more powerful and hence larger, faster vessels, both naval and merchant. Rudolf Diesel's highly efficient internal combustion engine was about to appear at sea in modest powered installations, which would be fuelled by easily handled oil. Oil

firing had already been applied to boilers, offering the prospect of eliminating coal bunkers taking up valuable space in the middle of the hull and of greatly reducing the number of stokers. The technical means now existed for significantly increasing the size and speed of any type of ship, wherever there was a demand.

Ship design and construction methods had been developed to the stage where a new vessel could be ordered, designed and completed in less than a year, and its performance assured. The professional engineering

The tanker had emerged in the late nineteenth century as the first truly specialised merchant vessel whose employment dominated – indeed dictated – the design. The Beme, *built on the Tyne in 1904 by Armstrong, Whitworth & Co, already displays the engines-aft/bridge-amidships layout that was to dominate tanker design for over half a century. The ship was built for the Burma Oil Co, then exploiting the oilfields of the East Indies.* (CMP)

bodies such as the Institution of Naval Architects and a burgeoning technical press, enhanced by the clear reproduction of photographs, helped transform shipbuilding from the mystique of an empirical craft to an engineering process based on scientific principles.

The last two decades of the nineteenth century had seen a bewildering array of dry cargo vessel concepts, each claiming to offer advantages of increased capacity and/or lower registered tonnages – awning deckers, spar deckers, well deckers, turret ships, trunk deck ships. Many of these designs exploited loopholes or anomalies in the regulations for calculating tonnage or freeboard in multi-deck ships. Some of the designs spawned what can be seen with hindsight to be vessels lacking in some measures of seaworthiness, for example the range of stability, that is the ability to recover from a large angle of heel induced by wind or wave. It became the practice about this time for the shipbuilder to provide detailed loading and stability information as guidance for a ship's master, albeit heavily qualified by phrases like 'Given in good faith but not guaranteed'.

In the first decade of the new century, the multitude of designs were about to be con-

solidated into three much simpler concepts, encouraged by revised load line regulations governing freeboard in 1906 and new tonnage regulations in 1907. The simplest was the *three island ship*, basically a single deck ship with a forecastle forward (sometimes still providing crew accommodation), a bridge amidships covering the machinery space and with officers' accommodation, and a poop aft (increasingly used for crew accommodation). Such a layout was particularly useful for medium size vessels often used for the coal and timber trades.

Where more decks were required, especially in liner trades for less dense general cargo such as manufactured products, a second deck added extra cubic capacity. The upper deck could be constructed as a 'shelter deck' with tonnage openings in such a way that the 'tween deck space was exempt from gross and net tonnage. Such a vessel could be adapted to carry dense cargoes by closing the tonnage openings in the shelter deck, resulting in a deeper draught and hence greater deadweight – disposable load (mainly cargo) – but of course greater registered tonnage. The resulting two-deck *shelter decker* concept remains to this day, although with changes in detail.

For small vessels, especially those with machinery aft, the *raised quarterdeck* vessel concept was popular. With the relatively long machinery spaces of the day tending to push the centre of gravity of the cargo forward, a flush deck vessel could trim by the head and become unseaworthy. This could be prevented by raising the depth of the hull

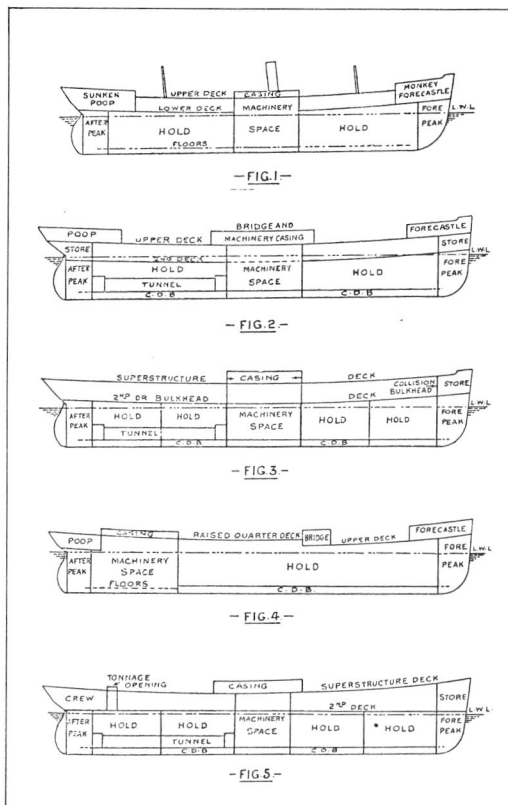

Alternative superstructure arrangements suited different cargoes, as well as producing different tonnage, capacity and freeboard figures. Fig 1 shows early steamships with a forecastle for the crew, poop aft for the officers and a casing amidships to protect the machinery. Fig 2 shows a three island ship with forecastle, bridge and poop. Fig 3 shows a spar deck ship with a light full-length superstructure to give extra space for low density cargoes; the awning decker was similar. Fig 4 shows a raised quarterdeck ship, which gave extra cargo capacity aft to avoid trim by the bow which would otherwise result from the long engine room aft, cargo being heavier than machinery. Fig 5 shows a shelter deck ship, whose substantial superstructure could be exempted from inclusion in the tonnage. This concept remained the predominant deep-sea cargo ship arrangement for half a century from about 1908. Illustration from a contemporary handbook, Merchant Ships and Shipping.

The turret ship design used by Doxford on the River Wear for 176 ships from 1892 to 1911 had a unique cross-section, which reduced tonnage, increased the height of the upper deck above the waterline, produced a longitudinally stiff structure and provided a grain feeder, although the beams and pillars interfered with the ease of cargo handling. Illustration from a contemporary handbook, Present Day Shipbuilding.

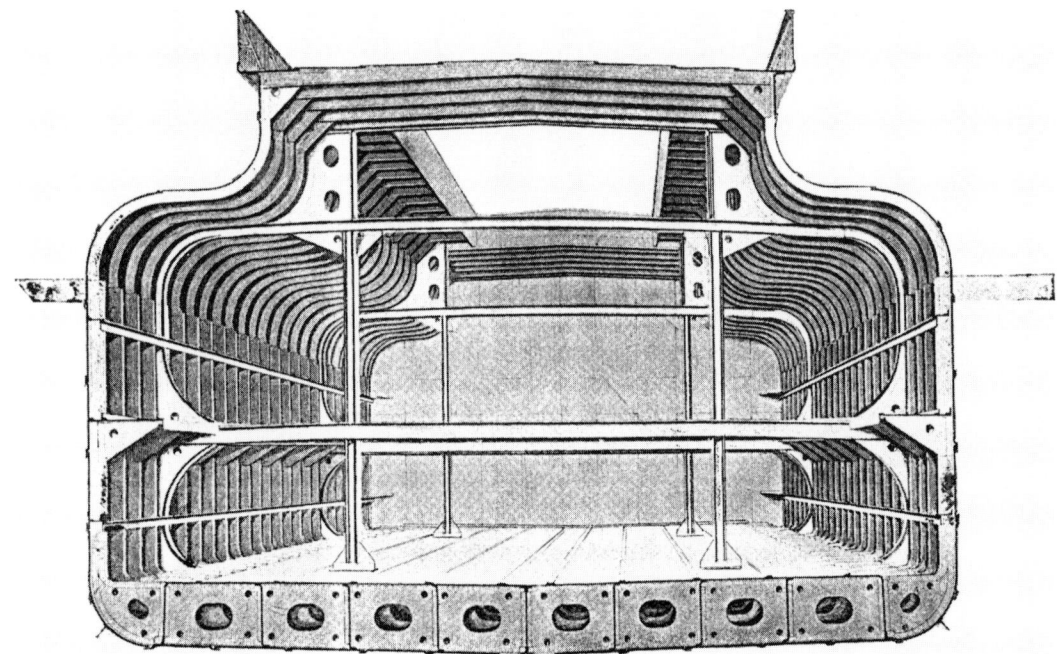

aft to increase the capacity of the after holds, the corresponding section of deck becoming the 'quarterdeck'.

Significant developments

For the next half century, merchant ship design and construction was largely an exploitation of techniques that had started to appear by around 1900. True, there were increases in ship size, speed and power, most notably in passenger liners and naval vessels, and the introduction of a few new vessel types such as ore carriers. But there were not the dramatic changes of the 1850–1900

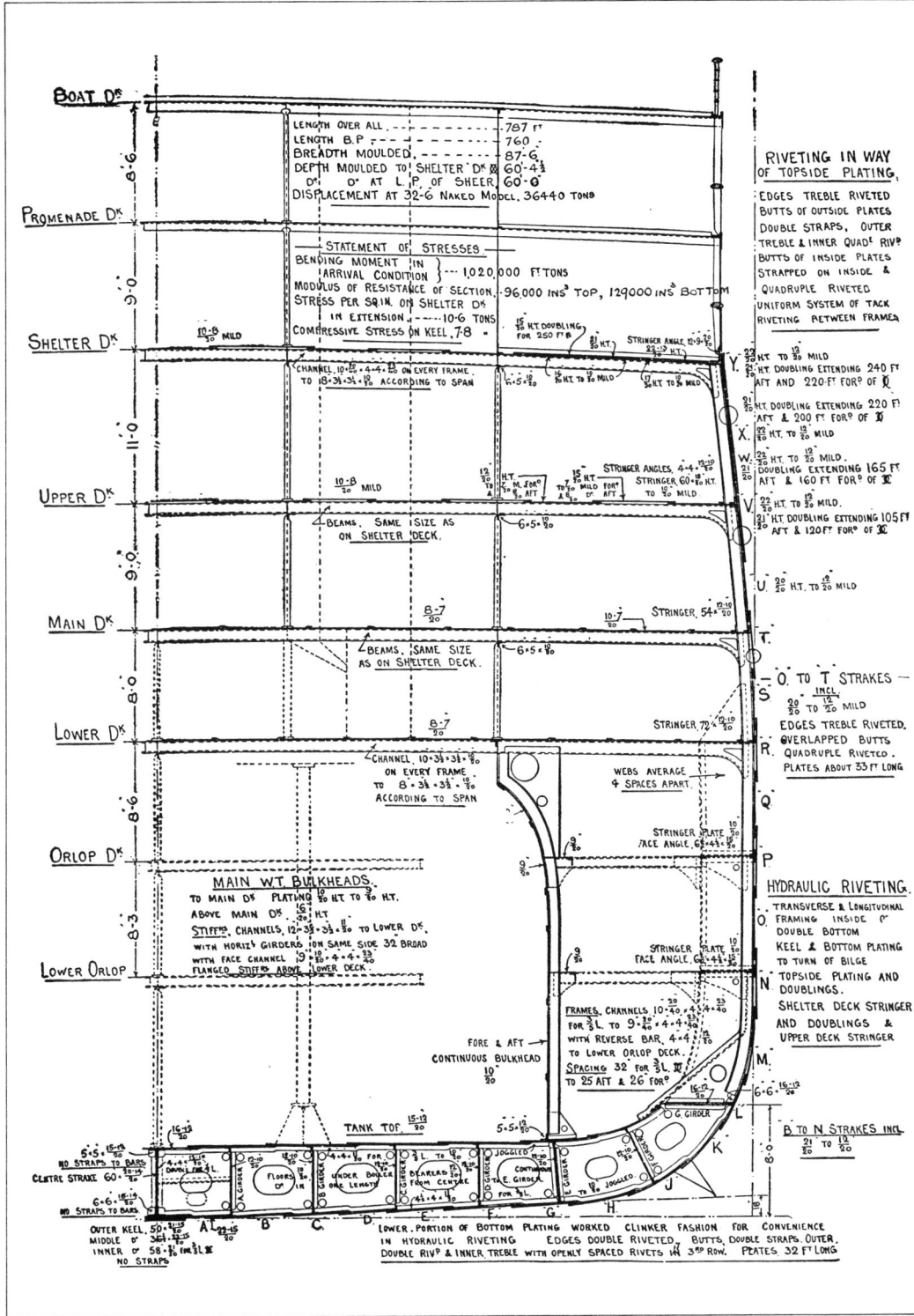

The midship section of the Cunarder Lusitania of 1907, showing her riveted construction (scantlings in inches) and extent of the newly introduced high tensile steel. The sheerstrake and deck stringer plates are double thickness, while the keel is treble thickness. Illustration from a contemporary handbook, Present Day Shipbuilding.

the machinery proportion of ship cost up from a quarter to a third.

Unlike today, the ordinary citizen of the major maritime countries took a great pride in shipping developments and bought his sons books with titles like *Shipping Wonders of the World*. Ocean-going vessels could be seen in the centre of many major cities such as London, Hamburg and New York. Progress was epitomised by the development of the transatlantic liner, which expanded from White Star's 17kt 20,000-tonners *Celtic* (1901) and *Cedric* (1903) to the 30kt 80,000 tonners *Queen Mary* and *Normandie* of the mid 1930s.

Mauretania and *Lusitania* were deservedly seen as technological marvels of their day. Their 32,000-ton 1903 design exhibited innovations on a grand scale, which a modern naval architect would hesitate to incorporate in a single design today. Their regular 25kts was only achievable by the use of steam turbines, albeit of 70,000 horsepower, 35 times the power of Parsons' prototype *Turbinia* of less than ten years earlier. Many experiments were carried out with models to determine the appropriate dimensions, hull form, propulsion system and power requirements. Unlike aircraft, ships do not have 'prototypes'; performance has to be predicted and achieved from the drawing board and small scale model.

The Cunarders, at 790ft (240m), were the longest ships yet built and very few shipyards had such long building berths. Such a length would induce high stresses in the hull, both at sea and during launching, so the newly introduced high tensile steel was used in the upper portions of the hull; parts of the structure were three plates thick or 3.2in (81mm).

period when steam and steel ousted sail and wood, nor the equally explosive growth of the 1950–80 period, when ship sizes expanded twenty-fold, and many new types were introduced, from the container ship to the liquefied gas tanker. The two mainstays of the world fleet, the freighter and the tanker, only increased in size by roughly half and little more than double respectively as the table of average (not largest) vessel particulars indicates. The increase in speed pushed

Dry cargo freighter	1900	1925	1950
Capacity, dwt	6200	8300	9500
Gross tonnage	3800	4800	6000
Service speed, kts	9.5	10.5	12.5
Machinery	coal fired	steam recip	diesel
Indicated horsepower (ihp)	1700	2250	4000
Machinery price £	11,000	20,000	150,000
Price per ihp	6.5	8.9	37
Typical ship price £	45,000	75,000	450,000
Price per ton dw £	7.2	9.0	47
Tanker			
Capacity, dwt	7500	9000	16,500
Service speed, kts	10	11	13.5

Their direct drive turbines rotated at
180rpm, the same speed as their four propellers, risking the newly recognised phenomenon of cavitation (high velocities and low
pressures causing erosion of the bronze propeller blades). The two engine builders
(Wallsend Slipway & Engineering on the
Tyne, and John Brown of Clydebank respectively) had to re-equip their shops to build
the massive machines with their huge cast-
ings and rotors, to say nothing of their 25
coal-fired boilers, which needed 324 stokers
to keep them supplied. Although Cunard
received a Government loan of £2.6 million
in view of their potential as armed merchant
cruisers, both the owners and the shipbuilders faced a huge financial risk. Indeed the
two Tyneside shipbuilders Swan & Hunter
and Wigham Richardson had merged in 1903
and taken a majority shareholding in
Wallsend Slipway for the express purpose of
bidding for one of the orders. The ships
turned out much more expensive than anticipated at £3.5 million the pair, no expense
having been spared to give them the best of
everything. Indeed they were the most expensive merchant ships built in Britain up to
that time.[1] In the event, the ships enhanced
the reputation of both owners and builders,
establishing themselves firmly in their respective markets.

During this first decade of the twentieth
century, many other shipbuilders were expanding their plant and facilities. Some like
Swan Hunter & Wigham Richardson built
covered berths (slipways), while others, including Harland & Wolff in Belfast and
Blohm & Voss in Hamburg built gantries
spanning their berths to give maximum lifting coverage, compared with the traditional
pole derricks ranged alongside the berths.
Some shipbuilders laid out brand new shipyards including Beardmore on the Clyde
and New York Shipbuilding Corporation at
Camden, New Jersey. Heavy fitting-out
cranes were installed, typically the newly
introduced hammerhead crane of 100–150
tons capacity, suitable for lifting heavy turbine components, boilers and, for naval builders, gun mountings. The actual construction
techniques remained unchanged, where each

steel plate and bar was worked individually
and erected piecemeal at the berth for riveting together. The ship as launched was thus
an empty steel hull, which needed installation of machinery and outfitting with accommodation and cargo equipment. However,
contemporary statistics all concentrated on
'launchings' as measures of shipbuilding
output, rather than the more realistic 'completions'. The published statistics usually omit-
ted naval vessels and non-propelled craft
such as floating docks (a rapidly expanding
alternative to graving docks for ship repair),
so did not give a complete picture of shipbuilding output.[2]

Technical advances

That first decade of the century also saw a
number of technical developments which
paved the way for further evolution. Experiments with welding were carried out, while
Joseph Isherwood, a former Lloyd's Register
surveyor, introduced a new system of longitudinal framing in place of the traditional transverse framing – the ribs which supported the
plates of the hull. This was particularly applicable to tankers, which were increasing in
length and prone to buckling in the bottom
and deck. Self-discharging single deck vessels
were introduced into deep-sea bulk trades,
adapting from Great Lakes experience. Such
vessels were used in the fast growing Scandinavian iron ore trades, offering much shorter
port times than conventional bucket dis-

charge using shore cranes. This greater efficiency compensated for the lack of a back-
haul cargo that a multi-deck freighter delivering ore might hope to obtain. Self-trimming
was introduced in vessels carrying grain and
coal, with the upper part of the hold sloped
at about 30 degrees to avoid men with shov-
els having to trim (level off) the cone of
loaded cargo out into the wings of the hold,
which could otherwise shift in a seaway and
possibly capsize the ship.

Some innovative hull forms were introduced, such as the corrugated hull in the
freighter *Monitoria* of 1909, where horizontal
troughs along the side of the ship were
thought to improve the flow of water to the
propeller and thus the propulsive efficiency,
as well having some tonnage-cheating features, still a popular quest for shipowners
and designers. Other naval architects ex-
pressed reservations about the claims, pointing out that the model experiments had been
carried out in a pendulum tank, in which a
rigid model was swung through a trough of
water to measure its apparent drag. The

1. Although battleships cost a similar amount, the
shipbuilder was only responsible for the hull and
machinery, or about half the cost, with the Admiralty
providing armament and armour plating separately.

2. One facet of the current work of the British
Shipbuilding History Project at Newcastle University is
to produce more comprehensive statistics of shipbuilding
and marine engineering output from a computer database
being created of the 100,000 ships built by the British
industry.

more reliable towing tank was now well established and, coupled with Froude's method of predicting full scale drag from model experiments, enabled shipbuilders to establish the necessary engine power and thus fuel consumption of a new design with greater confidence.

Until 1911, however, such facilities in Britain were only available to the Admiralty and a few private shipbuilders who had their own tanks, but in that year the National Physical Laboratory opened its Teddington tank near London, partly financed by torpedo boat builder Alfred Yarrow; it is still in use today. The United States Navy's facility at Washington was opened in 1900, where the British educated naval architect David Taylor conducted classic experiments, the results of which are still used today.[3] By using their own testing facilities, specialist builders like William Denny of Dumbarton on the Clyde were able to tender for high speed and unusual craft with much less risk of underestimating speed and power, which could lead to a loss on a contract, and thus came to dominate markets such as that of the cross channel ferry.

The years immediately prior to the First World War saw the application of the diesel engine to ships, first in coastal vessels such as Anglo-Saxon Petroleum's *Vulcanus* in 1910, then in 1912 to deep sea vessels with East Asiatic's cargo liners *Selandia* from Burmeister & Wain in Copenhagen and *Jutlandia* from Barclay Curle on the Clyde. A number of experimental designs were developed in that period both by traditional engine builders and by new companies, although the outbreak of war delayed both development and acceptance of the diesel engine in merchant ships.

The loss of *Titanic* in April 1912 sparked a re-examination of the whole question of passenger ship safety. The first International Convention for the Safety of Life at Sea, which was held in London in 1913, made a number of recommendations on life-saving appliances, such as lifeboats for all, greater subdivision (the number and arrangement of water-

tight bulkheads) to increase the chances of a vessel remaining afloat and reasonably upright after damage, enhancing the prospect thereby of safe evacuation, as well as improved firefighting provision and wireless equipment. Improved designs of lifeboat davit were introduced by Schat of Holland and Welin of Sweden, which required less effort and were more likely to get the boat into the water on an even keel. A number of these recommendations were either included in the design of new passenger liners or retrofitted in existing vessels, including *Titanic*'s sister *Olympic*.

This period was one of booming world trade, high freight rates and good profits for shipowners leading to the placing of newbuilding orders, and encouraging the expansion of shipbuilding facilities, not just in Britain but in Germany, France, Italy, the Netherlands and the United States. The year 1913 saw 1750 merchant ships launched around the world totalling 3.33 million tons gross, 58 per cent of them from UK yards.

During the First World War, merchant shipbuilding initially took second place to

3. A much larger tank was completed in Carderock, Maryland in 1939 named after Taylor, just in time for the Second World War.

An indication of the typical structure of an early twentieth-century merchant ship is provided by this dry-dock view of the Lochmonar, *a 9831grt Royal Mail cargo liner that broke her back after stranding in November 1927. A new 108ft bow section was built at Harland & Wolff, Belfast and attached in September 1928. The main structural elements – plates, angle bars and brackets – can be seen in the main, damaged, section of the ship, while the new bow clearly demonstrates the lapped in-and-out pattern of the plating.* (CMP)

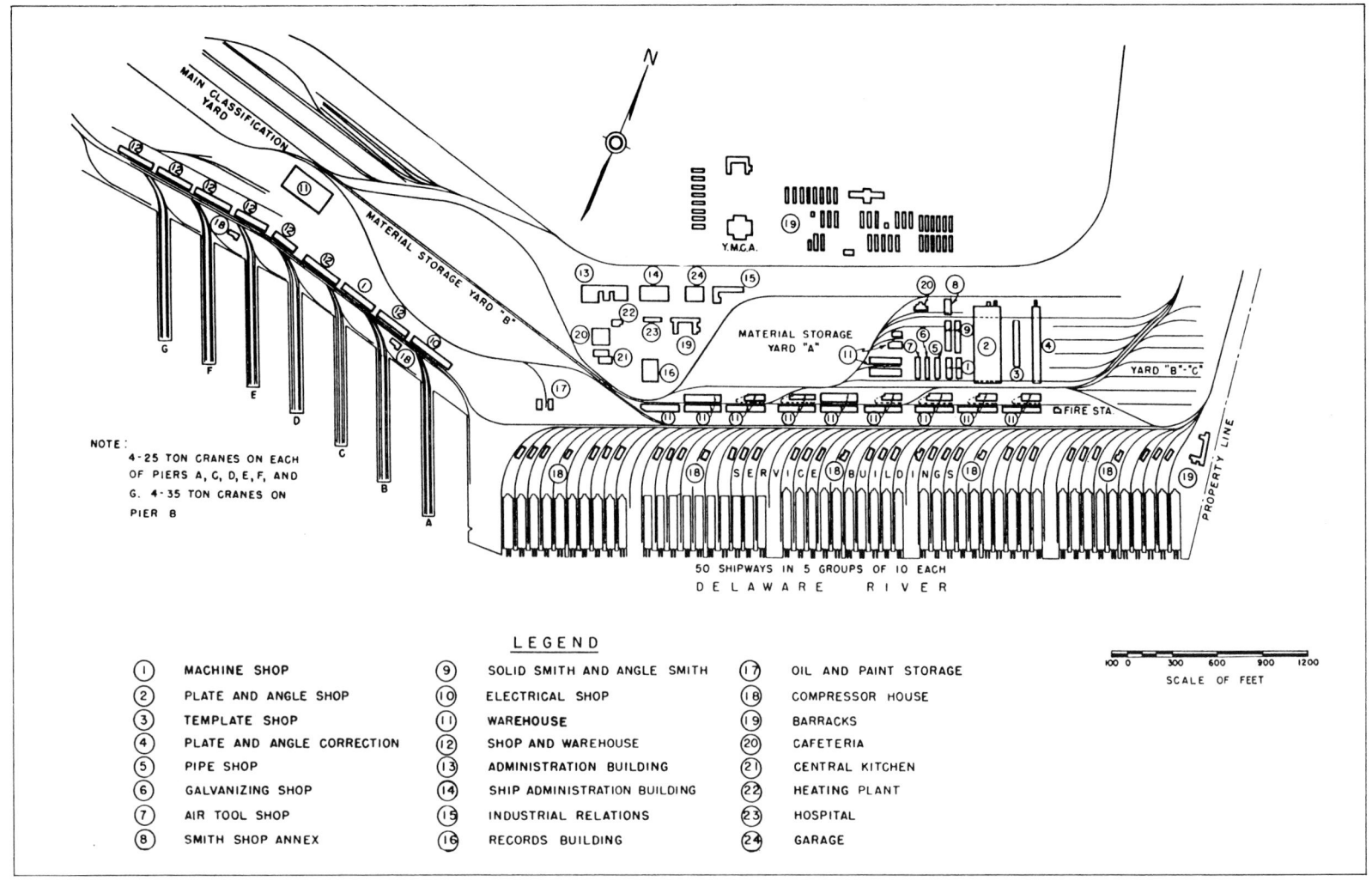

N

MAIN CLASSIFICATION YARD

MATERIAL STORAGE YARD "B"

Y.M.C.A.

MATERIAL STORAGE
YARD "A"

YARD "B"-"C"

PROPERTY LINE

FIRE STA.

NOTE:
4-25 TON CRANES ON EACH
OF PIERS A, C, D, E, F, AND
G. 4-35 TON CRANES ON
PIER B

SERVICE BUILDINGS

50 SHIPWAYS IN 5 GROUPS OF 10 EACH
D E L A W A R E   R I V E R

LEGEND

①	MACHINE SHOP	⑨	SOLID SMITH AND ANGLE SMITH	⑰	OIL AND PAINT STORAGE
②	PLATE AND ANGLE SHOP	⑩	ELECTRICAL SHOP	⑱	COMPRESSOR HOUSE
③	TEMPLATE SHOP	⑪	WAREHOUSE	⑲	BARRACKS
④	PLATE AND ANGLE CORRECTION	⑫	SHOP AND WAREHOUSE	⑳	CAFETERIA
⑤	PIPE SHOP	⑬	ADMINISTRATION BUILDING	㉑	CENTRAL KITCHEN
⑥	GALVANIZING SHOP	⑭	SHIP ADMINISTRATION BUILDING	㉒	HEATING PLANT
⑦	AIR TOOL SHOP	⑮	INDUSTRIAL RELATIONS	㉓	HOSPITAL
⑧	SMITH SHOP ANNEX	⑯	RECORDS BUILDING	㉔	GARAGE

100 0   300   600   900   1200
SCALE OF FEET

The Hog Island yard of the American International Shipbuilding Corporation on the Delaware river which was laid out from September 1917. It was over two miles long and had fifty slipways, capable of building standard cargo ships prefabricated at inland plants. It cost $65 million and employed 30,000 men. The first ship, the 5735grt Quistconck was launched on 5 August 1918. The yard is now the site of Philadelphia airport. Illustration from The Shipbuilding Business of the USA.

warship construction among the belligerents. Not until losses from U-boats mounted in 1916–17 was there a serious attempt to increase merchant shipbuilding output. Both in Britain and in the United States, emergency shipbuilding programmes were instituted. In the former case, existing designs were taken as a basis and re-engineered to be more suitable for rapid production, particularly of machinery, including one design with a straight frame hull. More spectacular was the US programme, involving the creation of 'greenfield' shipyards laid out for mass production. One of the most notable was the Hog Island yard near Philadelphia with no fewer than fifty berths, compared with a typical shipyard's four to eight.

The industry postwar

Relatively few of the standard vessels had been completed by the time of the Armistice in November 1918. Despite cancellations, large numbers of merchant ships were completed in 1919–20. Although immediate postwar demand was high, the boom was short-lived, freight markets peaking early in 1920 as supply of ships soon outstripped demand for their services. Ship prices, new and second-hand, fell sharply, triggering losses among both shipowners and shipbuilders. By contrast, shiprepairing, often seen as something of a cinderella industry overshadowed by more glamorous new construction, was still busy. Refurbishment of liners after military service continued for several years and many coal burners (including *Mauretania*) were converted to oil-firing. Oil reduced the weight and space occupied by bunkers as it had an energy content about 40 per cent higher than coal, it reduced engine room crews substantially and speeded the otherwise slow and dirty process of bunkering in port.

Time in port was also being reduced by more cargo-friendly ship structures and fittings. Hold obstructions like pillars, tie beams and stringers were gradually eliminated, making cargo handling easier and more suited to mechanical aids, while hatchways were increased in size. Cargo handling gear increased in capacity, typically with pairs of derricks now made of tubular steel instead of single wooden ones at each hatch, with one plumbing the hold and one the quayside, rigged in 'union purchase'. Non-essential features such as tumblehome (the slight sloping inwards of the hull above the waterline) and bar keels (awkward when drydocking ships and increasing the ship's draught) were eliminated in all except small vessels.

The first steps in applying welding to shipbuilding were taken. From about 1905, welding had been applied in ship repair, where it was useful for awkward components like boiler furnaces and sternframes. These early processes used both electric arc, developed in Sweden, and oxy-acetylene developed in France. The first all-welded vessel had been the 125ft (38m) barge *Ac 1320* built

From the 1930s, welding increasingly replaced riveting as a means of fastening ships. Initially welding was done by hand, but machines like this fuse-arc welder were gradually introduced from the Second World War onwards. This machine, being used in the construction of Union-Castle's Pretoria Castle *at Harland & Wolff's Belfast yard in March 1947, was then a recent innovation.* (CMP)

in 1918. The first all-welded ship was the 420 tons gross coaster *Fullagar* built by Cammell Laird at Birkenhead in 1920. She was a technical success, but lost her builders some £52,000 on a contract worth only £41,000! This was partly due to having to train the welders and subsequently pay them high wages; such demands retarded the application of welding to new construction in Britain. Riveting was seen as a more predictable process, the costs of which then were well understood, especially using the squad system, where a team of steelworkers contracted with the builder to carry out certain tasks like bending all the frames for a fixed price. The classification societies, like Lloyd's Register, responsible for the integrity of the hulls, were reluctant to authorise welding for critical hull structure until more experience had been gained. The Imperial Japanese Navy temporarily gave up using welding after major structural failures in its cruisers in 1935; quality control was more difficult to achieve than with riveting.

It was not until the 1930s that welding started to make headway in shipbuilding.

The traditional fastenings of steel ships were rivets. As late as 1947, when this photograph was taken in Bartram's Sunderland shipyard, vital parts of the ship, such as the stern, were still riveted by hand. In this process, red hot rivets were driven into pre-drilled holes from behind; the hand riveters then hammered the protruding end to form a head, while the rivet was held in place by a 'holder-up' on the other side of the plate. Pneumatic rivet guns, which made riveting a one-man operation, replaced hand riveters for most applications. (CMP)

Germany and Sweden led the way with partially welded tankers, where it was difficult to get oiltight riveting in cargo tank bulkheads, which were prone to leakage and corrosion. In Britain the first all-welded 'tanker' was the 720-ton oil lighter *Peter G Campbell* built by Swan Hunter & Wigham Richardson in 1933. Electric arc welding, using coated electrodes to shield the newly formed weld from oxidation, was introduced at this time, the technology being jealously guarded. In repair yards, special squads would be used, erecting screens around their work to shield it from prying eyes. Appreciable investment was required, not only in the welding plant itself, but in provision of electrical supplies and extra lifting appliances, as well as the training of welders. The cost of welded construction at that time was thus actually greater than that of riveting but the advantages included lighter hulls from eliminating overlaps (as much as 20 per cent) and thus greater deadweight from a given size of hull, plus reduced drag from the smoother hull.

The international scene

The 1920s witnessed considerable expansion in shipbuilding in countries other than Britain. This was partly due to their having been unable to buy British ships during the First World War but was also due to state encouragement, either with direct subsidies as in Italy, or support for shipping and import bans as in Japan. Other countries to expand included France, the Netherlands, Germany and Scandinavia. The United States contin-

ued to support shipbuilding but demand was so low with its higher costs that a number of shipyards closed, including all the emergency First World War yards. The British share of world merchant shipbuilding fell from over 60 per cent prewar to around 40–50 per cent in the 1920s, from about one hundred shipyards. A typical British annual output was around 500 ships aggregating some 1.4 million tons gross, employing some 150,000 men in shipbuilding and shiprepair. A number of small to medium sized British yards, as well as engine builders, went out of business at this time. Repair yards with small drydocks found it difficult to fill their capacity with the bigger ships being operated and several merged or closed.

Innovation in ship design was largely confined to specialist ship types and higher powered machinery. Two advanced ore carriers of 21,000 tons deadweight (over double the typical capacity) were built by Deutsche Werft at Hamburg in 1925 for £225,000 each for the Chile to US iron ore trade. So far ahead of the time were *Svealand* and her sister *Amerikaland* that the former remained in service for forty years. Unusually they had twin screw diesel propulsion for a speed of 11kts.

Indeed diesel propulsion was rapidly growing in popularity with a few dominant makes emerging as leaders, including Burmeister & Wain (Danish), Sulzer (Swiss), MAN (German), Doxford (British) and Werkspoor (Dutch). Extensive use of licensees was used to penetrate local markets; for example Harland & Wolff had the UK and Commonwealth B&W licence and, supported by Lords Pirrie

One of the technical developments of the inter-war period that gained temporary popularity was the cutaway Maierform bow, demonstrated perfectly by the Boschfontein, ex-Nieuwkerk, *of United Netherlands Navigation. This 1928 cargo-passenger ship was re-engined and lengthened in 1934 by de Schelde at Vlissingen, diesels replacing the original turbines. The new bow section, unpainted, stands out clearly from the original hull.* (CMP)

(chairman of the yard) and Kylsant (head of the Royal Mail Group, a major customer), developed their own design variants. There were still problems over reliability, maintenance costs, skilled engineers and the relatively high cost of diesel oil – a particular disadvantage to British owners with access to cheap coal bunkers.

Steam machinery responded to the challenge by increasing its efficiency to reduce fuel consumption – higher boiler pressures, use of exhaust steam from a conventional reciprocating engine led through a small geared turbine (Bauer-Wach), superheating and even reheating. Electric transmission was applied both to diesels and turbines, culminating in the 160,000shp turbo-electric installation in the transatlantic liner *Normandie*.

On the hull side, further efforts were made to reduce power requirements. Cruiser sterns increased the waterline length compared with counter sterns, streamlined rudders and sternframes increased propulsive efficiency, appendage design was improved and new

bow shapes evolved such as Maierform. The more efficient bronze propeller increasingly displaced the cast iron propeller, even in slow speed ships, while in the fastest ships, riveted seams and butts were smoothed off with composition.

The international ratification of prewar safety resolutions had been held up by the war, so there was somewhat patchy application of the recommendations by individual countries. British shipowners, while not averse to applying higher standards, were not pleased to find some of their commercial competitors not yet having to meet the same standards. In 1929, the second International Convention for the Safety of Life at Sea was held in London to agree improved standards on subdivision, life saving appliances, fire-fighting provisions and wireless equipment – which coincided with the rash

of Atlantic Blue Riband challengers including the Italian *Rex*, the German *Bremen*, French *Normandie* and British *Queen Mary*.

International agreement was also obtained on load lines, all countries agreeing to calculate and assign freeboard (height of deck above waterline) for both dry cargo ships and tankers according to the same, as opposed to local, regulations. These new load lines came into force on 1 January 1933, thus slightly changing the load draught, and hence deadweight capacity, of many vessels.

The Depression

The early 1930s were years of severe depression, with world trade falling well below prewar levels. Laid up tonnage mounted due to lack of cargoes and the shipbreakers, dominated by Britain, Italy and Japan, were not short of business. Shipbuilding orders virtually dried up, despite slashing of prices, apart from a few specialist vessels such as whale factory ships. Judicious placing of naval orders helped preserve several shipyards in Britain, Germany and the United States. The lowest point was reached in 1933, when only 330 merchant ships were launched worldwide, of a tonnage less than one sixth of only four years earlier. Unemployment in British shipbuilding and repair yards reached 60 per cent with employment down to about 66,000, less than a quarter of the 1920 figure.

In order to rationalise capacity and encour-

The biggest turbo-electric installation of its day was the 160,000shp plant in the French transatlantic liner Normandie, *seen here at Le Havre. As suggested by the plumes of smoke, only the first two funnels were genuine boiler uptakes, the third being a dummy, which actually contained the ship's kennels.* (CMP)

An example of the fast fruit carrier that became something of a Scandinavian speciality between the wars, the I K Ward *was built by AB Götaverken, Gothenburg, Sweden in 1929 for the Norwegian owner Chr Gundersen & Co. This twin-screw 14kt motorship was one of a pair that were improved versions of the* Gundersen *of 1927, the first motor fruit ship.* (CMP)

age firms to realise something from their assets and leave the industry, British shipbuilders, assisted by the Bank of England, set up National Shipbuilders Security Ltd. This company bought up redundant shipyards and closed them down to reduce overcapacity and competition, enabling the others to survive. One of the first yards to close was one of the newest, Beardmore's Dalmuir yard which had been laid out to generous standards barely twenty-five years earlier. Those shipyards with repair facilities, including Swan Hunter & Wigham Richardson, and Cammell Laird at Birkenhead, were better able to survive, since trading vessels, although reduced in number, still needed drydocking and maintenance. Some much needed cashflow and employment, not just for foremen and apprentices, could be maintained.

Modern designs

The more forward looking yards developed new designs during the lean years, for example the Ayre brothers at Burntisland on the Forth opposite Edinburgh and Doxford on the Wear with 'economy' ships. Innovation was not confined to the larger ships, with (Kort) nozzles being fitted around propellers in tugs to increase thrust. Steel hatch covers had been toyed with for some years, but in general the cheapness and ease of handling of conventional wooden boards on steel beams outweighed their slower operation and potential vulnerability in heavy seas. By the mid 1930s, however, more efficient designs of steel cover had been developed by the MacGregor brothers in the northeast of England. These speeded the turnround time of short-sea vessels like colliers, where low freeboard contributed to a relatively high loss rate when fitted with wooden covers. The concept soon began to be applied to deep sea ships, though it was not until the mid 1950s that steel covers had became almost universally adopted.

Dry cargo handling methods changed little between the wars: shipboard derricks and winches or shore cranes only lifting up to about 3 tons, still requiring much manual labour to stow cargo safely on board. In US coastal trades, fork lift trucks and other mechanical devices were introduced to counteract high wages; a novel design built in Britain in 1928 (*Seatrain New Orleans*) lifted whole railcars on board with a special gantry – a forerunner of the container ship concept of the 1950s.

Tankers developed steadily, with the increasing number of road vehicles requiring refined petroleum shipments. Scandinavian owners began to challenge the US and British dominance, introducing larger partially welded diesel vessels. These were often built in Britain, Sweden or Germany with loans raised on the strength of long term charters from oil companies – a method of finance to be further developed after the Second World War. The oil companies themselves built large classes of near standard ships, for example the 'three twelves' – 12,000 tons deadweight at 12kts on 12 tons of diesel fuel per day.

Scandinavian owners also developed the fast diesel fruit carrier, sleek refrigerated ships which also carried a few passengers at speeds of over 16kts. New yards capable of building such ships were often laid out with fewer constraints on sites or inherited restrictive labour practices than traditional yards in for example Britain. They used cranes instead of derricks, often travelling on tracks between the berths, and an increasing degree of welding, with its associated prefabrication. Welded structures lent themselves to the laying out in the workshops of large areas of plating to which the stiffeners could be attached in the efficient 'downhand' welding position. Whole units such as bulkheads could then be transported to the berth and erected quickly, reducing build time.

By 1937, 50 per cent of the world fleet was oil fuelled, both steam and diesel, with relatively few new ships being built for coal firing. The latter were largely local vessels with ready access to cheap supplies, although small Dutch motor coasters were beginning to challenge traditional British coaster owners and builders. Higher powers and speeds were much easier to achieve with liquid fuel, so that cargo liner speeds were increasingly in the 13–15kt range, although 10–11kts was still quite enough for tramps, given the low value of their bulk cargoes such as coal.

The number of vessel types began to expand, although Lloyd's Register of Shipping continued for another thirty years to record in its statistics only a few readily identifiable vessel types including tankers and fishing vessels. An indication of the mix of vessel types is given by a tonnage analysis of the 6692 merchant ships of 19.1 million tons gross built in British shipyards between 1920 and 1938:

	Percentage
Passenger carrying vessels	23.2
Dry cargo ships	50.8
Tankers	16.2
Colliers and coasters	3.9
Fishing vessels	1.2
Others	4.7

The car ferry was just beginning to emerge as a specific type, for example the 1939 Denny-built *Princess Victoria*, diesel powered and carrying 1500 passengers and 80 cars. She was lost in 1940 after conversion to a

The Denny-built car ferry Princess Victoria, *seen running trials in 1947, was almost a repeat of a 1939 vessel of the same name lost in 1940. The earlier ship was one of the first dedicated car carriers, which were to become far more significant in the automobile-dominated postwar world.* (CMP)

minelayer but a virtually indentical replacement was built in 1947, herself to be lost in heavy weather on her run from Stranraer to Larne in January 1953. This loss triggered design changes, in particular the closing in of vehicle decks with stern (and sometimes bow) doors.

By 1935–36, the worst of the slump was over, but government schemes to stimulate the marine industries were still needed. In Britain, the Scrap and Build loan scheme encouraged newbuilding on the basis of one ton gross for every two scrapped – providing further business for shipbreakers in the UK and on the Continent. In the United States, the newly formed Maritime Commission introduced modern designs of standard cargo vessels, offering construction subsidies, while selling off older cargo vessels from its laid-up fleet.

The Second World War

The outbreak of the Second World War in September 1939 saw a rather different pattern to world shipbuilding compared with 1914. The UK was still the world's largest shipbuilder with 34 per cent of the 3 million tons gross of merchant tonnage launched, but sustained largely by orders from British and Empire shipowners. Next came Germany (16 per cent) and Japan (15 per cent), whose industries had been protected from foreign competition for two decades. United States production had slumped to only 7 per cent, largely for local owners trading in home waters and whose shipping was protected by the Jones Act of 1916. Like most of the other shipbuilding nations, naval orders provided a welcome boost for production, especially as one ton (measured by standard displacement, or all-up weight excluding fuel) had about five times the value of one gross registered ton (grt as a measure of internal volume calculated at 100 cu ft = 1 ton). Naval orders were most important to the major engine builders, as machinery installations were typically 30,000 horsepower or more, compared with only around 3000 for a cargo vessel. More importantly, due to lack of international competition and some agreement among builders on minimum tender levels, prices included a reasonable measure of profit, which helped some British warship builders to survive lean years in the slump.

From before the outbreak of war, Britain recognised the threat from the U-boat and the need to maintain overseas trade, also the urgent need for convoy escorts. Since the shipbuilding industry was put under Admiralty control in October 1939, it was possible to balance merchant and naval demands and allocate material accordingly – a centralisation not adopted in the United States in the Second World War. Well respected shipbuilders such as James Lithgow and Amos Ayre were put in charge of merchant shipbuilding and encouraged the sixty or so remaining shipyards to concentrate largely on standard ships. The designs were simplified to speed production and to reduce the use of scarce materials such as imported timber.

With British shipyards fully extended and limited more by labour and materials than construction facilities, orders for cargo ships were placed in North America at the end of 1940, 'Ocean' type vessels being built both in Canada and the United States. This design was based on a Wearside design of 10,000-ton deadweight (7000 tons gross) riveted tramp with steam reciprocating machinery capable of 10.5kts. In 1941 this was re-engineered in the United States into the Liberty ship, all-welded for mass production in newly laid out assembly yards with components ordered centrally but manufactured nationwide. The US Maritime Commission financed eighteen new shipyards costing some $300 million, eight on the Atlantic coast totalling sixty-two slipways, six on the Pacific coast with sixty-two slipways and

The most famous of all the war standard merchantmen of either world war was the 10,000dwt Liberty ship, 2710 of which were built between December 1941 and October 1945. Based on a British design the ship was re-engineered for welded mass production in specially built new shipyards in the United States. At the height of the programme, it took about 60 days to build each ship, and by 1943 three ships per day were being completed. Not surprisingly, 'Liberties' formed the core of tramp and cargo liner fleets for decades after the end of the war. This is the Samarkand, *one of 385 'Liberties' built by Bethlehem-Fairfield at Sparrow's Point, Maryland, a yard that built the first Liberty of all. Initially* Samarkand *served under the British flag, being managed by Alfred Holt's of Liverpool, but under various names and flags survived until 1978.* (CMP)

four on the Gulf coast with thirty-five slipways.

The first Liberty, completed in December 1941, was *Patrick Henry* from Bethlehem-Fairfield at Baltimore. Early ships in the programme took around 230 days to build with about one million man hours but with mass production these figures were soon reduced to an average of 60 days and 400,000 man hours (including not a few woman-hours!). Average cost per ship was $1.78 million or about 2.5 times as much as a similar vessel built in wartime Britain with its more experienced but lesser paid labour. Peak output was in 1943 when over three 'Liberty' ships a *day* were being completed – more tonnage than had been lost each day by the Allies even at the height of the U-boat offensive. No fewer than 2580 'Liberties' were completed by the end of the programme in October 1945, plus 132 variants such as tankers, totalling 19.5 million grt or 28.7 million tons deadweight, with engines totalling 6.8 million horsepower. But even this huge output was only half the 38.6 million grt of merchant ships completed in US shipyards in 1939–45 – an annual average output roughly double the entire world shipbuilding output prewar. On top of this, US yards were producing a vast fleet of naval vessels, so that shipbuilding consumed 20 per cent of the nation's steel output during the war, compared with 1 per cent prewar. This massive achievement contributed hugely to the Allied victory in the Second World War – the 'arsenal of democracy' as Franklin Roosevelt called America.

Wartime designs reflected the military needs of vessels operating in convoy, for example heavy lift derricks for armoured vehicles, defensive measures such as self defence guns and extra lifesaving equipment, while shelter decks were closed in to provide extra deadweight for heavy cargoes and improve survivability if damaged. Existing shipyards were gradually re-equipped to reflect changes in construction – more welding, heavier lifts, greater storage areas, more cranes, more prefabrication and extended fitting out facilities, which reflected the longer construction times with all the extra equipment.

The postwar years

At the end of the war, German and Japanese shipyards were in ruins, and indeed banned from building ships other than small local craft. Yards in the Netherlands, France, Belgium, Denmark, Norway and Italy were still recovering from the war. In Europe, only Britain and Sweden were in a position to build in any quantity. Although the huge US wartime shipbuilding industry was still available, its prices were high – and dollars in short supply with potential customers. Wartime inflation in Britain meant that shipbuilding prices had nearly doubled – prewar, a typical 10,000dwt tramp cost about £130,000, but at the end of the war the price was around £250,000. With the uncertainties over material prices and labour costs, few shipbuilders would accept fixed price contracts, requiring 'cost plus', usually in the form of payment of actual material and labour costs plus a fixed sum for overheads and profit. Nevertheless shipowners had no choice but to pay; they needed the ships to replace tonnage lost during the war, and wished to re-establish services to former trading areas such as the Far East, while they had to refurbish tonnage like liners which had been converted to military purposes.

The vessels ordered were still much the same as prewar designs in type, size and speed, although tankers were beginning to get larger, partly spurred by the widely available war-built T2 tankers of 16,500 deadweight. Research and development were given a higher priority; in Britain, the shipbuilders formed the British Shipbuilding Research Association, while the engine builders formed the Parsons and Marine Engineering Turbine Research and Development Association, not surprisingly abbreviated to PAMETRADA. The former concentrated initially on hydrodynamic research, commissioning a systematic series of model tests on a range of hull forms, the latter on improved designs of steam turbine to exploit the higher steam pressures and temperatures widely used in US machinery. Wartime exigencies had exposed structural problems: brittle fracture of welded hulls especially at low temperatures, buckling of ship structures on heavy weather convoy routes in northern latitudes, particularly in the ballast condition. The development of notch tough steels and the increased use of longitudinal framing reduced such problems, assisted with full scale experiments on both riveted and welded hulls.

A third Safety of Life at Sea Conference was held in 1948, which not only brought the 1929 provisions up-to-date, but covered cargo as well as passenger vessels.

The Korean War in 1950 stimulated some

rearmament and further demand for raw materials and hence merchant ships. The United States was required to support the war from Japanese bases and they helped rebuild Japanese industry. Both Japan and Germany re-entered the shipbuilding market, initially for domestic owners. In both cases, they could develop yards unencumbered by trade unions made powerful by labour shortages, laying them out for welding and flow line production and with new management systems. In countries such as France, Italy and Norway, state support encouraged expansion in new and existing yards. In Britain, high profits encouraged significant investment in improved facilities for the first time for thirty years. Fewer, but longer and wider, berths were created on the usually cramped sites on river banks hemmed in by roads and railways, albeit at some disruption to output. New prefabrication sheds appeared together with improved fitting out facilities, as it became less common to tow newly launched hulls to engine builders' quays for machinery installation.

Ever larger ships

An important stimulus for this expenditure was the steadily increasing size of tankers, for by 1950, the largest had reached 30,000 tons deadweight (about 18,000grt) with an overall length of 640ft (196m). Such tankers were designed for transport of crude oil, to be refined at destination, which emphasised the economies of scale compared with the transport of oil products from refineries in producing areas. In parallel, ship repairers were encouraged to build new drydocks of suitable size – the postwar period had been one of unparalleled prosperity for them also.

Tankers had nearly always been built with machinery aft, to reduce the risk of fire, to assist trim and to avoid running the propeller shaft tunnel through cargo oil tanks. By the late 1950s, designers had begun to move the bridge aft as well, basically for economy of construction, concentrating all services in one area. The shelter deck vessel, while still useful for general cargo of low density, became increasingly unsuitable for large tonnages of bulk cargoes such as coal, grain and ore. The mid 1950s saw the evolution of the single deck short-sea collier into its big brother the 'bulk carrier'. The concept remained the same: a single deck, self trimming hoppered holds, machinery aft, steel hatch covers, but usually fitted with derricks due

After the war the trend in tanker size was upwards, initially in small increments but gathering momentum rapidly. Although no supertanker, the 42,000-ton British Duchess *of 1958 was the largest tanker so far launched from the Clyde. Two years earlier Japan's shipbuilding output exceeded Britain's for the first time, and much of that tonnage was in large tankers.* (CMP)

to their 'go anywhere' philosophy. Speed was modest at around 12kts, but size soon exceeded 15,000 tons deadweight.

The decade saw the end of coal firing, the steam reciprocator and riveting in new ships – although many ships had been built with a mixture of riveting and welding for some twenty years. The last parts to be riveted were frames to shell plating, deck plating connection to side plating, plus a few longitudinal crack arresting seams in the deck and shell plating.

The diesel engine could now offer over 10,000bhp with turbocharging and an ability to burn heavy residual fuel oil normally used only in boilers, which was little more

than half the price of the hitherto usual diesel oil. Continental and Scandinavian owners and builders were the keenest supporters of such machinery, with Britain and Japan not far behind, although the Americans remained faithful to the steam turbine for another twenty years. By 1959, 83 per cent of new construction by number was diesel propelled, although only 58 per cent by tonnage, as the turbine was generally more suitable for the higher powered vessels. This was particularly true of tankers, which needed steam anyway for cargo pumping; the turbine at that time was more reliable, had lower maintenance costs and used its gearing to get more efficient propeller rpm, compared with direct drive diesels.

Auxiliaries, including anchor windlass, cargo winches and pumps, were increasingly electrically powered, requiring much larger generators. Deck cranes were installed in some cargo liners giving faster cycle times and 'spotting ability'. They were not a new idea, as hydraulically driven deck cranes had been fitted in a few ships in the 1890s, but electric power gave much better control of all motions. Pallets (small wooden platforms holding a ton or so of cargo) handled by fork lift truck became popular, especially in Scandinavia. Navigational aids proliferated; radar had been fitted in merchant ships from the end of the Second World War, echo-sounders and direction finders were routinely fitted, while short-sea vessels often had high accuracy position fixing devices developed from wartime bombing aids, for example Decca Navigator. All contributed to reduced ship losses from stranding or collision. Indeed the annual casualty rate had fallen from around 1.4 per cent in 1905 to only 0.25 per cent by 1955. This meant that the probability of a ship surviving the perils of the sea for twenty-five years increased from 70 per cent to 94 per cent.

But ships did not live to significantly greater ages, because economic obsolescence with competition from increasingly efficient designs condemned more ships to the scrapyard. Shipbreakers' yards in the 1950s were full of steam trawlers, steam coasters and smaller tankers, not always physically worn out, and of course redundant Second World War-built naval vessels.

Cargo liner speeds increased steadily as world trade grew, partly to try to compensate for delays in port from slow cargo handling and outdated equipment and labour attitudes. The 20kt cargo liner was introduced with the US 'Mariner' class of 1952–56 (partly a

The postwar shape of things to come: the streamlined refrigerated motor ship Port Brisbane *of 1949, built for the Port Line's service between Britain and Australasia. The sophisticated, fast and expensive cargo liner enjoyed a brief Indian summer before the container revolution of the 1960s rendered them obsolete. In this photograph, the* Port Brisbane *is anchored in the Thames prior to her maiden voyage, making a pointed contrast with the sailing barge, many of which were still operating commercially in the postwar years.* (CMP)

defence requirement) but it was not long before such speeds were introduced by European operators, especially on the lucrative long-haul Far East route.

The new shipbuilders

Japan had already begun to flex its economic muscles. Industry was fast developing, with raw materials imports requiring ever more and larger ships. Her shipbuilding industry responded, assisted by official annual domestic shipbuilding programmes from 1954, which gave the industry a baseload from which it could seek export orders. The 56,000dwt ore-oil carrier *Sinclair Petrolore* was completed in 1955, while the 100,000-ton barrier was breached in 1959 with the tanker *Universe Apollo* with a length of 950ft (290m) and a draught of 50ft 9in (15.5m). Both ships were built by National Bulk Carriers using the former Kure Naval Dockyard leased by US shipowner Daniel K Ludwig, whose ships combined the maximum of efficiency with the minimum of beauty.

Early customers for Japanese shipyards were Greek and Norwegian owners ordering tankers or ore carriers on the basis of loans backed by long term timecharters from major oil companies or contracts of affreightment to US steel mills. Many of these vessels were registered under flags of convenience such as Liberia or Panama, not only to avoid tax but to bypass domestic regulations on, for example, manning requirements. Manning levels had yet to fall significantly, other than by removing stokers from engine room complements, but crew accommodation standards were beginning to rise; the single cabin, air-conditioning and the all-electric galley were introduced, making further demands on the auxiliary machinery, and requiring ever more specialist subcontractors to supply such equipment all over the world.

In 1956 Japan overtook the UK as the world's largest shipbuilding nation, a position it has yet to relinquish. This was achieved by dedication to purpose, new management methods applied to a co-operative well trained labour force, efficient plant, well engineered designs and good planning techniques. Sweden, Germany and the Netherlands had expanded output, the former concentrating on tankers. The league table for completions in 1960 showed 2005 ships of 8.745 million grt, with tankers making up 42 per cent of the tonnage.

Country	000 GRT	Percentage
Japan	1837	21.9
UK	1298	15.5
Germany	1124	13.4
Sweden	710	8.5
Netherlands	682	8.1
Italy	447	5.3
France	430	5.1
USA	379	4.5

In 1957, for the first time, more passengers crossed the Atlantic by air rather than by sea, signalling the end of the line voyage ship. The latter did not all become redundant, as many were converted for cruising. However, to make up for these declining vessel types, there were new types responding to demand in specialised trades such as car ferries, roll-on/roll-off vessels (adapted from the Second World War tank landing ship concept) and liquefied gas carriers, while the first container ship conversions entered service on US coastal routes. Each of these demanded new ideas from naval architects and marine engineers to meet problems of hull strength, cargo access, low temperatures, and low headroom in the engine room. Demand for service vessels expanded: cable layers, dredgers capable of maintaining channel depths of 50ft (15m) of water as ports adapted to deeper draught ships, and more powerful tugs both for harbour and for deep sea work.

Technical developments grew apace: compact medium speed diesel engines, controllable pitch propellers and bow thrusters for greater manoeuvrability, bulbous bows to reduce drag under particular conditions, higher tensile steel especially in ships with wide hatchways, data logging and remote control of machinery. The first digital computers were used by naval architects in the late 1950s, initially to mechanise routine calculations, but soon used to improve the design and construction processes themselves.

The final decade of the period saw the world shipbuilding industry already set for its greatest expansion yet. Output in 1960 was not only four times larger than at the turn of the century, but made up of a vastly different pattern in terms of vessel type, size, speed, propulsion, equipment and country of build. All these factors contributed to a great increase in ship efficiency and decrease in real costs of transport, which in turn contributed to global changes in raw material sources and development, manufacturing location and economic activity, which are described in the companion volume *The Shipping Revolution.*

Dr Ian Buxton

8

Marine Propulsion

S AIL AND the reciprocating steam engine were the only means of ship propulsion at the turn of the century. Large steel sailing ships were still being built for the Chilean nitrate and the Australian grain trades, with smaller wood and composite ships coming in considerable numbers from Baltic yards for carrying timber.

These were the days of both fierce competition between the British and German lines on the North Atlantic, and of massive emigra-

tion to escape severe ethnic repression in Russia, eastern and middle Europe. It was a period of increasing ship sizes and speeds, which called for machinery of correspondingly greater power. Oil had not come into use as a fuel, even for naval vessels, and the express ships required as many as twenty-five boilers, served by 300 firemen and trimmers handling some 1000 tons of coal per day.

The reciprocating engine reached its

zenith in the first decade with the machinery for Norddeutscher Lloyd's 19,360 tons gross *Kaiser Wilhelm II* which was introduced on

State of the art machinery at the turn of the century: one of the two 20,000ihp tandem-coupled six-crank quadruple-expansion engines of the Kaiser Wilhelm II, *the German transatlantic record-breaker of 1903. Note the high-pressure cylinders mounted above the first intermediate-pressure cylinders to save on engine room length. From* Der Schiffsmaschinenbau *by Gustav Bauer (Munich 1925).*

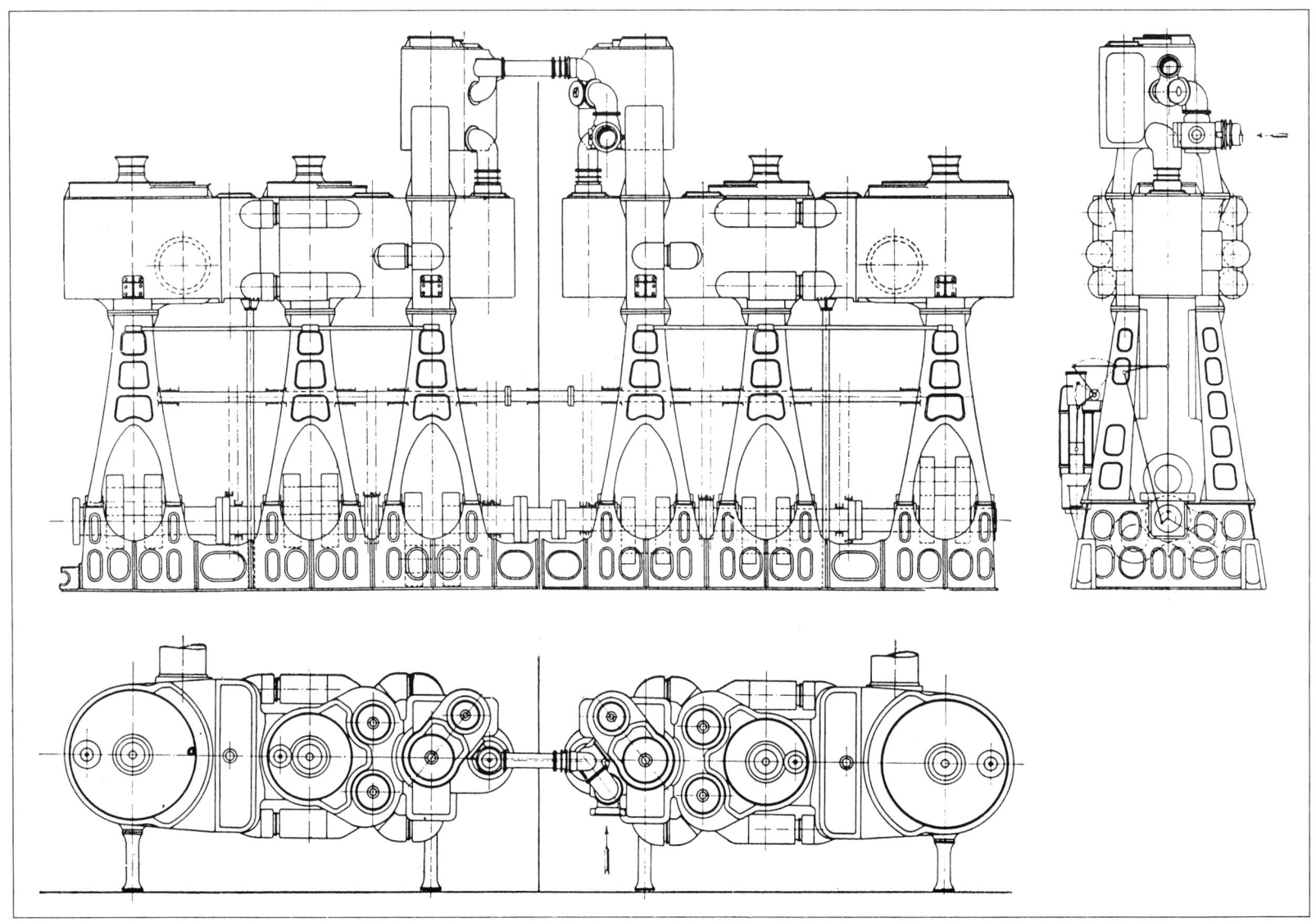

The Sloman cargo ship Barbara, *with a silhouette dominated by the three towers of the Flettner rotors. The rotors were intended as auxiliaries to the ship's diesel engines, but could drive the ship at 6kts without power assistance.* (Graeme MacLennan collection)

Second World War to improve on the rather low efficiency of the steam engine by add-on equipment such as reheaters to make use of higher steam temperatures, and turbines for recovering some of the energy otherwise lost to the sea when condensing the exhaust steam. Effectively, however, the marine steam engine's 150 years' life ended with the period under review.

A sectional end view of the Scott-Still machinery, a hybrid steam-diesel engine that saw some limited service between the wars. From The Marine Engineer and Naval Architect, *March 1922.*

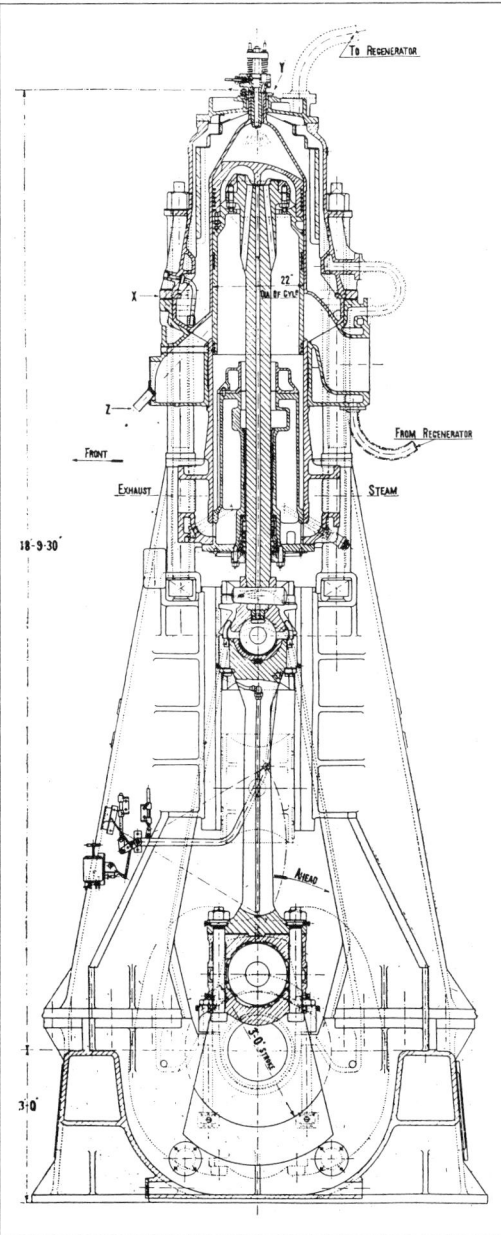

the North Atlantic in 1903. Built and engined by the AG Vulkan shipyard at Stettin to carry nearly 1900 passengers, some 40,000hp was required in order to attain a speed of over 23kts. This was needed to beat the then record holders, the Cunard Steam-Ship Co's 12,950 tons gross 22kt *Campania* and *Lucania* which had come from the Fairfield shipyard ten years earlier.

Power of this order could not be obtained from single quadruple-expansion engines, a problem solved by coupling two similar engines on end for each shaft. To reduce the length of these machines, the high-pressure cylinders were superimposed on the first intermediate-pressure cylinders so that the pistons worked in tandem. Even so, each engine was 72ft (22m) long. A transverse bulkhead extended across the middle of the engine room between the two high pressure and first IP cylinders on each shaft line. This was included for safety reasons, to reduce the volume of the vast space in case of flooding. Twelve double- and seven single-ended boilers in four boiler rooms, with coal bunkers between them, provided steam at 225psi.

Kaiser Wilhelm II took the Atlantic record in the year of her delivery and was followed by a sister ship *Kronprinzessin Cecilie* in 1907, but by that time Cunard had regained the record with the turbine-powered *Lusitania* and *Mauretania*. Surprisingly, both of these handsome German ships survived until 1940, having been first interned in New York, seized in prize and put into service as US troopships during the First World War.

The reciprocating steam engine continued to be built for lesser transatlantic liners up to the later 1920s, often in conjunction with a slow-running direct-coupled steam turbine which made use of the exhaust from the wing engines to drive a centre propeller. This was first used in the Denny-built *Otaki* for New Zealand Shipping Co in 1908 and the last to employ the system was White Star Line's *Laurentic*, built in 1927, only one year later than the completion of the last, and exceptional, large commercial sailing ship. This was Friedrich Laeisz's four-masted barque *Padua*, built in Geestemünde for the Chilean nitrate trade; she is still afloat today and a regular participant in the Tall Ships races as the Russian *Kruzenshtern*.

Among unorthodox hardware for applying wind power to ship propulsion, the most striking, physically, have been the towering hollow aluminium cylinders of Anton Flettner's rotor ships. They made use of the Magnus effect, whereby a fluid, in this case wind, flowing over a rotating cylinder will generate a force at right angles to that flow. Only very modest power was needed to rotate the cylinders. The Sloman cargo liner *Barbara*, with three Flettner rotors, made a number of trips to the Mediterranean in the later 1920s. The principle was not repeated, except in an experimental yacht, but has more recently been revived below the water-line, to enhance the effect of a rudder at slow manoeuvring speeds.

The reciprocator survived longer in the tramp shipping trades, where very much lower powers were required; typically around 2000hp. It was robust and could be repaired easily by the ship's engineers or in remote ports with few facilities. Moreover, speed was not a requirement and both coal and firemen were cheap. Efforts were made from the mid 1920s up to the outbreak of the

The steam turbine

The Hon Charles Parsons' bold demonstration of the marine steam turbine, by sending his experimental craft *Turbinia* to make an unauthorised dash through the lines of the fleets assembled off Spithead for Queen Victoria's Diamond Jubilee Review in June 1897, is well recorded, as is the suspicion that the intrusion was contrived. It was, however, effective, for the speed of over 32kts, which none of the guardships sent to arrest *Turbinia* could approach, brought the attention of the turbine to the world's navies in convincing fashion. At any rate, within a year turbine machinery had been ordered for the destroyer HMS *Viper* and the reciprocating engines for *Cobra* were cancelled in favour of turbines. That both ships were lost shortly afterwards had nothing to do with the machinery.

Merchant shipowners needed rather more convincing; indeed it required a larger-scale private venture commercial ship, the triple-screw passenger vessel *King Edward*, which entered service in 1901 on daily excursion duty on the Clyde estuary, before sufficient interest was aroused. The partners in The Turbine Syndicate were William Denny & Bros, noted builders of fast cross-channel ships, Parsons for the machinery and Captain John Williamson, who operated a fleet of paddle steamships on the Clyde. This ship was a considerable success, and the somewhat larger consort, *Queen Alexandra*, appeared in the following year, leading to several orders for turbine-driven cross-channel and Irish Sea ferries.

Most early turbine ships had triple screws, the centre one driven directly by the high-pressure turbine from which the steam passed to low-pressure turbines in the wings which powered the outer shafts. This compounding was necessary in order to spread the expansion of the steam over as many stages as possible. Reducing the number of stages would impair the efficiency of the turbines, which had many thousands of reaction blades. They were profiled so that the steam, in passing through the turbine, acted on the moving blades (those attached to the rotor) like a crosswind on the sails of a yacht. Fixed blades, attached to the stationary part of the turbine, restored the steam

flow to a direction appropriate for acting upon the next stage.

The Allan Line, later incorporated into Canadian Pacific Steamships, was the first to operate turbine ships on the North Atlantic. The 10,700 tons gross *Victorian* and *Virginian* entered service between Liverpool and Canada in 1905, and were also the first triple-screw steamers on the North Atlantic; the latter surviving, after passing through several ownerships, until she was scrapped in 1955.

Cunard saw in the turbine their means of regaining the Atlantic record and placed an order with John Brown & Co for a 'trial horse', the 20 + kt intermediate ship *Carma-*

nia, for comparison with the reciprocating engined sister *Caronia*. To gain experience with the turbine John Brown built a set of machinery for steaming tests ashore, and later built a ship to make use of it; the triple-screw *Atalanta* for the railway-operated ferry connection to the island of Arran.

The comparative trials in 1905 were convincing and Cunard planned two ships, much larger and faster than the German holder of the transatlantic record. Finance was a problem and after the UK Government had agreed to grant a £2.6 million loan over ten years at $2\frac{3}{4}$ per cent and an annual subsidy of £150,000 on top of the £68,000 mail contract, two 32,500 tons gross ships with a guaranteed

One of the first pair of turbine liners on the North Atlantic, the Allan Line's Virginian *of 1905, seen here at speed during her trials.* (CMP)

Cunard's famous Mauretania, *the turbine-driven record-breaker that held the Blue Riband of the Atlantic for twenty-two years from 1907 to 1929. The four-shaft direct-drive turbines generated 68,000shp, giving the ship a maximum speed of about 26kts.* (CMP)

speed of 24½kts were ordered. *Lusitania* was to be built and engined by John Brown & Co at Clydebank and *Mauretania* by Swan Hunter & Wigham Richardson on the Tyne, with Wallsend Slipway machinery.

The Cunard ships had turbines of 68,000shp and quadruple screws, the two outer high-pressure turbines driving the forward propellers and exhausting into the two inner low-pressure turbines, which drove the after propellers. Separate astern turbines were coupled in tandem forward of the low-pressure turbines, so that only the after propellers were used for running astern. The initial steam pressure was 195psi, provided by twenty-three double- and two single-ended cylindrical boilers installed in four boiler rooms, with coal bunkers in the wing spaces and forward in the case of the narrow No 1 boiler room. Four 375kW Parsons steam turbine generators were sufficient to support the auxiliary and hotel services. Ships carrying the same number of passengers today require ten to twelve times this generating capacity.

Lusitania's trials, in July 1907, were extensive and included a running-in voyage at various speeds around Ireland, followed by four runs over a measured distance of 303 miles from Corsewall Point at the entrance to the Clyde estuary to Land's End. The maximum recorded speed was 26kts, 25.4kts sustained over 48 hours, fully satisfying a large number of official observers, including representatives from the Admiralty, who had called for certain naval features to be incorporated.

When the Cunarders *Lusitania* and *Mauretania* appeared in September and November 1907, they immediately took the Atlantic records. *Lusitania* was sunk in 1915, but *Mauretania* went on to hold the record for twenty-two years, raising it again in 1924, after she had been converted to oil-firing, and only losing the title in 1929 to Norddeutscher Lloyd's *Bremen*.

That ship had four sets of geared turbines totalling 90,000hp, a power probably well exceeded for the record-breaking maiden voyage in July 1929, which returned an average speed of 27.86kts. Here the steam was expanded in three separate turbines which were geared together for each shaft, an arrangement enabling both the turbine and propeller speeds to be optimised.

As mentioned above, all the early Parsons turbines were directly coupled to their respective propellers. However, it was clear to Parsons that, while the steam turbine was a much more efficient machine than the reciprocating engine, the speed of rotation at which it delivered its output was inconveniently high for driving a correspondingly efficient propeller. This resulted in the direct-drive turbines for large and fast passenger ships being of immense size and weight and quite unsuitable for cargo vessels. Very high speed steam turbines had been successfully adopted for generator drive ashore but not for the output shaft speeds required for ship propulsion. In fact a 10hp reversing turbine, driving twin screws through gearing, had been built for a 22ft long launch in 1897.

Parsons accordingly purchased the twenty-two year old cargo steamship *Vespasian*, fitted with a triple-expansion steam engine. The first step was to run a lengthy series of performance trials, including a commercial voyage loaded with coal to Malta. On return to the UK, the engine was removed and replaced by plant consisting of two turbines in series, each driving a gear pinion engaging with an 8ft 3½in diameter gearwheel connected to the original propeller. An astern turbine was incorporated in the low-pressure casing, and the usual auxiliaries, condenser circulating and air pumps, feed and bilge pumps, were driven from a crank attached to the forward end of the gearcase. Comparison of the water rates (the amount of water supplied to the boiler and hence used for all purposes on board at sea) showed the geared turbine to have a clear advantage, which increased with the shaft revolutions and power. An increase of one knot was obtained at full power for the same coal consumption. *Vespasian*'s successful results led to the general adoption of geared turbines in succeeding years, the first units being fitted to the London and South Western Railway Co's cross-channel steamers *Normannia* and *Hantonia* in 1911. This was of particular advantage to naval authorities for whom the direct-drive turbines by then necessary to produce the powers required, were too cumbersome and inflexible. The new form of propulsion was taken up with enthusiasm by cargo liner companies, and even by a few tramp shipping operators – the first cargo ship installation was in Cairn Line's *Cairnross* built by Doxford in 1913 – although, by then, the diesel engine was offering greater advantages in terms of economy of fuel and staffing.

Trouble was experienced in the early 1920s when double-reduction gearing was introduced as a measure to enable the turbines to run at higher speeds for maximum efficiency. This resulted in hesitancy on the part of some liner companies, who opted for electrical transmission from high-speed turbo-generator sets to the slow-speed motors which drove the propellers, thereby offering the possibility of direct control of the machinery by simple lever from the bridge. This was adopted by the French Line for their striking transatlantic flagship and record-breaker *Normandie*, which appeared in 1935 with four land power station-type generator sets, each providing power for a 40,000shp propulsion motor. There were twenty-nine boilers and six turbo-generators providing 13,200kW. The record was taken on the first voyage, in 4 days, 3 hours and 2 minutes – 29.94kts, but aft-end vibration arising from the propellers plagued the ship for some time.

Although Cunard had employed double-reduction gearing for their intermediate liners in the 1920s, their *Queen Mary*, which entered service in 1936 after some years lying idle on the building berth due to the depression, had four series-connected turbines of 50,000shp, arranged around a single-reduction gearcase, for each of the four shafts. Her four days, twenty-seven minutes crossing raised the record speed to 30.14kts. There

were twenty-four Yarrow-type main boilers and seven generators of 9100kW.

The Second World War, particularly the later stages in the Pacific when British ships were working closely with those having US-designed machinery, had a great influence on marine steam turbine construction. Most of those ships, both naval and mercantile, had steam turbines supplied by the major electric utility suppliers – General Electric, Westinghouse, Allis Chalmers and others using impulse turbines and double-reduction gearing. These showed to great advantage in terms of fuel consumption and led to an association being set up with Government support in the United Kingdom to develop designs for improved performance and ease of manufacture. The Parsons and Marine Engineering Turbine Research and Development Association (PAMETRADA) produced

standard and special designs of turbine machinery which members in the UK and overseas built for all classes of ship from Great Lakes traders with only 1500shp to fast cross-channel ferries, large tankers and cargo liners. The penultimate, and most powerful, examples were the two 55,000shp sets which were the original machinery of *Queen Elizabeth 2*.

The US liner *United States*, which made the Atlantic crossing in July 1952 at an average speed of 35.59kts, one unlikely ever to be challenged by any conventional ship, was a remarkable and uneconomic exercise, supported by massive construction and operating subsidies. The striking profile dominated by

The layout of the 160,000shp single-reduction Parsons geared turbines in the forward and after engine rooms of Cunard's original Queen Elizabeth. *From* The Marine Engineer, *November 1946.*

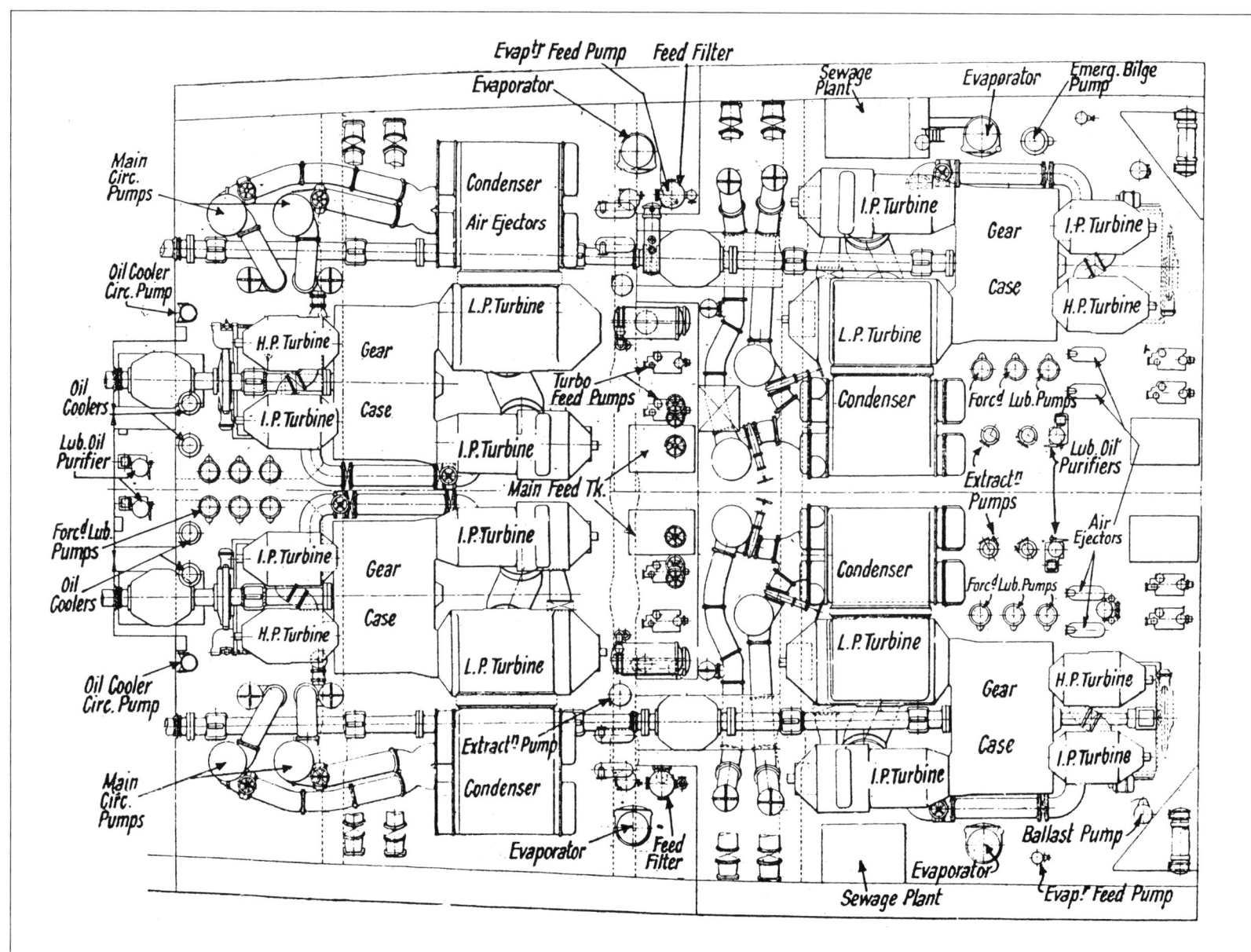

A manufacturer's photograph of the Westinghouse double-reduction steam turbines of 60,000shp as fitted in the United States. The casings have been removed.

After only seventeen years in service *United States* was laid up and, in spite of several abandoned proposals, has not sailed in the past twenty-three years except in tow in 1992 to Turkey, from where she has since been moored for removal of tons of asbestos as part of a revitalising project. She has been transferred to a yard in the Crimea for this to be undertaken, following environmentalist pressure.

The French Line's flagship *France* of 1961, with four turbines of 160,000shp, also employed single-reduction gearing, some twelve years after it had gone out of fashion. As the cruise ship *Norway* she continues in service, but with her two outer shafts and their corresponding forward sets of machinery out of commission.

Steam turbines were the choice machinery for the larger tankers in the 1950s because of the availability of steam for heating heavy oil cargoes in cold weather and for the turbine-driven pumps needed for discharging the cargo at the end of the voyage. The first tankers of over 100,000 tons deadweight capacity were already building in Japan, and for which General Electric of the US were supplying 25,000shp machinery.

The diesel engine – slow starter outliving all others

A century ago, in February 1893, Rudolf Diesel was granted the patent covering a 'Rational Heat Engine', for which he had applied a year previously. He had earlier contracted with the forerunners of the present MAN concern at Augsburg to build a test engine and granted them a licence to build engines for sale in certain areas of Germany. Further licences were taken up shortly afterwards by Krupp, Sulzer and other major European engineering companies, but these were for the manufacture of industrial oil engines which, by then, had demonstrated a clearly superior efficiency over the Otto petrol and kerosene engines of the time.

Diesel engines were first applied to ship

two huge and widely-separated funnels was, and is, unique. As with all other post Second World War liners, she was not a giant in terms of gross tonnage but very fine-lined and fitted with the most powerful machinery ever to be installed in a merchant ship; four sets of Westinghouse turbines, of the type which had been supplied for the aircraft carriers of the US Navy some years earlier. For a number of years technical details of the machinery were restricted, in view of the ship's potential as a fast troop-carrier. The

quite conventional cross-compound turbines, with double-reduction gearing of locked-train configuration (which shared the power in the intermediate stages between two parallel gear trains in order to avoid high tooth loadings) developed 240,000shp and were supplied with steam at the high pressure and temperature of 888psi and 1000°F (61bar and 540°C) by eight Foster Wheeler boilers. The machinery was widely spread over the ship's length in order to improve survivability in the event of damage.

The Danish Selandia *was fitted with the first large marine diesels, the revolutionary nature of her propulsion system being symbolised by the absence of a conventional funnel. The diesel exhaust was carried up thin trunking alongside the main mast.* (CMP)

propulsion in 1904 and exclusively to inland waterways vessels. They were installed in a Swiss lake cargo ship, by Sulzer, and the first of very many tank lighters for the Nobel brothers, who had a virtual monopoly of the oil business in Russia and who were themselves one of the seven original diesel engine licensees. These craft were engaged in carrying oil from Baku on the Black Sea coast and up the Volga to St Petersburg, a distance of some 3000 miles and an excellent reference for the new prime mover.

The first sea-going motorship was also a tanker, *Vulcanus*, built in 1910 to distribute the Shell Co's products in the Netherlands East Indies. Quite a small ship, she had a 460hp engine built by Werkspoor of Amsterdam, whose workshops remain active today in diesel engine manufacture. This was an open-framed engine, with exposed connecting rods and crankshaft, like those of the contemporary steam engine, and the cylinder block supported by cross-braced round steel columns.

The manufacturer's photograph of one of the two 1250bhp Burmeister & Wain diesels of the Selandia. *The diesel, using pumped oil fuel, did away with the need for gangs of boiler room firemen and with the fuel tanks in the double bottom and other awkward spaces, freed more of the ship's internal volume for revenue-earning cargo than was possible with coal.* (Graeme MacLennan)

The Danish licence was taken up in 1898 by Burmeister & Wain of Copenhagen, in which city was based A/S Det Ostasiatiske Kompagni (The East Asiatic Company), a major international trading concern whose steamships made long voyages to the Far East. Oil firing was not generally employed in cargo ships of the time and the need to provide space for considerable quantities of coal, which with its weight, had an adverse effect upon the earning capacity of ships making lengthy passages.

Burmeister & Wain were soon able to convince The East Asiatic Company that the diesel engine would overcome these prob-

lems at a stroke, as well as dispensing with a large number of firemen. In February 1912 the 4950 tons gross cargo motorship *Selandia*, first of a pair ordered with two eight-cylinder engines of 1250bhp each, sailed for Bangkok. These were the first large marine diesel engines and the ship made a special call in London so that representatives of shipping lines, the Admiralty, including the then First Lord, Winston Churchill and others interested could examine the revolutionary machinery. The ship herself was no less unusual in appearance having, instead of a funnel, two thin exhaust pipes led up alongside the centre of the three masts. The first round

voyage was uneventful and therefore a commercial success.

In the meantime Burmeister & Wain received contracts for several more of these first-generation motorships from Scandinavian owners, among them Johnson Line of Sweden which did not order another steamship after they took delivery of *Suecia* in 1912. Further progress was delayed by the outbreak of the First World War and it was not until the early 1920s that the activity was resumed. Many shipyards and engine builders in Europe and the United States took licences to build marine diesel engines according to the six leading designs of marine engines which had, in the meantime, evolved independently from the original Diesel agreements, and accordingly differed quite widely in concept and principle. These secondary licensees received drawings and technical assistance in exchange for fees based on the horsepower of the engines which they built.

The diesel engine was well suited to the tramp shipping trades which frequently involved voyages of long duration at quite modest speeds – from Australia or the Far East to northern Europe via the Cape for instance. Numbers of so-called standard 'economy' motorships introduced by several yards were built for owners in Great Britain which then had the largest fleet of tramp ships but, as noted earlier, the steam engine was still very popular.

Passenger ship owners were immediately attracted by the diesel engine which offered economy, a much reduced demand on space and a lower manning requirement. The pioneer transatlantic passenger motorship was *Gripsholm*, built in 1925 on the Tyne for Svenska Amerika Linien (Swedish America Line) and fitted with two six-cylinder B&W double-acting four-stroke engines developing, together, some 12,500bhp. In a double-acting engine the lower part of the cylinder is enclosed and a combustion cycle also takes place below the piston on the up-stroke. This requires fewer cylinders and shortens the engine for any required power, but at some mechanical complication in the case of four-cycle models, which require inlet and exhaust valves and their operating gear for both the top and bottom of each cylinder. Nevertheless *Gripsholm*'s original machinery remained in the ship throughout her life of some forty years and was a pattern for that installed in many passenger motorships during the ensuing eight years. In the same year *Parkeston*, first of four passenger motorships to operate across the North Sea be-

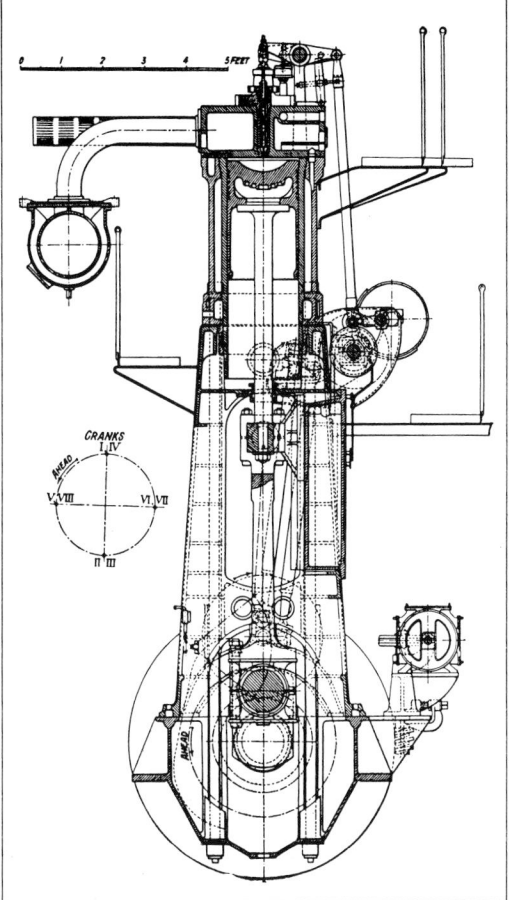

Section through a first generation Burmeister & Wain marine diesel. (Barclay Curle & Co Ltd, by courtesy of Graeme MacLennan)

tween Harwich and Denmark, entered service. Much lower powers were required and single-acting versions of the B&W four-stroke engine were adequate. The owners, DFDS, never built another steamship and others operating longish ferry routes soon followed, but it was not until 1934 that motorships appeared on the short-sea channel routes.

Another important pioneer passenger motorship was *Aorangi*, built at the Fairfield shipyard on the Clyde for the much longer trans-Pacific service from Vancouver to New Zealand – a link in the 'All-Red' route from the UK via Canada. *Aorangi* had machinery of 13,000bhp developed by four six-cylinder engines employing the single-acting two-stroke cycle adopted by Sulzer Bros of Switzerland and which, because of its greater simplicity requiring no inlet and exhaust valves, became a much more popular and long-lasting design. MAN of Germany, FIAT in Italy and others also built two-stroke engines which were installed in large and intermediate passenger ships, cargo liners and tankers.

In the mid 1920s the Scott-Still engine, fitted in two Blue Funnel cargo liners made use of an integrated combined cycle which did achieve a modest improvement in fuel consumption, but at considerable complexity. *Dolius* had two four-cylinder double-acting two-stroke engines, in which fuel was burned on the down-stroke (above the pistons), while steam, generated in the cylinder jackets and held in a receiver, was applied to the piston undersides. In the later *Eurybates* a simpler configuration was adopted with the steam functions performed in separate two-cylinder non-compound double-acting engines coupled to the forward ends of the diesel engines. The introduction of turbocharging a few years later provided a much simpler means of increasing specific outputs with improved economy.

A popular engine which used the two-stroke principle, but applied it in a different way, was that designed and built by Wm Doxford, of Sunderland and licensed for manufacture by very many builders in the UK, Europe and as far afield as Australia and the Far East. The cylinders were without covers, each being closed by a working piston at top and bottom, combustion taking place between them. The lower piston and connecting rod were connected conventionally to the crankshaft, while the upper piston bore a yoke from which depended a pair of side rods leading to crossheads and connecting rods which worked on crank-throws at 180 degrees to that for the lower piston. The forces were thus balanced, the frame was relieved of all combustion loads and there were no cylinder covers; a frequent source of cracking problems in the early designs.

An important step in the development of the diesel engine, enabling it to produce much greater specific output, was the introduction of turbocharging. This, too, dates from the mid 1920s which may come as a surprise to those who have associated it with recent automobile engines. Dr Alfred Buchi, a former Sulzer engineer considered how to recover some of the dynamic and thermal energy lost in the exhaust of a diesel engine. His patent, essentially simple, embraced passing the exhaust through a gas turbine which was coupled directly to drive a centrifugal fan. The system was self-regulating for, as the power increased so did the exhaust flow, increasing the speed of the turbine and the delivery from the fan or blower to provide the air required for complete combustion of the extra fuel. Initially, commercial success was slow but by the mid-1950s nearly all

A view of the half-platform between two MAN double-acting two-stroke engines of an immediately post Second World War intermediate liner. (Wilton-Fijenoord, Schiedam)

which needed clear decks unobstructed by machinery casings which would have been inevitable with the taller, conventional diesel engines.

Electric drive

Electric transmission was employed afloat as far back as 1904, but not initially for the reasons it is adopted today. The early Nobel diesel engines built under licence in Russia for tank lighters operating on the Volga were non-reversing, but propeller reversal was made possible by the Del Proposto system which consisted of a generator attached to the engine crankshaft, which continued through a clutch to an electric motor coupled to the propeller shaft. The clutch was engaged so that the whole assembly rotated with the engine when going ahead. For running astern the clutch was disengaged and the generator excited so that it supplied current for opposite rotation of the motor. Soon afterwards the first true diesel-electric ship, the 650dwt shallow-draught *Vandal* was put into service carrying kerosene from Baku to St Petersburg with three generators and three propeller motors.

Later, diesel-electric machinery was installed in a variety of vessels: tugs and river ferries where easy and rapid control from the wheelhouse was the advantage; suction dredgers in which the generating plant could also power the large pumps, and three ships of the United Fruit Co for which the reason given was an increase of 26 per cent in cargo capacity. In one of them, the original British Thomson-Houston electrics outlasted three different sets of diesel engines, in some thirty years.

Steam turbo-electric drive enjoyed a brief spell of popularity in passenger liners built in the UK. P&O had experienced problems with their first geared turbine ships in the early 1920s and reverted to reciprocating engines for succeeding classes. Turbo-electric drive, by BTH, was chosen for *Viceroy of India* (1929) intended for the Bombay mail service and similar plant of greater power was adopted two years later for the Australian service 'white sisters' *Strathnaver* and *Strathaird*.

diesel engines, whether for propulsion or driving generators, were turbocharged.

Many cargo shipping companies soon operated fleets which were entirely diesel powered but there were some who strongly resisted the trend. Steam ruled supreme in the US merchant fleet, possibly due to unhappy memories of less than satisfactory experience with engines fitted in connection with the US Shipping Board's Conversion Programme after the First World War, but also because of the entrenched position of the large American electrical engineering concerns which supplied steam propulsion packages as a sideline to their production of utility power stations.

By the end of the period under review several engines were being built which were capable of applying 20,000bhp to a single screw and with cylinder diameters of 900mm (35.5in), for installation in then large and fast tankers. Shortly afterwards the Europe–Far East trade was demanding cargo liners with sustained sea speeds of 20kts, calling for machinery of this order and many of these impressive machines were built for this duty.

Medium-speed engines – derived from the submarine

The existence of a considerable number of submarine engines which had been built for installation in boats not yet ready to receive them, was a situation which occurred at the end of both World Wars. These were utilised in many ways, for power generation and pumping ashore, as well as for restoration of the German merchant fleet. On both occasions these stimulated the development of suitable reduction gearing and flexible couplings to protect the gear teeth from violent torsional oscillations arising from 'rough running' of the engine as it passed through certain speeds.

The success and flexibility of these applications led to the development and introduction of ranges of very high-performance, faster-running (200 to 900rpm) engines by half a dozen makers, developing then up to 370kW (500bhp) per cylinder and up to 6000kW (8000bhp) per power unit[1] which could be used for duties varying from generator and bow thruster drive to main propulsion, either through reduction gearing or one of several forms of electric transmission. Johnson Line was the first to adopt the principle after the Second World War for deep-sea cargo liners, with their *Rio de Janeiro* class of ships having four 12-cylinder PC1 Pielstick engines driving twin controllable-pitch propellers through gearing. These engines were of a French design, developed from the last of the German wartime submarine engines. The application of geared medium-speed engines was to become of considerable significance in succeeding years, particularly for drive-through car ferries,

---

1. Present outputs are three times these figures.

In the period immediately before the outbreak of the Second World War, Hamburg-Amerika Linie became convinced that electric drive, with both diesel and steam prime movers, was the solution to operating problems and put in hand a programme which included cargo liners, intermediate passenger and cargo vessels and even their flagship-to-be, the 36,000 tons gross *Vaterland*. By specifying the same model of diesel engine, MAN's GZ52/70 trunk-piston two-stroke, in different numbers and with varying numbers of cylinders, servicing became well understood and the spares inventory was simplified.

The many T2 tankers built in the US during the war years with turbo-electric machinery driving a single screw and also powering the electrically-driven cargo pumps in harbour were much liked by the engineers who served in them.

Under construction at Belfast in 1960 was P&O's 45,000 tons gross *Canberra*, by a considerable margin the company's largest ship. She was designed primarily for the Australian trade but with provision for up-market worldwide cruising in mind. Delivered in the following year, she has 85,000shp BTH (by then AEI) turbo-electric machinery, and is still a major force in P&O Cruises' operations.

Gas turbines

The gas turbine was proposed in 1938 as a prime mover for naval vessels, advocates citing its high power/space and weight characteristics and few working parts as particular benefits. Some work was done in Germany towards the development of a gas turbine for E-boats but the first vessel to be so powered was the British *MGB 2009*, which ran trials in 1947. This was the conversion of a 36m long triple-screw motor gunboat, in which the centre Packard Merlin 1250hp petrol engine was replaced by a 2500hp turbine, built by Metropolitan-Vickers using one of their existing jet engines as a gas generator for a four-stage power turbine and single-reduction gearing. The craft was purely a test bed for the turbine, and encouraging results led to the construction of two purpose-built light craft with Bristol-Siddeley Proteus gas turbines.

For larger combatant ships it was felt that aero-derived engines would be too fragile for this application and an elaborate full-scale heavy-duty gas turbine of 6500shp was ordered from English Electric Co, with a view to eventual installation afloat. By the time this machinery had been tested it became clear from sea trials of the light craft that the aircraft turbine was very robust indeed, requiring only anti-shock mountings, changed blade materials to resist the salt content of the inspired air and heavier bearings, since the machine would always be operating at sea level in dense instead of rarified air.

Parallel shore development of gas turbines suited to merchant ship propulsion was being undertaken in the UK, France and the US, but none of these went to sea. It was the Shell and British Thomson-Houston (BTH) companies which had practical results to share. The tanker *Auris* was built with diesel-electric machinery consisting of four 1300hp diesel-generator sets supplying power to one propulsion motor. Later, as was intended from the outset, one of the diesel sets was replaced by a BTH gas turbine generator set of the same power which, on occasions, powered the ship on its own. The third stage was to replace the machinery

The new 1200shp BTH gas turbine generator unit labelled up for a press visit to the newly converted Shell tanker Auris in January 1952. This was the first stage of the experiment, the gas turbine replacing one of the ship's original four diesel-generators. (CMP)

A model of the final all-mechanical drive BTH gas turbine installed in the Auris. *(BTH, by courtesy of Graeme MacLennan)*

Nuclear power

Nuclear power was first applied to ship propulsion in 1955 when the submarine *Nautilus* joined the US Navy. It conferred continuous underwater capability limited only by the endurance of the ship's company and the need to replenish supplies. The nuclear reactor serves simply as a boiler to produce steam for conventional turbines driving the now usually single propeller through gearing. The promise of almost unlimited range due to independence of fuel supplies was an attraction to the designers of larger surface ships and the aircraft carrier *Enterprise* with eight reactors and Westinghouse turbines of 280,000shp for a speed of 36kts was under construction at Newport News, for delivery in 1961.

The possibility of applying nuclear power to fast merchant ships led to the order by the US Maritime Administration of a prototype

entirely by a BTH gas turbine of 5500bhp with *mechanical* transmission to the propeller. This incorporated a hydrodynamic astern torque converter of the type built, but not installed in time, for a steam turbine battle-

cruiser of the Imperial German Navy during the First World War. Much experience was gained but by the time the tests were complete, the ship had become too small to trade economically and was withdrawn.

The US Savannah — *named after the first steamer to cross the Atlantic — was the world's first nuclear powered merchant ship, and is shown docking at Southampton in July 1964 after her transatlantic maiden voyage. The economics of nuclear power, with its rigorous safety requirements, run counter to the needs of merchant shipping and no vessel so equipped has been run under properly commercial conditions.* (CMP)

for development and training purposes. This was *Savannah*, with a Babcock pressurised water reactor and de Laval steam turbines of 22,000shp.

In practice however, it was only for the special duty of state-owned Polar icebreakers which could operate far from fuel supplies that nuclear power has been applied to non-military vessels. The Soviet Union's *Lenin*, built by Baltic Shipbuilding at Leningrad in 1959, was fitted with three reactors providing steam for four turbines, each driving four 1920kW 600V generators, a cumbersome all-direct-current system requiring numbers of machines in tandem for both generators and propulsion motors; 19,600shp on the centre shaft and 9800shp on each of the wing shafts. *Lenin* has since been followed by several larger nuclear propelled icebreakers but the only other nuclear merchant ships built have been the German bulk carrier *Otto Hahn* in 1968 and the Japanese research ship *Mutsu* in 1972.

Machinery conversions

Fundamental machinery replacements were unusual in the earlier days of the period but have become commonplace later as the gap in daily fuel costs has widened between steam and diesel engines. Most of the machinery conversions which took place in the 1920s and 1930s were from steam reciprocating engines or steam turbines to diesel engines in the case of cargo vessels, particularly those regularly engaged on long voyages. In the 1920s several unsatisfactory diesel engines were introduced by the builders of traditional steam engines, who did not appreciate that the higher working pressures and temperatures involved in the diesel cycle required a different design approach and much improved materials. Some of them never got beyond the test bed, others were exchanged for steam engines after a voyage or two.

In passenger ships, diesel machinery was more frequently replaced by diesel engines of more up-to-date design with greater power for increased speed to meet competition on their particular routes. The earlier large passenger ship engines were worked hard and did not have great reserves of power. Moreover, they were mechanically complex and the sailing schedules called for a great deal of maintenance effort. Notable diesel-to-steam conversions took place in 1934 when the Royal Mail Line's 18+kt motorships *Asturias* and *Alcantara* had their original double-acting four-stroke engines of 1925–26 replaced in 1934 by steam turbines of greater power. This was said to be to in order to compete with newer and faster German and French ships which had been introduced on the South American service.

Propeller developments

The Voith-Schneider cycloidal propeller which provided both propulsion and steering was made by J M Voith of Heidenheim, near Lake Constance, where it was first fitted in excursion ships and ferries. It took the form of a rotating disc, suspended horizontally below water level and carrying a number of streamlined vertical blades which were 'feathered' by an internal mechanism as they moved against the direction of motion and could produce full azimuthing thrust. They were and still are widely used for river ferries where V-P propellers fore and aft enable them to cross a strong current directly without losing the line of advance. For floating cranes and minesweepers they offer precise positioning and shallow draught capability.

Graeme Maclennan

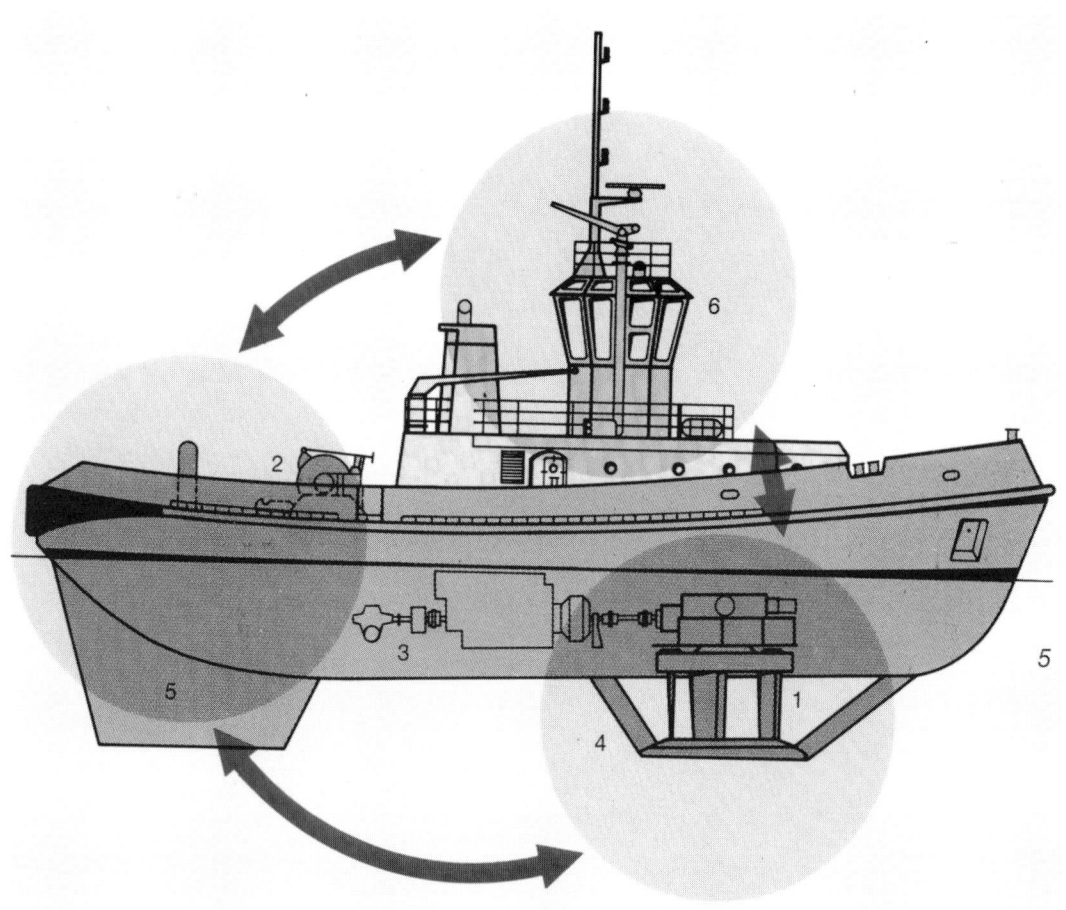

The principles of the Voith-Schneider propeller, as applied to a 'water tractor' (tug):

1 *The Voith-Schneider propeller is arranged in the forebody, with free inflow and outflow in all directions. The thrust forces act ahead of the pivot point of the vessel.*

2 *The towing gear (bollard, hook, winch) is located abaft the pivot point of the vessel. The exact location depends on the particular operating conditions of the tractor.*

3 *The hull should ideally serve only as a support for the propulsion system and towing gear. For this reason it is desirable to obtain the smallest dimensions necessary for the task to be performed.*

4 *Fitted underneath the propellers is a nozzle plate whose nozzle effect increases the propeller thrust. It also protects the propeller against grounding and supports the vessel in the dock.*

5 *Located underneath the aft body is an effective stabilising fin. This provides adequate course stability and shifts the centre of lateral resistance aft, thus increasing the lever arm between propeller thrust and pivot point. As an otter board it also helps to increase the towline forces during shiphandling. The bottom edge of the fin and the underside of the nozzle plate are at the same level, thus permitting simple docking of the vessel.*

6 *The tractor is controlled from the bridge. The control stand in the wheelhouse – one of several control stands connected in synchronism, depending on the size and design of the vessel – is usually connected mechanically to the propellers by a control rod system. This ensures that the captain has direct control over the vessel.*

Shipping Economics

THE PERIOD from 1900 to 1960 was dominated by the British mercantile marine, which reached its zenith in the decade prior to the First World War. Severely shaken by two World Wars it maintained the premier role, although slow decline set in and was to accelerate after 1960.

The stage for this had been set many years previously, when the Whig Government of 1848 came to power with a mandate for free trade. The repeal of the Navigation Acts that followed saw complacent, sheltered British owners facing the virile strength of the United States merchant fleet, a challenge only removed by the American Civil War (1861–65) which largely destroyed the US fleet. Thereafter America turned West and ceased to look to the sea. The depredations of the Napoleonic wars, leaving a shattered Europe, had given British industry a fifty-year lead in the Industrial Revolution and with it shipbuilding, although this was now being steadily eroded.

A most important stimulus during the second half of the nineteenth century was the growth of the British Empire, reflected on a smaller scale in other European colonial powers. New settlements needed material support from the homeland, people, supplies and capital investment. The early one-way trade gave way to a growing volume of colonial produce to pay for manufactured goods. A colonial industry economy would develop during the twentieth century and, ultimately, play a role in changing the face of shipping.

Technically the steamship had advanced to the stage of being able to totally replace sail, with economical and reliable triple- and quadruple-expansion machinery and turbines, soon to be joined by the diesel. After 1880 refrigeration made rapid strides, changed the economies of many pastoral

Symbolising the pattern of British trade, which dominated the shipping world in 1900, a Blue Funnel cargo liner is shown being berthed in Singapore's aptly named Empire Dock between the wars. The basic exchange was between raw materials from the colonies and manufactured goods from the mother country, rubber being one of Singapore's principal exports at this time. (CMP)

Launched on 22 February 1905 by William Doxford & Sons Ltd, Sunderland, the 5600grt turret ship Wellington *was completed in April 1905 for W J Tatem & Co, Cardiff. She was employed as a tramp in the bulk trades from South Wales, with coal a major export cargo. She remained in Tatem service until torpedoed and sunk by U 118 on 16 September 1918. (Welsh Industrial & Maritime Museum)*

countries and introduced a new trade for shipowners. A small fleet of tankers was to grow steadily and in due course have its own influence on the shipping scene. In 1900 there were still 7.3 million tons of sailing ships afloat, 28 per cent of the total world tonnage of 25.9 million tons. The early years of the century saw this share rapidly eroded, and in 1914 the 3.7 million tons under sail was only 7.5 per cent of the world total of 49.1 million tons. Under the Red Ensign the fall had been even more dramatic, from 25 to 2.5 per cent.

The situation in 1900

The twentieth century opened with the British merchant marine holding the premier position in world shipping and during its first decade ships flying the Red Ensign carried 70 per cent of trade within the Empire and 30 per cent of cross trades, in total over 50 per cent of world trade. Shipping was a growth industry for the entrepreneur, with British export trade doubling between 1880 and 1914.

British entrepreneurial activities extended beyond the confines of Empire and shipping and this was a vital factor. British capital played a major investment role in foreign undertakings, such as railways and meat packing plants in Argentina and nitrates in Chile, and hence these looked to Britain for consumable supplies, carried in British ships, as well as cargo in the reverse direction. British capital also organised the network of coaling stations, repair yards and services required to support shipping, once again drawing their consumables from Britain on British ships. This close link between shipping and other interests was maintained throughout the period in all the colonial empires. Few liner services ran from Britain to French, Portuguese or other colonial destinations, and for all practical purposes it was necessary to direct what trade existed for transshipment through the appropriate motherland.

Shipping, especially the tramp trades, has always operated balanced delicately on a knife edge. Being international in character, it is largely uncontrollable and one ship too many is often sufficient to change a seller's

into a buyer's market, a situation well described by Charles Dickens in *David Copperfield*, where Mr Micawber defines the difference between happiness and misery. The failure of a crop could flood the market with unwanted ships. Consequently the history of shipping has been a series of cycles, with boom years soon followed by slump. The effect rapidly rippled through the maritime field with shipyards reflecting such conditions within a short time.

In 1900 the industry was experiencing a boom after many years of steadily falling freight rates, although this fall, long term, was to a large extent offset by the improved level of technology and efficiency of ships. During the closing years of the nineteenth century a series of wars made great demands on shipping: the Sudan campaign (1898), the Spanish–American War (1898), South African War (1899–1902) and Boxer Rebellion in China (1900). The South African Boer War was the largest overseas military expedition ever dispatched by Britain, involving the transport of 380,000 men, 460,000 animals and over one million tons of equipment and supplies. This was soon surpassed by the First World War when the British authorities alone, between 1914 and 1918, moved 23.7 million men, 2.2 million animals, 500,000 vehicles and 50 million tons of stores. This was equivalent to a year's British imports trade or a 25 per cent rise in demand over the war period; hence the impact on shipping is all too apparent.

British shipping played a major role in the tramp or bulk trades, seconded by the growing Norwegian fleet (a role later to be as-

sumed by the Greek flag). Seasonally, grain moved from Russian ports on the Black Sea, from Australia, North America and the relatively new sources around the River Plate. Rice was loaded in Indo-China and Burma, sugar from Java, India, the Philippines, West Indies, United States, Australia and Fiji. Cotton featured from the United States and Egypt, jute from India, nitrates from Chile and phosphates from the United States. Hardwood timber from the tropics was overshadowed by the large softwood trades of the Baltic and North America, whilst the flow of ore from Spain, India, Sweden, Brazil and other sources was growing. But, by far the most important was the movement of coal, which provided the major energy source of the world. British production had for many years been the largest in the world, only dropping to second place in the closing years

of the nineteenth century when the United States assumed the premier position. Other developing sources included mainland European countries, India, South Africa and Australia.

The volume of British coal exports was a vital factor in the economy of British shipping, providing the means for many ships to both arrive and depart with paying cargo. Over the years as this trade decreased it played a major role in changing the character of British shipowning, as the growing oil trade was controlled to a large degree by the oil companies. They chose to own and oper-

Coal exporting was vital to British trade, and this business was centred on the ports of South Wales. This view of loading coal at Cardiff's Queen Alexandra Dock was taken in May 1948, but would have been a familiar sight at the turn of the century when Cardiff was the second busiest port in Britain after London. (CMP)

Shipping losses during the Great War forced the British government to organise emergency shipbuilding programmes, mostly to standard designs. The most common were the two 400ft bp Type A (single deck) and B (two decks) dry freighters. Towards the end of the war potential oil shortages led to the adaptation of some of these as tankers, with cylindrical tanks built into their holds; they were then known as Types AO and BO, some thirty of them being under construction in March 1918 although only twenty-four of the former and one BO were completed by the Armistice. War Ruler, shown here, was an AO design, built by Vickers-Armstrong at Barrow and completed in May 1919; the 7885dwt ship was driven at 11kts by triple-expansion machinery. The ship enjoyed a long career under six names and was not broken up until 1959. (CMP)

ate their own tankers rather than rely on chartering as in the coal trade. In addition the number of independent British tanker owners was never large, in contrast with Norway with the Shell 'sale and charter back' agreements of 1927. In 1913 the world export trade in coal totalled 171 million tons, of which 73 million tons was from Britain. Only in one year, 1923, was the British export tonnage (79 million) to match or pass that of 1913. The Great Depression saw the world figure drop as low as 120 million tons in 1936 (Britain 34 million tons).

As with all bulk cargo the shelter-deck tramp was never the most efficient vehicle and the growth in numbers of the more suitable bulk carrier after the Second World War, especially in the 1960s, was to erode the British tramp fleet. The tonnage of coal exported continued to fall – 13.6 million tons in 1950 and only 5.1 million a decade later. As we close this account in 1960 it was a mere shadow of the past, with a tonnage of less than 74 per cent of the peak.

The shipping slump after the Boer War was protracted, a slight recovery about 1908 was not sustained and it was to be about 1912 before owners could report a healthier climate. Few orders were placed and the effect on shipbuilders was catastrophic. For example, Doxford's Sunderland yard had twenty-six orders (108,000grt, £1.1 million) in hand at the end of December 1906, but in the following summer the west section of the yard was shut down and in January 1908 a mere five orders (19,800grt, £208,000) remained.

The First World War

Conditions were to take on a completely different hue with the outbreak of war in Europe in the summer of 1914 and soon to affect most major countries of the world. This paralysed the shipping of Germany and her allies, caught in ports of refuge and later confiscated. Initially British shipping was also largely brought to a standstill, owners being uncertain of the risks involved and their insurance position. Rapidly the Government need to dispatch forces to France saw the chartering of a growing number of ships and the industry entered the most prosperous financial period ever known. The key to this was not freight rates, although free market prices spiralled, but ships were fully employed and not swinging at anchor earning nothing whilst waiting for a cargo. Government chartered and requisitioned ships were paid 'Blue Book Rates' on time charter. An important tool in getting shipping back to sea was the inauguration of the State Insurance Scheme against war risks, which in the course of the conflict received £80.2 million in premium, paid claims of £64.2 million and made a profit for the Government of £16 million.

A brief glance at some of the freight rates compiled by Angier Brothers over the period gives a clear indication of fluctuations in the first two decades of the century. The good rates for coal outward to the Plate peaked in 1900 and by 1904 fixtures were being made at a mere 25 per cent of the peak. The 1900 figures were not to be repeated until 1912 but rates went wild during the war with 150

shillings (£12.50) being paid on the free market in 1918. Homeward steamer freight on grain from Australia and South America followed a broadly similar pattern, the Australian high of 1912 being the best rate ever to that date, as was the Plate rate for 1914. But the war had the same effect as on coal, although in 1917–18 no charters were taken for Australian grain as it was all shipped under Government control and the low rates for 1919 reflect the figures paid to British Government 'directed' tonnage.

Like most industrialists, shipowners accumulated embarrassing cash assets during the war, partially offset by the introduction of Excess Profits Tax levied on the difference between current and the last three prewar years' profits. For shipowners these three years had been good, enabling them to retain more of the profits than otherwise. These assets were, in part, distributed to shareholders as dividends or paid-up shares. In many instances part was invested and gave wise managers an investment income which proved invaluable to offset poor trading results in the inter-war years.

At the Armistice on 11 November 1918 Lloyd's of London recorded losses to British, Allied and neutral shipping by enemy action at 6471 ships of 12.8 million tons, plus 1349 ships of 1.5 million tons untraced, missing or lost through marine risk. The majority of the losses took place after unrestricted submarine warfare commenced early in 1917. The replacement of lost tonnage by large numbers of emergency ships ordered from shipyards in Britain, the United States, Japan and Hong Kong never had time to take full effect. Another source was chartering from neutral Norway, Sweden, Denmark and the Netherlands: by November 1918 nearly 1.4 million tons gross. Some of this was under duress, the lever being rationed coal supplies and restrictions on the import of other vital goods imposed by a maritime blockade. By November 1918 some 40 per cent of Swedish shipping was active in Allied service, plus 870,000 tons of Norwegian.

Wartime newbuilding costs and second-hand prices reflected the market, with an average tramp of 4,000grt, costing £40,000 prewar, attracting prices approaching £200,000 in 1916 and nearing the £250,000 mark in 1919. Those buying at these enhanced prices were to regret the decision when sanity returned, some owners going on record and stating that some such ships never recovered their cost before they were sold for scrapping.

Many new shipping enterprises commenced business in the boom of the war. Views of owners varied, some considered the future with optimism and others took a pessimistic view of trade when peace returned. Amongst the latter were to be found well known figures such as Lewis (of Furness Withy), Burrell, Runciman, Tatham and Sutherland. Lewis pruned the Furness Withy newbuilding programme heavily at the end of the war, the others sold their fleets and, if they returned to owning, waited for some years. The optimists, including Lord Kylsant (Royal Mail Steam Packet), made insufficient provision for depreciation and finished up with bankrupt undertakings, the assets of which bore no relationship to capital and liabilities. Examples of this can be briefly mentioned, although the ultimate collapse was that of the Royal Mail Group in 1930

with losses of over £50 million. Edgar Edwards formed the Western Counties Shipping Co in 1915; by 1920 it was capitalised at £2.5 million having purchased the Runciman and Sutherland fleets. Forecasting profits of £1 million a year, the receiver was in control two years later. Amalgamated Industrials Ltd, formed in 1919, likewise purchased companies in many industries at enhanced prices, including the Cork Shipping Co and the Ulster Steamship Co, only to crash within a few years. In shipbuilding Sperling & Co were instrumental in promoting the Northumberland Shipbuilding Group, which included Workman, Clark & Co, William Doxford & Sons, Blythswood Shipbuilding Co and Fairfield Shipbuilding & Engineering Co. This group crashed in 1926.

Such collapses pulled others down with them. Traditionally shipbuilders played an important role in the finance of shipping, accepting post-dated bills of exchange or shares in companies and ships in lieu of cash. These bills or shares would, over a period, be redeemed from the earnings of the ships and, in the meantime, could be discounted with banks to provide operating capital for the builders. Doxfords alone, in February 1906, had £939,952 of such bills discounted with the banks, plus a further £131,064 held in their safe, or the equivalent of the total value of orders in hand. In the winding up of D & W Henderson & Co in 1935 a major factor was the inability of two Royal Mail Group companies to meet discounted bills totalling £204,000 (Elder Dempster & Co's

African Steam Ship Co and Lamport & Holt's Liverpool, Brazil & River Plate Steam Navigation Co).

If anything, the return of peace briefly increased the demand for shipping as the war-ravaged countries returned to normality. Demand remained high for over a year, whilst an increasing flow of ships entered service from the emergency programmes of Britain and the United States. Many of the US ships were destined to spend their lives laid up, in many instances going straight from builder to lay-up. The greatly enhanced world fleet, 53.9 million tons gross in 1920 compared with 43.1 million in 1914, faced the prospect of competing for the same volume of cargo as existed before the war, a recipe for disaster. The Allied seizure of the fleets of Germany and her allies as reparations, and selling them on the open market, further aggravated the situation. The new owners took over ships which had, in many instances, been interned and had received little or no maintenance since 1914. These were overshadowed when German owners were allowed to return to trade, as they commissioned newly built, more efficient ships.

The interwar years

In the summer of 1920 the freight market collapsed, plunging many owners into receivership and the industry commenced a decade of recession. It soon became apparent that support for shipowners and shipbuilders was needed, and most countries made suitable arrangements to support their fleets and builders. In the United Kingdom the only help came from the Trade Facility Acts, under which the Treasury guaranteed loans raised from commercial sources. Initially not intended for shipping it was extended to cover that area, benefiting a short list of British owners, as well as some from abroad in respect of ships ordered in the United Kingdom which would not compete with British vessels.

The Federal SN Co's 10,892grt Cambridge *was one of many ex-German ships sequestered after the 1918 armistice and sold cheaply among the victorious allies. Built in 1916 as the* Vogtland *for Hamburg-America, she was laid up immediately after completion, due to the allied blockade, and ceded to Britain in January 1919. Initially she was managed by the Glen Line for the government's Shipping Controller, until sold to Federal in May 1921 for conversion to a frozen meat carrier.* (Ambrose Greenway collection)

A development of great potential for shipping economics was the adoption of the marine diesel, which after slow beginnings just before the First World War was to take hold gradually during the 1920s and '30s. The East Lynn *of 1928 was a typical motorship of the time, built by the British firm of Doxford, which went on to develop an 'economy' motor tramp.*

The early years of the 1920s saw many ships laid up for lack of employment, peaking in July 1921 with nearly 1.9 million tons idle in the principal British ports alone. The number slowly reduced over the years, 1926 closing with unemployed tonnage standing at 400,000 tons. Shipyards were hungry for work and closing, whilst the constant threat of reactivating laid-up vessels effectively kept rates down. The decade was one of uncertainty, maritime trade unions feeling their strength and not hesitating to take strike action. The General Strike of 1926 was reflected briefly by a rising freight market as coal exports fell to 40 per cent of normal, 20.6 million tons as against 50.8 million the previous year. Although the strike lasted for only a few days, the miners remained out for many months. The resultant coal shortage led to the importation of over 20 million tons from the United States and elsewhere, balancing lost exports.

Early in 1927 the Chamber of Shipping's Annual Report stated the cost of supplies, maintenance and repairs for liner companies was 75 per cent up on the 1914 level, but freight rates were only up 20 per cent. The tonnage of Britain's import and export trade also illustrates the latent problems for shipowners. In 1913 the total was 149.6 million tons, but by 1925 it had fallen to 124 million and the following year was down again to 110.3 million tons. Table 9/1 shows that the British fleet rose from 16.8 million tons in 1910 to 20.3 million tons in 1930: a larger fleet chasing a smaller volume of trade.

Soon thereafter the considered opinion of many owners, that the cyclical nature of shipping heralded a boom, led to an increase in orders placed with builders to be ready to benefit. Unfortunately, however, the boom was to remain in the eye of the beholder, as the effects of the Wall Street Crash in October 1929 drove the fragile recession into the Great Depression. Typical of the owners to go under in this period was Pardoe-Thomas & Co Ltd of Newport. Having operated a small fleet of six ships built in 1911–14, all sold during the war, they decided to re-enter shipowning and built a fleet of fifteen ships. Orders were placed for eight with Lithgows and Priestman. The first entered service in 1929, but soon they found themselves unable to earn sufficient to service the builder's loans and the ships were taken back by their builders as creditors, remaining on their hands until 1933 and later before they were able to sell them.

Many countries supported their national fleets for economic or strategic reasons, among them Japan, Italy, Germany and the United States. In Japan, Italy and Germany the rise of nationalism was to lead to the Second World War. In Britain there was further limited support through the 'Scrap and Build' scheme. The British Shipping (Assistance) Act of 1935 made available loans for the building of new ships (fifty were built) and £2 million a year for three years to be distributed as a tramp voyage subsidy (payment for the third year, 1937, was cancelled owing to the rise in freight rates). The subsequent Shipping Loan proposals of 1939 were largely nullified by the outbreak of war, although another forty-eight ships were built under its provisions.

The economic development of Germany, in the years following the rise of Hitler to power, was to have an effect on British shipyards. Unable to remit profits from German subsidiaries, companies used the blocked Sperrmarks to buy goods in Germany and export them for sale. Unilever was an outstanding example of this, placing orders for sixty-eight ships in the two-year period commencing November 1934. The following

One of the inter-war 'Empire Food Ships', the 12,791grt Brisbane Star, *built in 1936 by Cammell Laird, Birkenhead. These large and relatively fast refrigerated ships were in great demand during the Second World War, both* Brisbane Star *and her sister* Melbourne Star *taking part in the famous Operation Pedestal to resupply Malta in August 1942. Despite losing her bow to torpedo attack, the* Brisbane Star *survived to reach Malta; after repairs she continued to serve for another two decades until broken up in 1963.* (John G Callis)

year 32 per cent of ships building in German yards were for their account. Although some were employed in company trade many were sold, including tankers to Norwegian owners. Norway was also a major seller of whale oil to Germany, much of it bartered for yet more tankers. In Parliament questions were raised as the orders had 'repercussions on British shipyards which can no longer be overlooked'. By the summer of 1936, 49 per cent of German output was for export, in Britain only 2.4 per cent. A decade earlier the British order book had contained many tankers for Norwegian account and the net result of placing these orders in Germany between 1934 to 1939 was probably, for British shipyards, equivalent to the loss of orders for a hundred or more ships ranging from 4000 to 22,000grt.

The economic climate of shipping was clearly reflected in shipbuilding. After the completion of the First World War emergency programmes, world shipbuilding production averaged about 2 million tons a year, compared with a British capacity alone of double that tonnage. Expansion of British yards in the war had increased their capacity by over a third. The consequent unemployment, coupled with the threat of suicidal competition, led British shipbuilders to form National Shipbuilders Security Ltd to rationalise the industry by buying, dismantling and 'sterilising' excess capacity, financed by a debenture issue repaid from sale proceeds and a levy on members' output. Consequently by 1939 the capacity of the industry had been reduced by about 30 per cent.

An interesting index of prices was compiled by the shipping periodical *Fairplay* at regular intervals, the editor requesting builders to quote for a 7500dwt single-deck steam tramp of very plain specification (the latter was not updated until 1945, hence the interest). At the end of 1914 the price quoted was £54,000, rising steadily through the war until reaching £258,750 in March 1920. A year later it had collapsed to £97,500 and continued to drop until bottoming in 1925 at

Table 9/1: World and British Shipping Tonnage

All figures 000,000 grt						
Year	World tonnage	British tonnage	percentage	Next countries	tonnage	percentage
1900	22.4	11.5	51.5	Germany	2.2	9.8
	(0.4)	(0.2)	(58.4)	France	1.1	4.9
				USA	0.9	3.9
1910	37.3	16.8	45.0	Germany	4.0	10.7
	(0.8)	(0.4)	(55.6)	USA	1.6	4.4
				France	1.4	3.8
1920	53.9	18.1	33.6	USA	12.4	23.0
	(3.4)	(1.1)	(33.9)	Japan	3.0	5.6
				France	3.0	5.5
1930	68.0	20.3	29.9	USA	10.6	15.6
	(7.5)	(2.2)	(29.3)	Japan	4.3	6.3
				Germany	4.2	6.2
1939	68.5	17.9	26.1	USA	8.9	13.0
	(11.4)	(2.9)	(25.4)	Japan	5.6	8.2
				Norway	4.8	7.1
1950	84.6	18.2	21.5	USA	25.2	29.8
	(16.9)	(3.8)	(22.5)	Norway	5.5	6.5
				Panama	3.4	2.8
1960	129.8	21.1	16.3	USA	22.3	17.2
	(17.4)	(2.9)	(16.7)	Liberia	11.3	8.7
				Norway	11.2	8.6

Source: Lloyd's Register of Shipping
Notes: 1. Tanker tonnage, in brackets, is shown under World and British figures. Lloyd's Register compiled tanker statistics after 1923; for earlier years the list of ships fitted to carry petroleum in bulk has been used.
2. USA excludes Great Lakes shipping, but include the laid-up Reserve Fleet (13.1 million grt in 1948). For much of the period, 90 per cent of active tonnage was in coastal, not international, trade.
3. Sail has been excluded. In 1900 it was 6.1 million grt (23 per cent) of world tonnage (UK 1.7 million grt), rapidly falling to 4.6 million grt (11 per cent) in 1910 (UK 0.7 million grt), through 3.4 million grt (6 per cent) in 1920 (UK 0.2 million grt) to 1.6 million grt (2.3 per cent) in 1930 (UK 0.1 million grt).
4. The British figure is for the United Kingdom only, and excludes Dominion and colonial fleets.

Table 9/2: Freight Rates 1900–1950

	Coal				Grain			
	Wales to Plate		Australia to UK/Cont.			Parana to Europe		
Year	High	Low	High	Low		High	Low	
1900	25s	9s 3d	37s 6d	32s 6d		29s 6d	17s	
1905	12s	6s 3d	26s 3d	22s 6d		20s	11s	
1910	18s	11s	27s	20s 6d		14s 6d	7s 6d	
1915	41s 3d	17s 6d	110s	85s		125s	42s 6d	
1920	58s 9d	22s 6d	150s	100s		200s	40s	
1925	20s	10s 8d	55s	27s 6d		25s 6d	10s 9d	
1930	15s	9s 6d	37s 6d	20s		20s	9s 6d	
1935	9s 9d	8s 6d	28s	18s 6d		17s	11s 6d	
1940	38s	27s 6d	150s	55s		155s	42s 6d	
1945	57s	40s 8d	120s	95s		86s 6d	82s 6d	
1950	57s 6d	28s 9d	87s 6d	52s 6d		67s 6d	40s	

Notes: All figures in shillings and pence per ton.

£60,000. The price fluctuated between that figure and £67,750 right through the Great Depression and rose to around £100,000 in the years before the outbreak of war in 1939. Government controls on shipping through that conflict ensured prices did not run away as they had in the previous war, but even so the quote had risen to £180,000 by 1945. After that time, changes in the *Fairplay* specification make it difficult to compare price levels but in 1982 an equivalent vessel might have been Austin & Pickersgill's SD-9, a smaller version of the SD-14 which was never built, costed at about £5.5 million.

At the height of the Great Depression such a new vessel would have attracted a price of only 50 per cent on the second-hand market. Numerous examples of ships only months old were reported, built at prices of £60,000 to £76,000, selling for between £29,500 and £46,500. One of the Pardoe-Thomas ships mentioned above, *Knight of the Cross* cost £60,000 to build in 1929 and realised only £29,500 when sold.

One of the numerous technical developments designed to give greater carrying capacity or more strength was the arch deck. This close-up of the Philipp M *(1924/2085grt) shows the hull configuration of a typical arch deck steamer. She was one of the last of some two dozen built over a twelve year period. A Burntisland-built ship, she had an overall length of 283ft and a deadweight tonnage of 3880, this on a load draught of only 18ft 9in. (Laurence Dunn collection)*

Table 9/3: Shipping Company Financial Data 1909–1948

Five year average	Capital per cent	Dividend per cent	Fleet grt*	Depreciation	
				Actual*	at 5 per cent*
Liner and cargo liner companies					
1909–13	22.8	6.83	4.3		
1914–18	34.5	11.26	5.0		
1919–23	45.5	9.42	4.6		
1924–28	73.4	5.68	6.4		
1929–33	86.7	3.41	6.6		
1934–38	66.7	3.00	5.8		
1939–43	62.0	5.74	4.7		
1944–48	60.0	7.32	3.7		
Tramp companies					
1904–08	8.6	3.74	1.4	£0.3	£0.8
1909–13	10.0	5.69	1.9	1.2	0.9
1914–18	13.2	14.59	1.9	2.1	1.0
1919–23	22.6	7.89	1.3	1.3	1.6
1924–28	26.8	4.80	2.1	1.5	2.0
1929–33	15.8	2.76	2.0	0.5	1.4
1934–38	12.6	3.58	1.5	0.9	1.0
1939–43	11.9	6.61	1.2	0.9	0.8
1944–48	10.3	10.01	0.9	2.5	0.7

Note millions.

In accord with its original role of advocating fair play for shareholders, *Fairplay* published regular summaries of shipowners' earnings, and their 'Annual Summary of British Shipping Finance' is enlightening. The average dividends paid for the two war periods, and the years immediately thereafter, were never matched at any other period, whilst the difference between actual depreciation incorporated into the accounts for some periods leaves much to be desired. The depreciation was not included in the *Fairplay* liner figures, but over the whole period from 1904 to 1948 the tramp owners only managed to allow 90 per cent of the desirable 5 per cent figure which would have recovered the cost of ships over a twenty-year period. However, some owners managed to show a good return on the sale of their ships, in a number of instances managing to show a profit on the newbuilding costs in addition to depreciation.

Table 9/2 illustrates the problem faced by shipowners, with outward rates for coal in 1935 ranging from 9s 9d to 8s 6d. In the decade prior to 1914 only 1904 had seen rates to match this low figure. In the meantime operating costs had risen. Many owners, with no prospects of profitable employment for their ships, chose the alternative of laying them up, whilst tales abound of ships manned entirely by crews holding masters qualifications, with all the seamen lining the rail to take sextant sights and practise their navigational skills.

Leafing through a volume of voyage estimates prepared in the Newcastle office of Runciman's Moor Line gives a clear picture of the state of affairs (see Table 9/4). Typical is the estimate prepared on 23 February 1933 for the motor vessel *Jedmoor* (4392grt, 8100dwt), completed by Doxford in June 1928. *Jedmoor* had arrived at Dunkirk on 14 December 1932, from Saigon, and over twenty estimates in two months witness the effort expended in seeking further employment for what became voyage 10. In the event she sailed from Dunkirk on 21 January 1933 in ballast for Durban, refuelling at Dakar en route. She was being positioned where prospects for further employment were considered better than in Europe, even if an initial loss was sustained.

Unfortunately there is not a detailed voyage estimate for the passage home to complete the story. But with an estimate of £5 18s (£5.90p) profit per day it can be considered one of the more profitable, others showing a far smaller profit margin and many resulting in losses. It must also be remembered that these figures are limited to the direct operation of the vessel and do not make any provision for depreciation, dividends to shareholders, etc. The £29 per day mentioned in the expenses covers wages, victualling, insurance and expendable deck and engine room stores.

The Great Depression saw a number of ideas mooted to alleviate the ills of the industry. The only one to really work was that devised by H T Schierwater in 1934 and operated by the International Tanker Owners'

Table 9/4: Voyage Estimates for MV Jedmoor

		Jedmoor		23 February 1933
Voyage:	Dunkirk–Durban in ballast			
	Durban–Diego Suarez and Saigon			
	1000 tons @ 12s 6d, 6000 tons @ 8s (probably coal)			£3025
	390 tons oil @ 41s			800
				£3825
Days				
To + at				
	at Dunkirk 170 tons oil @ 45s		£ 382	
11 + 1	to/at Dakar 540 tons oil @ 40s		1110	
20 + 6	to/at Durban		150	
	150 tons oil @ 50s		375	
	5 days dispatch @ £10		50	
7 + 4	to/at Diego Suarez		175	
21 + 10	to/at Saigon		500	
	4 days dispatch @ £10		40	
80 days	@ £29 per day		2320	
	8 7/12% total commission out		256	
	Management		96	
	Sundries		163	5615
		Loss		£1790
	Profit Melbourne–UK @ 27s	£3700 in 80 days		
	Loss arriving Melbourne (20 days from Saigon)	2650 in 100 days		
		Profit £1050 in 180 days		
	About £5 18s 0d per day.			
				WCP

Note: Jedmoor voyage 10 was Dunkirk (sailed 21 January 1933), Dakar (fuelled, arrived 1 February/sailed 2 February), Durban (23 February/25 February), Diego Suarez (4 March), Saigon (25 March/3 April), Singapore (fuelled, arrived and sailed 6 April), Geraldton (15 April/26 April), Fremantle (27 April/4 May), Dakar (fuelled 16 June), Dublin (30 June/6 July), Manchester (7 July/13 July), Cardiff (arrived, drydocked 15 July).

Association. Applicable only to oil tankers, owners paid a levy on their freight earnings into a central fund which was used to recompense owners who laid up their vessels and avoiding glutting the market. The key to the success of the scheme was the desire of the oil companies to see independent tanker owners maintain a healthy financial state and in a position to provide them with a good quality fleet for charter. The oil companies showed their support by giving preference to members of the plan when chartering. Improved conditions and, finally, war in 1939, ended the scheme.

The inter-war years saw many technical advances which helped owners meet their economic stringencies of the time. Attention was given to the hull lines of tramp steamers and it soon became apparent that improvements of up to 30 per cent could be achieved. To this was added the efforts of the marine engineer, giving attention to materials and lubricants used in marine engines, valve gear, superheating of steam supplies and the use of the reheater and exhaust turbines to extract the last energy before the steam entered the condenser. The mid 1930s saw Doxford's 'economy' motor tramp, Burntisland's steam 'economy' ship and others such as *Embassage* from Thompson's yard (Thompson had co-operated with Laing on experimental work during the height of the Great Depression) which led directly to the ubiquitous 'Liberty' ship. Burntisland publicised the results for their design. An older steamer of the same size would burn 25 tons of coal a day. Their standard 'economy' ship of 7800dwt consumed 18 tons, which reduced to 15.8 tons if balanced slide valves were fitted, then to 13.6 tons using superheated steam, whilst an exhaust turbine was worth a further reduction to 11.25 tons. Needless to say the saving in fuel was also reflected in the ability to carry more cargo (680 tons of coal outward and 265 tons grain home from the Plate). Thompson also provided data for their *Embassage* which confirmed these findings.

The Second World War and after

The outbreak of war in September 1939 saw, in many instances, a repeat of 1914. The German fleet was swept from the seas, sunk, seized or interned in neutral ports. But the British Government had learned from the previous conflict in various ways. No longer would a free freight market be allowed, and all ships were taken under Government control, although managed and operated by their owners. Charter was at a rate calculated to

The Shell tanker Diloma, *built by Cammell Laird in 1939, followed a standard inter-war pattern known as 'Three Twelves' – 12,000dwt, 12kts on 12 tons of bunker fuel per day. This formula was satisfactory for the 1930s, but the war was to place a premium on greater speed.* (FotoFlite)

The massive number of Liberty ships built during the war meant that they were to dominate the tramp trades after 1945. The Soviet Baku, *seen here in February 1948, still has the wartime gun tubs and liferaft chutes although the wartime equipment itself has been removed. The ship was launched in 1943 by the Oregon SB Corporation, Portland, as the* David Douglas. (CMP)

In 1945 peace returned, although the left-over war risks such as stray mines caused casualties for many years afterwards. Owners were concerned for the future, memories recalling events twenty-five years before when the market collapsed. Although ship-yards were busy reconditioning ships after war service and had full order books, the once cautious owners refrained from placing orders until they were certain another collapse was not due to take place. In the event, circumstances dictated continued prosperity. A number of reasons can be identified: the Marshall Plan of 1947 under which $13 billion of US aid flowed to sixteen war-ravaged countries over a five-year period called for the services of a large number of ships; and in addition the war to end all wars failed to do so. Continued fighting in French Indo-China, leading to independence in 1954, as well as the Korean War (1950–53) kept demand for shipping high. Controlled infla-

give a reasonable return on investment, rather than have the runaway profits clawed back by an Excess Profits Tax as previously. Services considered essential were maintained by owners using tonnage allocated, not always their own. Soon there was not the need to look for neutral tonnage as few countries avoided being drawn into the conflict.

Losses were expected to be heavy and without delay arrangements were made to build emergency tonnage in North America. In September 1940 R C Thompson and H Hunter sailed on *Scythia* to head a Merchant Shipbuilding Mission which ordered sixty 'Ocean' ships to be built in the United States

and a further twenty-six 'Forts' in Canada. The plans were those of Thompson's *Dorington Court*, a development of their prewar series starting with *Embassage* of 1935. In the United States the plans were further refined to produce the 'Liberty' ships which played a vital role in the war. Meanwhile in Britain, as new Government tonnage was commissioned it was allocated to owners to manage. A certain amount of private building was permitted under licence, whilst a Tonnage Replacement Scheme was introduced to allocate chosen newly built 'Empire' ships to owners with heavy losses. Initially acting as managers they would purchase these ships at the end of the war.

The Suez Crisis of 1956–57 had both short- and long-term effects on the shipping world. The six BP tankers laid up in the River Fal, Falmouth, in August 1957 demonstrates one of them – they had only just been able to unload their cargoes of furnace oil because stockpiling prior to the conflict took up available storage. Longer term, the incident encouraged the existing trend towards larger tankers. (CMP)

tion, used to maintain employment and the economy, was reflected in shipping. Then in 1956 Egypt nationalised the Suez Canal and later in the year British and French forces intervened to protect the canal from fighting between Israel and Egypt. The closure of the waterway, from November 1956 until March 1957, raised the demand for shipping, which now had to take the long route around South Africa. Further fighting in the Middle East was to have greater effect on shipping in 1967 and 1973.

The postwar period was also to witness the phenomenon of the flag of convenience. The first of these was Panama, used by the United States to circumvent the prohibition on US ships operating in the war zone prior to Japanese forces attacking Pearl Harbor in December 1941. The world shipping table clearly shows the appearance of both Panama and Liberia at the top of the list, as US owners also sought means to limit taxation and other restrictions such as crewing and building (US flag ships had to be built in the United States) which made it uneconomic to operate under their own flag in competition with others. Greek and other owners also saw the advantages and rapidly flags of convenience became an accepted institution.

The postwar period to 1960 was to be the Indian summer of British shipping. Thereafter a tide of change was to become increasingly apparent; the appearance of new flags flown by the fleets of newly independent nations, the changing flow of trade as the European Common Market grew and the appearance of new technology in containerisation, liquefied gas transportation and the bulk carrier field. Many owners with traditional views on shipping, regardless of flag or home port, found the change too drastic and withdrew as shipping entered the first of several decades which were to be more volatile than anything previously experienced.

David Burrell

The North Atlantic passenger trade enjoyed a postwar boom. On 10 July 1958 six liners, carrying 8029 passengers left New York, setting a postwar record. From top to bottom the ships are the Ocean Monarch, Britannic *(almost hidden behind a warehouse),* Queen Elizabeth, Olympia, United States, America, Constitution *and* Vulcania; *all except* Ocean Monarch, Olympia *and* America *took part in this mass departure, the sixth vessel being* Maasdam *which sailed from Hoboken. However, the writing was on the wall: in the previous year for the first time more people crossed the Atlantic by air than by sea.* (CMP)

10

Navigation 1900–1960

OCEAN navigation underwent no dramatic change with the gradual introduction of steam, but a form of power less capricious than the wind enabled the practice of navigation to become less of what King Charles II had called an 'arte and mysterie', and more of a science.

This was chiefly due to the variables of course and speed becoming increasingly predictable, enabling far more accurate dead-reckoning, which in turn enhanced the accuracy of astro-navigation. From the time that James Cook proved Harrison's fourth chronometer, a mariner's ability to calculate his longitude with its use ousted the older, complex and infrequently-practised method using lunar observations. Latitude had been determinable from ancient times, using either the altitude of Polaris, the pole star, or by the altitude of the sun when it 'culminated', or reached its maximum elevation above an observer's horizon at noon. This occurs as it crosses the observer's meridian, but the determination of that meridian had vexed navigators until the availability of an accurate timepiece impervious to the motion of a ship.

During the nineteenth century, a number of refinements were added to the common stock of navigational skills, notably by the American, Captain Thomas Sumner, and the

French Captain Marc St Hilaire, whose development of the 'position line' for practical purposes combined with the chronometer to enable a high degree of accuracy to be obtained by the ordinary navigator in the humblest of ships. All he needed was a sextant, chronometer, almanac and tables.

Charts, especially those produced by the Hydrographic Department of the British Admiralty, had already reached a high standard of accuracy and reliability by the end of the nineteenth century, arguably the Royal Navy's most lasting and beneficial achievement.

The gradual supremacy of the steamship with its ability to steer a straight course at a known speed was an important factor in improving the quality of navigation and it also enabled shipowners to advertise sailings which could now be run to schedules much more dependable than those attempted across the Atlantic by the crack sailing packets of the Victorian age. These liner services spread all over the world and were not restricted to passengers, many shipping companies from the major maritime nations in

Europe, America and the Far East, instituting cargo liner services.

No advance in human affairs comes unalloyed, and the very ability of ships to maintain consistent, and often high speeds, introduced competition and a consequent pressure upon ship-masters to regard the keeping of schedules as more important than anything else. Fog remained the greatest natural hazard encountered by ships until the end of the period under review, and its conquest by radar was not itself without its own unique tragedies.

Radar, like many of the other devices increasingly used by the 1960s, was a product of war, but at the dawn of the twentieth century, few aids were in general use, and 'lead, log and lookout' remained the basic tools of the navigator, though 'latitude and longitude' could now be added, since even the meanest tramp ship carried a chronometer and the competence of masters and mates was a matter of flag-state certification. Nevertheless, dead-reckoning, or the estimation of a ship's progress across the ocean's surface, underpinned all other forms of navigation

The wheelhouse of an Atlantic liner at the beginning of the century: the Cunard Aquitania of 1914. As befits a prestige ship, the bridge was better equipped than many more humble merchantmen, but the wheel and compass binnacle takes pride of place as it would on any ship. Aquitania has a second binnacle forward of the steering position, and the engine room telegraphs have repeaters above the bridge windows (note the mechanised linkages running across the deckhead). One piece of new technology fitted to the ship – and visible on the two stands in the right foreground – was the patent Navyphone which allowed voice contact with the forecastle, crowsnest and poop (nearest set) and the engine-room and secondary steering position. This would have allowed manoeuvring orders to be more precisely timed during tricky operations like docking. (NMM)

until the supercession of the sextant as a primary tool by electronics. Irrespective of anything else, once a ship lost sight of land (and poor visibility may bring this to pass long before she is out of its vicinity), the maintenance of a running record of progress dominated the navigating officer's life, on cruiser or collier. It could be reduced to two components: direction and distance, which, once resolved into differences of latitude and longitude by means of a 'traverse table' and applied to the last known position, called a 'departure', updated the estimated position of the ship. The early twentieth century navigator derived his knowledge of direction from a vessel's course, and distance from a calculation of time and speed.

The compass

A ship's course was largely what she steered by compass. In coastal seas, tides would affect the end result and in pelagic waters oceanic currents could have a lesser influence. Wind, in the form of a sideways pushing known as 'leeway', might also impinge on the course made good, though all these variables reduced with speed and in deep-sea navigation allowance for them was largely a matter of informed estimation based on experience. Direction was therefore, principally derived from the compass.

The magnetic compass had been used since the discovery of the 'magical' properties of the lodestone in ancient times. Refinements had improved its ability to serve as an instrument of direction-finding, but it was always subject to 'variation', caused by the

The gyrocompass was adopted relatively slowly by the merchant service but was more readily taken up by navies. This Sperry naval compass, of about 1949 is shorter and less bulky than the usual wartime master gyro, but shows the form of the basic unit. (NMM)

earth's magnetic field, and to 'deviation', caused by iron and steel within a vessel, a fact made worse by the adoption of the materials for the entire fabric. Moreover, just

Where magnetic compasses were duplicated as necessary about the ship (at the emergency steering position, for example) only a single master gyro was necessary, with repeaters positioned where needed. This pelorus stand and repeater dates from about 1943. (NMM)

as variation altered with a ship's position on the earth's surface, so did deviation with differing courses, the raised or lowered status of derricks and additional iron or steel carried as cargo. This complex situation necessitated the officer of the watch taking 'a compass error', or 'azimuth', during every duty period (and successive 'errors' if the ship altered course during his watch), each of which were meticulously recorded with the condition and position of the ship. The primitive compass served until well into the century, but was superseded, except as a failsafe provision, by the gyrocompass.

The principal of the gyrocompass was developed from the properties of the gyroscope, invented by the Frenchman Jean Bernard Léon Foucault in 1852. Foucault discovered that a heavy wheel rotating freely at high speed within a system of gimbals allowing its axis to take up any direction, will resist a considerable force before its axis will submit to change. If the axis is pointed at a fixed star, such as Polaris, the gyroscope becomes a compass, capable of maintaining alignment with the true meridian, and this circumvented the tedious reliance upon the earth's vaguer, so-called 'magnetic pole'.

The first proper gyrocompass was developed by the German engineer Dr Anschutz in 1908, with Dr Elmer Sperry's model being patented in the United States in 1911 and S G Brown's following in Britain in 1916. Introduction of the gyrocompass to merchant ships was very slow, and they were not commonplace until after the technological explosion immediately following the Second World War, but it soon attracted the notice of warship designers, both for use as a compass, and also for weapon control, most notably that of the torpedo. By the 1950s its incorporation into early automatic pilots removed the necessity of a helmsman in open waters and marked the first device which would, in the post 1960 period, make the seaman increasingly redundant.

The log

Following the more accurate control of a ship's course by gyrocompass, the measurement of speed remained almost as much a matter of inspired guesswork. Determination of speed between two known fixes, measuring the distance and dividing by the time elapsed is a straightforward solution, and was used to work out the 'day's run', or noon-to-noon progress of a ship, but it gives only historical information. For accurate

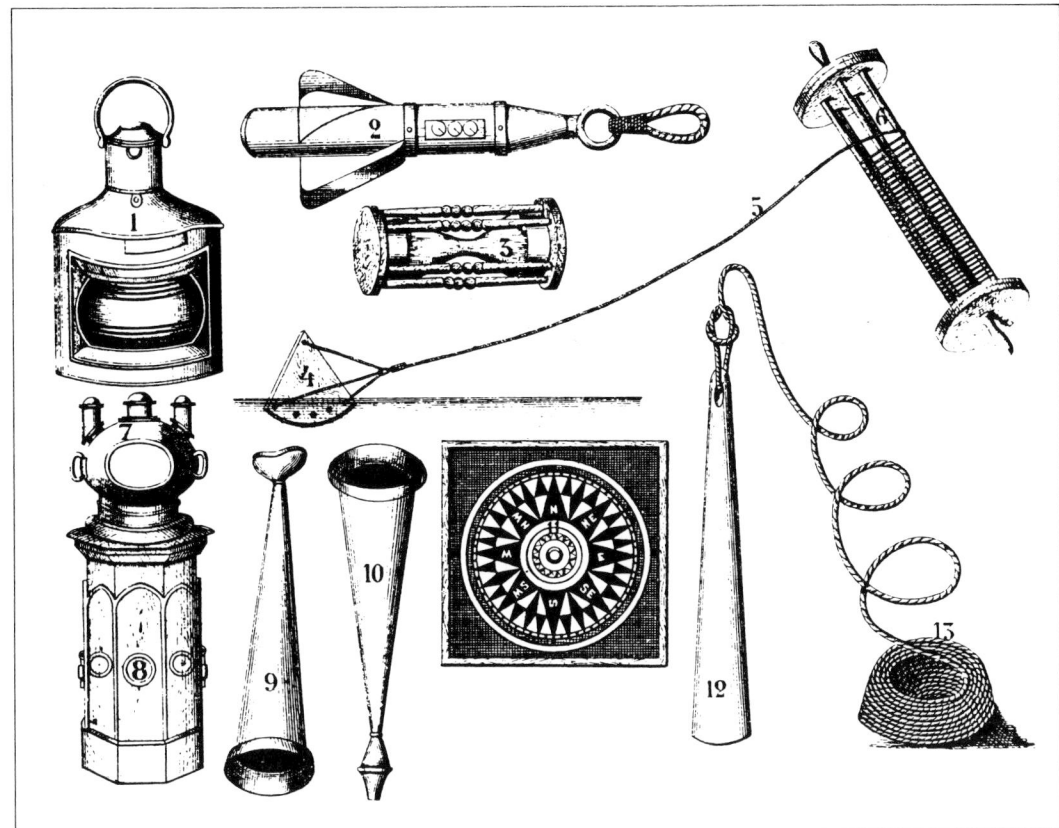

The basic items of navigational equipment carried by any seagoing merchantman about 1900:

1. Port and starboard side lantern
2. Walker's patent 'Harpoon' log – impeller (note dials which registered the distance made good through the water)
3–6. The predecessor of the patent log, the glass (3), 'ship' (4), line (5) and reel (6) of the traditional log
7. Compass binnacle
8. Standard or steering magnetic compass binnacle
9. Speaking trumpet
10. Foghorn
11. Compass rose
12–13. Lead and line (note left-handed lay of rope for use by a right-handed leadsman)

(From Paasch's *Illustrated Marine Encyclopedia* of 1890)

dead-reckoning the navigator required to know the speed of his ship at any given moment and he had two methods of doing so. The mechanical properties of a ship's screw were well known by 1900 and its 'pitch' (the forward movement of a screw propeller conceived as going through solid matter), combined with its revolutions per minute, gave an arithmetical solution of speed. But the sea is not a solid object, and if it is itself moving over the earth's surface impelled by tide or current, the progress thus measured is inaccurate, a situation worsened by the retarding effects of the pitch and roll of the ship. Equally inaccurate, because it is similarly related to 'speed through the water', not 'speed over the ground', was the measurement determined by a towed log.

The towed log consisted of an impeller, usually streamed astern of a ship, which spun as the ship moved forwards. The impeller was constructed in such a way that its revolutions recorded the distance made good through the water. In Thomas Walker's 'Harpoon' log of 1861, this registered within the impeller itself; on later types, such as Walker's 'Cherub' of 1884 and later 'Trident' models, it showed on a dial mounted on the taffrail.

Liable to be torn away in bad weather, fouled by weed, eaten by sharks, and subject to 'slip' resulting from the length of the log-line itself, the towed log inhibited a ship from manoeuvring astern and was only streamed on a long passage. An early improvement, intended to give speed when manoeuvring, was made by Captain Chernikeeff of the Russian navy in 1917. Chernikeeff designed a 'bottom log', consisting of an impeller on a retractable tube lowered through a watertight gland and sluice valve in a ship's bottom. In rotating, the impeller made electrical contacts which registered as speed and distance on the bridge. Substitution of a 'rodmeter', measuring pressure, produced the pitometer log, actually named after Henry Pitot who discovered the principle in 1730. Both types were fitted to warships during the Second World War. Their introduction to merchant ships was not common until some time afterwards, the Swedish 'SAL' log being used increasingly by 1960. But all these devices were limited in their ability to measure only 'speed through the water'. The determination of 'speed over the ground' had to wait until after the period under review, and the 'Doppler' log.

Dead-reckoning

Possessed of course and speed and an accurate 'departure position', the early twentieth century navigator next worked a traverse, the solution of a simple triangle by tables which, by applying a difference in latitude and longitude to his original departure position, allowed him to update his estimate of a ship's position. This 'dead-reckoning' was always worked from the last *known* position. It was required at the end of every watch, and for the working of azimuths and astronomical 'sights'.

Dead-reckoning was fundamental to astro-navigation during the first half of the present century, not least because, in the first instance, its practice is dependent upon actually seeing the sun, moon or stars! Obvious though this seems, in some localities and at some seasons, such as the North Atlantic in winter, this is an uncertain matter. However, it was important to the navigator in working out almost all calculations that he *assumed* he was in a certain position, and the nearer he was to this, the more accurate would be his final conclusions. Only latitude can be found without this assumption, the determination of which is a relatively simple matter, and for this he needed only a sextant.

Beyond the substitution of the micrometer for the vernier on the sextant, the instrument remained basically as James Hadley had refined it from the eighteenth century quadrant. In all astro-navigation the sextant was used to measure the angle between a known heavenly body and the observer's horizon. This was noted with the exact Greenwich Mean Time of the 'sight' shown on the chronometer. It was latitude which was traditionally found at noon, without a chronometer, by a 'meridian altitude'. The application of sextant 'altitude', corrected for such things as the height of the observer, refraction and so forth, when applied to the sun's celestial latitude, or declination, easily yields the observer's latitude. To produce a noon position,

Electronics and navigation

It was realised early in the century that in the propagation of radio waves lay a possible solution to this dilemma, but early exploitation of the phenomenon was confined to communications. Guglielmo Marconi succeeded in transmitting a message in morse code across the Atlantic from Poldhu in Cornwall to St John's in Newfoundland in 1901. The system was quickly adopted by shipping companies, the British and Italian navies and Lloyd's for commercial, strategic and tactical communications. Wireless telegraphy, using Morse code, had its obvious application from ship to shore and inter-ship. The radio officer made his debut in the first decade of the century and remained for the next seventy years. By 1960, however, very high frequency (VHF) plain language transceivers were being widely adopted in merchant ships in equipment developed from the naval TBS (Talk Between Ships) system developed during the Second World War for tactical control of convoy escorts and task forces. Radio propagation could, however, be used for navigation by establishing radio beacons at known positions on land and transmitting medium frequency signals of 250–420 kHz. Prefixed and suffixed by a Morse code identifying signal, the transmissions of such beacons could be picked up by vessels fitted with direction-finding receivers, the conspicuous feature of which was a double-loop aerial, at ranges of up to some 200 miles offshore. The first of these was fitted to the British Cunard liner *Mauretania* in 1911, the year before her White Star rival *Titanic* transmitted her infamous distress message by wireless telegraphy. Several radio bearings thus obtained could give a navigator a fix, though they were subject to certain limitations affecting their accuracy.

Whilst the proliferation of radio beacons greatly enhanced the safety of navigation in coastal waters and the approaches to continental land masses, such as Europe and North America, they were not capable of extreme range. The 'Consol' system, produced long range bearings up to a distance of 1000 miles, but was awkward to use and considered inferior to 'Loran' (Long Range Navigation), developed in the United States in 1943. Loran shore stations generated low fre-

a difference of longitude derived from a 'longitude by chronometer' observed some three or four hours earlier, was worked up from the course and speed in the interim. Using an assumed latitude shortly after the sun has risen, or before it sets, a navigator could calculate the hour angle between his meridian, and that at Greenwich, the zero-standard, and thus determine his longitude 'by chronometer'. But in the more accurate method pioneered by Sumner and developed by St Hilaire, the navigator worked out 'an intercept'.

This was customarily used in the 'stellar observations' regularly taken at morning or evening twilight and only by these almost simultaneous observations of a number of stars, could a really accurate 'fix' be made.

Since every heavenly body is directly overhead at the zenith of some point on the earth's surface at a given moment (and this can be determined from the ephemeris tabulated in a nautical almanac), if an observer can measure his angular distance from such a zenith, his position must lie on a circle of equal angular 'zenith distance' which has this position as its centre. This was an enormous circle and the navigator was only concerned

with that part of it which crossed his bearing of the heavenly body at right angles and passed through his own position. For all practical purposes, unless his dead-reckoning was more than 60 miles adrift, this was considered to be a straight line.

Assuming his dead-reckoning position was correct, the navigator calculated the theoretical angle between the heavenly body he observed, and his own zenith, or the point in the heavens directly above his own head. This 'zenith distance' was then compared with the one he actually measured. The difference was known as an 'intercept' and if the true intercept was greater than the observed, the navigator knew he was further away from the sun or star, on the line of bearing, or 'azimuth' of the body, which was also calculated. If several stars were observed during a period of a few minutes, and a small course and distance correction applied for the varying times the actual observations were made, then a fix, accurate to within two miles (and usually a great deal less) was possible. Such a method was acceptable when visibility was good; long periods of fog or overcast skies increased risks and made navigation progressively uncertain.

quency transmissions to a range of 700 miles by day, doubling at night due to skywave reflections. Shipboard receivers measured the elapsed time between the origin and reception of a signal which was then plotted on a hyperbolic lattice based on the time base in microseconds. Simultaneous readings from two or more stations enabled the navigator to obtain a fix but shipboard receivers were expensive and therefore rare, unless a ship was continually employed in the trades of the North Atlantic or northeast Pacific.

A second hyperbolic, though shorter ranged, navigation system developed during the Second World War was 'Decca', which originated in the United States as 'Gee'. The hyperbolae, overprinted on the navigator's chart, derived from the interrelation between the 'phase comparison' of radio transmissions from one master and up to three slave stations. The onboard receiver consisted of a number of 'decometers' capable of measuring the phase differences between the signals, to produce a fix.

Another device used when navigating 'in soundings' and born of an earlier war was the echo-sounder. This depth measuring instrument had been developed by an Anglo–French team during the First World War in the hunt for an effective antisubmarine weapon, and finally superseded the hand thrown lead line which was as ancient as the magnetic compass.

But by far the most significant electronic development affecting the post 1945 period was that of radar. Radio detection had been mooted as early as 1903 by a Herr Hulsmeyer of Germany and advocated by Marconi in 1922. Early sets were fitted to the British battlecruiser *Repulse* and the German *Panzerschiff* (pocket battleship) *Admiral Graf Spee* in 1936, but they were disappointing, as was that fitted to the liner *Normandie* of the Compagnie Générale Transatlantique, the maximum ranges being limited to no more than five miles.

In 1940, British scientists invented the magnetron, which enabled short wavelengths to be produced in shipborne radar sets. By 1943, wavelengths of less than two centimetres could detect U-boat periscopes, and surface detection and gunnery control by radar secured its place in history.

In the postwar period British merchant ships were increasingly fitted with three centimetre radar, while the Americans favoured the ten centimetre set. Radar was hailed as the conqueror of fog, except that early misunderstandings as to relative motion derived from the 'plan position indicator', or radar screen, led to several so-called 'radar-assisted' collisions, perhaps the most notorious of these being that between two liners, the Italian *Andrea Doria* and the Swedish *Stockholm*, which occurred in fog off the eastern seaboard of the United States in 1956. Following another incident, a well-known British shipping company abandoned the fitting of radar to its ships until proper training persuaded them that the fault lay, not with

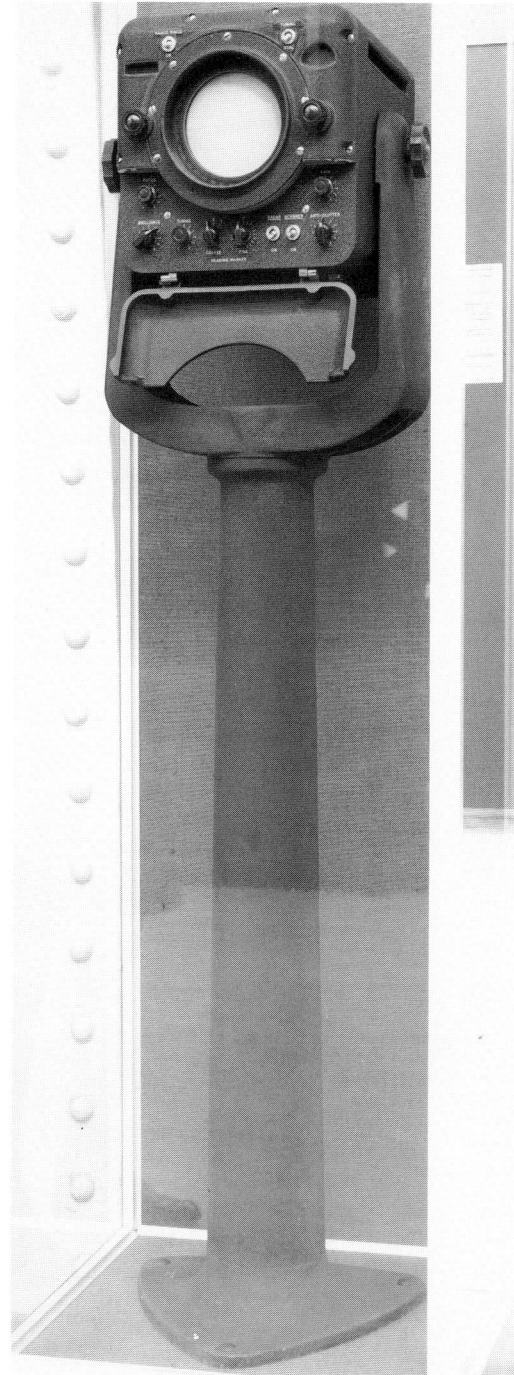

An early commercial radar set for merchant ships, the Decca Type 159. This particular unit was fitted to the British collier Birdwood *in 1949, a relatively small (2862grt) vessel built in 1945. That radar was thought worthwhile for such a workaday craft says much for the relative cheapness of the Type 159, and a growing awareness among owners of radar's potential value.* (NMM)

Another piece of electronics more rapidly adopted by navies than merchant marines was the echo sounder. This was not only more convenient than casting the lead, but was also more accurate, and could be set to give warning when the water beneath the ship reduced beyond a predetermined depth. This is an Admiralty Type 765 of the 1944–1958 period from the light fleet carrier Triumph. (NMM)

radar, but the human element. In the relative motion display, the navigator's own ship lay at the centre of the screen, with all other vessels moving past, or across it, not as they actually did, but as they appeared to. Such misconceptions of other vessels's courses and speeds, was determinable only by careful plotting and subsequent analysis.

Radar not only became invaluable as an anti-collision aid in the open ocean but as a navigational aid in coastal waters, enabling bearings to be taken of prominent features in the same way as the officer of the watch could take a gyrocompass bearing of a lighthouse, or other seamark. Combining this with its primary purpose of determining range, allowed a fix to be obtained from a single, known object. By 1960, the first steps were being taken to produce the 'true motion' radar that obviated the relative displays that had so confused early operators and all the basic components of the electronic age were in place, awaiting the full impact of the technological revolution. Thus the first six decades of the twentieth century had produced a steadily increasing improvement in navigational facilities, both at sea and ashore.

Making a landfall

As a merchant vessel approached her landfall after an ocean passage, her watch-keeping officers would be obeying the routine established from the last departure fix. This, in the North Atlantic winter, with no sights for a week, might have been Sable Island, off Novia Scotia, or Cape Race, Newfoundland. Equally it might have been the chief officer's stellar fix at 0730. At 0800, the third officer, or third mate (depending upon company usage), would take over the watch from the chief officer. The log would have been read and the logbook filled in with the DR position, weather, course and speed. At about 0830 the third mate would take a morning sight, either a longitude by chronometer, or a position by the intercept method, and, using the chief officer's star fix, obtain either a longitude or an intercept for running up to cross with the noon latitude.

The ship's captain, and in some vessels the off-duty officers, would come up and take an observation, so that the noon position was the result of consensus. Simultaneously with his sight, the officer of the watch would take an azimuth, and work out the compass error. If the ship bore apprentices or cadets, they would take their own observations. The third mate would also work out the estimated time of local noon, so that all the navigating officers would be on the bridge at the correct time. This would be close to 1200 ship's time, but might be up to half an hour adrift, depending upon what time the ship was keeping, itself a subject of continuous review. Towards noon, master, chief, second and third mates, with any apprentices so ordered, would assemble on the bridge and take the noon sights, work out the day's run, speed and the course and distance made good. This message was customarily transmitted to the ship's owners. By mid-afternoon the second mate would take a sight and azimuth, a mirror of the third mate's morning observation, particularly valuable if the sky clouded over before the chief officer obtained stars. He might switch on the radio direction-finder and obtain bearings of the radio beacons on the lighthouses at Bishop's Rock in the Scilly Isles and the Ile d'Ouessant off Brittany. He might also make use of the echo-sounder, in the expectation of picking up the hundred fathom line that marked the edge of the continental shelf.

Proximity to the land would once have brought apprehension to the old sailing ship navigator, but the sturdy Victorian engineered lighthouses on both sides of the English Channel, the lightvessels and their fog signals and the buoys that crowded the shoal-littered Strait of Dover far ahead, would have reassured him. The chill in the air which presaged fog reminded him both of the master's orders and the probability of fishing boats being about and he would have turned on the radar, so that the hum and dim glow of it filled the wheelhouse. Reminding the apprentice of the necessity to keep a sharp lookout, he would have rung the telephone to the master's cabin. 'Ship's in soundings, sir, and the visibility's closing in a touch . . .'.

Richard Woodman

The bridge of one of the last conventional cargo liners, the Glenogle, *11,918grt, of 1962. Much of the control equipment is concentrated on the steering console itself, an Arkus autopilot with gyro-repeater. However, out of sight abaft this unit was an open-plan chartroom with the radar and hold-condition monitoring equipment. Above the engine room telegraph to starboard is a tachometer showing engine revs, and there is a periscopic reflector of the magnetic compass on the monkey island above projecting from the deckhead.* (Ocean Travel)

Bibliography

Edited by Roger Jordan from material supplied by the contributors.

GENERAL

FRANK C BOWEN, *London Ship Types*, East Ham Echo (London 1938).
Pen sketches of all types of vessel using the London River.

LAURENCE DUNN, *Merchant Ships of the World in Colour 1910–1929*, Blandford Press (London 1973).
Descriptions and superb paintings of ninety-six carefully chosen ships ranging from passenger liners to coasters.

A C HARDY, *The Book of the Ship*, Sampson, Low, Marston (London 1947).
In depth descriptions of all types of ship. Well illustrated.

PASSENGER VESSELS

A. PASSENGER LINERS

A great many books have been written on this ever popular subject. The following is a brief selection:

FRANK O BRAYNARD and WILLIAM H MILLER, *150 Famous Liners* (3 vols), Patrick Stephens (Wellingborough 1987).
Histories and pictures of 150 individual liners in worldwide service from the late nineteenth century to present day.

N R P BONSOR, *North Atlantic Seaway* (5 vols), Brookside Publications (Jersey 1980).
Extremely comprehensive survey of companies and ships involved in the North Atlantic passenger trade. A few illustrations and line drawings.

——, *South Atlantic Seaway*, Brookside Publications (Jersey 1983).
As above but dealing with passenger ships trading Europe–Brazil, Uruguay and Argentina.

LAURENCE DUNN, *Passenger Liners*, Adlard Coles (2nd ed London 1965).
A classic work, designed for use by the travel trade, and since widely imitated. Gives particulars, including accommodation, and good photographs of all contemporary passenger liners.

ARNOLD KLUDAS, *Great Passenger Ships of the World* (Vols 1–5), Patrick Stephens (Cambridge 1975).
Comprehensive and well-illustrated chronological listing of all passenger liners of over 10,000grt since the *Great Eastern*.

JOHN M MABER, *North Star to Southern Cross*, T Stephenson (Prescot 1967).
Describes the companies and ships involved in the passenger trade to Australia and New Zealand.

NEIL McCART, *Twentieth Century Passenger Ships of the P&O*, Patrick Stephens (Wellingborough 1985).
Describes and illustrates ships engaged in the Far East and/or Australian trades.

C F MORRIS, *Origins, Orient and Oriana*, Teredo Books (Brighton 1980).
An insight into passenger ship design, mainly Orient Line ships, by the company's chief naval architect.

PETER PLOWMAN, *Passenger Ships of Australia & New Zealand* (2 vols), Conway Maritime (London 1981).
Chronological listing with description of each ship's history facing illustration.

P RANSOME-WALLIS, *North Atlantic Panorama 1900–1976*, Ian Allan (Shepperton 1977).
A superb pictorial account of twentieth century North Atlantic passenger liners. Accompanying chronological text gives insight into development of the vessels and a history of each.

EUGENE W SMITH, *Passenger Ships of the World, Past & Present*, George H Dean (2nd ed, Boston 1978).
Valuable reference source with comprehensive listing.

CDR C R VERNON-GIBBS, *British Passenger Liners of the Five Oceans*, Putnam (London 1963).
A concise survey of ships carrying 50 or more passengers, listed under companies arranged in different trades.

ROSS WATTON, *The Cunard Liner Queen Mary*, Conway Maritime 'Anatomy of the Ship' series (London 1989).
Detailed description of the structure of the famous liner with excellent line drawings.

E A WILSON, *Soviet Passenger Ships 1917–1977*, World Ship Society (Kendal 1978).
This book lists all Soviet passenger vessels, including those inherited from the tsarist era, war reparations and the many vessels built postwar. For each vessel there is detail of builders, dimensions, career, and many interesting, some rare, photographs.

B. CROSS-CHANNEL STEAMERS

RIXON BUCKNALL, *Boat Trains & Channel Packets: The English Short Sea Routes*, Vincent Stuart Publishers (London 1957).
A survey of the Dover Strait services from early days to the 1950s including ships, port developments and railway connections.

C L D DUCKWORTH and G E LANGMUIR, *Railway & Other Steamers*, T Stephenson (2nd ed Prescot 1977).

Still regarded by many as the channel-steamer 'Bible'. Contains short descriptions and comprehensive fleet lists of the ships owned by UK railway companies. Some illustrations.

RICHARD GARRETT, *Cross-Channel*, Hutchinson (London 1972).
A history of Dover Strait cross-channel shipping services development from Roman times to the late 1960s.

DUNCAN HAWS, *Merchant Fleets: Britain's Railway Steamers* (3 vols), TCL Publications (Hereford 1993–94).
Listing of companies and individual ships with line drawings and comprehensive histories.

DAVID LYON, *The Denny List* (4 vols), National Maritime Museum (Greenwich 1975).
Chronological listing of all the ships built by Wm Denny, giving brief details with elevation plan. Includes many cross-channel steamers.

D B McNEILL, *Passenger Steamship Services* (Vols I and II), David & Charles (Newton Abbot 1969).
Good overall survey of Irish cross-channel and coastal services covering the North and South respectively.

ROBERT C SINCLAIR, *Across the Irish Sea*, Conway Maritime (London 1990).
A detailed history of the Belfast Steamship Co and some of its rivals.

The following are selected from the many titles dealing with individual routes:

CONNERY CHAPPELL, *Island Lifeline 1830–1980*, T Stephenson (Prescot 1980).
History of Isle of Man Steam Packet Co.

JOHN HENDY, *The Dover–Ostend Line* and *Harwich–Hook of Holland – 100 years of Service*, Ferry Publications (Kilgetty 1991 and 1993).

FRASER G MACHAFFIE, *The Short Sea Route: Stranraer–Larne*, T Stephenson (Prescot 1975).

B M E O'MAHONEY, *Newhaven–Dieppe 1925–1980*, Capella Publications (2nd Edition, Stowmarket 1981).

KEVIN LE SCELLEUR, *Channel Islands Railway Steamers*, Patrick Stephens (Wellingborough 1985).

CARGO SHIPS

A. CARGO LINERS

DAVID BURRELL, *Furness Withy 1891–1991*, World Ship Society (Kendal 1992).
Comprehensive account of this shipping group, whose component fleets owned many cargo liners.

LEONARD GRAY, *85 Years of Shipping under the Maltese Cross*, World Ship Society (Kendal 1967).
Short history and fleet list of Hansa Line, which specialised in heavy-lift ships.

DUNCAN HAWS, *Merchant Fleets* (Hereford).
A series of reference books devoted mainly to well-known UK shipping companies such as British India, Blue Funnel, Ellerman, T & J Harrison, New Zealand Shipping/Federal, Shaw Savill etc, most of which were heavily involved in liner shipping. Chronological company history and individual ship careers illustrated with line drawings.

CAPTAIN A W KINGHORN, *Before the Box Boats*, Kenneth Mason (Emsworth 1983).
Interesting reminiscences of the author's career spent mainly in Blue Star Line cargo liners.

THORSTEN RINMAN, *The Johnson Line*, Rinman & Linden (Gothenburg 1990).
An informative history of this innovative Swedish shipping company, including descriptions of its early motorships and later well-known cargo liners.

I G STEWART, *The Ships that serve New Zealand Vol 1: British & European Lines*, A H & A W Reed (Wellington 1964).
A well-illustrated survey of passenger and cargo ships (mainly refrigerated) in the Europe–New Zealand trade.

MICHAEL STRACHAN, *The Ben Line 1825–1982*, Michael Russell Publishing (Norwich 1993).
The inside story of this famous company, concentrating mainly on the post Second World War period. Includes information on its later ships, including heavy lifters.

RICHARD WOODMAN, *Voyage East*, John Murray (London 1988).
A fictitious story, strongly based on fact, of a round voyage to the Far East in a Holt cargo liner.

B. FRUIT SHIPS

P BEAVER, *Yes! We Have Some: The Story of Fyffes*, privately published (1976).
The history of the banana company from the early days of Sir Alfred Jones of Elder Dempster.

MARK GOLDBERG, *Going Bananas*, American Merchant Marine Museum (New York 1993).
Volume 3 of a series of authoritative books on US merchant shipping history. Describes development of Caribbean–USA banana/fruit trade, concentrating on passenger carrying ships but also covers cargo ships and the mainly chartered 'mosquito' fleet.

ARNOLD KLUDAS and WITTHOLM, *Die Deutsche Kuhlschiffe*, Koehlers Verlag (Herford 1981).
Illustrates and gives brief historical details of all German reefer ships from A to Z. German language.

R M PARSONS, *The White Ships*, City of Bristol Museum & Art Gallery (Bristol 1992).
A history of the banana trade into Avonmouth, mainly concerned with the ships of Imperial Direct Line and Elders & Fyffes.

HANS PEDERSEN, *The French Fully Refrigerated Fleet 1861–1980* (Le Havre 1990).
An illustrated alphabetical survey of French reefers with individual histories. A photographic section covers many other reefers, particularly Scandinavian.

SOREN THORSOE, *J Lauritzen 1884–1984*, World Ship Society (Kendal 1984).
Short company history with listing of all vessels, including reefers.

C. TRAMPS OR GENERAL CARGO SHIPS

LEONARD GRAY and JOHN LINGWOOD, *The Doxford Turret Ships*, World Ship Society (Kendal 1975).
An account of the building and history of the Doxford turret deck vessels with notes on the careers of all 182 vessels built.

K J O'DONOGHUE and H S APPLEYARD, *Hain of St Ives*, World Ship Society (Kendal 1986).
The history of this leading owner of cargo vessels is traced from its humble beginnings in the Cornish fishing village of St Ives to its integration into the P&O General Cargo Division in 1971.

J LINGWOOD and H S APPLEYARD, *Chapman of Newcastle*, World Ship Society (Kendal 1985).
This history of a typical Northeast shipowning concern covers its business and fleet's fortunes from the 1860s until the 1970s.

D C E BURRELL, *The Thistle Boats*, World Ship Society (Kendal 1987).
This account of the Albyn Line of Sunderland gives a detailed insight into the operation of a typical twentieth-century tramp company. It draws extensively on company records and memories of employees to consider in detail the ships, men and trades of the fleet, and there is much financial background.

NORMAN J MIDDLEMISS, *Travels of the Tramps*, (4 vols) Shield Publications (North Shields).
The heyday of British tramp shipping is recalled with histories of eighty major British tramp companies – each of the four volumes containing twenty companies.

BULK CARGO CARRIERS

A. OIL TANKERS

J L ADAM, *Structural Design of Oil Tankers*, North-East Coast Institution of Engineers and Shipbuilders (Newcastle-upon-Tyne 1942–3).

HARALD ALMQVIST, *Ludvig Nobel och världens Första Oljeångare, Unda Maris 1973–74*, Sjöfartsmuseet (Gothenburg).
A detailed account of the Nobel family business in Russia with much information on the early history of the oil industry and the Caspian ships. Swedish language.

C R H BONN, *The Oil Tanker*, Association of Engineering & Shipbuilding Draughtsmen (1921–22).
A monograph containing a very abridged history of the tanker. The main usefulness of the document is in the detailed information it contains of the tanker and tanker practice of the period.

JOCHEN BRENNECKE, *Tanker*, Koehlers Verlag (Herford 1980).
A useful general history of the tanker particularly with regard to German built vessels and German owned companies. German language.

E H CRAGGS, *On Vessels Constructed for the Over-sea Bulk Oil Trade*, Cleveland Institute of Engineers (Middlesbrough 1893–94).

LAURENCE DUNN, *The World's Tankers*, Adlard Coles (London 1956).
An authoritative account of the development of the tanker from the days of sail to the mid 1950s, illustrated with numerous photographs and the author's own excellent drawings.

A C HARDY, *Bulk Cargoes*, Chapman & Hall (London 1926).
A textbook on the different types of bulk cargo and descriptions of the specialised vessels (ie tankers, ore carriers, etc) required for their carriage.

ROBERT HENRIQUES, *Marcus Samuel, First Viscount Bearstead and Founder of the 'Shell' Transport & Trading Company 1853–1927*, Barrie & Rockliff (London 1960).
A biography of Marcus Samuel describing the foundation and development of the 'Shell' company.

J D HENRY, *Thirty-five Years of Oil Transport*, Bradbury, Agnew (London 1907).
The standard reference work on the history of the tanker up to the time of publication.

STEPHEN HOWARTH, *Sea Shell – Shell's British Tanker Fleets 1892–1992*, Thomas Reed (London 1992).
This is a comprehensive account of the British Shell tanker fleet from the launch of *Murex* in 1892, and the related business history.

BASIL LUBBOCK, *Coolie Ships and Oil Sailers*, Brown, Son & Ferguson (Glasgow 1955).
Details of sailing case-oil vessels and sailing tankers.

B ORCHARD LISLE, *Development and History of the Tankship*, Institution of Petroleum Technologists (London 1935).
A good general history of the tanker up to 1935.

B ORCHARD LISLE, *Tanker Techniques 1700–1936*, (London 1936).
A book on tanker history developed from Orchard Lisle's paper to the Institute of Petroleum Technologists.

H F ROBINSON, J F ROESKE, A S THAELER, *Modern Tankers*, Society of Naval Architects and Marine Engineers (New York 1948).
A very full survey of American tankers of the period with a great deal of tabular information.

S W RYDER, *Blue Water Ventures*, Hodder & Stoughton (London 1931).
An autobiographical account which includes Commander Ryder's experiences on some of the early tankers. Among them are details of a voyage through the Baltic, the Mariniski Canal and the River Volga to the Caspian Sea with one of the Russian tankers.

W R G WHITING, 'The Origins of the Tanker', *Transactions of the Institution of Naval Architects* 76 (London 1934).

B. BULK CARRIERS

SIR JOSEPH W ISHERWOOD and WILLIAM ISHERWOOD, 'The Bracketless System'; *Transactions of the Institute of Engineers and Shipbuilders in Scotland* (Glasgow 1926).
The paper in which the details of the Isherwood Bracketless System were presented.

GERALD MANNERS, *The Changing World Market for Iron Ore 1950–1980*, Johns Hopkins University Press (Baltimore, MD 1971).
Bulk shipping seen from the perspective of the users, the large commodity shipping corporations which often encourage industrial services controlled by these same corporations.

ERLING D NAESS, *Autobiography of a Shipping Man*, Seatrade Publications (Colchester 1977).
Fascinating revelation of the ambitions, strategies and career reflections of a very successful entrepreneur who built up what was at one time the world's largest bulk carrier fleet and who was a champion of 'flags of convenience'.

JAMES C WORKMAN, 'Shipping on the Great Lakes', *Society of Naval Architects and Marine Engineers, Historical Transactions 1893–1943*, p363, (New York 1945).
A general review of shipping on the Great Lakes.

COASTAL AND SHORT-SEA SHIPPING

A. COASTAL CARGO VESSELS

A BOERMA, *Coasters*, Uitgeverij De Alk bv (Alkmaar 1985).
A history of Netherlands coastal shipping in the twentieth century, with many excellent photographs. Includes brief histories of major fleets (in Dutch).

TOM COPPACK, *A Lifetime With Ships*, T Stephenson (Prescot 1973).
An autobiography of coasting shipowner Tom Coppack, whose firm operated from the now defunct port of Connah's Quay, North Wales. It chronicles the personal and business experiences of a small shipowner through much of the twentieth century.

GERT UWE DETLEFSEN, *Vom Ewer zum Containerschiff*, Koehlers Verlag (Herford 1983).
The evolution of the German coastal motorship. An interesting innovation is the inclusion of histories of each German shipyard which built motor coasters, with lists of vessels built for German owners (in German).

R S FENTON, *Cambrian Coasters*, World Ship Society (Kendal 1989).
A survey of the steam and motor coasters owned in North and West Wales, with histories of the ships and their owners, and short accounts of the area's ports and trades.

K S GARRETT, *Everards of Greenhithe*, World Ship Society (Kendal 1991).
F T Everard was one of the pioneers of the motor coaster, and the company grew to become the leading British owner in the coastal and short-sea bulk trades. An illustrated history of the company and its ships.

J A MACRAE and C V WAINE, *Steam Collier Fleets*, Waine Research Publications (Albrighton 1990).
A companion to *Steam Coasters and Short Sea Traders* concentrating on vessels in the coal trade, with much detail on individual fleets, ports and installations.

BARRY PEMBERTON, *Australian Coastal Shipping*, Melbourne University Press (Melbourne 1979)
A detailed history of the coastal shipping services around, between and sometimes beyond the states of Australia, with a full list of the vessels involved.

DOUGLAS RIDLEY-CHESTERTON and ROY S FENTON, *Gas and Electricity Colliers*, World Ship Society (Kendal 1985).
Chronologies of the British gas and electricity undertakings which owned coastal colliers and histories and details of their ships.

OWEN G SPARGO and THOMAS H THOMASON, *Old Time Steam Coasting*, Waine Research Publications (Albrighton 1982).
Two first-hand accounts of serving in British steam coasters in the 1920s and 1930s: detailed, highly readable, and illustrated with photographs, drawings and maps.

CHARLES V WAINE, *Steam Coasters and Short Sea Traders*, Waine Research Publications (Albrighton 1976).
A comprehensive account of the British steam coaster, concentrating on vessels in the bulk trades. The emphasis is on constructional detail, with many general arrangement and other drawings, but there is much on the owners and their trades.

B. COASTAL PASSENGER VESSELS

MIKE BENT, *Coastal Express – The Ferry to the Top of the World*, Conway Maritime (London 1987).
A well-researched history of the Norwegian coastal serv-ice from its early beginnings to the present day, with many excellent photographs and drawings.

FRANK BURTT, *Cross-Channel and Coastal Paddle Steamers*, Tilling (London 1934).

——, *Steamers of the Thames and Medway*, Tilling (London 1949).
Excellent accounts of cross-channel paddle steamers, coastal passenger vessels, and the passenger vessels of the Thames and Medway.

ALAN D CUTHBERT, *Clyde Shipping Co – A History*, Maclehose (Glasgow 1956).
Although it had deepsea and towage interests, Clyde Shipping was also one of the foremost operators of coastal passenger ships.

C L D DUCKWORTH and G E LANGMUIR, *Clyde River and Other Steamers*, T Stephenson (2nd edition Prescot 1977).
Brief descriptions and comprehensive fleet lists of several companies involved in the coastal carriage of passengers including Burns & Laird, Coast Lines, Langland, British & Irish, Sloan and Clyde Shipping.

C L D DUCKWORTH and G E LANGMUIR, *West Highland Steamers*, Brown, Son & Ferguson (Glasgow 1987).
Same format as above but mainly concerned with David MacBrayne's ships.

G E LANGMUIR and G H SOMNER, *William Sloan & Co Ltd, Glasgow 1825–1968*, World Ship Society (Kendal 1987).
Short history and illustrated fleet list.

ROBERT TURNER, *The Pacific Princesses*, Sono Nis Press (Victoria, BC 1977).
A beautifully produced and well illustrated study of the west coast passenger steamers of the Canadian Pacific Railway.

C. EXCURSION VESSELS

C L D DUCKWORTH and G E LANGMUIR, *Clyde River and Other Steamers*, T Stephenson (Prescot 1977).
Brief descriptions and comprehensive fleet lists of several companies involved in the coastal carriage of passengers.

IAN MCCRORIE, *Clyde Pleasure Steamers – An Illustrated History*, Orr, Pollock & Co (Greenock 1986).
A concise history of the Clyde 'steamer' fleet from Henry Bell's *Comet* to the car ferry *Isle of Arran* of 1984.

J S PATERSON, *Classic Scottish Paddle Steamers*, David & Charles (Newton Abbot 1982).
This book covers in detail twelve well-known Clyde steamers, from *Iona* (1864) to *Jeanie Deans* of 1931.

E C B THORNTON, *Thames Coast Pleasure Steamers*, T Stephenson (Prescot 1972).
Good summary of Thames excursion vessels from early paddle steamers to the last General Steam Navigation Co motorship.

THE WORLD'S FISHING FLEETS

A VON BRANDT, *Fish Catching Methods of the World*, Fishing News Books (3rd ed London, 1984).
A survey of methods of all descriptions from bare hands to pumps and attraction by electric light, by way of cormorants, lines, trawls, indeed every imaginable method. A comprehensive and well illustrated book, which covers subsistence as well as commercial fishing.

A C HARDY, *Seafood Ships*, Crosby Lockwood & Son (London 1947).
A general account of the larger fishing vessels of the world and their equipment in the 1930s and '40s.

A C HARDY, *The Book of the Ship*, Sampson, Low, Marston (London *c*1950).
Chapters on fishing and whaling within a survey of ships. The whaling account includes a description of the factory ship *Balaena* in some detail.

JOHN H HARLAND, *Catchers and Corvettes. The Steam Whalecatcher in Peace and War 1860–1960*, Jean Boudriot Publications (Rotherfield 1992).
A detailed study of whalecatcher history, including a full examination of design, propulsion, equipment operation and much else. Copiously illustrated, photographs, drawings, plans.

PETER HJUL (ed), *The Stern Trawler*, Fishing News Books (London 1972).
A technical survey of the world's stern trawlers by various authors with additional chapters on the mechanisation of trawl gear handling, the handling and processing of fish and on small stern trawlers.

J A TØNNESSEN and A O JOHNSEN, *The History of Modern Whaling*, C Hurst (London 1982).
This is a shortened edition in English, translated by R I Christophersen, of the four volume *Den Moderne Hvalfangsts Historie* (Vol 1 by A O Johnsen, Aschehoug & Co, Oslo 1959; Vols 2, 3 and 4 by J N Tønnessen, Norges Hvalfangstforbund, Sandefjord 1967–70). Volume 1 is a quite separate account of Finnmark whaling. Volumes 2–4 cover whaling worldwide. The English edition omits the local Norwegian material, but is still an extensive account of the industry, in economic, social and technical terms.

JAN-OLAF TRAUNG, *Fishing Boats of the World*, Fishing News Books, on behalf of the United Nations Food and Agriculture Organization (Vol 1 1955, reprinted 1975).
An exhaustive survey of fishing vessels and their methods, large and small, by contributors from all over the world in the form of essays with discussions.

JEREMY TUNSTALL, *The Fishermen*, MacGibbon & Kee (London 1962).
This is a social account of fishing, particularly from Hull, and concentrates on the recruitment, working conditions, domestic life and economics relating to deep sea fishing up to about 1960. It contains much background information on fleets and companies.

W VAMPLEW, *Salvesen of Leith*, Scottish Academic Press (Edinburgh 1975).
A good account of Salvesen's merchant fleets and whaling operations but the book does not cover the company's involvement in stern trawling with *Fairtry* and her sisters.

WILLIAM W WARNER, *Distant Water. The Fate of the North Atlantic Fisherman*, Little, Brown & Co (2nd ed Boston, MA 1983).
Readable and entertaining account of the last days of large scale deep sea fishing in the mid 1970s. It covers stern trawler development, and operations by US, British, West German and Soviet stern trawlers and Spanish pair fishing.

SERVICE VESSELS

A. OCEAN-GOING AND SALVAGE TUGS

M J GASTON, *Tugs and Towing*, Patrick Stephens (Sparkford 1992).
A description of tugs, machinery and equipment in considerable detail. Well illustrated with drawings, and black and white and colour photographs.

JOSEPH N GORES, *Marine Salvage*, Doubleday & Co (Garden City, NY).
Detailed and very readable stories of salvages carried out all over the world, many of them being submarines.

STEVEN LANG and PETER H SPECTRE, *On the Hawser*, Down East Books (Camden, ME).
Described as a 'Tugboat Album', this is 490 pages of tug photographs going back to the very early days, mainly from the US point of view, although a section is devoted to other countries. Each photograph has a short descriptive note.

R E SAUNDERS, *The Practice of Ocean Rescue*, Brown, Son & Ferguson (Glasgow).
Well illustrated with drawings and diagrams, this volume shows how it is done generally from a British point of view.

P N THOMAS, *British Steam Tugs*, Waine Research Publications (Albrighton 1983).
Standard work on both ocean and ship handling tugs of steam era.

J VAN EIJK (ed), *Tugs: 3000hp and over*, Lekko (Ijmuiden, Netherlands 1986).
Listing of some 1700 vessels giving their owner, flag, date of build, bollard pull, horsepower, gross tonnage, length and speed.

B. SHIP HANDLING TUGS

EDWARD M BRADY, *Tugs, Towboats and Towing*, Cornell Maritime Press (Cambridge, MD).
After briefly discussing tug types and their design, the volume gives considerable details of towing equipment and operational methods.

TIM NICHOLSON, *Take the Strain*, The Alexandra Towing Co (Liverpool).
A history of the company and its vessels covering 150 years, well illustrated with black and white and colour photographs.

RICHARD PARSONS, *The Story of Kings*, Redcliffe Press (Bristol).
The history of C J King & Sons, a family business which dominated the stevedoring and tug owning scene in Bristol after its foundation in 1850.

GEORGE H REID, *Shiphandling with Tugs*, Cornell Maritime Press (Cambridge, MD).
A comprehensive guide to the safe and effective employment of tugs doing ship work. Intended for pilots, tug captains and ship masters.

JEFFREY N WOOD, *Caldwell's Screw Tug Design*, Hutchinson (London 1969).
This is an update of a famous book by A C Caldwell, which looks at every aspect of the design of a tug. There are very few such books.

C. CABLE SHIPS

K R HAIGH, *Cable Ships and Submarine Cables*, Standard Telephones & Cables (2nd ed London 1978).

W H RUSSELL, *The Atlantic Telegraph* (1865), reprinted by David & Charles (Newton Abbot 1972).

D. ICEBREAKERS

T ARMSTRONG, 'The Northeast Passage as a commercial waterway 1879–1979', *Ymer* (Stockholm 1980).

L BRIGHAM, 'Arctic Icebreakers: US, Canadian and Soviet', *Oceanus* 29, No 1 (Spring 1986).

SHIP DESIGN AND CONSTRUCTION

The international shipbuilding industry has been well served this century by its technical press, including: *The Shipbuilder* (from 1906, now *Shipping World and Shipbuilder*); *Shipbuilding and Shipping Record* (1913–1977); *The Motor Ship* (from 1920).

The transactions of the professional engineering institutions are a mine of information on practical and theoretical developments, including Royal Institution of Naval Architects (London), Institute of Marine Engineers (London), Society of Naval Architects and Marine Engineers (New York) and Schiffbautechnischesgesellschaft (Berlin).

A large number of shipbuilding company histories have been written from bland public relations glossies to in-depth studies of the company, its performance and products. A selection published in English includes: *Bath Iron Works* (R L Snow, 1987), *Beardmore* (I Johnston, 1993), *Blohm & Voss* (H G Prager, 1977), *Harland & Wolff* (M Moss and J R Hume, 1986), *Hawthorn Leslie* (J F Clarke, c1979), *Scotts of Greenock* (1906, 1920, 1950 and 1961), *Thornycroft* (K C Barnaby, 1964), *Wilton Fijenoord* (P J Bouwman, 1954).

W ABELL, *The Shipwright's Trade* (Cambridge 1948; reprinted Conway Maritime Press, London 1981).
Historical overview of building of ships from prehistoric times.

E W BLOCKSIDGE, *Merchant Ships and Shipping*, Ernest Benn (London 1933).
Comprehensive review of development in ship construction and associated regulations on tonnage, freeboard and safety.

I L BUXTON, 'The Development of the Merchant Ship 1880–1990', *The Mariner's Mirror* 79 (Feb 1993).
Trends of technical and economic performance of dry cargo ships and tankers.

CASSIERS MAGAZINE.
Popular monthly technical journal pre First World War, with special Marine Numbers in 1897, 1908 and 1911, with a large number of articles on current developments written by prominent naval architects and marine engineers.

J F CLARKE, *A Century of Service to Engineering and Shipbuilding: A Centenary History of the North East Coast Institution of Engineers and Shipbuilders 1884–1984*, NECIES (Newcastle 1984).
Describes the contribution of a professional engineering institution to the improvement of ships and their machinery.

5000 Weeks of Fairplay (28 June 1979, London).
Celebratory issue of a weekly maritime journal with sixteen overview articles on the preceding century, from naval architecture to maritime safety.

H G FASSETT (ed), *The Shipbuilding Business in the United States of America*, 2 vols, Society of Naval Architects and Marine Engineers (New York 1948).
Comprehensive description of the American shipbuilding industry and its operations, with extensive statistics.

A C HARDY, *The Book of the Ship*, Sampson, Low & Marston (London nd c1950).
Well illustrated view of the postwar shipping scene with not too technical descriptions of ship types, their construction, machinery and operation.

J A HIND, *Ships and Shipbuilding*, Temple Press (London 1959).
Concise popular account of ships, their design and construction.

A C HOLMS, *Practical Shipbuilding: A Treatise on the Structural Design and Building of Modern Steel Vessels*, Longmans Green (London 1904 and 1917).
Detailed textbook on shipbuilding technology, with one volume of text and a large volume of plates.

L JONES, *Shipbuilding in Britain: Mainly between the two World Wars*, University of Wales Press (Cardiff 1957).
Scholarly analysis of the change in the British shipbuilding industry, with many statistics.

J M MURRAY, 'Merchant Ships 1860–1960', *Transactions of the Royal Institution of Naval Architects* 100 (London 1960).
Good summary of a century of technical developments, as seen by Lloyd's Register.

J R PARKINSON, *The Economics of Shipbuilding in the United Kingdom*, Cambridge University Press (Cambridge 1960).
A description, in non-technical language, of the state of British shipbuilding, its prospects and how it stands in relation to its competitors. It covers the growth of the industry from the 1850s, its organisation, the demand for ships, and the supply, touching on such questions as technical change, industrial organisations, labour, and competition.

Shipbuilding and Ships, Worshipful Company of Shipwrights (London 1947).
Forty-two articles on all aspects of current marine technology, to accompany exhibition.

P N THOMAS, *British Ocean Tramps*, Vol 1: *Builders and Cargoes*. Waine Research Publications (Wolverhampton 1992).
Competent review of the design, construction and operation of the less glamorous cargo vessels. Well supported by drawings.

F M WALKER, *Song of the Clyde: A History of Clyde Shipbuilding*, Patrick Stephens (Cambridge 1983).
Account of one of the world's foremost shipbuilding regions and its 400 shipbuilders.

T WALTON, *Steel Ships: Their Construction and Maintenance*, Charles Griffin (London; many editions from 1st in 1901 into the 1960s).
Covers shipbuilding materials, ship structure and construction, with many drawings.

MARINE PROPULSION

DENIS GRIFFITHS, *Power of the Great Liners – A History of Atlantic Marine Engineering*, Patrick Stephens (Sparkford 1990).

SHIPPING ECONOMICS

DAVID BURRELL, *Scrap and Build*, World Ship Society (Kendal 1988).
This is an important and fascinating book for anyone interested in ships and shipping in the immediate pre Second World War period. It describes attempts made by

government to aid the depressed British shipping industry in the 1930s, both the Scrap and Build scheme of 1935 and the Shipping Loan scheme of 1939. There is much historical background to the schemes, an assessment of their success and much additional information in ten appendices.

R CRAIG, *Steam Tramps and Cargo Liners*, Volume 5 in 'The Ship' series, HMSO (London 1980).
A concise examination of developments from 1850 to 1950 covering technical developments, commercial organisation, trades and operations.

EDWIN GREEN and MICHAEL MOSS, *A Business of National Importance – The Royal Mail Group 1902–1937*, Methuen (London 1983).
Traces the rise and fall of the Kylsant Group of companies and its complex corporate financial structure.

R HOPE, *A New History of British Shipping*, John Murray (London 1990).
A remarkably good and extensive history, it contains much on the golden age of shipping, as well as what succeeded it and what is likely to occur in the future with regard to British shipping.

FRANCIS E HYDE, *The Cunard Line*, Macmillan Press (London 1975).
A business history of the celebrated company.

DAVID JENKINS, *Jenkins Brothers of Cardiff. A Ceredigion Family's Shipping Ventures*, National Museum of Wales (Cardiff 1985).
The author produces here a well researched and easy to read account of a small tramp company in which his own family had an interest. He untangles the complexity of family shipowning, the single ship companies, the 64 shares, and the movement of capital.

L JONES, *Shipbuilding in Britain*, University of Wales Press (Cardiff 1957).
Mainly concerned with the 1919 to 1939 period, covering production, competition, labour, subsidies, etc.

ERLING D NAESS, *Autobiography of a Shipping Man*, Seatrade Publications (Colchester 1977).
Fascinating revelation of the ambitions, strategies and career reflections of a very successful entrepreneur who built up what was at one time the world's largest bulk carrier fleet and who was a champion of 'flags of convenience'.

J R PARKINSON, *The Economics of Shipbuilding in the United Kingdom*, Cambridge University Press (Cambridge 1960).
A description, in non-technical language, of the state of the British shipbuilding industry, its prospects and how it stands in relation to its competitors. It covers the growth of the industry from the 1850s, its organisation, the demand for ships, and the supply, touching on such questions as technical change, industrial organisation, labour, and competition.

T RINMAN and R BRODEFORS, *The Commercial History of Shipping*, Rinman & Linden (Gothenburg 1983).
Essentially a shorter volume on the same lines as *A New History of British Shipping*.

S G STURMEY, *Shipping Economics: Collected Papers*, Macmillan (London 1975).
A classic study which focuses on British shipping but has wider implications. It provides an incisive account of shipping as it passed from the golden age to the revolution.

P N THOMAS, *British Ocean Tramps*, Waine (Wolverhampton 1992).
The history of the British steam tramp, covering design and construction, builders and owners, cargoes and trades.

NAVIGATION

Admiralty Manual of Navigation, Volumes 1 and 2, HMSO (London 1955).
A contemporary Royal Navy training manual. Volume 1 covers the chart, coastal navigation, tides, radio aids to navigation and instruments associated with navigation with the exception of the sextant. Volume 2 covers the sextant, meteorology and the mysteries of astro-navigation. Contrasts in emphasis with *Nicholls's Concise Guide* (see below). A third volume covers more abstruse aspects of navigation.

E W ANDERSON, *The Principles of Navigation*, Hollis & Carter (1966).
Written by an aeronautical navigator and concerned with air, as well as conventional surface navigation, this book nevertheless provides comprehensive cover of all aspects of pre- and early electronic navigation.

CHARLES H BROWN, *Nicholls's Concise Guide*, Volumes 1 and 2, Brown, Son & Ferguson (Glasgow 1958).
The British merchant navy officer's *vade mecum* of the period. Known colloquially as 'Nicholls's Confused Guide', the first volume was the principal book by which they learned their trade and which covers all aspects of navigation with worked examples.

D H SADLER, *Man is not Lost*, HMSO (London 1968).
A joint publication of the National Maritime Museum and the Royal Greenwich Observatory to celebrate 200 years of astronomical navigation with the *Nautical Almanac* produced by the British Admiralty. It gives a good layman's guide to the history of astro-navigation.

RICHARD WOODMAN, *Voyage East*, John Murray (London 1988).
An account based on first-hand experience of a voyage made by a typical cargo liner in the early 1960s with information on navigation, cargo-work, etc.

Glossary of Terms and Abbreviations

Compiled by Roger Jordan. This list assumes some knowledge of ships and concentrates on terms and abbreviations used in this volume.

Flag abbreviations

Aus	Australia
Bel	Belgium
Can	Canada
Den	Denmark
Dzg	Danzig
Fin	Finland
Fra	France
Ger	Germany
Gre	Greece
Ind	India
Ita	Italy
Jap	Japan
Lib	Liberia
Mor	Morocco
Ne	Netherlands
Nor	Norway
Pan	Panama
Por	Portugal
Rus	Russia
SA	South Africa
Sp	Spain
SU	Soviet Union
Swe	Sweden
Tur	Turkey
UK	United Kingdom
US	United States

A/B. Aktiebolag (Swedish, limited company).

ABS. American Bureau of Shipping (see *Lloyd's Register of Shipping*).

aftercastle. Raised portion or island at after end of vessel; also known as poop.

arcform. Ships in which the topsides are given a considerable amount of tumblehome, the arc of which continues far below the waterline, so eliminating the traditional near-squareness of the bilge area.

arch deck. Steamer design dating from 1912–24, with a bulge in the hull above the waterline, and main recognition features were very slight reverse sheer, short forecastle and poop and midships superstructure set between four hatches.

ARS, ATA, ATF, ATR. Designations of US-built standard design tugs of the Second World War.

A/S. Aksjeselskap (Norwegian, limited company).

A/S D/S. Akties. Dampskibsselskab (Danish, steamship limited company).

athwartships. Across a vessel; at right angles to centreline.

B&W. Burmeister & Wain, Copenhagen shipbuilders and engine builders.

ballast. Usually water, used to stabilise a vessel not carrying cargo.

beam trawler. A fishing vessel employing a beam trawl, a trawl net in which the net is kept open during towing by a beam fitted to the headline.

bhp. Brake horsepower (see *horsepower*).

BISCO. British Iron & Steel Corporation.

Blue Riband. Until 1934, when H K Hales presented a fine trophy (the Hales trophy), the coveted Blue Riband was entirely a nominal title awarded to the passenger ship recording the fastest passage of the North Atlantic.

boilers-on-deck. Boilers placed well up in the superstructure instead of in front of the main engine.

bp. Between perpendiculars (length).

bridge deck. Mid-castle or island about amidships.

BTU. British Thermal Unit.

bulk cargo. Heavy dry cargo such as ore or coal, or bulky such as grain or timber.

bulk carrier. A single deck cargo vessel designed for and employed in the carriage of dry bulk commodity cargoes, such as grain, ore etc.

bulk/oil carrier. See *combined carrier*.

bulkhead. Vertical watertight wall (partition) which sub-divides the hull, and prevents flooding spreading from one compartment to another. It also strengthens the hull and is usually transverse.

bulwarks. The sides of a vessel extending above the deck, to give shelter or protection in place of railings.

bunkers. Fuel for a vessel.

'C' types. C1, C2, C3 and C4 type cargo vessels, with variations, were standard series cargo vessels built in the US during the Second World War.

cargo liner. A vessel which operates a regular schedule service on a fixed route between designated ports and carries many consignments of different commodities. It appeared significantly after the mid nineteenth century when steam propulsion, and the opening of the Suez Canal in 1869, made international schedules more possible.

castle. Raised portion or island above upper deck.

catwalk. Raised gangway connecting castles, above the upper deck, especially in tankers.

centreline. Imaginary line drawn on deck from stem to stern.

CGT. Compagnie Générale Transatlantique; leading French shipping company.

CMB. Compagnie Maritime Belge; leading Belgian shipping company.

collier. A carrier of coal cargoes. The term collier is an ancient one and the first recorded shipment of coal from the River Tyne was in about 1340. The first steam collier appeared in 1852. Thames 'down river' colliers, unlike the flatiron (*qv*), traded mainly from the UK northeast coast to the Thames but were restricted to discharge at locations down river of London's low bridges.

combined carrier. A term applied to *bulk/ oil* and *ore/oil* vessels. A bulk/oil carrier is a single deck vessel designed with dual purpose holds which can be used for the carriage of both dry and liquid bulk commodities; most vessels of this type are also strengthened for the carriage of ore and referred to as OBOs (*ore/bulk/oil*). An ore/oil carrier is a single deck vessel designed for the carriage of ore or oil, the former in centre holds.

compound steam engine. See *reciprocating steam engine*.

condensers. The apparatus in which the returned steam from the cylinders is condensed back into water.

CRDA. Cantieri Riuniti dell'Adriatico. Italian shipbuilder at Trieste and Monfalcone.

crosstrees. Platform on top of lower mast or kingpost to which lifting gear is rigged.

Danish seine. Fishing method originated in Denmark and suited to shallow waters with sandy or muddy bottom and relatively few obstructions.

DD. Drydock (in company title).

dead-reckoning. The estimation of a ship's progress across the ocean surface.

deadweight tonnage. A measurement of weight of cargo, fuel, stores, etc carried by the vessel when loaded to her maximum summer loadline.

Decca Navigator. A co-ordinated navigation system developed in the UK.

demersal fishery. A fishery for fish which feed on the seabed.

derrick. A long spar attached to the foot of a mast or kingpost and used for handling cargo.

Det Ostasiatiske Kompagni, A/S (The East Asiatic Company). Leading Danish shipping company with considerable trading interests in eastern Asia.

DFDS. Det Forenede Dampskibsselskab A/S (The United Steamship Co); leading Danish shipowner.

diesel-electric. Propulsion plant in which diesels drive electric generators which, in turn, drive electric motors connected to the propeller shaft.

displacement. The actual weight of the vessel – the weight of water displaced. When quoted for merchant vessels it is usually the light displacement, ie without cargo, stores, etc.

DR. dead-reckoning (*qv*); double-reduction gearing.

drift net. A gill net which floats just below the surface and is fastened to the fishing vessel while fishing. Both vessel and gear drift with wind and current while fishing.

D/S A/S. Dampskipsaksjeselskap (Norwegian, joint stock steamship company).

dwt. Deadweight tons.

'Economy' vessels. General term applied to cargo ship designs from certain British shipbuilders in the 1930s, and which, with the adoption of several improvements saw, among other things, fuel consumption economies on increased deadweight tonnage.

'Empire' type vessels. Term applied initially to British cargo vessels of about 9000–10,000dwt in the Second World War, but later encompassing a wide range of vessels, from passenger liners to tugs, and including several enemy vessels captured during the war and numerous enemy merchant vessels taken over by Britain following the capitulation. Given names prefixed with *Empire*.

Empire Malta type. A series of nine standard type cargo steamers built in the UK during 1944–45, and of about 3550grt.

Eng. Engineering (in company title).

fifie. A Scottish sailing drifter.

flare. Slope outwards of ship's hull from waterline to upper deck, particularly at bows and stern.

flatiron colliers. Flatiron colliers or 'flatties', were mainly employed in carrying coal from the UK northeast coast to gas and electricity works on the River Thames. In order to pass under London's low bridges, they were of low profile, with the minimum of superstructure. The funnel (if any) and masts could be lowered and there were no derricks on board.

flush deck. A flat-topped hull without raised islands.

fly dragging. Seine net fishing method developed mainly in the 1930s in Scotland and which gradually replaced the inshore small and to some extent long line fishing. The gear suits operation in deeper water on relatively restricted patches of sandy bottom surrounded by rocky or hard bottom.

forecastle. Raised portion or island at forward end of vessel.

'Fort' type. A series of standard construction general cargo vessels of about 10,400dwt, built in Canada during the Second World War. Given names prefixed with *Fort*.

freeboard. Depth from upper deck to water line.

freeing ports. Openings on ship's side or bulwarks to allow water to run off, also known as *scuppers*.

geared turbine. A method of propulsion in which a fast-running steam turbine is geared down to a more efficient propeller speed.

GRT. Gross Register Tonnage. The internal capacity of a vessel. Although the word ton is used it is not an expression of weight, but of cubic capacity (100cu ft = 1 ton). Open decks and the like do not form part of a vessel's gross tonnage, although deck cargoes may be carried. It is widely accepted that the origin of the word ton in this context is *tun*, being a measure of capacity of a certain cask of wine.

'Hansa' type. German standard cargo steamer of the Second World War, of about 1920grt, 3200dwt; built in Germany and occupied countries from 1943.

horsepower. The rate of doing work. One horsepower = 500 foot pounds per second. Early steam engine builders equated the power of their engines to that of a horse, showing how many could be replaced. They chose weak horses to enhance the value of their engines and initially, the numerical value differed. Eventually the formula above, thanks to James Watt, became universal. The horsepower in a propulsion unit will depend on where, and to some extent how, it is measured.

– **brake horsepower (bhp)** is the effective or useful horsepower developed by a prime-mover or electric motor, as measured by a brake or dynamometer.

– **indicated horsepower (ihp)**. This measures the pressure and volume of gas within a cylinder and gives the power available within the engine. This power is then reduced by internal losses (such as friction) and by power needed to work auxiliaries such as the fuel pump, air extraction pump, etc; ihp may be some 25 per cent more than the power output. It is normally only quoted for steam reciprocating engines though it can be measured for internal combustion engines.

– **shaft horsepower (shp)**. This is the power at the forward end of the propeller shaft. It will only differ significantly from bhp if there is a gearbox (with power losses) between the two points of measurement.

Hurtigruten. (Norwegian Coastal Express Service). Since 1893 has linked Bergen with all the main ports and settlements on the west coast and around the North Cape to Kirkenes, and often the only link between some communities and the 'outside' world.

ihp. Indicated horsepower (see *horsepower*).

IMCO. Inter-governmental Maritime Consultative Organization (1954); the predecessor of IMO (*qv*).

IMO. International Maritime Organization, based in London, is a United Nations specialised agency which provides machinery in respect of technical matters concerning international shipping, maritime safety and prevention and control of marine pollution from ships. It also drafts international maritime conventions.

island. A raised portion of the hull, either poop, bridge deck or forecastle.

jumboising. The act of increasing a vessel's size by lengthening, usually by the addition of an additional cargo section.

kingpost or **sampson post.** Vertical post supporting derricks (*qv*) and resembling a stump mast. Often placed in pairs athwartships.

KK. Kabushiki Kaisha (Japanese, joint stock company).

klondyking. The practice of buying fish directly from fishing vessels and shipping the cargoes directly to market without landing at an intermediate fishing port.

Kort nozzle. Dating from 1932, this was a tube fixed around the propeller, and carefully shaped to control the flow of water and so producing a substantial increase in the thrust or pulling power of the tug. Originally a fixed tube, it eventually became part of the rudder and turned with it, increasing efficiency even more.

Lend-Lease. US legislation to get round the neutrality act so that supplies could be sent to Britain and her allies in the Second World War, in return for leases on bases in the Americas. Effectively gave generous supplies free of charge.

length. Length overall is the extreme length of the vessel; length between perpendiculars (bp) is the distance on the summer load waterline from the fore side of the stem to the after side of the rudder post, or to the centre of the rudder stock if there is no rudder post.

'Liberty' type. A series production standard type of general cargo vessel of about 7200grt, of which 2710 were built in the USA during the Second World War. Some of the vessels were completed as tankers.

line fishing. A generic term which includes long line, hand line and trolling. Long line fishing involves laying stationary lines on the bottom, mid-water or below the surface and hauling these at intervals. Hand line fishing involves hand-held lines operated at any depth, along a vertical plane. Trolling involves towing relatively short lines just below the surface.

liner. Usually accepted as referring to a large fast passenger vessel.

Lloyd's Register of Shipping. The oldest (founded 1760) and largest of the ship classification societies. It has its origins in the Lloyd's of London insurance market, but during the 1830s became a separate organisation and was reconstituted in 1834. In March 1949 the British Corporation Register of Shipping and Aircraft (established 1890) was merged with Lloyd's Register. The Register Book of Lloyd's Register of Shipping, published annually with monthly supplements, contains details of the majority of sea-going commercial vessels over 100grt and all vessels with a Lloyd's Register classification. Other classification societies include American Bureau of Shipping (USA, established 1867), Bureau Veritas (France, 1828), Germanischer Lloyd (Germany, 1867), Nippon Kaiji Kyokai (Japan), Det Norske Veritas (Norway, 1864) and Registro Italiano Navale (Italy).

loadline. Horizontal lines painted on hull amidships to indicate depth to which vessel may be loaded under varying conditions.

lpg carrier. A carrier of liquefied petroleum gasses, the most common being propane and butane.

MAN. Maschinenfabrik Augsburg-Nürnberg. West German marine diesel engineers.

Maierform hull. Late 1920s hull form designed by an Austrian and distinguished by convex lines, especially forward; the stem, always raked, was also generally curved. It was designed to reduce resistance and therefore engine power required.

Mek. Verk. Mekaniska Verkstad (Swedish, machine/engineering works).

nhp. Nominal horsepower (see *horsepower*).

nicky. A Manx sailing drifter.

nobby. A Manx sailing drifter.

NRT. Net Register Tonnage. This is gross register tonnage (*qv*) minus the space occupied by crew, engines, navigation equipment, bunkers, etc. Broadly speaking, the space available for carriage of cargo or passengers – the earning capacity of the vessel.

OBO. Ore/bulk/oil carrier (see *combined carrier*).

'Ocean' type. A standard type of general cargo vessel of about 7150grt of which sixty were built at shipyards on the US west coast for Britain during the earlier years of the Second World War. Given names prefixed *Ocean*.

ore/oil carrier. See *combined carrier*.

orlop deck. The lowest deck in a vessel.

otter trawl. A bag-shaped net in which the net opening is kept open during towing by two otter boards or trawl doors placed either side and ahead of the net by warps.

P&O. Peninsular & Oriental Steam Navigation Company; leading British shipowner.

PAMETRADA. (Parsons and Marine Engineering Turbine Research and Development Association), formed as a branch of the Department of Scientific and Industrial Research and UK marine engine builders after the Second World War, and concentrating initially on improved designs for steam turbines; it was supported by government grants and partly financed by the marine engineering industry.

'Park' type. A series of standard construction general cargo vessels of about 10,400dwt built in Canada during the Second World War. Given names with the suffix *Park*.

part-awning deck. Found on a vessel with two decks, the main and awning, forward of the superstructure, but only one aft. The quarterdeck was several feet above the main deck.

pelagic fishing. Open sea fishing.

poop. Raised castle at stern; same as *after-castle*.

purse seining. A method of encircling fish using a large stationary net drawn together at the bottom by a purse line, while the top of the net is maintained at the surface by a large number of floats.

quadruple-expansion steam engine. See *reciprocating steam engines*.

reciprocating steam engines. Are of the single, compound, triple-expansion and quadruple-expansion (one, two, three or four cylinder) types, and low pressure or high pressure according to the amount of power desired. In the most numerous, triple-expansion, steam is expanded doing work in three stages. Initially, each stage of expansion was carried out in a single cylinder, but in many later engines, the large, low pressure cylinder was replaced by two cylinders of more moderate size.

reefer (refrigerated) vessels. Vessels in which the cargo carrying space is largely or wholly refrigerated.

Rep. Repairers, repairing (in company title).

rpm. Revolutions per minute. Rate at which shaft turns.

rubbing strake. Heavy permanent wood, metal or rubber guard along the hull to protect plating when going alongside. Prominent feature in coasters and other small vessels.

SB. Shipbuilding, shipbuilders (in company title).

scaffy. A Scottish sailing drifter.

'Scandinavian' type. British built standard cargo vessel of the Second World War, of about 2850grt, 4500dwt.

schuyt or **schoot.** Pronounced *skoot*. Popular name for a type of Dutch coaster.

scuppers. Same as *freeing ports*.

SD-14. A standard type of general cargo vessel designed and built in the UK, and under licence in Greece and Brazil, as a 'Liberty replacement'. Originally conceived as 14,200dwt, on a laden draught of 28ft 6in (8.68m) and with a speed of 14kts.

seine nets. A bag-shaped net with two wings, made from relatively lightweight mesh, used for fishing on the seabed, by means of towing.

seiner. A term applied to fishing vessels which operate purse seines or seine nets (*qv*).

sheer. The rise of a ship's deck at the bow and stern above the midship portion.

shelter deck. A structure above the principal deck; not regarded as part of the enclosed hull for tonnage measurement purposes, and which facilitates ready conversion from the open to the closed shelter deck condition or vice versa. In the open condition the greater part of the upper 'tween-decks space is exempt and not included in the tonnage; in the closed condition the upper 'tween-decks space is included and consequently the tonnages in the closed condition are greater than in the open condition. Shelter deck vessels became popular in the 1950s providing owners with a higher cubic capacity on the same gross tonnage.

shp. Shaft horsepower (see *horsepower*).

SR geared turbines. Single-reduction geared turbines.

steam turbines. Steam engine in which steam is passed over sets of blades, alternately fixed and rotating, which by changes in pressure over the blading causes the shaft to rotate.

stern trawler. A fishing vessel in which the trawl gear is shot over the stern, rather than over the side (*side trawler*, or colloquially, *sidewinder*).

stevedore. A person employed to load or unload ships.

Stülcken derrick. Developed by Hamburg shipbuilders and engineers H C Stülcken Sohn in the 1950s, consisting of two tapering masts angled outwards allowing the derrick mounted between them to serve the hatches both forward and aft of it and with a lifting capacity far greater than conventional derricks.

Sulzer. Swiss designer and manufacturer of marine diesel engines. The majority of Sulzer engines are built under licence outside Switzerland.

'Sunderland' type. A term loosely describing a type of vessel sought by a British mission to the USA in 1940. The mission's purpose was arranging the urgent building of cargo steamers and had as its basic plan those of the British steamer *Dorington Court*, built in Sunderland, and of about 10,000dwt.

superheater. Ordinary steam is called saturated steam, but if it passes through a compartment at a higher temperature, it will be raised in energy without the pressure being altered; it is then superheated.

supertanker. A term loosely applied to the largest tankers of the era, notably the 1950s and into the '60s. Tankers described as supertankers would have included *Tina Onassis* (built 1953, 27,853grt), *World Glory* (1954, 28,323grt), *Universe Leader* (1956, 51,400grt), *Universe Apollo* (1959, 72,133grt), *Manhattan* (1962, 65,740grt) and *Nissho Maru* (1962, 74,869grt).

'T2' type. A US-built standard type tanker, full designation T2-SE-A1; 525 were built during the Second World War. Propelled by turbo-electric machinery, of about 16,600dwt.

'T3' type. A US-built standard type tanker, full designation T3-S2-A1, commenced in the late 1930s and of 18,300dwt.

three-island ship. Basically a single deck ship with forecastle, bridge amidships covering the machinery space and with officers' accommodation and poop (usually with crew accommodation). This layout was particularly useful for medium size vessels involved in the coal and timber trades.

tonnage. See *deadweight, displacement, GRT, NRT, shelter deck*.

tramp. As distinct from the cargo liner (*qv*), the traditional tramp is a vessel which is built to go anywhere and pick up any type of cargo which is available, often at relatively short notice. Pre Second World War it was accepted as a vessel of over 2000grt with a speed of 10–12kts.

trawler. Originally a fishing vessel operating a beam or otter trawl. The term is often applied generally to vessels operating towed gear, including seine nets (*qv*).

triple-expansion steam engine. See *reciprocating steam engine*.

trunk deck cargo vessel. Dating from 1896, a vessel with a continuous trunk topped by a short raised forecastle, but no poop. The absence of this latter feature and conspicuous edges to the harbour deck distinguished trunk deckers from Doxford's turret ships. There were later variations to the type, and latterly to be found in many coastal tankers.

tug/tender. Developed from the ship towage tug, and limited in numbers, these were a combination of harbour tug and small passenger ship, and used to ferry passengers and baggage to and from ocean liners anchored in the stream or in open roadsteads. They came to prominence in the early part of the twentieth century when tugs were granted passenger certificates for the purpose.

tumblehome. The inward slope of the ship's side above the level of the greatest beam.

turbo-electric. A propulsion system in which a steam turbine drives an electrical generator which, in turn, supplies power to an electric motor connected to the propeller shaft. It was used extensively in the Second World War, mainly because of a shortage of gear cutting machinery, but it was heavy and inefficient. It was adopted in T2 type tankers (*qv*).

turret ship. A cargo vessel patent type developed in the 1890s. It had one long turret, its width being about half that of the ship. Flanking this turret and not far above the load line was the so-called 'harbour deck', the sides of which joined the main vertical plating in large radius curves. This type was popular with owners as net tonnage was low in relation to deadweight and Suez Canal dues were based on the breadth of the main deck and not on the lower harbour deck.

'tween deck. The space between the decks.

USCG. United States Coast Guard.

'Victory' type. A standard series general cargo vessel built in the USA during the Second World War. A total of 531 were built, of which 414 were cargo vessels and 117 were a military transport variant. They were about 10,750dwt with a speed of 16kts.

Voith-Schneider. A propeller used on small vessels such as ferries from the 1930s and mainly on tugs since 1955, consisting of a series of blades hanging vertically from a tube, the whole unit revolving rather like an egg-beater. By adjusting the pitch of the blades the water flow is directed in different directions through 360 degrees.

washports. Same as *freeing ports* and *scuppers*.

weather deck. A term for a light deck enclosed by plating; frequently used to refer to upper deck.

well deck. Portion of hull between castles or islands and about 7–8ft lower.

whaleback. A curved deck placed above the main forecastle deck on certain classes of fishing vessel.

whale catcher. A small hunting vessel equipped with a harpoon gun operated in conjunction with a whale factory ship in the open sea. Usually about 120ft to 170ft in length and 200–600grt.

zulu. A two-masted fishing vessel formerly used in northeast Scotland (reputed to have been introduced during the Zulu war, 1878–79).

Index